D0891948

MAKING RIGHTS REAL

Ten years after the passing of the Human Rights Act 1998, it is timely to evaluate the Act's effectiveness. The focus of *Making Rights Real* is on the extent to which the Act has delivered on the promise to 'bring rights home'. To that end the book considers how the judiciary, parliament and the executive have performed in the new roles that the Human Rights Act requires them to play and the courts' application of the Act in different legal spheres. This account cuts through the rhetoric and controversy surrounding the Act, generated by its champions and detractors alike, to reach a measured assessment. The true impact in public law, civil law, criminal law and on anti-terrorism legislation are each considered. Finally, the book discusses whether we are now nearer to a new constitutional settlement and to the promised new 'rights culture'.

Volume 15: Human Rights Law in Perspective

HUMAN RIGHTS LAW IN PERSPECTIVE

General Editor: Colin Harvey

The language of human rights figures prominently in legal and political debates at the national, regional and international levels. In the UK the Human Rights Act 1998 has generated considerable interest in the law of human rights. It will continue to provoke much debate in the legal community and the search for original insights and new materials will intensify.

The aim of this series is to provide a forum for scholarly reflection on all aspects of the law of human rights. The series will encourage work which engages with the theoretical, comparative and international dimensions of human rights law. The primary aim is to publish over time books which offer an insight into human rights law in its contextual setting. The objective is to promote an understanding of the nature and impact of human rights law. The series is inclusive, in the sense that all perspectives in legal scholarship are welcome. It will incorporate the work of new and established scholars.

Human Rights Law in Perspective is not confined to consideration of the UK. It will strive to reflect comparative, regional and international perspectives. Work which focuses on human rights law in other states will therefore be included in this series. The intention is to offer an inclusive intellectual home for significant scholarly contributions to human rights law.

Making Rights Real

The Human Rights Act in its First Decade

IAN LEIGH AND
ROGER MASTERMAN

·HART·
PUBLISHING

OXFORD AND PORTLAND, OREGON
2008

Published in North America (US and Canada) by
Hart Publishing
c/o International Specialized Book Services
920 NE 58th Avenue, Suite 300
Portland, OR 97213–3786
USA
Tel: +1 503 287 3093 or toll-free: (1) 800 944 6190
Fax: +1 503 280 8832
E-mail: orders@isbs.com
Website: www.isbs.com

Hart Publishing, 16C Worcester Place, OX1 2JW
Telephone: +44 (0)1865 517530 Fax: +44 (0)1865 510710
E-mail: mail@hartpub.co.uk
Website: http://www.hartpub.co.uk

British Library Cataloguing in Publication Data

Data Available

ISBN: 978–1-84113- 353–9

Typeset by Columns Design Ltd, Caversham, Reading
Printed and bound in Great Britain by
TJ International Ltd, Padstow, Cornwall

To Sue and Laura

Series Editor's Preface

The tenth anniversary of the enactment of the Human Rights Act 1998 is an appropriate time to reflect on its contribution to enhancing the promotion and protection of human rights in the UK. The ambitious cultural shift promised makes any evaluation of impact difficult and measuring effectiveness even more problematic. This significant new work offers a balanced assessment of progress so far, concentrating on the relationship between the legislature, judiciary and executive, with a particular focus on the case law. The Act has certainly encouraged constitutional conversations, but debates have at times simply revealed the depth of misunderstanding of the nature and role of human rights.

The Act was never likely to deliver the scale of change many anticipated, due primarily to the political, legal and social cultures and contexts it was born into. Nevertheless, the Act remains impressive and results have been achieved but much more remains to be done. With talk of constitutional reform on the agenda this book provides a firm basis for discussion of the impact and effectiveness of the Human Right Act 1998.

Colin Harvey
August 2008
Belfast

Preface and acknowledgements

The Human Rights Act 1998 (HRA) has generated enormous interest among academics and the legal profession and a wealth of commentary, criticism and analysis in its first decade. Several hundred (perhaps thousands) of cases have been decided using the Act, some of fundamental importance. Arguably, a legal revolution is taking place.

In a book of this kind we could not hope to survey the whole range of developments that have taken place since October 2000 (the date on which the Act came into force). Our purpose therefore is not so much to focus on particular areas of substantive law (where there is already a vast and growing literature); rather, it is to critically assess more broadly whether the Act is achieving the objectives set in the White Paper, *Rights Brought Home* and whether it is living up to the claims made by the judiciary and others when it was introduced. We take the core objective of the HRA to be to provide an accessible and effective domestic remedy for violations of Convention rights. This litmus test is highly practical. It is also somewhat removed from much of the theoretical commentary that has grown up around the Act.

For this purpose it is necessary to examine both the techniques that the judiciary is employing (notably in statutory interpretation and use of Convention jurisprudence) and the impact of the HRA in terms of procedures and remedies. These are fundamental if rights are to be more than rhetorical devices. The emphasis throughout the book is therefore on the questions of what has the judiciary made of the European Convention on Human Rights under the HRA and how effective is this in delivering protection of rights?

The book is in two parts, with a concluding chapter. In Part I we are concerned with the architecture of the Act. An opening chapter describes the main features of the HRA and examines underlying causes that shaped the legislation and the expectations at the time of enactment. Chapters 2–4 continue with an examination of both the new political procedures for vetting policy and legislation for compatibility with human rights and the new judicial techniques of reasoning (the duties to take account of Convention jurisprudence and to interpret legislation so far as possible compatibly with Convention rights). Chapter 5 deals with the broad constitutional impact of the Act on the role and relationships between the judiciary, Parliament and the executive, as a result of the declaration of incompatibility and remedial order processes.

Part II examines the effectiveness of the Act as interpreted by the courts in providing protection in the different settings of challenges to public authorities through judicial review (chapter 6), the criminal trial and anti-terrorism legislation (chapters 7 and 8), and in private litigation, ie against private individuals and companies (chapters 9 and 10).

The conclusion evaluates the overall trends and considers questions for the future. We have endeavoured to state the law as at 1 January 2008.

The inspiration for a book with this title and theme came from an article that Ian Leigh wrote with Laurence Lustgarten a decade ago ('Making Rights Real: The Courts, Remedies and the Human Rights Act', (1999) 58(3) *CLJ* 509–545). Parts of the book (especially parts of chapters 3 and 6) benefited from our involvement in a research project and seminars on Judicial Reasoning under the Human Rights Act funded by the Arts and Humanities Research Council (now published as H Fenwick, G Phillipson and R Masterman, *Judicial Reasoning under the UK Human Rights Act* (Cambridge, Cambridge University Press, 2007). We are grateful to the participants in that project, and to academic colleagues in seminars at Dunedin, Glasgow, Keele, Melbourne, Ottawa, Trento and Wolverhampton who listened to and commented on earlier versions of some of these ideas.

We are grateful also to our colleague Professor Gavin Phillipson, who read and commented on a number of chapters in draft, and to Hélène Tyrrell for discussions on the content of chapter 3. Several people also supplied useful materials or references: thanks to Andrew Butler, Helen Fenwick, Lorna Fox, Stephen Gardbaum, Andrew Geddis, Grant Huscroft, Richard Mahoney, Aidan O'Neill and Alison Young. Our thanks are also due to Jenny Leigh for her assistance in compiling the tables and bibliography.

In addition to providing a collegial home for academically-minded human rights scholars in the Human Rights Centre, the University of Durham awarded us research leave, during which time we were able to bring the writing to a conclusion.

Finally, we gratefully acknowledge the forbearance of Richard Hart: as the project overran its promised delivery date (more than once) he kept faith with us and with the idea.

Contents

Table of Cases

European Court and Commission of Human Rights

Part I

The Architecture of the Human Rights Act

Chapter 1

Great Expectations

INTRODUCTION

INTRODUCING THE HUMAN Rights Bill for its second reading in the House of Lords in November 1997 the then Lord Chancellor and one of the architects of the Act, Lord Irvine of Lairg, said the following:

> This Bill will bring human rights home. People will be able to argue for their rights and claim their remedies under the [European Convention on Human Rights] in any court or tribunal in the United Kingdom. Our courts will develop human rights throughout society. A culture of awareness of human rights will develop. Before Second Reading of any Bill the responsible Minister will make a statement that the Bill is or is not compatible with Convention rights. So there will have to be close scrutiny of the human rights implications of all legislation before it goes forward. Our standing will rise internationally. The protection of human rights at home gives credibility to our foreign policy to advance the cause of human rights around the world.[1]

Although the Bill was much-fêted during its passage through Parliament,[2] 2006 saw the Department for Constitutional Affairs forced to mount a belated counter-offensive in support of the Human Rights Act 1998 (HRA)[3] – a piece of legislation which is broadly perceived as the cause of a miscellany of ills by the Conservative opposition and popular press. Recently, the Conservative party, under the leadership of David Cameron, has announced a policy to repeal the HRA and replace it with a home-grown Bill of Rights which – we are told – would better balance rights with responsibilities and 'would strengthen our hand in the fight against crime and terrorism.'[4] Support for the HRA has not even been

---

[1] HL Debs, vol 582, col 1228 (3 November 1997).

[2] Ewing has noted that the Human Rights Bill – as it then was – was in Parliament '[v]ariously described as "brilliant"; "a masterly exposition of the parliamentary draftsman's art"; and even "a thing of intellectual beauty"' (KD Ewing, 'The Human Rights Act and Parliamentary Democracy' (1999) 62 *MLR* 79, 79).

[3] Department for Constitutional Affairs, *Review of the Implementation of the Human Rights Act* (July 2006).

[4] David Cameron, 'Balancing Freedom and Security – A Modern British Bill of Rights', Speech to the Centre for Policy Studies, 26 June 2006.

consistently found within its parent administration – indeed, as early as 2000 it was written that

> the Human Rights Act bears the hallmark of a proposal conceived in opposition that comes to be viewed differently in the cold harsh light of government.[5]

Successive Home Secretaries have lamented the ability of the judiciary to question 'democratically endorsed' government policies dealing with asylum seekers and suspected terrorists under the terms of the Act[6] – even though the carefully-crafted provisions of the Act preclude US-style de facto judicial supremacy. The former Prime Minister Tony Blair spoke on a number of occasions of introducing legislation to dictate to the judiciary how the Act should be interpreted, and of how the balance between the interests of individuals and the interests of state and national security needs to be further weighted in favour of the state.[7] The Premiership of Gordon Brown has brought with it further discussion of constitutional renewal, including the possibility of taking steps towards a 'British Bill of Rights and Duties'.[8]

Criticisms have also been widespread in the popular press. A spectacular failure to appreciate the significance of the word 'human' has seen the HRA widely portrayed as a charter for terrorists, paedophiles and other criminals[9] – apparently deeming them unworthy of the protections it offers against detention without trial, cruel and unusual punishments and discriminatory laws. The Act is increasingly referred to as an inequitable piece of legislation under which the rights of unpopular minorities are said to be 'elevated' above the rights the majority, as if civil rights and fundamental freedoms have become an entitlement based on behaviour and attitudes that are acceptable to the majority. One of the Act's most passionate supporters has welcomed the discussions which will be prompted by the Conservative's 'British Bill of Rights' initiative, as the HRA has – 'in the

---

[5] J Croft, *Whitehall and the Human Rights Act 1998* (London, Constitution Unit, 2000) 27.

[6] For perhaps the most striking example, see the response of David Blunkett MP to the decision of Collins J in *R (Q) v Secretary of State for the Home Department* [2003] EWCA Civ 364 (on which see: A Bradley, 'Judicial Independence Under Attack' [2003] *PL* 397).

[7] See, eg, 'Revealed: Blair attack on human rights law' *Observer*, 14 May 2006.

[8] *The Governance of Britain* (Cm 7170, July 2007), pp 60–63. See also: Gordon Brown MP, Speech on Liberty, University of Westminster, 25 October 2007 (available at <http://www.number-10.gov.uk/output/Page13630.asp> accessed 12 May 2008); Jack Straw MP, The MacKenzie Stuart Lecture, Faculty of Law, University of Cambridge, 25 October 2007 (available at <http://www.justice.gov.uk/news/sp251007a.htm>) accessed 12 May 2008.

[9] For an important counter-perspective, see British Institute of Human Rights, *The Human Rights Act – Changing Lives* (London, British Institute of Human Rights, 2007) (available at <http://www.bihr.org/downloads/bihr_hra_changing_lives.pdf> accessed 12 May 2008).

absence of prior consultation' – 'failed to attract sufficient symbolic significance to become embedded in the national consciousness.'[10]

Barely 10 years into the life of an Act which was the product of a 30-year campaign for incorporation and hailed as the United Kingdom's 'Bill of Rights,'[11] the HRA faces an uncertain future.

THE PLACE OF DOMESTIC AUTHORITIES WITHIN THE ECHR SYSTEM

Signed in Rome in 1950 and ratified by the United Kingdom – the first country to do so – the following year, the European Convention on Human Rights forms '[a] classical statement of what British people have taken for granted as their rights in relation to the state.'[12] Yet for British citizens the rights and freedoms contained in the Convention could only be successfully realised through the exhaustion of domestic judicial remedies and the slow and costly trip to the European Court of Human Rights in Strasbourg. Until the HRA came into force in October 2000, the common law – so trusted by Dicey as a mechanism of rights protection – and the democratic process provided the front-line of domestic protection of human rights; in the face of a sovereign Parliament, struggling against an increasingly mighty executive branch, residual liberties were being slowly eroded.[13] Until the HRA came into operation, the effects of the Convention on domestic law had either been enforced – following an adverse ruling from the Strasbourg enforcement bodies[14] – or indirect – by judicial recourse to the Convention in the event of a statutory uncertainty or in other specific circumstances.[15]

From 2 October 2000[16] the Convention rights became directly enforceable against the acts or omissions of public authorities in domestic

---

[10] Francesca Klug, 'Enshrine These Rights' *Guardian*, 27 June 2006, and letter to *Observer*, 'Parliament – A Danger to Freedom', 9 April 2006.

[11] See generally: F Klug, *Values for a Godless Age: the Story of the United Kingdom's New Bill of Rights* (London, Penguin, 2000).

[12] Joint Committee on Human Rights, Minutes of Evidence, 14 March 2001, 3 (Jack Straw MP).

[13] R Dworkin, *A Bill of Rights for Britain* (London, Chatto and Windus, 1990); KD Ewing and CA Gearty, *Freedom Under Thatcher* (Oxford, OUP, 1990).

[14] Of which there were many; introducing the Human Rights Bill at Second Reading, Lord Irvine noted that the United Kingdom had been found to be in breach of the Convention on 50 occasions, more than any other party to the Convention bar Italy (HL Debs, vol 582, col 1227 (3 November 1997)).

[15] See text to n 32 below.

[16] The HRA came into force in England and Wales on this date. Since 1999, when they were established under the Scotland Act 1998, the Scottish Parliament (s 29(2)(d)) and Executive (s 57(2)) will be acting ultra vires should they pass legislation or otherwise act incompatibly with the Convention Rights. The National Assembly for Wales (Government of

courts.[17] The HRA 1998 therefore saw the redefinition of liberty in the United Kingdom; to the protections afforded by the developing common law constitutional rights jurisdiction and the democratic process were added the 'Convention rights'[18] which were to be given 'further effect' in domestic law under its terms.

At the time of the parliamentary passage of the Human Rights Bill, the United Kingdom was one of only two signatories to the Convention in which the rights and freedoms contained within that document could not be directly relied upon in domestic litigation.[19] In a number of monist Member States – France and Germany for example – the Convention took direct effect in law upon being signed by the government. Others had taken steps to incorporate the Convention into their domestic laws. The United Kingdom's dualist system required Parliament to legislate on incorporation before international law obligations could be enforceable in domestic courts: 'the making of a treaty is an executive act, while the performance of its obligations, if they entail alteration of the existing domestic law, requires legislative action.'[20] Successive UK administrations had failed to take such a step; and without primary legislation to incorporate, or give effect to, the provisions of the European Convention in English law, domestic courts had long shown reluctance to enhance the role of the rights and freedoms contained within the Convention in domestic law, as to do so would be a usurpation of the democratic process.[21]

The Convention bodies themselves however, do not require Member States to amend domestic laws to allow citizens to assert the Convention rights in domestic courts;[22] member states are only obliged to amend national law or practice in the event of a finding of incompatibility by the European Court of Human Rights. As such, under the terms of the Convention, the United Kingdom was only strictly bound to 'abide by' those decisions of the Strasbourg court in which it has been involved as a

---

Wales Act 1998 s 107(1)) and Northern Ireland Assembly (Northern Ireland Act 1998 s 6(2)(c)) and Executive (Northern Ireland Act 1998 s 24(1)(a)) are similarly bound.

[17] HRA s 6.

[18] HRA s 1(1) defines the 'Convention Rights' as Arts 2–12 and 14, Arts 1–3 of the First Protocol and Arts 1 and 2 of the Sixth Protocol (as read with Arts 16–18 of the Convention). The failure to include Art 13 – the right to an effective remedy – in this list is discussed in ch 10, pp 265–266.

[19] The other was the Republic of Ireland, which has since passed the European Convention on Human Rights Act 2003.

[20] *A-G for Canada v A-G for Ontario* [1937] AC 326, 347 (Lord Atkin).

[21] See, eg, *R v Secretary of State for the Home Department ex p Brind* [1991] 1 AC 696 (HL). *Cf* M Hunt, *Using Human Rights Law in English Courts* (Oxford, Hart Publishing, 1997).

[22] *Ireland v UK* (1979–80) 2 EHRR 25, [239].

party to the proceedings.[23] Further, the 'essentially declaratory'[24] nature of judgments of the Strasbourg organs – stating whether a given decision or action of domestic authorities is either compatible with the Convention standards (or falling within a State's margin of appreciation) or in breach of those standards – presents a hurdle to the direct application of such authority in national law: decisions of the Convention bodies are by no means 'self-executing'.[25] As such, for the purposes of the Strasbourg organs, a domestic court is 'not obliged to give [a decision of the Strasbourg institutions] direct effect in the national law of the defendant state', as a party is free to implement such decisions 'in accordance with the rules of its national legal system.'[26] This flexibility is entirely in keeping with the position of the Court as a court of review: a supervisory court adjudicating on the compatibility of members States' law and practice with the terms of an international treaty. In the Convention system therefore, it is the domestic authorities of the States parties that are primarily responsible for upholding the Convention rights – with the Convention institutions themselves providing a secondary, or supervisory, layer of protection – as the European Court noted in its judgment in the *Handyside* case:

> by reason of their direct and continuous contact with the vital forces of their countries, State authorities are in principle in a better position than the international judge to give an opinion on the exact content of these requirements as well as on the 'necessity' of a 'restriction' or 'penalty' intended to meet them.[27]

The inability of UK courts to place direct reliance on the Convention rights in domestic proceedings had arguably subverted this system; as the former Labour Minister Mike O'Brien noted during the parliamentary debates on the Human Rights Bill:

> the proper role of the Strasbourg Court is to act as a backstop but, at present, the Strasbourg institutions are often placed in the front line, as the first bodies to consider issues arising under the Convention.[28]

---

[23] Art 46(1) ECHR provides: 'The High Contracting Parties undertake to abide by the final judgment of the Court in any case to which they are the parties.' Art 46(2) provides the task of supervising the execution of such a judgment is exercised by the Committee of Ministers.

[24] DJ Harris, M O'Boyle, C Warbrick, *Law of the European Convention on Human Rights* (London, Butterworths, 1995) 26.

[25] C Warbrick, 'The European Convention on Human Rights and the Human Rights Act: the View from the Outside', in H Fenwick, G Phillipson and R Masterman (eds), *Judicial Reasoning under the UK Human Rights Act* (Cambridge, CUP, 2007) 34.

[26] DJ Harris, M O'Boyle, C Warbrick, above n 24, 26, where the example given is of *Vermeire v Belgium* (1993) 15 EHRR 488.

[27] *Handyside v UK* (1979–1980) 1 EHRR 737, [48].

[28] HC Debs, vol 306, col 859 (16 February 1998) (Mike O'Brien MP).

That domestic courts had in effect been precluded from dealing with Convention issues in the vast majority of cases was almost certainly a factor which had contributed to the large number of occasions on which the United Kingdom had been found to be in breach of the Convention by the Strasbourg Court. International obligations aside therefore, the Convention could only be utilised in domestic courts prior to the coming into force of the HRA in certain, limited, circumstances.[29] First, in the event of a statutory ambiguity, the courts would presume that Parliament had intended to legislate compatibly with the United Kingdom's treaty obligations and would give effect to the Convention-compatible reading of the law. In a similar vein, those Acts which sought to achieve compatibility with the Convention could be interpreted in the light of their aim. The exercise of judicial discretion would also seek to avoid an outcome which was non-compliant: a lack of clarity in the common law could similarly be remedied through judicious use of the Convention,[30] while – in the determination of an issue of public policy – 'widely accepted treaties ... may point the direction in which such conceptions, such as applied by the courts, ought to travel.'[31] Finally, where EC law gave effect to ECHR obligations, domestic courts would be obliged to give effect to those measures in domestic law under the terms of the European Communities Act 1972.

However, research published in 1997 was less than optimistic about the positive effects of the Convention under such a constricted regime; despite being raised in argument in some 316 cases decided between 1973 and 1996, the impact of the Convention on the outcome of the case – 'in the sense that the decision of the court might well have been different if the ECHR had not been taken into account' – was limited to only 16 of that number.[32] Without pressure from the Strasbourg organs to take steps to allow the individual to have direct recourse to the ECHR at the domestic level, the myth was perpetuated in the courts that the common law was the equal of the ECHR in terms of the protections it offered for individual liberty.[33] As a consequence, many took the view that liberty was adequately protected in the United Kingdom prior to the enactment of the

---

[29] *Bringing Rights Home: Labour's Plans to Incorporate the European Convention on Human Rights into United Kingdom Law* (December 1996); HL Debs, vol 573, col 1465–7 (3 July 1996) (Lord Bingham of Cornhill). See generally, M Hunt, *Using Human Rights Law in English Courts* (Oxford, Hart Publishing, 1998).

[30] See, eg, *Derbyshire CC v Times Newspapers* [1992] QB 770.

[31] *Blathwayt v Baron Cawley* [1976] AC 397, 426 (Lord Wilberforce).

[32] K Starmer and F Klug, 'Incorporation through the Back Door' [1997] *PL* 223, 225.

[33] See, eg, *Attorney-General v Guardian Newspapers (No 2)* [1990] 1 AC 109, 283–284 (Lord Goff of Chieveley); *Derbyshire v Times Newspapers* [1993] AC 534, 551 (Lord Keith of Kinkel). Cf *Sunday Times v UK* (1979–80) 2 EHRR 245; *Sunday Times v UK* (1992) 14 EHRR 229.

HRA: as the Rt Hon John Major MP is reported to have said with Diceyan confidence, 'we have no need of a Bill of Rights because we have freedom.'[34]

THE BILL OF RIGHTS DEBATE IN THE UNITED KINGDOM[35]

For Dicey the liberty of the individual was rooted in the flexibility of the common law: this malleability – alongside the sovereignty of Parliament – was seen as one of the great strengths of the unwritten constitution. Under this system the citizen was free to do whatever he or she might chose – provided it was not prohibited by either statute or common law.[36] As Lord Browne-Wilkinson noted in *Wheeler v Leicester CC*:

> Basic constitutional rights in this country such as freedom of the person and freedom of speech are based not upon any express provision conferring such a right but on freedom of an individual to do what he will save to the extent that he is prevented from so doing by the law ... These fundamental freedoms therefore are not positive rights but an immunity from interference by others.[37]

Liberties were therefore residual; only existing in the void left after parliamentary statements through legislation. To the extent that these 'liberties' could be defined, cases such as *Entick v Carrington*[38] and *Beatty v Gilbanks*[39] illustrate the strengths of the common law – working in tandem with the rule of law – in this regard. However, as liberties were negatively defined under the common law, reliance on a 'right' in court was often precluded on the grounds that it was not positively recognised by English law.[40] Such 'rights' were also on a precarious footing; in the face of the sovereign Parliament, the common law was powerless to challenge encroachment into these areas of liberty:

> There are two obvious limits to what the common law can achieve by way of protecting human rights. The first is a matter of law – the principle of parliamentary sovereignty. Any legislation can override rights recognised and protected by the common law. The second is a matter of technique and attitude. By and large the common law courts have not reasoned from the premise of

[34] The Rt Hon John Major MP, quoted by Lord Irvine of Lairg QC, HL Debs, vol 582, col 1228 (3 November 1997).

[35] For more detailed commentary on these issues than space allows here see: M Zander, *A Bill of Rights?* (London, Sweet and Maxwell, 1997); F Klug, above n 11; H Fenwick, *Civil Liberties and Human Rights* (4th ed) (London, Routledge Cavendish, 2007), chs 3 and 4.

[36] See, eg, *A-G v Guardian Newspapers (No 2)* [1990] 1 AC 109, 178 (Sir John Donaldson MR).

[37] *Wheeler v Leicester CC* [1985] AC 1054, 1065.

[38] (1765) 19 St Tr 1030.

[39] (1882) 9 QBD 308.

[40] For two notorious examples see: *Malone v Metropolitan Police Commissioner (No 2)* [1979] Ch 344; *Kaye v Robertson* [1991] FSR 62.

specific rights. Our boast, that we are free to do anything not prohibited by law, and that official action against our will must have the support of law, reflects the fact that our rights are residual – what is left after the law (and in particular, legislation) is exhausted. Our thinking does not proceed from rights to results – rather, our rights are the result.[41]

Bradley and Ewing have written that the late nineteenth century, when Dicey wrote his famous treatise, 'was in many ways the high-water mark of an independent Parliament acting as a watchdog of the executive.'[42] Since then, the deficiencies of the common law to protect human rights have only been highlighted by the increasing power of the executive branch vis-a-vis Parliament.[43] The apparent failure of the democratic process to protect rights,[44] coupled with the perception of the increasing weakness of Parliament in the face of an increasingly strong executive branch ensured that the campaign for incorporation of the European Convention on Human Rights steadily gathered momentum.[45]

By the mid-1990s the impotency of the common law in the face of the sovereign Parliament had provoked a number of influential commentators, including senior judges, to raise questions about the future of public law adjudication – specifically that dealing with questions of rights – in the United Kingdom.[46] Yet the continued inertia displayed by the democratic branches to legislate to give effect to positive rights – and the subsequent narrowing of the residue of liberty – saw the suggestion raised that the 'sovereign' power of Parliament was not, in fact, absolute, and that

> ultimately there are even limits on the supremacy of Parliament which it is the courts' inalienable responsibility to identify and uphold.[47]

Lord Woolf's conception of Parliament enacting the 'unthinkable' was reminiscent of the famous words of Lord Coke in *Dr Bonham's case*:

---

[41] J Doyle and B Wells, 'How far can the common law go towards protecting human rights?' in P Alston (ed), *Promoting Human Rights through Bills of Rights* (Oxford, OUP, 1999) 17.

[42] AW Bradley and KD Ewing, *Constitutional and Administrative Law* (London, Longman, 2003) 405.

[43] The famous phrase coined by Lord Hailsham to describe the effect of the growth in power of the executive branch was 'elective dictatorship': see *The Dilemma of Democracy* (London, Collins, 1978).

[44] On the effect of this growth in executive power on liberty in the United Kingdom, see R Dworkin, above n 13; KD Ewing and CA Gearty, above n 13.

[45] See, eg, A Lester, *Democracy and Individual Rights* (London, Fabian Society, 1969); Lord Scarman, *English Law – The New Dimension* (London, Stevens and Sons, 1974).

[46] See, eg, J Laws, 'Is the High Court the Guardian of Fundamental Constitutional Rights?' [1993] PL 59; T Bingham, 'The European Convention on Human Rights: Time to Incorporate' (1993) 109 *LQR* 390; Lord Woolf, 'Droit Public – English Style' [1995] PL 57; S Sedley, 'Human Rights: A Twenty-First Century Agenda' [1995] PL 386.

[47] Lord Woolf, above n 46, 69.

In many cases, the common law will control Acts of Parliament, and sometimes adjudge them to be utterly void: for when an Act of Parliament is against common right and reason, or repugnant, or impossible to be performed, the common law will control it, and adjudge such Act to be void.[48]

For some, recourse to such a pre-civil war authority on the respective status of common and statute law was dubious at best,[49] but for others the words of Lord Coke symbolised the latent potential of the common law in the face of unbridled executive power.[50] The response of the common law came gradually in an increased intensity of review in administrative law cases and the recognition of a category of 'fundamental common law rights'. Through cases such as *Leech*,[51] *Witham*[52] and *Simms*[53] the courts gradually expounded the interpretative presumption that Parliament would not inadvertently legislate to constrain the exercise of certain fundamental rights: to do so successfully, express words would be required.

Prior to the implementation of the HRA then, the domestic case law on fundamental, or constitutional, common law rights had become – in UK terms – a relatively sophisticated statement of positive rights, in comparison to the largely residual state of liberty in the UK at that time.[54] As Lord Steyn has noted extra-judicially, the classification of a right as constitutional

is a powerful indication that added value is attached to the protection of the right. It strengthens the normative force of such rights. It virtually rules out arguments that such rights can be impliedly repealed by subsequent legislation.[55]

Yet – as tacitly indicated by Lord Steyn – the protection that the common law could afford these 'fundamental rights' was not without its limits, as Lord Hoffmann also recognised in *Simms*:

parliamentary sovereignty means that Parliament can, if it chooses, legislate contrary to fundamental principles of human rights ... But the principle of legality means that Parliament must squarely confront what it is doing and accept the political cost. Fundamental rights cannot be overridden by general or

---

[48] (1610) 8 Co Rep 113b, 118a.
[49] See: J Goldsworthy, *The Sovereignty of Parliament: History and Philosophy* (Oxford, Clarendon Press, 1999) 111–17.
[50] See, eg, Lord Woolf, above n 46, 67–9. For a more recent example see Lord Woolf, 'The Rule of Law and a Change in the Constitution' (2004) 63(2) *CLJ* 317, 327–9. See also the speeches of Lord Steyn and of Baroness Hale in *Jackson v Her Majesty's Attorney-General* [2005] UKHL 56.
[51] *R v Secretary of State for the Home Department ex p Leech (No 2)* [1994] QB 198.
[52] *R v Lord Chancellor ex p Witham* [1998] QB 575.
[53] *R v Secretary of State for the Home Department ex p Simms* [2000] 2 AC 115.
[54] Lord Cooke of Thorndon 'The Road Ahead for the Common Law' 53 *ICLQ* 273, 276–8.
[55] Lord Steyn, 'Dynamic Interpretation amidst an orgy of statutes' [2004] *EHRLR* 245, 252.

ambiguous words. This is because there is too great a risk that the full implications of their unqualified meaning may have passed unnoticed in the democratic process. In the absence of express language or necessary implication to the contrary, the courts therefore presume that even the most general words were intended to be subject to the basic rights of the individual.[56]

The challenges posed by the doctrine of parliamentary sovereignty to those wishing to see the Convention given further effect in domestic law were, however, various and constant. First, as noted above, in the event of the use of the Convention as an aid to construction, clear and unambiguous words of primary legislation could – in the absence of an adverse finding against the State – be deployed to effectively trump any authority from Strasbourg relied upon by counsel. Those hoping for the judiciary to develop a coherent and principled basis on which the Convention might be used in domestic litigation were therefore countered with the decision of the House of Lords in *Brind*: the Convention might be relied in certain closely defined circumstances, but to give further effect to its terms in domestic law – in the absence of legislation permitting it – would see the courts straying beyond interpretation of the law into its implementation.[57]

Secondly, the argument for an entrenched bill of rights – protected from future amendment or revocation – was met with assertions of the unfettered sovereign power of Parliament, and the suggestion that any legislative measure in favour of protecting human rights would itself be open to future repeal or amendment:

British constitutional law has long held to the principle that ... entrenchment is impossible ... Only by not having a concept of entrenchment of any sort has it been possible to protect the full power of Parliament's sovereignty from the passing desires of temporary majorities.[58]

Thirdly, the conviction that to allow the judiciary to decide upon questions of rights would be a usurpation of the democratic processes of Parliament – judges being neither elected by nor accountable to those whom Parliament is said to represent – was similarly deployed against those in favour

---

[56] [2000] 2 AC 115. These fundamental common law rights continue to 'exist quite apart from the Human Rights Act' (Lord Cooke, above n 54, 276). In *International Transport Roth GmbH v Secretary of State for the Home Department* [2003] QB 728, [71], Laws LJ stated: '... the common law has come to recognise and endorse the notion of constitutional, or fundamental rights. These are broadly the rights given expression in the Convention for the Protection of Human Rights and Fundamental Freedoms, but their recognition in the common law is autonomous ...'; and although the HRA has brought certain of the Convention Rights into play in domestic law, as the House of Lords recognised in *R (Anufrijeva) v Secretary of State for the Home Department* [2004] 1 AC 604, [27], 'the Convention is not an exhaustive statement of fundamental rights under our system of law'.
[57] *R v Secretary of State for the Home Department ex p Brind* [1991] 1 AC 696, 718 (Lord Donaldson of Lymington MR), 762–3 (Lord Ackner).
[58] KD Ewing and CA Gearty, 'Rocky Foundations for Labour's New Rights' [1997] *EHRLR* 146, 147.

of incorporation.[59] The transfer of political 'power from Westminster to the Strand, from Parliament to the Courts',[60] which critics argued would accompany any Bill of Rights would be detrimental to the democratic process for the reason that power would be shifted away from the elected representatives of the people to a body who would have 'ultimate authority to make political decisions for a community' while not being 'in any sense representative of the community they serve.'[61] In the absence of wholesale reform of the judiciary and its appointments process,

> the effect of a Bill of Rights or incorporated European Convention is to empower the judges to unsettle decisions made in the political arena by the people's representatives and thereby frustrate the democratic process.[62]

Public law adjudication in the United Kingdom has long been characterised by the doctrine of deference most evident in *Wednesbury*-style[63] judicial review, and the fact that the validity of Acts of Parliament cannot be questioned in courts of law.[64] The incorporation of the European Convention on Human Rights would, objectors argued, unsettle the status quo by, at best, removing considerable political power from elected bodies, and, at worst, allowing the (unelected, unrepresentative and unaccountable) judiciary to strike down decisions – including Acts of Parliament – produced in the political realm.[65]

BRINGING RIGHTS HOME

May 1997 saw the election of the first Blair administration with manifesto commitments to implement an unprecedented array of constitutional reforms. The abolition of the hereditary principle as a criterion governing membership of the House of Lords, the enactment of Freedom of Information legislation, devolution to Scotland, Wales and Northern Ireland, reform of the party funding mechanisms, and reform of the House of

---

[59] See, eg, JAG Griffith, 'The Political Constitution' (1979) 42 *MLR* 1; Lord McCluskey, *Law Justice and Democracy* (London, Sweet and Maxwell, 1987).

[60] KD Ewing, 'The Bill of Rights Debate: Democracy or Juristocracy in Britain?' in KD Ewing, CA Gearty and BA Hepple (eds), *Human Rights and Labour Law: Essays for Paul O'Higgins* (London, Mansell, 1994) 147.

[61] *Ibid*, 152.

[62] *Ibid*, 156.

[63] *Associated Provincial Picture Houses v Wednesbury Corporation* [1948] 1 KB 223.

[64] *British Railways Board v Pickin* [1974] AC 765. *Cf* the limited exceptions to this rule in *Factortame (No 2)* [1991] 1 AC 603 and *Jackson v Attorney-General* [2006] 1 AC 262.

[65] For a sample of 'rights sceptical' literature see: T Campbell, KD Ewing and A Tomkins (eds), *Sceptical Essays on Human Rights* (Oxford, OUP, 2001); JAG Griffith, above n 59; J Waldron, 'A Rights-Based Critique of Constitutional Rights' (1993) 13(1) *OJLS* 18; J Allan 'Bills of Rights and Judicial Power – A Liberal's Quandary' (1996) 16(2) *OJLS* 337; J Allan, 'Portia, Bassanio or Dick the Butcher? Constraining Judges in the Twenty-First Century' (2006) 17 *KCLJ* 1.

Commons were all a part of the new Government's ambitious scheme.[66] The enactment of a statute designed to incorporate the European Convention on Human Rights into domestic law was one of the key elements of this new constitutional landscape. The proposals to incorporate the Convention were a part of the legacy of the leadership of John Smith who, in 1993, had advocated such a step and effected a significant change in Labour party policy.[67]

The Labour Party consultation paper, *Bringing Rights Home*,[68] written by Jack Straw and Paul Boateng – then Shadow Home Secretary and Shadow Minister for the Lord Chancellor's Department respectively – was published in December 1996. It outlined a proposal for incorporation which would, its authors said, 'cut costs, save time and give power back to British courts.'[69] The proposed method of incorporation would not systematically scour domestic law for inconsistency with Strasbourg, but – in harmony with the incremental nature of common law development:

> allow case law to develop over time, and ... point the way to any areas where Parliament might need to amend existing law.[70]

The interpretative mechanism that would become section 3(1) HRA was apparent even at this early stage:

> the courts would be required to construe all existing (as well as future) legislation, so far as is possible, consistently with the Convention.[71]

The proposals were attacked by Ewing and Gearty, who suggested that it was by no means evident that this 'constitutional revolution' would either cut costs, increase efficiency or in fact improve the state of civil liberty in the United Kingdom, pointing to the unsuitability of the judiciary to determine questions of human rights:

> Until quite recently, democracy was taken sufficiently seriously in this country for it to be considered wrong in principle to allow unelected, unrepresentative and unaccountable lawyers to determine the validity of parliamentary legislation.[72]

---

[66] *New Labour: Because Britain Deserves Better* (London, Labour Party, 1997).

[67] *A New Agenda for Democracy: Labour's Proposals for Constitutional Reform* (1993).

[68] J Straw and P Boateng, *Bringing Rights Home: Labour's plans to incorporate the European Convention on Human Rights into United Kingdom Law* (London, Labour Party, 1996).

[69] *Ibid*. In 1996 it was estimated that, after exhausting domestic remedies, it would take 'some six years from the time when an individual complains to the Commission until the Court gives judgment' (Lord Lester, 'The European Convention in the New Architecture of Europe' [1996] *PL* 5, 5).

[70] *Ibid*.

[71] *Ibid*.

[72] KD Ewing and CA Gearty, 'Rocky Foundations for Labour's New Rights' [1997] *EHRLR* 146, 148.

Under the proposed measure, direct reliance on the Convention rights would be available against public authorities – 'government departments, executive agencies, quangos, local authorities and other public services'[73] – as 'the central purpose of the ECHR is to protect the individual against the misuse of power by the State.'[74] Importantly however, the consultation document anticipated a scheme of incorporation which would not afford the judiciary a power to invalidate or otherwise 'disapply' primary legislation. As a result, Straw and Boateng claimed, '[t]his new Act would not alter Parliament's sovereignty.'[75] This claim may have underplayed the significance of the proposed measure, as it would also apply not only to Acts passed prior to its enactment but also to measures which had been passed later in time. As such, Ewing and Gearty argued, parliamentary sovereignty would in fact be significantly altered by the proposed measure:

> ... sovereignty is anything but unaffected by the Labour proposal ... Labour seem prepared to contemplate the jettisoning of the doctrine of implied repeal, so as to permit the courts to strike down legislation [sic] passed not only before but also after incorporation where such Acts are found by the courts to be inconsistent with the terms of the Convention.[76]

RIGHTS BROUGHT HOME

The White Paper on the Human Rights Bill, published in October 1997, restated the case for incorporation, based on the central issues of costs and delay to those seeking redress. The Government estimated that the average cost of taking a case to Strasbourg was £30,000, and that to do so would take in excess of five years, following the exhaustion of domestic remedies.[77] It was argued that these facts deterred many of those who felt their rights had been infringed from attempting to obtain a remedy. In addition, and in spite of the fact that British lawyers had played a leading role in the drafting of the Convention, the new Government suggested that the Convention rights were 'no longer seen as British rights',[78] further deterring those who may have suffered a breach from seeking a remedy. Allowing domestic courts to enforce the Convention rights would therefore provide both a benefit to those seeking a remedy in the jurisdiction and,

[73] The White Paper and Bill which followed – and the HRA – offered no comprehensive definition of 'public authority'. See ch 6 below.

[74] J Straw and P Boateng, *Bringing Rights Home* (London, Labour Party, 1996).

[75] *Ibid.*

[76] KD Ewing and CA Gearty, 'Rocky Foundations for Labour's New Rights' [1997] *EHRLR* 146, 147.

[77] White Paper, *Rights Brought Home* (October 1997), Cm 3782, para 1.14. See <http://www.archive.official-documents.co.uk/document/hoffice/rights/rights.htm> accessed 20 May 2008.

[78] *Ibid.*

more widely, would have the effect of enabling British judges to make a 'distinctively British contribution to the development of the jurisprudence of human rights in Europe.'[79] Equally it was hoped that a more rights-orientated process of litigation in domestic courts would lead to fewer embarrassing findings of incompatibility at Strasbourg.

A collaborative exercise?

During the Second Reading debates on the Human Rights Bill in the House of Lords, Lord Irvine stated that 'the Bill is carefully drafted and designed to respect our traditional understanding of the separation of powers',[80] no doubt partly to placate those who felt the Bill heralded the transfer of political power to the judges. But looking beyond the debate over the boundary between sections 3 and 4 of the Act,[81] it is clear that the doctrine of the separation of powers *would* in a sense be altered by the passing into effect of the HRA. At least in the eyes of the Government, the HRA formed the hub of a collaborative exercise involving all three branches of Government in the promotion and protection of the Convention Rights. The HRA was seen by those in Government as a tool for creating a 'human rights culture' in the UK: a mechanism to halt the 'decline in the culture of liberty' that had come to prompt critics of residual liberty to advocate incorporation by the 1990s.[82] Ministers were keen to stress that the HRA would not just affect those with the resources to challenge the acts or omissions of public authorities for non-compliance with the Convention rights, but would bring about a sea-change in public body decision-making processes that would be beneficial to society as a whole. As Lord Irvine later elaborated before the Joint Committee on Human Rights:

> a culture of respect for human rights is to create a society in which our public institutions are habitually, automatically responsive to human rights considerations in relation to every procedure they follow, in relation to every decision they take, in relation to every piece of legislation they sponsor.[83]

It became clear that the implementation of the HRA was not intended to be the within the sole jurisdiction of the courts, but was to encourage a collaborative exercise toward the promotion and protection of human rights involving the three arms of government. At the parliamentary level, section 19 HRA was designed to ensure that the human rights dimensions

---

[79]   *Ibid.*
[80]   HL Debs, vol 582, col 1228 (3 November 1997).
[81]   On which see ch 4.
[82]   R Dworkin, above n 13, 1.
[83]   Joint Committee on Human Rights, Minutes of Evidence, 19 March 2001, 38 (Lord Irvine of Lairg).

of proposed legislation were to be explored fully prior to introducing a bill into the legislature,[84] and it soon became evident that central to parliamentary involvement in this enterprise would be a human rights committee, the creation of which was proposed during the passage of the Human Rights Bill by the Government.[85] Perhaps the clearest indication that the HRA was intended to spark a collaborative exercise at the apex of government was in the design of what are arguably the Act's key provisions: sections 3 and 4. As is now well-known, section 3 affords the judiciary the power to interpret statutory language to achieve compatibility with the Convention Rights, or, if such an interpretation is not possible, the Act allows for Parliament to resolve the issue following the issue of a declaration of incompatibility by the higher courts.

However, if the Government did see the implementation of the HRA 1998 as a collaborative exercise, it was unclear at the time whether one of the main partners in this enterprise – the judiciary – shared the same view. From the outset it was evident that aspirations for the HRA differed markedly between personnel in the three branches of government. In a notable appearance before the fledgling Joint Parliamentary Committee on Human Rights in March 2001 the Lord Chief Justice, Master of the Rolls and Senior Law Lord were asked to comment on the views expressed by the Lord Chancellor at a previous evidence session, when he had stated that the HRA would prompt a 'dialogue' between the three branches of government. Lord Woolf acknowledged that the Act would alter the traditional balance in the separation of powers, but would not be drawn on how that change might manifest itself, saying:

[a]s I see it, the judges have got a role, Parliament has a role and the executive has a role, and the Human Rights Act is going to affect all three in the performance of that role.[86]

Lord Bingham was more dismissive of the idea of the HRA as a collaborative exercise, saying:

---

[84] Section 19 is discussed more fully in ch 2.

[85] Mike O'Brien MP, HC Debs, vol 307, col 857 (16 February 1998). Ultimately, the decision to establish such a committee, and the remit of that body, were decisions to taken by Parliament. The Joint Parliamentary Committee on Human Rights was established in January 2001 with a broad remit to scrutinise 'matters relating to human rights in the United Kingdom', albeit one which fell short of a power to investigate individual complaints (although the potential for such a power was discussed in Parliament: HL Debs, vol 583, col 1153 (27 November 1997)). The terms of Reference of the Joint Committee are as follows: 'To consider: (a) matters relating to human rights in the United Kingdom (but excluding consideration of individual cases); (b) proposals for remedial orders, draft remedial orders and remedial orders made under s 10 and laid under Sch 2 to the Human Rights Act 1998; and (c) in respect of draft remedial orders and remedial orders, whether the special attention of the House should be drawn to them on any of the grounds specified in Standing Order 73 (Joint Committee on Statutory Instruments).

[86] Joint Committee on Human Rights, Oral Evidence (21 March 2001), 78.

> I would not myself think in terms of a dialogue at all. The business of the judges is to listen to cases and give judgment. In doing that, of course, they will pay attention to the arguments that are addressed to them and one hopes they will be alive to the currents of thought which are prevalent in the community, but I do not myself see it as the role of the judges to engage in dialogue.[87]

Lord Phillips of Worth Matravers added: 'I do not think that dialogue is the right word either, but I do think there is a spirit of co-operation rather than adversarial feeling so far as the judiciary and executive are concerned; we are both trying to do the same thing.'[88]

Parliamentary Sovereignty – and Rights Sceptics – Assuaged?

A more nuanced conception of the separation of powers doctrine may therefore have been envisaged by the Government in its design of the Act, but this realignment of constitutional principle came with clear limits. Revolutionary the HRA may be, but it is not a Bill of Rights in the US or Canadian sense: the courts cannot use it to override statutes. Parliamentary sovereignty, theoretically, remains the cornerstone of the constitution. As the then Home Secretary, Jack Straw, outlined during the Bill's second reading debate:

> The sovereignty of Parliament must be paramount. By that, I mean that Parliament must be competent to make any law on any matter of its choosing. In enacting legislation, Parliament is making decisions about important matters of public policy. The authority to make those decisions derives from a democratic mandate. Members of this place possess such a mandate because they are elected, accountable and representative ... To allow the courts to set aside Acts of Parliament would confer on the judiciary a power that it does not possess, and which could draw it into serious conflict with Parliament.[89]

Vitally, therefore, the HRA does not therefore promote the *de facto* judicial supremacy which characterises adjudication surrounding other Bills of Rights. Instead, there is the duty of the courts to read and give effect to primary and subordinate legislation 'in a way which is compatible with the Convention rights', in the words of section 3(1), '[s]o far as it is possible to do so'. This carefully-crafted provision strengthens the influence of the Convention in at least two ways. First, the courts previously required legislation to be ambiguous before they would refer to the Convention to settle differences of meaning, on the assumption (which could be displaced) that Parliament intended to legislate in accordance with the Crown's international treaty obligations. Section 3 no longer requires there to be a

---

[87] *Ibid.*
[88] *Ibid.*
[89] HC Debs, vol 306, col 772 (16 February 1998) (Jack Straw MP).

statutory ambiguity before the threshold can be crossed. The Convention must be considered in all cases by all courts and tribunals and even where to adopt a Convention-friendly reading might seem unnatural, provided it is *possible*.

The second main extension under section 3 of the courts' duty is that legislation *in all fields* is to be read in a Convention-friendly way. This applies as much in the private sphere, for example, to landlord and tenant and family legislation, where there is on the face of it no clash between the individual and the state. This is one of several ways in which the Act may apply 'horizontally.'[90]

Section 3 – and the interpretative exercise it sanctions – does not affect the 'validity, continuing operation or enforcement of any incompatible primary legislation.'[91] The prospect that it may be impossible to read some statutes to conform is the escape-hatch that the HRA has left for parliamentary sovereignty. In these cases the superior courts may issue a curious order – a declaration of incompatibility,[92] which again upholds the sovereignty of Parliament, since the Act states clearly that even legislation declared incompatible remains valid and effective.[93] The practical effect of the declaration is to signal to Parliament that there is a problem and to allow Ministers to expedite changes in the law[94] – if they choose to do so. The fact that Parliament is given the task of remedying the incompatibility reinforces the role played by the democratic process in protecting rights and freedoms: although the courts may declare an Act to be incompatible, the resolution of that incompatibility lies in the hands of the democratic arms of the state. For those rights sceptics concerned that the incorporation of the Convention would amount to a 'constitutional revolution' under which the powers of the elected arms of the state would be placed at the mercy of the judicial branch, this carefully constructed balance between judicial enforcement of the Convention and parliamentary democracy was key to an acceptance of the HRA.[95]

Although the use of the 'declaration of incompatibility' mechanism nominally ensures that the ultimate resolution of the issue lies in Parliament, it is apparent the recourse to this route was – at least in the eyes of the Government – not to be the norm; most 'inconsistencies' between the

---

[90]   See ch 9.

[91]   HRA s 3(2)(a).

[92]   HRA s 4. For the purposes of s 4, 'court' is taken to mean the House of Lords, Judicial Committee of the Privy Council, Courts-Martial Appeal Court, High Court of Justiciary (sitting otherwise than as a trial court) or Court of Session in Scotland, or the High Court or Court of Appeal in England and Wales and Northern Ireland.

[93]   HRA s 4(6).

[94]   HRA s 10 and Sch 2.

[95]   Contrast the views of Professor Gearty as expressed in n 76 above, with his *Principles of Human Rights Adjudication* (Oxford, OUP, 2004).

Convention rights and domestic legislation could be dealt with through the interpretative power in section 3(1). During the parliamentary debates on the Human Rights Bill Lord Irvine referred to the 'rare cases where the courts have to make declarations of incompatibility,'[96] and early indications were that this view was shared by members of the senior judiciary.[97] While section 3(1) may therefore fall well short of a power of legislative override, if it were to be used with regularity – with the declaration of incompatibility consigned to be a 'measure of last resort'[98] – then the compromise between parliamentary sovereignty and 'juristocracy'[99] might not in practice be as carefully balanced between the judicial and democratic arms as might be appear to be in theory.[100]

THE PREPARATORY STAGES FOR IMPLEMENTING THE ACT

In the run-up to October 2000, significant steps were taken across Whitehall to prepare for the coming into force of the HRA.[101] Various bodies – Cabinet Committees, Lawyers co-ordination groups – met to discuss the potential impact of the Act on central government; while the Civil Service College implemented a training scheme for Civil Servants aimed at increasing awareness across government more generally. The lead implementation department – the Home Office – set up the Human Rights Task Force, a combination of government and NGO representatives charged with assisting Whitehall departments and wider public bodies in their preparations for October 2000,[102] and with increasing public awareness of the rights to which the HRA would give further effect.

The Human Rights Task Force, along with the Home Office, published guidance and information material on the Act for public authorities and the general public, made recommendations to Departments, collected and

---

[96]   HL Debs, vol 582, col 1231 (3 November 1997) (Lord Irvine of Lairg).

[97]   *R v A (No 2)* [2002] 1 AC 45, 68 (Lord Hope), 106 (Lord Hutton).

[98]   *Ibid*, 44 (Lord Steyn).

[99]   KD Ewing, 'The Bill of Rights Debate: Democracy or Juristocracy in Britain?' in KD Ewing, CA Gearty and BA Hepple (eds), *Human Rights and Labour Law: Essays for Paul O'Higgins* (London, Mansell, 1994).

[100]   This debate – and a more detailed examination of the cases involving ss 3 and 4 HRA – will be returned to in chs 4 and 5.

[101]   See generally: A Hammond, 'The Human Rights Act and the Government Legal Service' 20(3) *Statute Law Review* 230, 235–36.

[102]   Its members were: Mike O'Brien MP (Chair), Lord Bach (Lord Chancellor's Department), Ross Cranston MP (Solicitor General), Francesca Klug (Human Rights Act Incorporation Project), Anne Owers (JUSTICE), Pam Giddy (Charter88), Sarah Spencer (IPPR), Heather Vaccianna (The 1990 Trust), John Wadham (Liberty), Officials from the Home Office, Lord Chancellor's Department and the Cabinet Office, and representatives from the Association of Chief Police Officers, the Crown Prosecution Service and The Local Government Association.

passed on information on good practice, assisted with training, including establishing a Human Rights Act helpdesk and website, and organised publicity for the Act.[103] In doing so – as Croft has observed – it fulfilled one of the main functions of a Human Rights Commission, namely, the promotion of human rights. It would not however, take responsibility for 'the conduct of inquiries into human rights issues' nor 'assist ... users of the HRA in the Courts' and was 'deliberately steered away from the broader policy issues in relation to the HRA that might overlap with the proposed Joint Parliamentary Committee on Human Rights.'[104]

By far the largest task however in the run-up to the implementation of the Act was the audit of statutory provisions designed to highlight areas of potential incompatibility. As Lord Irvine subsequently noted before the Joint Committee on Human Rights:

> the truly remarkable amount of preparation that went in, in Whitehall, across all departments, to estimate and evaluate major statutory provisions, practices, procedures of the departments, to audit for Human Rights Act compliance is itself a yardstick of success of the Act itself.[105]

This exercise fulfilled two major roles: firstly as a precaution against challenge to existing measures and practices on the ground of incompatibility with one of the 'Convention rights'; secondly as a mechanism for 'mainstreaming' human rights – making officials familiar with the language and implications of the HRA – one of the first steps towards the Government's 'culture of human rights.' Some commentators have however argued that the first of these aims took priority,[106] with, in the run-up to implementation, there being 'no incentive at the centre to become too deeply engaged in matters relating to the future operation of the Act';[107] instead the focus was placed very much on damage limitation. Croft wrote in 2000 that:

---

[103] Memorandum by the Home Office, *Implementation and Early Effects of the Human Rights Act 1998*, Joint Committee on Human Rights, Minutes of Evidence, 14 March 2001.

[104] J Croft, *Whitehall and the Human Rights Act 1998* (London, Constitution Unit, 2000) 22.

[105] Joint Committee on Human Rights, Minutes of Evidence, 19 March 2001, 43 (Lord Irvine of Lairg).

[106] Although Lord Irvine has written that the task was one of 'sensible auditing, training and moderate reform, with the aim of achieving sufficient, rather than excessive, compliance' ('The Impact of the Human Rights Act: Parliament, the Courts and the Executive', in *Human Rights, Constitutional Law and the Development of the English Legal System* (Oxford, Hart Publishing, 2003) 118).

[107] J Croft, *Whitehall and the Human Rights Act 1998* (London, Constitution Unit, 2000) 28.

a containment strategy would now appear to be in effect that will realise the objective of avoiding or reducing successful challenges but will not provide the springboard for further steps to be taken a part of a proactive human rights policy.[108]

This reluctance to engage fully with the promotion of a 'human rights culture' can, at least in part, be attributed to the fact that the majority of Whitehall departments did not see an increase in their budgets to deal with incorporation. The same cannot be said of the preparations undertaken by the judiciary in the run-up to implementation. The Judicial Studies Board (JSB) programme of training for the senior judiciary cost £4.5 million and amounted to the 'largest programme in the history of the official training body',[109] involving some 3,500 judges and 30,000 magistrates.

All full and part-time judges were able to attend a JSB-organised series of 58 seminars on specific sections of the Act and Articles of the Convention which ran during 2000:

> the seminars included opening lectures by leading practitioners and academics on the methodology and structure of the Act and Convention, followed by syndicate exercises to enable judges to work on criminal, civil and family (public and private) law ... The training was carefully structured to engage the participants and develop understanding of the Act in a short timeframe.[110]

Magistrates and tribunal members also participated in various events and training schemes organised by, among others, Liberty and JUSTICE.[111]

But beyond the initial deployment of governmental resources, a questionable commitment to the ongoing ideal of a human rights culture can also be discerned. While the Human Rights Task Force undoubtedly conducted vital work in raising awareness in the run-up to implementation, the Government evidently felt that its usefulness post-October 2000 was limited: it last met in April 2001. The Government's ambivalence to the longer term success of their human rights project is also arguably evident in their initial reluctance to establish a specific human rights commission.[112] While the Lord Chancellor's Department – subsequently

---

[108]   *Ibid*, 27. The Government's 'damage limitation' policy is in evidence in its motivations for enacting the Regulation of Investigatory Powers Act 2000 (see the Home Office Consultation Paper, 'Interception of Communications in the United Kingdom (1999), Cm 4368). For the more explicit steps taken by the Scottish Parliament see the Convention Rights (Compliance) (Scotland) Act 2001.

[109]   F Klug, *Values for a Godless Age* (London, Penguin, 2000) 33–34.

[110]   Memorandum from the Lord Chancellor, Lord Irvine of Lairg, to the Joint Committee on Human Rights (March 2001), Minutes of Evidence, Joint Committee on Human Rights, 19 March 2001.

[111]   F Klug, *Values for a Godless Age* (London, Penguin, 2000) 34. See also: Lord Hope, 'The Human Rights Act 1998: The Task of the Judges' (1999) 20(3) *Statute Law Review* 185, 188–9.

[112]   See, eg, Lord Irvine of Lairg, HL Debs, vol 582, col 1233 (3 November 1997); Lord Williams of Mostyn, HL Debs, vol 583, cols 850–851 (24 November 1997). See now the

the Department for Constitutional Affairs, most recently the Ministry of Justice – retained 'ownership' of the HRA, the lack of a body charged with promoting the so-called 'human rights culture' allowed a series of damaging myths and misconceptions to develop surrounding the effects and abilities of the HRA – many perpetuated by Government Ministers themselves.[113] During 2006 the Department for Constitutional Affairs belatedly announced its intention to, 'lead a major push on guidance and training within departments, and within wider public sector agencies' and recognised the

> urgent need for the public to be better informed about the benefits which the Human Rights Act has given ordinary people, and to debunk many of the myths which have grown up around the Convention rights and the way they have been applied, both domestically and in Strasbourg.[114]

If the implementation of the HRA was to be a collaborative exercise, by 2006 it was unclear whether the Government was effectively holding to its side of the bargain.

Equality and Human Rights Commission, provided for in the Equality Act 2006, which became operational in October 2007 (<www.cehr.org.uk> accessed 15 May 2008).

[113] For discussion see H Fenwick, G Phillipson and R Masterman, 'The Human Rights Act in Contemporary Context' in H Fenwick, G Phillipson and R Masterman (eds), *Judicial Reasoning under the UK Human Rights Act* (Cambridge, CUP, 2007); F Klug, 'A Bill of Rights: Do we need one, or do we already have one?' [2007] *PL* 701.

[114] Department for Constitutional Affairs, *Review of the Implementation of the Human Rights Act* (July 2006) 6–7.

Chapter 2

Human Rights and the Political Process

INTRODUCTION

IT WAS AN avowed intention of the Labour Government in introducing the Human Rights Act 1998 (HRA) that human rights culture would become central to the UK's public life and political discourse. Equally, though, as we have seen in chapter 1, there was a desire to avoid judicial supremacism. Rather, the proposed model was one in which the courts, Parliament and the executive shared responsibility for promoting human rights:

> The enforcement of Convention rights will be a matter for the courts, whilst the Government and Parliament will have the different but equally important responsibility of revising legislation where necessary. But it is also highly desirable for the Government to ensure as far as possible that legislation which it places before Parliament in the normal way is compatible with the Convention rights, and for Parliament to ensure that the human rights implications of legislation are subject to proper consideration before the legislation is enacted.[1]

In this chapter we examine the ways in which that objective has been carried forward, both through provisions in the HRA itself and through other institutions and parliamentary processes. We discuss the procedures both at Westminster – through the use of compatibility statements under HRA section 19 and the operation of the Joint Committee on Human Rights – and in the devolved assemblies. The latter – the Scottish Parliament, the National Assembly for Wales and the Northern Ireland Assembly, together with their respective governments – are the other most notable feature of the Labour Government's grand constitutional reform project.

We begin, however, with the road not travelled. There has been no attempt to tie together protection of human rights with the major reform of Parliament itself that has been underway since 1997: reform of the House of Lords. Not only, we argue, does this represent a failure of

---

[1] *Rights Brought Home: the Human Rights Bill* (Cm 3782, 1997), para 3.1.

joined-up thinking but also, when judged by international standards, it underlines the relative weakness of the protection granted to human rights under the HRA.

HOUSE OF LORDS REFORM AND HUMAN RIGHTS

In its 2000 Report on reform of the House of Lords the Royal Commission on Reform of the House of Lords (the Wakeham Commission) quotes Professor Sir William Wade:

> One safeguard conspicuous by its absence from the constitution is the entrenchment of fundamental rights.[2]

That remains the case despite both the introduction of the HRA[3] and the partial implementation of reform of the second chamber. It is worth identifying at the outset why the connection between rights protection and parliamentary reform has not been made in the United Kingdom. A superficially attractive answer would refer, of course, to parliamentary sovereignty and the design of the HRA itself. It is true that a distracting and sterile debate about the (im)possibility of entrenching a Bill of Rights delayed incorporation of the European Convention for decades.[4] However, the issue here is not the respective powers of the courts and parliament, but rather the powers and role of each House of Parliament. In that discussion 'parliamentary sovereignty' is a doubly-encrypted term: it is code for House of Commons' supremacy and (behind that), executive dominance.

Consequently, when the government established a Royal Commission to examine reform of the House of Lords in 1999, one reform that it did *not* contemplate was increasing the powers of the Lords to scrutinise or delay legislation that interfered with human rights – this was put beyond the terms of reference of the Wakeham Commission.[5] Nevertheless the Commission was instructed to take particular account 'of the present nature of the constitutional settlement, including ... the impact of the Human Rights Act 1998.'[6]

---

[2] Report of the Royal Commission on the House of Lords, *A House for the Future*, Cm 4534 (2000) para 5.2. See <http://www.archive.official-documents.co.uk/document/cm45/4534/4534.htm> accessed 20 May 2008.

[3] See the discussion of the potential impact of a Bill of Rights in ch 11.

[4] pp 12–13 above. *Rights Brought Home* summarily dismissed the idea of entrenchment: 'an arrangement of this kind could not be reconciled with our own constitutional traditions, which allow any Act of Parliament to be amended or repealed by a subsequent Act of Parliament. We do not believe that it is necessary or would be desirable to attempt to devise such a special arrangement for this Bill.' (para 2.16).

[5] These referred to maintaining 'the position of the House of Commons as the preeminent chamber of Parliament': *A House for the Future*, preliminaries.

[6] Idem.

The Commission decided not to support the calls that it received for a reformed second chamber to be given additional powers over constitutional or human rights legislation, for example, an absolute veto or a suspensory veto for two years. These proposals were rejected 'both for practical reasons and also on principle'.[7] As regards the latter, the Commission saw procedures of this kind as fundamentally altering the existing balance of power between the two chambers. The Commission was also unsympathetic in part because it would introduce or formalise in effect a process for constitutional amendments.[8] The practical objections concerned the difficulties of delineating what was a 'constitutional' or 'human rights' question in the absence of a written constitution and a constitutional court.[9] In view of the wide scope of Convention rights and the large numbers of Bills that the Joint Committee on Human Rights (JCHR) has analysed for Convention compatibility this objection may appear to have some force. The Commission also considered more limited alternatives, such as listing legislation protected by any such provision, to be undesirable. A list would in its view either be very short and incomplete or, if more complete, give unwarranted protection against amendment by many 'inoffensive' Bills.[10] Instead the Commission looked to the (then pending) establishment of the JCHR and the Constitution Committee in the House of Lords as sufficiently underwriting the role of the reformed second chamber as a 'constitutional long-stop'.

Although several parliamentary committees have considered detailed schemes for Lords' reform in the aftermath of the Commission, these have been pre-occupied with the debate over *composition* of the second chamber. None of them has given detailed consideration to the issue of human rights protection[11] or dissented from Wakeham's conclusions. The relative lack of protection within the UK legislative process against legislation affecting fundamental rights that this leaves is anomalous from an international perspective. In a study comparing the powers of second chambers in twenty countries worldwide, Meg Russell found that in most of these states constitutional amendments required at least a qualified majority vote in both chambers of Parliament[12] and that in all other cases except the UK the second chamber's consent by a simple majority was required (thus

---

[7] *A House for the Future*, para 5.6.

[8] *Ibid*, paras 5.7 and 5.8.

[9] The alternative of certification by the Speaker was rejected for similar reasons: para 5.11.

[10] Para 5.10.

[11] Eg *Fifth Report of the Public Administration Committee*, Cm 494 (2001–02), para 72 ff.

[12] M Russell, *Reforming the House of Lords: Lessons From Overseas* (Oxford, OUP, 2000) 34–41, discussing Austria, Belgium, the Czech Republic, Germany, India, Italy, Japan, Mexico, Netherlands, the Russian Federation, South Africa, and the USA.

giving it a veto) or a referendum had to be held.[13] In a number of countries there was also a power for parliamentarians to refer the constitutional validity of draft legislation to the constitutional court with the effect of a veto if the legislation was found unconstitutional.[14] Naturally, in all the comparator states there was a written constitution,[15] since the United Kingdom stands virtually alone in not possessing such a document; but, that difference notwithstanding, the lack of any formal equivalent protection at Westminster is a grave and idiosyncratic defect that it is too easy to overlook from a position of detached Anglo-Saxon superiority.

Behind the Government's refusal to countenance an increase in the powers of the House of Lords to underpin its constitutional watchdog role lay a telling distinction in its diagnosis of the need for added protection for human rights. The White Paper *Rights Brought Home* made clear that the main defect it sought to address was the ease of access for individuals to the Convention.[16] There was, then, no official acknowledgement that excessive curtailment of human rights through repressive legislation by Parliament was part of the problem to be addressed. Bearing that in mind, it is unsurprising that the HRA relies upon enhanced human rights *scrutiny* rather than formal parliamentary hurdles to promote rights protection. We turn now to examine the devices for scrutiny under the Act and at Westminster, beginning with the requirement for a ministerial statement to Parliament.

COMPATIBILITY STATEMENTS UNDER SECTION 19

The Human Rights Act borrows from earlier parliamentary rights schemes the requirement for certification of human rights compatibility of draft legislation. This device is a feature of both the Canadian and New Zealand Bills of Rights. Section 19 HRA requires the responsible minister to make a statement before the second reading of a Bill. This is either, in his or her view, that the provisions are 'compatible with Convention rights',[17] or:

---

[13]   *Idem*, discussing Australia, Canada, Ireland, Poland and Switzerland.

[14]   Russell, above n 12,187–88, discussing procedures for referral in Spain, Germany and France.

[15]   A written constitution invariably includes protection for individual rights although Australia has a written constitution but (as yet) no Commonwealth (federal) Bill of Rights.

[16]   'Our aim is a straightforward one. It is to make more directly accessible the rights which the British people already enjoy under the Convention': *Rights Brought Home*, para 1.19.

[17]   S 19(1)(a). Strictly, the effect is to require *two* statements, ie before the Second Reading in each House, with the possibility that if the Bill has been amended the statements may differ. This happened in the case of the Local Government Bill 2000 when, a statement of compatibility having been given before the Bill's introduction in the House of Lords, the statement was withdrawn on introduction in the Commons following Lords' amendments, which removed a provision intended to repeal 'section 28' (the provision preventing a Local

that although he is unable to make a statement of compatibility the government nevertheless wishes the House to proceed with the Bill.[18]

This provision carefully preserves parliamentary sovereignty. The statement is a procedural requirement rather than a substantive bar on Parliament legislating in way incompatible with Convention rights. It is intended to draw Parliament's attention to the consequences for human rights of its law-making. If properly applied it should prevent Parliament from enacting legislation that inadvertently overrides human rights, without ultimately constraining political choice. In the words of Lord Irvine, section 19

> guarantees an informed consent on the part of Parliament. It will not legislate incompatibly with the Convention, without being absolutely clear that it is doing so.[19]

The natural consequence is to carry debates about the interpretation and application of human rights out of the courts and into the policy-making and parliamentary arenas. Legislative proposals will be vetted for compatibility before being unveiled by government, and legislators will inevitably probe and challenge the reasoning underlying the statement of compatibility. That the Government intended this to be the case is clear from the White Paper, which spoke of a shared responsibility to uphold human rights lying not but on the courts but also on the executive and Parliament.[20]

The text of section 19 gives an impoverished view of this process, but, as so often with the UK constitution, it is profoundly misleading without an appreciation of the parliamentary procedure and the inner working of government, both of which help to place it in context. The White Paper foreshadowed the creation of a parliamentary human rights committee (discussed below).[21] It also predicted that the statement procedure would have a 'significant and beneficial impact on the preparation of legislation within Government'. Human rights considerations would influence policy-making in *all* departments[22] and new collective procedures would be established to vet policies for human rights compatibility and to ensure

---

Education Authority from promoting homosexuality). As Feldman argues, this was a clear example of political misuse of s 19: D Feldman, 'The Impact of the Human Rights Act on the UK Legislative Process' (2004) 24 *Stat LR* 91, 98. Nevertheless the episode is a clear reminder of the political context of the process and the potential for the government (as well as it opponents) to mobilise human rights arguments in support of its policies.

[18]   Section 19(1)(b).

[19]   Lord Irvine of Lairg, 'The Impact of the Human Rights Act; Parliament, the Courts and the Executive' [2003] *PL* 308, 311.

[20]   *Rights Brought Home*, ch 3.

[21]   *Ibid*, para 3.6

[22]   There was an implied reproach that this had been the specialist preserve of the Home Office and Foreign and Commonwealth Office.

that awareness of developments in the courts was disseminated throughout Whitehall. We will return shortly to examine the extent to which these aspirations have been fulfilled.

One consequence of the statement of compatibility procedure has been to give enhanced prominence in the policy-making process to vetting on human rights grounds.[23] Central guidance to government departments advises that a 'general assessment' for Ministers of the human rights implications should be prepared by the senior administrator in charge of a Bill so that 'Ministers are always alerted to substantive ECHR considerations before the policy is determined.'[24] At the drafting stage a more detailed analysis of ECHR points is prepared by departmental lawyers, in consultation with the Law Officers and the Foreign and Commonwealth Office as appropriate. This again is cleared with ministers and goes to the Legislative Programme committee of the Cabinet when approval is sought for the inclusion of the Bill in the Government's parliamentary programme.[25] This memorandum

> must set out the Convention rights likely to be engaged by the policy embodied in the Bill and explain how the proposed legislative scheme ensures that any interference with the identified right does not result in a breach. It will do this by demonstrating that the interference is legitimate, necessary, proportionate and non-discriminatory.[26]

Together with any comments from the Cabinet committee, it then informs the Minister's section 19 statement to Parliament.

A review by the Department of Constitutional Affairs in 2006 argued that the Act had had 'a significant, but beneficial, effect' on policy-making, although it admitted that it was hard to pinpoint specific consequences because human rights considerations were one of several influences on the policy process. The review highlighted as an example the development of a policy allowing schools to search pupils for weapons, claiming that in particular consideration of proportionality had produced a more 'tailored' solution, ie ensuring that searches only took place where necessary. This, the review argued, was illustrative of a more general trend: that the influence of the HRA was not to defeat the policy in question but rather to affect the way in which it was delivered.[27] The Act could be seen therefore

---

[23] For earlier reviews see J Croft, *Whitehall and the Human Rights Act 1998: the First Year* (London, The Constitution Unit, 2002).

[24] *Human Rights Act: Guidance to Departments*, para 34.

[25] *Ibid*, 35.

[26] *Review of the Implementation of the Human Rights Act* (London, Department for Constitutional Affairs, 2006) 20.

[27] *Ibid*, 21–22.

'as part of a framework which promotes greater personalisation and therefore better public services.'[28]

Overall, it is hard to accept these conclusions unquestioningly, not least because of some of the legislative proposals, especially in the counter-terrorism and criminal justice fields, that have presumably been vetted in this way and have nevertheless emerged to general criticism on human rights grounds. Moreover, the conclusion that the HRA affects mainly the process and delivery of policies, perhaps too neatly, has something for everyone. Politicians are reassured that they can nevertheless achieve their objectives, whereas human rights advocates can claim credit for having improved the policy and legal process resulting.

Claims of major impact on the policy process also sit uncomfortably alongside the conclusions of the Joint Committee on Human Rights in 2006 that, by and large, its own technical reports on Convention compatibility had come too late in the policy cycle to have any serious impact on the government's thinking.[29] This conclusion was buttressed by candid official evidence that the government's mind was usually made up by the time a section 19 statement had been made. In response the Joint Committee partially reoriented its work to allow greater opportunity to comment on Green and White Paper proposals, an area that it had been unable to devote much attention to because of its main emphasis on tracking Bills introduced into Parliament.

Some other shortcomings in the section 19 process are apparent from the legislative design. It does not apply to Private Member's Bills,[30] nor to subordinate legislation laid before Parliament. The statement is a snapshot of the Bill as introduced and there is no continuing duty to publicly assess amendments before, for example, the Report or Third Reading stages. In view of the propensity of modern governments to use the legislative timetable for continuous re-drafting of Bills – sometimes introducing wholly new provisions at a very late stage – this is a serious defect. Unlike the procedure under the New Zealand Bill of Rights Act on which it was modelled, the statement process under the HRA is a partisan one. Sceptics might argue that the responsible minister has a conflict of interest in making a statement of compatibility, since giving the statement will significantly ease the parliamentary passage of the Bill. By contrast, under the New Zealand Bill of Rights Act, a more detached perspective is ensured

---

[28]   *Ibid*, 21.

[29]   F Klug and H Wildbore, 'Breaking new ground: the Joint Committee on Human Rights and the role of Parliament in human rights compliance' [2007] *EHRLR* 231.

[30]   However, the House of Commons has brought pressure to bear to require comparable statements by refusing to discuss Private Member's Bills without them: D Feldman, 'Parliamentary Scrutiny of Legislation and Human Rights' [2002] *PL* 323, 339; and see Lord Lester, 'Parliamentary Scrutiny of Legislation under the Human Rights Act 1998' [2002] *EHRLR* 432, 446, discussing the reporting of the Joint Committee on Private Member's Bills.

by placing responsibility on the Attorney-General, whose constitutional position is independent, to draw any inconsistency to the attention of Parliament.[31]

A further difference from the New Zealand arrangements is the absence of a statutory duty under section 19 for ministers to give reasons for their conclusions. This lacuna has been partially filled through the practice of the Parliamentary Joint Committee, which is to test the reasoning underlying a section 19 statement through correspondence with departments and to publish it own legal conclusions. Ministers were reluctant to publish the underlying reasons routinely at an early stage, as the Committee suggested because of concerns over the confidentiality of legal advice. However, they conceded some ground and since 2002 this has led to to fuller reasons for the Government's conclusions concerning compatibility appearing in the Explanatory Memoranda that are published with Bills.[32]

The White Paper suggested that uncertainty over whether legislation was Convention-compatible might lead to use of the 'nevertheless' statement in a case where there was a risk of violation on Convention rights. In practice, however, the Government has operated a '51 per cent rule'.[33] It has therefore reserved 'nevertheless' statements for instances where in its view there is a *probability* of incompatibility. Where there is a risk but not a probability, ministers sign statements of compatibility. The decision to interpret section 19 in this way has important consequences. First, it weakens the internal human rights vetting within government by lowering the bar.[34] Secondly, it means that the reliance that Parliament is able to place on these statements is weakened and the need for its own independent assessment is correspondingly strengthened.

Statements given under section 19 do not bind the courts. In the words of Lord Hope they are

> no more than expressions of opinion by the [responsible] minister. They are not binding on the court, nor do they have any persuasive authority.[35]

There is no impediment therefore to a declaration of incompatibility being issued in respect of legislation which Parliament had passed following a ministerial statement of compatibility. Indeed this is exactly what happened in the *Belmarsh* detainees case, where the House of Lords found provisions

---

[31] NZBORA s 7; see P Rishworth, G Huscroft, S Optican, and R Mahoney, *The New Zealand Bill of Rights* (Oxford, OUP, 2003) ch 6.

[32] Lord Lester, above, 447–8; Feldman, 'Parliamentary Scrutiny of Legislation and Human Rights' [2002] *PL* 323, 339.

[33] Home Office, *Human Rights Act Guidance for Departments* (2nd ed, 2000) para 36.

[34] Note, however, that in Canada practice requires only that there a be 'a credible argument' that legislation is Charter compliant for the Attorney-General to give certificate: Feldman, 'The Impact of the Human Rights Act on the UK Legislative Process', (2004) 24 *Stat LR* 91, 98.

[35] *R v A (No 2)* [2001] 1 AC 45, 75.

in Pt IV of the Anti-Terrorism Crime and Security Act 2001 (ATCSA 2001) to be incompatible with Article 5 of the Convention.[36]

On the other, since Parliament has legislated presumably placing some reliance on a ministerial statement of compatibility, this strengthens the position of the courts under the interpretive duty in section 3. The presumption that Parliament thought that the legislation was compatible gives permission for the courts to go the beyond conventional interpretation of the statutory language. In a 2007 decision on control orders, for example, Baroness Hale stated:

> when Parliament passed the 2005 Act, it must have thought that the provisions with which we are concerned were compatible with the convention rights. In interpreting the Act compatibly we are doing our best to make it work. This gives the greatest possible incentive to *all* parties to the case, and to the judge, to conduct the proceedings in such a way as to afford a sufficient and substantial measure of procedural justice.[37]

It would seem, however, that the opposite is not the case. Where legislation has been passed following a statement that the minister was unable to state that it was Convention compatible this does not preclude the courts from later holding that is compatible.[38]

Despite the fact that section 19 imposes a legal duty on ministers it seems unlikely that this could enforced in court, for example by questioning the legislation if no statement was in fact made or, still less, by suggesting that that a misleading or incorrect statement was invalid itself or a somehow affected the validity of an Act. All such an arguments would be barred by Article 9 of the Bill of Rights 1689,[39] whether or not they could be said to call into question parliamentary sovereignty as such.[40] On this basis the New Zealand courts refused to consider whether the Attorney-General should have reported alleged incompatibility to Parliament under the comparable provision in the New Zealand Bill of Rights.[41] Although there are some differences between the provisions[42] it is likely that UK courts would decline any challenge for the same reason.

---

[36] *A v Secretary of State for the Home Department* [2004] UKHL 56. See ch 8 below.

[37] *Secretary of State for the Home Department v MB* [2007] UKHL 46, para 73; see further 215–16 below.

[38] *Animal Defenders International v Secretary of State for Culture, Media and Sport* [2006] EWHC Admin 3069; [2008] UKHL 15.

[39] 'Proceedings in Parliament shall not be questioned or impeached in any other place'.

[40] For further discussion see N Bamforth, 'Parliamentary Sovereignty and the Human Rights Act 1998' [1998] *PL* 572, 575–82.

[41] *Mangwaro Enterprises v Attorney-General* [1994] NZLR 451.

[42] HRA s 19 requires a statement concerning all government legislation, whereas under NZBORA s 7 the duty only arises where the Attorney-General perceives that there is an incompatibility.

As indicated above, in large part because of the '51 per cent rule', ministerial statements of compatibility have been the invariable rule even where there is scope for debate over compatibility with Convention rights. One notable exception concerned the prohibition on political advertising on television, which is maintained under the Communications Act 2003.[43] On this occasion ministers made a 'nevertheless' statement. Although this no more pre-determines the outcome of any legal challenge than where a compatibility statement is made, it presents a high hurdle to using section 3 to achieve compatibility. There would seem to be little point, however, in a domestic court making a declaration of incompatibility either, since Parliament has legislated with its eyes wide open – unless circumstances have changed materially since the passing of Act (perhaps including an intervening change of government).[44] A 'nevertheless' statement on the other hand might be thought to be a virtual invitation to the Strasbourg court to decide against the UK.

Faced for the first time with such a statement the Joint Committee used the occasion to give detailed guidance. It argued that 'strong justification as a matter of principle' was required. It highlighted several relevant factors:

—making a section 19(1)(b) statement does not evince a lack of respect for human rights standards. It shows that the Government is taking the task of assessing the human rights implications of its legislation seriously, and considers that there are reasons (which it should be ready to share with Parliament) for considering that it is desirable in the public interest to take the risk of incompatibility;

—this may be justifiable if its reasons for taking the risk of incompatibility are sufficiently compelling and are consistent with the general objective of maintaining respect for rights;

[43]   Ss 319 and 321. See further: A Scott, '"A Monstrous and unjustifiable infringement"? Political expression and the broadcasting ban on advocacy advertising' (2003) 66 *MLR* 240; T Lewis, 'Political Advertising and the Communications Act 2003' [2005] *EHRLR* 290; H Fenwick and G Phillipson, *Media Freedom under the Human Rights Act* (London, 2006) 1015–33.

[44]   It seems that the Administrative Court may agree. In a striking decision it refused to make declaration of incompatibility in respect of section 321 of the Communications Act 2003 despite the agreement of the parties that the provision was so clear as to leave no room for reading down under s 3 HRA: *Animal Defenders International v Secretary of State for Culture, Media and Sport* [2006] EWHC Admin 3069. Ouseley J's conclusion captures the reasoning: 'Whether the decision of Parliament in enacting s 321 of the Communications Act 2003 is seen as strong evidence for the necessity for the prohibition in an area of its primary experience and expertise or as a judgment in an area where a wider margin of discretion should be accorded to it, its decision should be respected by the Courts. It is not incompatible with the ECHR.' (para 125) (discussed in T Lewis, Rights Lost in Translation? Fact-insensitive Laws, the Human Rights Act and the United Kingdom's Ban on Political Advertising' [2007] *EHRLR* 663). See also *R (Animal Defenders International) v SS for Media, Culture and Sport* [2008] UKHL 15.

—section 19(1)(b) makes it clear that it is the Government, not the individual Minister, who takes the responsibility for inviting Parliament to consider a Bill notwithstanding a substantial risk that it is incompatible with a Convention right. In other words, this is a matter for which the Government as a whole is collectively responsible to Parliament;

—a section 19(1)(b) statement does not mean that the Government considers that the provision in question would be held to be incompatible with a Convention right. It only means that the Minister is unable to say, with the requisite level of confidence,[footnote omitted] that the provision is compatible;

—it follows that, where a section 19(1)(b) statement is made, the Government remains free to argue in subsequent litigation that the provision in question is actually compatible with Convention rights;

—where the Government is prepared to do that, and to amend the Act if it is held to be incompatible, it evinces an appropriate level of respect for human rights, as long as its reasons for taking the risk of incompatibility in the first place are sufficiently compelling and are consistent with the general objective of maintaining respect for rights.[45]

Applying these considerations the Joint Committee reconciled itself to the Statement in this case, partly because the Government could be seen to be reserving its position to ague that the relevant Strasbourg jurisprudence[46] was incorrectly decided. Professor David Feldman (who was the Committee's Legal Adviser at the time) has argued that the process demonstrated the government's 'careful assessment' of the risk of incompatibility and a 'respect for rights, rather than a lack of respect'.[47] Nevertheless, the Committee's conclusion dilutes the force of the argument that section 19 was intended to ensure Parliament's 'informed consent' to incompatible legislation. By introducing the intermediate category of incompatible (but-perhaps-only-for-now) the Committee sent an ambiguous message to Parliament and created an escape route for Ministers to use on future occasions.

The Joint Committee's approach also provokes the question, of course, of what would happen in the hypothetical case of an unequivocal refusal by the government to follow the Convention. From the Joint Committee's comments it can be surmised that their view would be that this is a possibility deliberately left open by the HRA, but that the ministerial

---

[45] Joint Committee on Human Rights, *First Report for 2002–03*, HL 24; HC 191, para 15.

[46] *Vgt Verein Gegen Fabriken v Switzerland* (2002) 34 EHRR 159, holding that the case for a blanket prohibition on political advertising on radio and television had not been justified under Art 10.2. The Administrative Court in *Animal Defenders International v Secretary of State for Culture, Media and Sport* [2006] EWHC Admin 3069 also found the rationale for this decision hard to discern and preferred instead to distinguish it.

[47] D Feldman, 'The Impact of the Human Rights Act on the UK Legislative Process', (2004) 24 *Stat LR* 91, 100.

statement should nonetheless explain why the latitude within the Convention, particularly to restrict qualified rights where appropriate, was insufficient to secure the legislative goals.

Overall, the section 19 procedure is premised on an unnaturally simplified view of the Convention and its jurisprudence. While in some instances it will be possible to say with certainty that a proposed law either complies with or breaches the Convention (imagine a law licensing torture, which would clearly violate Article 3, for example), in many other instances it will be a question of probabilities.[48] This may be for a variety of reasons: because the exact point is not explicitly covered by the Convention text and has not previously arisen before the Court; because of divergent trends in the jurisprudence; due to the margin of appreciation; or because of a clash of Convention rights is involved, and so on. Moreover, in making a section 19 statement Ministers are attempting to second-guess *both* the domestic and the Strasbourg courts. Extending Lord Irvine's informed consent analogy: as with a physician discussing medical treatment with a patient, it is perhaps more realistic to recognise that the probabilities of a law being found compatible or not, and the underlying reasons, are more informative and helpful than the bare conclusion or prediction that section 19 requires. The true value of the provision is that it has made this process of calculation more transparent and, in practice, has compelled the Government both to share its reasoning and to justify and defend it from informed criticism. This has sometimes turned the parliamentary process into a dress rehearsal for Convention challenges that will be resumed later in the courts. The lack of an independent perspective has been remedied to some extent by the Joint Committee on Human Rights, which we discuss below.

THE PARLIAMENTARY JOINT COMMITTEE ON HUMAN RIGHTS IN PRACTICE[49]

The parliamentary Joint Committee on Human Rights is not a creature of the HRA as such. This is partly for reasons of constitutional propriety: parliamentary select committees are usually established and governed by Standing Orders (the internal working rules of Westminster) rather than by

---

[48]   *Ibid*, 98.

[49]   For assessments by a member of the Committee and its first legal adviser, see respectively Lord Lester, 'Parliamentary Scrutiny of Legislation under the Human Rights Act 1998' [2002] *EHRLR* 432 and D Feldman 'Parliamentary Scrutiny of Legislation and Human Rights' [2002] *PL* 323. For a comparative perspective: J Hiebert, 'Parliament and the Human Rights Act: can the JCHR help facilitate a culture of rights?' (2006) *Int. J of Constitutional Law* 1. The 2006 review of the JCHR's work and priorities is described in F Klug and H Wildbore, 'Breaking new ground: the Joint Committee on Human Rights and the role of Parliament in human rights compliance' [2007] *EHRLR* 231.

legislation. Nor is it remit limited to *Convention* rights – it includes, for example, monitoring other human rights treaties such as the UN covenants on Civil and Political and Economic and Social Rights and the UN Conventions of Torture, Rights of the Child and on the Elimination of Discrimination against Women. Nevertheless, the creation of the Joint Committee was an integral institutional reform, designed to complement at the political level the enhancement of human rights in the judicial sphere under the Act.

The Government had raised the possibility of the creation of a parliamentary committee in its 1997 White Paper, *Rights Brought Home*.[50] The format and terms of reference were agreed through parliamentary discussions. The committee came into operation in January 2001 – 15 months after the HRA's full implementation in the courts. It is a Joint Committee of both Houses of Parliament, comprised of equal numbers of MPs and Peers. Joint parliamentary committees are a constitutional device used relatively sparingly to deal with bi-partisan questions or issues of constitutional significance in which each chamber has a stake. The Joint Committee on Human Rights is a slight departure of previous precedents, in that is established for the life of a Parliament (rather than ad hoc) and has relatively wide terms of reference. Due to the Joint Committee's composition the Government does not have a majority, and this, together with other factors, has enabled it to work in a bi-partisan fashion.[51] Undoubtedly its status as a joint committee and the seniority and experience of some its members, together with the specialist expertise of its advisers (from its inception the committee has employed a full-time senior legal adviser) have also enhanced its perceived independence and stature.

The Joint Committee's terms of reference are framed widely, to include

> matters relating to human rights in the United Kingdom (but excluding consideration of individual cases); proposals for remedial orders, [consideration of] draft remedial orders and remedial orders.[52]

As will be explained shortly the areas of emphasis within this portfolio have shifted over time.

In the early stages the Committee gave priority to human rights scrutiny of Bills. These were vetted by the Committee's legal adviser who, drew any with implications for Convention compatibility to the attention of the Chairman. The Chairman in turn would write to the relevant Minister, and the correspondence, together with the report of the Legal Adviser, would

---

[50] Home Office, *Rights Brought Home: the Human Rights Bill 1997*, Cm 3782 (1997), paras 3.6–3.7. See also Jack Straw MP and Paul Boateng MP, *Bringing Rights Home, Labour's Plan to Incorporate the ECHR into UK Law* (Labour Party, December 1996) 12.

[51] Hiebert, *op cit*, 16.

[52] <http://www.parliament.uk/parliamentary_committees/joint_committee_on_human_rights/jchrabout.cfm> (accessed on 14 January 2008).

be considered by the Committee. Under pressure from the Committee in the early years of its operation, most government departments have become more forthcoming concerning the reasons underlying section 19 statements, so that exchanges have become more focused on exploring areas of possible disagreement between the committee and the government over Convention compatibility. The Committee's first Legal Adviser Professor David Feldman characterised the role as being to give 'advice' on Convention rights rather than interpretation.[53] These Bill scrutiny reports have rightly drawn praise for providing Parliamentarians with high level independent advice on human rights to facilitate parliamentary debate.

Nevertheless, and despite heroic efforts by the Joint Committee on Human Rights to produce timely and detailed reports for Parliament, there has been something of a mismatch between the operation of the legislative process and the scrutiny work of the Committee. This is primarily because of the frenzied and unyielding parliamentary timetable which produces continuous and rapid technical amendments to a Bill as it progresses, often leaving inadequate time for proper deliberation on the merits of the proposed law and of any changes. There has been some improvement in recent years with growing use of draft Bills tabled a session in advance, but these are still very much in the minority. A flavour of what is involved can be gained from David Feldman's description of the progress of the Nationality, Immigration and Asylum Bill 2002 towards the end of the 2001–02 parliamentary session. Despite extensive earlier government amendments tabled at each preceding stage in both Houses:

> After the Bill had passed through its Committee Stage in the Lords the Government announced that it would introduce major new clauses by amendments on Report in the Lords ... these were intended to require the Secretary of State to withhold assistance from destitute asylum-seekers unless they had applied for asylum as soon as practicable after arriving in the UK, and to empower the Secretary of State to withhold assistance if they failed to give a full and credible account of the way they had entered the UK. The new clauses also introduced a statutory presumption that certain countries are safe places to which a failed asylum-seeker can be returned without risk of torture or persecution, and changed the law retrospectively to reverse the effect of a judicial decision about the right to be free of detention. ... The Joint Committee on Human Rights, working at great speed, produced a report drawing attention to the risk that the proposed clauses posed to rights under ECHR Articles 3, 6 and 8, and the International Covenant on Economic, Social and Cultural Rights, Article 11.1. But despite the grave reservations expressed ... the Government steamrollered the clauses through without redrafting[54]

---

[53]   D Feldman, 'Parliamentary Scrutiny of Legislation and Human Rights' [2002] *PL* 323.
[54]   Feldman, n 47 above, 110.

Although extreme, this example is not unique. Suggestions that the parliamentary timetable be amended to make space for adequate consideration by the Joint Committee and for Parliament to digest its reports before debate have gone largely unheeded. In this climate it is inevitable that the influence of the Committee's Bill scrutiny reports is reduced. Insiders acknowledge that that once a Bill has reached the stage of a section 19 statement the government is unlikely to be persuaded by human rights arguments to amend it unless there a combination of factors producing overwhelming parliamentary opposition.

A study conducted for the Joint Committee in 2006 concluded that the visible influence of the Committee's reports on Bills was relatively minor. In a detailed analysis of the parliamentary session 2005–06 it was found that reports had been relied upon during fewer than 30 interventions in the House of Commons Bill debates (and around 70 times in the House of Lords). Of some 500 Bills introduced up until 2005–06 the Committee's reports had led to amendments in perhaps 18.[55] While this was a worthwhile contribution to parliamentary scrutiny, consideration focused on whether it was a good return for the considerable effort expended. The Committee acknowledged that the impact in the parliamentary process had been perhaps disappointing and that some change in priorities might make more effective use of the committee's expertise, with greater impact.[56] Accordingly, it has adopted more selective criteria for deciding on when to report on Bills. These include:

> whether the issue is one on which the European Court of Human Rights or one of the higher courts in the UK has recently given a judgment; the broad political or public impact of the bill, including the extent to which it has attracted public and media attention ...; the extent to which reputable NGOs or other interested parties have made representations ...; the particular interests or expertise of the members of the Committee and the degree to which the Committee can add value to the scrutiny which the bill might receive from other committees; the completeness of the Explanatory Notes or Human Rights Memoranda (if the Government agrees to provide these) accompanying the Bill ...; the extent to which the bill furthers the promotion or protection of human rights, or could have contained provision to that effect but does not; whether the issue is one on which the Committee has previously reported, particularly if there is a clear pattern of incompatibility.[57]

The second strand of the Joint Committee's work directly relating to the HRA is consideration of remedial orders made or proposed under section

---

[55] Klug and Wildbore, above n 49, 241.

[56] Klug and Wildbore, 'Breaking New Ground: the Joint Committee on Human Rights ands the role of Parliament in human rights compliance' [2007] *EHRLR* 231.

[57] JCHR, *The Committee's Future Working Practices*, Twenty-Third Report, Session 2005–06, para 29.

10 of the Act.[58] Necessarily this has occupied less of the Committee's time than Bill scrutiny. The Committee has resolved in effect to extend this consideration a stage further back to include Declarations of Incompatibility.[59]

In addition to Bill scrutiny, the Committee has engaged in useful and important thematic work[60], for example, producing reports on deaths in custody, human trafficking, the rights of elderly people in healthcare, the human rights of adults with learning disabilities, and the case for a human rights commission. The last of these in particular is credited with having influenced the functions and powers of the Equality and Human Rights Commission, established under the Equality Act 2006. Here, as elsewhere in its work, the Committee has, through its evidence-gathering, operated as an important parliamentary focus by which human rights expertise in NGOs and the universities can influence policy.

After its 2006 review the Joint Committee determined to change the emphasis of its work. In addition to the more selective analysis of human rights compatibility of draft legislation, it decided to change the type of reporting. Two aspects are significant: first, the Joint Committee's decision to give greater prominence to consideration of proposals at an earlier stage (ie, White or Green Papers), when it might have greater influence on government thinking;[61] secondly, its decision to move away somewhat from legal commentary on Convention compatibility, to give greater consideration to the arguments of proportionality that are often the nub of any dispute between the government and those claiming that a particular measure will infringe human rights.

Professor Danny Nicol has criticised the Committee for excessive attention to predictions concerning whether legislative provisions are compatible, and argues that Parliament should give greater attention to what human rights could mean and spend less time imitating judicial interpretation, particularly of Convention rights.[62]

---

[58] See, eg, the JCHR, *Sixth Report for 2001–02* HL 57, HC 472, discussing the Mental Health Act (Remedial Order) 2001.

[59] See further 146–7 below,

[60] Klug and Wildbore, op. cit., 237.

[61] For a recent example: *Second Report for 2007–08, Counter-Terrorism Policy and Human Rights: 42 Days*, HL 23, HC 156.

[62] D Nicol, 'The Human Rights Act and the Politicians' (2004) 24(3) *LS* 452. See also D Nicol, 'Law and Politics After the Human Rights Act', [2006] *PL* 722, 742–3: 'A more genuinely pro-dialogue reading would involve breaking open the courts' interpretative monopoly, and recognising Parliament's potential to interpret the Convention rights. Rights issues involve the choice between competing moral maps, the struggle between competing notions of the common good. Traditional legal discourse which categorises judgments as "correct" or "incorrect", "rightly decided" or "wrongly decided", is inappropriate for such a contestable, value-laden exercise. ... *Elucidating the meaning of the Convention rights should therefore be seen as a shared responsibility between judiciary and legislature.*' (footnotes omitted, emphasis supplied).

This is part of a larger argument about 'dialogue' between the courts and Parliament, but it is nevertheless important to be clear about the implications, since to some extent the argument uses a false antithesis between legalistic interpretation and political interpretation. There is little space for a useful role for Parliament's distinctive interpretation of what Convention rights *mean* (eg whether a practice constitutes torture or amounts to a manifestation of religious belief etc, or whether a provision creates a criminal offence or civil obligation) in the sense of the *scope* of rights. There is an important difference here from some of the other purely domestic Bills of Rights, from which commentators tend to borrow in discussing relations between politicians and judges. Political conceptions of the scope of rights that differed from the Convention jurisprudence would simply end up in domestic declarations of incompatibility or Strasbourg rulings against the UK. There is room, however, for an informed debate about proportionality in the case of qualified rights, but against a clear legal background that explains the parameters of the Strasbourg jurisprudence. With that groundwork done, there could then be serious discussion within Parliament about the human rights implications of government proposals and possible less intrusive means of achieving similar objectives. Once again, however, to undertake this type of dialogue about proportionality (and then to give it some type of presumptive force through a concept of deference in the courts) would be misguided if it were to take place in a vacuum without accurate analysis of the Strasbourg jurisprudence. When commentators speak of Parliamentarians being under the interpretive duty in HRA section 3,[63] this helps to underline Parliament's shared responsibility for protecting human rights, but within the scheme of the Act as a whole. It does not help to set this duty as somehow in opposition to the courts' duties.

The confusion of roles of the Joint Committee on Human Rights and the fact that its members are active parliamentarians perhaps makes a tension between the legal and the political aspects of its work inevitable. The antidote, however, is not to deny a proper place for accurate legal information concerning the Convention and its jurisprudence to inform the parliamentary process. Rather, it would be preferable to separate this valuable legal advisory function more clearly from the speculative or evaluative parts of human rights scrutiny. This could be achieved by enhancing the independence of the legal adviser. An institutional reform that would achieve this would be to make the legal adviser more clearly a resource for Parliament as whole, rather than the Joint Committee. Legal adviser reports could be published separately, leaving the Committee to

---

[63] See, eg, D Feldman, 'Institutional Roles and Meanings of Compatibility under the Human Rights Act' in Fenwick, Phillipson and Masterman, op. cit.

engage in the type of proportionality analysis where its members could more distinctively add value and bring political and policy expertise to bear.

A reform of this type might be more coherent if coupled with parallel reform of section 19, placing the onus, for example, for reporting on compatibility on the Speaker in each House, rather than the minister sponsoring the Bill. These reports would then become an independent legal commentary on the compatibility of legislation. To be practical, any such reform would, of course, involve at least creating a breathing space in the frantic legislative process between introduction of a Bill and debates at Second Reading. If that is impractical then a report of this type could inform the Committee stage.

A more radical version of the same idea might link Speaker's reports on compatibility with the procedural discussion of a Bill – for example, giving the House of Lords an enhanced power of delay under the Parliament Acts where a Bill was certified as incompatible.[64] This would be a development of the parliamentary rights model both in keeping with parliamentary sovereignty and with increased parliamentary responsibility for rights scrutiny.[65] Realistically, however, institutional reform of this type is unlikely to appeal to a government already on the back foot in defending the HRA. Much more modestly, and without any institutional or significant procedural reform, the Joint Committee could simply begin to publish legal advice of this kind either as a report in its own right or as a memorandum of evidence.

Despite the debate concerning how to integrate high quality independent legal advice into the parliamentary process, commentators acknowledge that the Joint Committee has proved its worth. The presence of an expert independent parliamentary committee has given the compatibility statement process a cutting edge and has provided an incentive for the executive to take pre-legislative review of compatibility seriously. This has gone some way towards creating the conditions for the much-trumpeted human rights culture in the UK.

---

[64] This would in effect place the Speaker in the reverse position to when certifying a Bill as a 'money Bill' under the Parliament Act 1911 (with the consequence that it becomes law automatically without House of Lords' approval).

[65] The delay power could either constitute a cooling-off period or be designed to allow for consultation of the electorate.

HUMAN RIGHTS SCRUTINY IN THE DEVOLVED ASSEMBLIES[66]

The scrutiny of human rights compatibility operates in a radically different context in the devolved assemblies than in Westminster. This is because in each case it is beyond the powers of the assemblies to legislate contrary to the Convention rights. In their case, therefore, the HRA takes the form of a constitutional restraint, and comparisons with 'strong-form judicial review'[67] are apposite. The implication according to Aidan O'Neill QC is that there are 'two wholly divergent constitutional models in relation to the protection of fundamental rights' in the UK. Writing of Scotland (but his comments are equally true as regards Northern Ireland and Wales) he explains:

> One model under the Human Rights Act 1998 … is based on the idea of delicate constitutional dialogue and a dance of deference between judiciary and legislature but one where ultimately Parliament has the last word. The other model, under the Scotland Act … is one in which the courts are supreme and are required to strike down all and any 'unconstitutional' acts of the devolved legislature and administration.[68]

The Scottish Parliament, the Northern Ireland Assembly and the National Assembly for Wales each have different legislative powers. Commentaries tend to differentiate between the legislative devolution in Scotland and Northern Ireland on the one hand and executive devolution in Wales on the other.[69] Formal differences in the law-making powers turn crucially upon whether the assembly is able to amend Westminster Acts of Parliament within its field of legislative competence (as is the case with the Scottish Parliament, whose measures are termed 'Acts' of the Scottish

---

[66] We are not concerned in this section with broader aspects of the extent to which the devolution legislation protects human rights or with human rights challenges to the actions of devolved governments or in general with the means by which devolution issues may be brought before the courts. See P Craig and M Walters, 'The Courts, Devolution and Judicial Review' [1999] *PL* 274; B Winetrobe, 'Scottish Devolved Legislation in the Courts' [2002] *PL* 31.

[67] M Tushnet, 'Judicial Review of Legislation' in P Cane and M Tushnet (eds), *The Oxford Handbook of Legal Studies* (Oxford, OUP, 2003) 174–78.

[68] Aidan O'Neill QC, '"Stands Scotland where it did?": devolution, human rights and the Scottish constitution seven years on' (2006) 57 (1) *NILQ* 102–137.

[69] This is a partly outdated distinction. Following the enactment of the Government of Wales Act 2006 there is the possibility of the National Assembly exercising primary law-making powers either ad hoc through Legislative Competence Orders to extend the 'matters' upon which the Assembly may legislate by Measures within specified 'fields' (the current position, discussed further below), or in future under Pt 4 (following a referendum), which would introduce Acts of the National Assembly for Wales, similar to Acts of the Scottish Parliament. Once passed, both Measures and Assembly Acts have similar effect to an Act of Parliament; however Legislative Competence Orders are subject to approval at Westminster, whereas if Pt 4 is brought into effect this layer of control will be removed. See A Trench, 'The Government of Wales Act 2006: the next steps on devolution for Wales' [2006] *PL* 687.

Parliament and receive Royal Assent) or whether its legislative powers are secondary in nature. Seen, however, from the perspective of the HRA these distinctions are less important: under section 21(1) the Acts of the Scottish Parliament and the Northern Ireland Assembly are deemed 'subordinate legislation' in the same way as Measures of the National Assembly for Wales.[70] The significance is that, whereas Acts of the Westminster Parliament cannot be quashed or annulled by the courts for incompatibility, legal instruments from the devolved assemblies can be, whatever their designation.[71]

Lord Rodger of Earlsferry has confirmed the similarities between the Scottish Parliament and other statutory bodies and the contrast to the sovereign Parliament at Westminster:

> the [Scottish] Parliament [i]s a body which – however important its role – has been created by statute and derives its powers from statute. As such, it is a body which, like any other statutory body, must work within the scope of those powers. If it does not do so, then in an appropriate case the court may be asked to intervene and will require to do so, in a manner permitted by the legislation. In principle, therefore, the Parliament like any other body set up by law is subject to the law and to the courts which exist to uphold that law. ...

> While all United Kingdom courts which may have occasion to deal with proceedings involving the Scottish Parliament can, of course, be expected to accord all due respect to the Parliament as to any other litigant, they must equally be aware that they are *not* dealing with a Parliament which is sovereign: on the contrary, it is subject to the laws and hence to the courts.[72]

The formal limitations are found in section 29 of the Scotland Act 1998 and equivalent provisions in the other legislation:[73]

> (1) An Act of the Scottish Parliament is not law so far as any provision of the Act is outside the legislative competence of the Parliament.

> (2) A provision is outside that competence so far as ...

> (d) it is incompatible with any of the Convention rights ... .

---

[70]   Cf C Himsworth, 'Rights versus Devolution', in T Campbell, KD Ewing and A Tomkins (eds) *Sceptical Essays on Human Rights* (Oxford, 2001) 149–151, who argues, however, that this can produce anomalous consequences in the status of identical legislation emanating from either Edinburgh or Westminster that amends a UK Act of Parliament. O'Neill argues that the effect of s 21(1) is to impliedly repeal Acts of the Scottish Parliament that are incompatible with Convention rights to the extent of the incompatibility: op. cit., 108.

[71]   Note, however, the power to suspend judgments when legislation is found to be outside legislative competence, to enable the defect to be cured: Scotland Act 1998, s 102; Government of Wales Act 2006, s 153; Northern Ireland Act 1998, s 81.

[72]   *Whaley and others v Lord Watson of Invergowrie and the Scottish Parliament* 2000 SC 125, OH; 2000 SC 340, 348H, 350B–C, IH (Lord Rodger).

[73]   Northern Ireland Act 1998, s 6(2)(c); Government of Wales Act 2006, s 94(6)(c).

Moreover, the HRA has in effect an entrenched status, since it is among the scheduled provisions which the assemblies cannot amend or repeal.[74] In theory these hurdles could be overcome by a devolved body requesting that Westminster override the HRA on its behalf, but such a request is most unlikely to be granted. The limitations on legislative competence are complemented by provisions that direct the courts to interpret legislation from the devolved assemblies narrowly: in instances where any provision 'could be read in such a way as to be outside competence' it is instead to be read as narrowly as is required for it to be within competence, if such a reading is possible, and is to have effect accordingly'.[75] So far as Convention rights affected by devolved legislation are concerned this mirrors the interpretive obligation under section 3 Human Rights Act.

Bearing this context in mind, the Scotland Act 1998, the Northern Ireland Act 1998 and the Government of Wales Act 2006 (GWA 2006) each contain complex processes for pre-legislative scrutiny and challenge, designed to prevent the enactment of incompatible legislation.

Under the Standing Orders of the Scottish Parliament Executive Bills must be accompanied by a Policy Memorandum setting out an assessment of any effects on human rights.[76] These Memoranda sometimes draw attention to relevant parts of Bills that might be thought to raise human rights concerns and give brief reasons with reference to the Convention text (and in general terms to the Convention jurisprudence) for the executive's conclusion that the Bill is compatible. On other occasions, however, they inscrutably assert compatibility without analysis in a way that does little to inspire confidence in the robustness of the policy process.[77] Scrutiny of Bills takes place in Committees but there is no one committee that has a remit comparable to the Joint Committee on Human Rights at Westminster. These arrangements plainly allow for differing degrees in the seriousness with which human rights scrutiny is undertaken both by executive departments and the lead subject committees to which the consideration of Bills is committed.[78] This is perhaps explained in part

---

[74] Scotland Act 1998, Sch 4; Northern Ireland Act 1998, s 7(1)(b); Government of Wales Act 2006, Sch 5, Pt 2 and Sch 7, Pt 2.

[75] Scotland Act 1998, s 101(1) and (2); cf. Northern Ireland Act 1998, s 83; Government of Wales Act 2006, s 154.

[76] *Standing Orders of the Scottish Parliament*, 3rd ed (1st rev, 2007), rule 9.3 (c) (iv).

[77] Eg the Policy Memorandum to the Family Law (Scotland) Bill 2005, para 103, which simply states: 'The Bill does not give rise to any issues under the European Convention on Human Rights (ECHR)', despite the obvious relevance of Art 8.

[78] For an example, detailed scrutiny by a committee see the consideration of provisions for Risk of Sexual Harm Orders in the Protection of Children and Prevention of Sexual Offences (Scotland) Bill, by the Justice 1 Committee, *5th Report for 2005 (Session 2)* <http://www.scottish.parliament.uk/business/committees/justice1/reports-05/j1r05–05-vol01–00.htm> accessed 22 May 2008.

by the lack – to date – of a successful human rights challenge in the courts to an Act of the Scottish Parliament,[79] despite the Parliament's extensive use of its powers since commencement. The Scottish Parliament has, however, passed legislation to create a Scottish Commission for Human Rights with general responsibility for promoting human rights, including monitoring the law in Scotland and the policies of Scottish authorities.[80] This role could potentially include commenting upon draft Bills before the Scottish Parliament, but no explicit power or duty to do so is created by the legislation.[81] The omission is surprising in view of fact that the prior consultation paper described this as a 'key function' of the Commission.[82]

Under the GWA 2006 the person in charge of an Assembly Measure (usually a minister of the Welsh Assembly Government) must state whether the provisions would be within the Assembly's legislative competence and the Assembly Presiding Officer must make a similar determination.[83] So far as Convention compatibility is concerned[84] this is the equivalent process to section 19. There is a significant difference, however: the Presiding Officer's statement adds an independent element to the process that the Westminster provision lacks. Moreover, these determinations will be legally contestable: the legislation allows the Counsel General (the Welsh Assembly Government's chief legal adviser) or the UK Attorney-General to refer the question of competence of a Measure that has been passed to the Supreme Court.[85] Equally there would appear to be no bar (except the development of a potential field of judicial deference) to an application for judicial review of a determination by the Presiding Officer that a Measure

---

[79] For unsuccessful challenges, see: *A (A Mental Patient) v Scottish Ministers* 2001 SLT 1331 (PC) (unsuccessful challenge to Mental Health (Public Safety and Appeals) (Scotland) Act 1999); *Adams v Scottish Ministers* 2004 SC 665, IH (unsuccessful challenge to the Wild Mammals (Scotland) Act 2002); *DS v Her Majesty's Advocate*, Privy Council Appeal No 12 of 2007, PC 22 May 2007 (unsuccessful challenge to section 10 of the Sexual Offences (Procedure and Evidence) (Scotland) Act 2002).

[80] Scottish Commissioner for Human Rights Act 2006, see s 4 especially. The Commission commenced work in spring 2008, chaired by Professor Alan Miller.

[81] Contrast the Northern Ireland position, described below.

[82] F MacDonald and E Thomson, *The Scottish Human Rights Commission: Analysis of Consultation Responses* (Scottish Government Research, 2004) para 3.19; the Scottish Executive, while recognising that the decision was for the Parliament, considered that it was unnecessary to create a Parliamentary Human Rights Committee: *Ibid*, 3.20: <http://www.scotland.gov.uk/Publications/2004/05/19320/36686>.

[83] GWA 2006, s 96 (2) and (3).

[84] This is not of course the sole consideration: controversy may also arise over whether a proposed Measure is within the 'fields' specified under the GWA, whether it is compatible with Community law, or whether it has consequences outside Wales.

[85] GWA 2006, s 99. In addition, the Secretary of State may also intervene under s 101(1)(d) where there reasonable grounds to believe that a proposed Assembly Measure would be incompatible with an international obligation of the UK. Any such order will bar the Assembly Measure from being submitted for approval. Judicial review of the Secretary of State's intervention may be more problematic, since it is subject to Parliamentary negative resolution.

is beyond the Assembly's legislative competence. These procedures – which follow on from the implementation of the recommendations of the Richard Commission that the Assembly be given enhanced law-making powers[86] – are relatively new since they have only been in operation since the 2007 elections for the third Assembly, which produced a Labour–Plaid Cymru coalition. Consequently, the Assembly has yet to develop detailed or separate human rights scrutiny processes for the Presiding Officer's statements of legislative competence.

In the case of the Northern Ireland Assembly the independent scrutiny of Bills is taken a stage further. Not only is the Speaker of the Assembly required to report on matters of legislative competence (including Convention compatibility),[87] but there is also a requirement for the Northern Ireland Human Rights Commission to give its advice to the Assembly on whether a Bill is compatible with human rights.[88] The Commission is one the institutions established under the Northern Ireland Act 1998, following the Good Friday agreement, with a broad mandate to promote human rights.[89] Owing to the long periods during which work of the Northern Ireland Assembly was suspended until the resumption of the devolved arrangements in 2007, this aspect of scrutiny, like the arrangements in Wales, is at an early stage.[90]

One final striking feature of the devolution legislation is the procedure by which disputes over legislative competence can be referred to the courts before the provisions take effect. Under section 33 of the Scotland Act 1998 the Advocate-General, the Lord Advocate or the Attorney-General may refer to the Privy Council the question of whether a Bill passed by the Parliament is within its legislative competence. Clearly this is one route by which arguments of compatibility with Convention rights could be aired, particularly in a dispute with Westminster, but the procedure has yet to be

---

[86] *Report of the Richard Commission on the Powers and Electoral Arrangements of the National Assembly for Wales*: <http://www.richardcommission.gov.uk/content/finalreport/report-e.pdf> accessed 17 May 2008. See further: R Rawlings, "Hastening Slowly: The Next Phase of Welsh Devolution' [2005] *PL* 824; B Hadfield, Devolution and the Changing Constitution: Evolution in Wales and the Unanswered English Question' in J Jowell and D Oliver (eds), *The Changing Constitution* (6th ed, Oxford, 2007); A Trench, op. cit.

[87] Northern Ireland Act 1998, s 10.

[88] *Ibid*, s 69(4).

[89] Northern Ireland Act 1998, s 69. This has included intervening in litigation (following the decision of the House of Lords that it was competent to do so: *Re Northern Ireland Human Rights Commission* [2005] UKHL 25) and promoting an extensive and detailed debate on a proposed Bill of Rights for Northern Ireland: see Northern Ireland Human Rights Commission, *Making a Bill of Rights for Northern Ireland* (2001); 'Symposium, the Proposed Bill of Rights for Northern Ireland' (2001) *NILQ* 230.

[90] A proposal under the Good Friday Agreement that an equality/human rights committee be created within the Northern Ireland Assembly has yet to be implemented: C McCrudden, 'Northern Ireland and the British Constitution Since the Belfast Agreement', in J Jowell and D Oliver (eds), *The Changing Constitution* (6th edn, 2007), 257 n 114.

used.[91] Nevertheless, it is an important innovation that places the Privy Council (soon to be replaced by the new Supreme Court[92]) in the position of a constitutional court on a continental model, ie in the position of pronouncing on validity of legislation before it becomes law.

CONCLUSION

Political and parliamentary scrutiny of policy and legislation at Westminster operates under the HRA in a context where the judicial protection of rights is relatively weak. Part of the defence for these arrangements by the government was that the full responsibility for protecting rights should not fall on the judiciary alone. Commentators have argued that the UK has embarked on a unique experiment in protecting rights through inter-institutional dialogue or through what Professor Janet Hiebert has termed the 'political rights' model:

> Its principal innovation. ... lies in its attempt to broaden the scope of rights review beyond judges to include political and public actors. A second innovative feature of this model, which relates to this idea of dispersed responsibility for judgments about rights, is the creation of dialectical tensions between the government and Parliament, and between the judiciary and Parliament, when determining if legislation is compatible with rights or, alternatively, is warranted despite judicial declarations of incompatibility. Together these features create incentives for a critical examination of the relative merits of legislation from a broader spectrum of institutional actors – and in a more reflective manner – than is normally associated with a Bill of Rights[93]

At its most generous this model requires that the executive honestly reports its views concerning compatibility to Parliament and that Parliament in turn exercises independent scrutiny. Some elements of this system have operated relatively successfully, notably the Joint Committee on Human Rights.

In other respects, however, the HRA has proved disappointing in its impact on the political process. Section 19 statements have operated as a formal and procedural defence of a pre-determined policy, rather than an informative exercise in dialogue. The House of Commons has shown relatively little interest in rising above party tribal affiliations to use the independent assessments provided to it by the Joint Committee. Parliamentarians have been unwilling to make the necessary reforms to the parliamentary process to make the aspiration of rights scrutiny of legislation into

---

[91]   For equivalent procedures: Government of Wales Act 2006, s 112; Northern Ireland Act 1998, s 11.

[92]   Constitutional Reform Act 2005, s 40 and Sch 9.

[93]   J Hiebert, 'Parliament and the Human Rights Act: can the JCHR help facilitate a culture of rights?' (2006) *Int J of Constitutional Law* 1, 5 (footnotes omitted).

a reality. The House of Lords has been more assertive but, naturally, within a context where its powers are limited and there is no likelihood that they will be extended. Significant elements of the political rights model are therefore simply dysfunctional and it would more accurate to talk of a *politicised* rights model.

Although implementation of devolution and incorporation of the European Convention went hand in hand in places, the fit between these two constitutional reform projects is untidy. In theory, the devolution legislation provides for stronger systems of pre-legislative review than at Westminster and within schemes where, because of the limited powers of the assemblies, greater attention is given to ensuring Convention compatibility. It is too early to say in the cases of Northern Ireland and Wales how these models are working, because of the effects of suspension and changes to the scheme respectively. In Scotland the results are decidedly mixed and, if anything, the Scottish Parliament has demonstrated less interest in rights scrutiny than Westminster.

Chapter 3

The Courts (I): Sources of Law

INTRODUCTION

THE UNITED KINGDOM'S adoption of the Human Rights Act 1998 (HRA) was markedly different to the earlier experiences of legal systems – in Canada, New Zealand and South Africa – coming to terms with the adoption of a newly created Bill of Rights, for the reason that the 'rights' given further effect by the HRA were already to be found in the text of an established international treaty. Nor however, in Britain's case, was the exercise merely one of incorporating into domestic law the European Convention on Human Rights. Alongside the text of the 'Convention Rights'[1] themselves, came also a significant body of jurisprudence from the European Court of Human Rights and the European Commission.[2] This voluminous body of case law has not been however 'incorporated' into domestic law, and therefore domestic courts are not obliged to implement decisions of the Strasbourg bodies under the terms of the HRA. Instead, jurisprudence of the Convention organs is given the status of persuasive authority in domestic law; under s 2(1) of the Act courts and tribunals are bound only to 'take into account' such decisions when the Convention Rights are in play.

SECTION 2(1) AND THE DUTY TO 'TAKE INTO ACCOUNT' STRASBOURG DECISIONS

In 'determining a question which has arisen in connection with a Convention right' under the HRA, section 2(1) obliges domestic courts to 'take into account any' judgment, decision, declaration or opinion of the Strasbourg organs, 'whenever made or given, so far as, in the opinion of the Court or tribunal, it is relevant to the proceedings in which that question has arisen.'[3] Domestic courts are therefore not bound to follow

---

[1] 'Convention rights' are defined in HRA s 1(1).
[2] The latter was abolished under the 11th Protocol to the Convention.
[3] The full text of s 2(1) is as follows: 'A court or tribunal determining a question which has arisen in connection with a Convention right must take into account any – (a) judgment,

decisions of the Convention organs:[4] the duty imposed is to 'take into account' appropriate Convention jurisprudence, insofar as it is considered to be of relevance to the case in hand.

On the face of it this obligation may appear to be relatively weak – 'since it is open to the judiciary to consider but disapply a particular decision'[5] – but equally it remains open to the domestic judiciary to directly apply the principles of a pertinent Strasbourg decision to domestic proceedings. In the words of Buxton LJ in *R (Anderson) v Secretary of State for the Home Department* the courts

> will take the [Strasbourg] court's jurisprudence into account whether we determine the case in accordance with it; or on the other hand decline, on a reasoned basis, to apply that jurisprudence.[6]

In deceptively simple terms section 2(1) creates a significant judicial discretionary power to apply Strasbourg jurisprudence directly, to take it 'into account' but fail to apply it, or to come to a decision somewhere between the two extremes by either applying (or being influenced by) the Convention jurisprudence to a greater or lesser degree.

Section 2(1) therefore gives the Convention jurisprudence the effect of persuasive authority in domestic law. The court's discretion lies in the degree of consideration to afford to the Strasbourg authority. Certain characteristics of the 'relevant' authority, or circumstances of the case in hand, may lead the court to place differing degrees of reliance on decisions of the Strasbourg organs. For example, in deciding whether or not to take into account seemingly conflicting decisions of the Commission and the European Court of Human Rights, a domestic court might legitimately decide to give more weight to the decision of the European Court as the superior and final court of review. Equally, considerations of time are apt: the effect of the Convention may alter over time; it is a 'living instrument' to be given a 'dynamic interpretation in the light of conditions prevailing at the time a matter falls to be considered.'[7] As Lord Irvine stated at the

---

decision, declaration or advisory opinion of the European Court of Human Rights, (b) opinion of the Commission given in a report adopted under Art 31 of the Convention, (c) decision of the Commission in connection with Art 26 or 27(2) of the Convention, or (d) decision of the Committee of Ministers taken under Art 46 of the Convention, whenever made or given, so far as, in the opinion of the court or tribunal, it is relevant to the proceedings in which that question has arisen.'

[4] See, eg, *R (Alconbury Developments Ltd) v Secretary of State for the Environment, Transport and the Regions* [2001] UKHL 23, para 76; *Huang v Secretary of State for the Home Department* [2007] UKHL 11, para 18.

[5] H Fenwick, *Civil Liberties and Human Rights* (3rd ed) (London, Routledge Cavendish, 2002) 146–47.

[6] *R (Anderson) v Secretary of State for the Home Department* [2001] EWCA Civ 1698, [88].

[7] S Grosz, J Beatson and P Duffy, *Human Rights: The 1998 Act and the European Convention* (London, Sweet and Maxwell, 1999) 18.

report stage of debates on the Human Rights Bill, a judgment given by the European Court of Human Rights 'decades ago' may contain 'pronouncements which it would not be appropriate to apply to the letter in the circumstances of today.'[8] Similarly, in terms of the hierarchy of pronouncements emanating from the Strasbourg institutions,

> a judgment of the European Court has more authority than a decision of the Commission, particularly a decision on admissibility ... [A] decision of the Chamber of the European Court has more authority than a decision of the Committee of the Court.[9]

Domestic courts might therefore legitimately afford increased weight to a recent decision of the Grand Chamber of the European Court than to, say, a decision of the Court handed down 20 years ago.

Various factors might in practice affect the degree of weight to be afforded to a Strasbourg decision in the circumstances of an individual case, yet in terms of the construction of section 2(1) the courts' obligation could arguably be satisfied by simply considering the Strasbourg authority put before it; having taken the decision into account it would not be obliged to follow or apply its reasoning. What is striking about those Human Rights Act decisions that engage with the requirements of the section 2(1) obligation is that they contain little or no discussion of this process of attributing weight to the Strasbourg case law. As will be seen, the general focus of the courts' enquiry has been the decision of whether to follow the Convention authority in question.

THE MARGIN OF APPRECIATION AND UK COURTS

Early decisions under the HRA did however, reflect the view that:

> [c]aution is needed where the European Court relied on the 'margin of appreciation' doctrine in concluding that there was no violation of the Convention because the doctrine has no direct application in domestic law.[10]

The margin of appreciation doctrine forms a key element of the jurisprudence of the Strasbourg organs. It refers to the degree of discretion that national authorities will be afforded by the supervisory organs at Strasbourg as to the scope of protection that will be afforded to a Convention

---

[8] HL Debs, vol 584, col 1272 (19 January 1998). And see: *R v Ministry of Defence ex p Smith* [1996] QB 517.

[9] K Starmer, *European Human Rights Law: The Human Rights Act 1998 and the European Convention* (London, LAG, 1999) 27.

[10] Starmer, above n 9, 27.

right in a given set of circumstances. The justification for this degree of discretion was set down by the European Court of Human Rights in the *Handyside* case:

> ... the machinery of protection established by the Convention is subsidiary to the national systems regarding human rights ... by reason of their direct and continuous contact with the vital forces of their countries, State authorities are in principle in a better position than the international judge to give an opinion on the exact content of these requirements as well as on the 'necessity' of a 'restriction' or 'penalty' intended to meet them.[11]

The margin of appreciation afforded in a given area, taken with the status of the Convention as a 'living instrument,' may make it increasingly likely that the range of permissible responses or restrictions may accordingly differ from one State to the next over time. As the application of the doctrine inherently involves a degree of respect for the judgment of the national decision-maker – one which takes into account the prevailing circumstances in that State[12] – it is arguable that domestic courts would be advised not to adopt unquestioningly similar reasoning without noting the breadth of the margin afforded in such circumstances, especially where the judgment of the Strasbourg authorities is addressed to another State party. As Fenwick and Phillipson have suggested, in the context of direct action protest, the tendency of the Strasbourg institutions to afford a wide margin of appreciation to States parties has a number of consequences:

> Review of the 'necessity' of State interferences is not intensive, at times appearing to be confined to ensuring actions were taken in good faith and were not manifestly unreasonable ... States are typically not required to demonstrate that lesser measures than those actually taken would have been inadequate to deal with the threats posed ... the effect of this 'light touch' review may also be seen in the tendency to deal with crucial issues – typically proportionality, but also in some cases the scope of the primary right – in such a brusque and abbreviated manner that explication of the findings is either non-existent or takes the form of mere assertion.[13]

On the one hand therefore, there are strong arguments that the margin of appreciation should have no domestic equivalent since its whole rationale lies in the limits of the Strasbourg court and in a recognition of domestic legal differences throughout Europe. Judicial recognition of this position would enlarge the scope for creative interpretation since, with the margin of appreciation discarded, domestic judges would, in theory, have a freer

---

[11] *Handyside v UK* (1979–1980) 1 EHRR 737, para 48.

[12] Although, in the words of the Commission, those circumstances 'cannot of themselves be decisive': *Dudgeon v UK* (1981) 3 EHRR 40, para 114.

[13] H Fenwick and G Phillipson, 'Direct Action, Convention Values and the Human Rights Act' (2001) 21 *LS* 535, 553–54.

hand to determine for themselves the meaning of the limitations on Convention rights in a uniquely British context. Similarly, UK laws which have been upheld or would be upheld at Strasbourg because of the margin should be open to be given a more rights-friendly reading at the domestic level. Put simply by Lord Hoffmann in *A and others v Secretary of State for the Home Department* when confronted by Strasbourg authority shaped by the margin of appreciation, 'we, as a United Kingdom court, have to decide the matter for ourselves.'[14]

Initially, the signs were encouraging. Recognising the position of the margin of appreciation as a tool of international law, early in the life of the HRA the courts accordingly declared that the doctrine has no application in domestic law. In *Kebilene* Lord Hope stated that 'this technique is not available to the national courts when they are considering Convention issues arising within their own countries.'[15] However, it soon also became clear that recognition that the margin of appreciation was not applicable in domestic proceedings would not necessarily be accompanied by active steps to disentangle the margin from decisions of the Strasbourg organs.[16] Nor would the enforcement of the HRA be accompanied by a jettisoning of home-grown techniques of affording respect to the elected branches of government. Deference to Parliament and respect for the executive are quintessential features of the UK legal system that have shaped the role of judges since the Glorious Revolution in the 17th century, and it seemed unlikely that this tradition would be transformed overnight. As much was confirmed by Lord Bingham in *Brown v Stott*:

> While a national court does not accord the margin of appreciation ... it will give weight to the decisions of a representative legislature and a democratic government within the discretionary area of judgment accorded to those bodies.[17]

In similar vein were Lord Hoffmann's remarks in *Alconbury*, reflecting a fear that the charge of judicial supremacism would be laid: 'the Human Rights Act 1998 was no doubt intended to strengthen the rule of law but not to inaugurate the rule of lawyers.'[18] In practice, discussion of the notion of deference to the democratic arms of the government – or, 'the

---

[14] [2004] UKHL 56, para 92.

[15] *R v DPP ex p Kebilene* [2000] 2 AC 326, 380–81 (HL).

[16] Fenwick and Phillipson have written that, 'In numerous appellate decisions under the HRA, the courts have paid lip service to the notion that the margin of appreciation has no role to play in domestic decision-making. In nearly every case ... the courts have then gone on to apply Strasbourg case law heavily determined by that doctrine, thus precisely applying the margin of appreciation.' (H Fenwick and G Phillipson, *Media Freedom under the Human Rights Act* (Oxford, OUP, 2006) 146.)

[17] [2001] 2 WLR 817, 835 (PC).

[18] *R (Alconbury Developments Ltd) v Secretary of State for the Environment Transport and the Regions* [2001] UKHL 23; [2003] 2 AC 295, para 129.

discretionary area of judgment'[19] – has become one of the hallmarks of adjudication under the HRA and a much-covered area of academic comment and criticism which will be returned to in subsequent chapters.[20]

DOMESTIC RECEPTION OF THE STRASBOURG CASE LAW

Prior to the coming into force of the HRA, a minority of judges clearly thought that the Convention had little to add to domestic law and tried to dissuade counsel from even citing relevant cases. This is a phenomenon which predates the HRA: in the area of freedom of expression the House of Lords in 1990 declared itself satisfied that the common law was identical to Article 10 of the Convention, so there was little point in engaging seriously with the (extensive) Strasbourg case law.[21] Even rulings from Strasbourg pointing out where common law doctrines had failed to meet the standard of the Convention had apparently done little to shake this breezy self-confidence.[22]

Early decisions under the HRA demonstrated mixed responses to the obligation to consider the Convention case law. In some cases counsel were told that domestic legislation already fully took into account the Convention so that it was unnecessary to cite relevant jurisprudence. One case in particular – decided shortly before the Act came into force – did not bode well for judicial receptivity to the Convention jurisprudence. In the family law appeal of *Re F (Care: Termination of Contact)*,[23] the mother of children in care (aged three and five) appealed against a justices' order giving the council leave to terminate contact with her. She argued that the making the order was premature and would be an infringement of her rights under Articles 6(1) and 8 of the European Convention. Mr Justice Wall said that, while the Children Act 1989 had to be read and given effect in a way that was compatible with the Convention rights, it was for the English courts applying what he called 'English criteria of fairness and justice' to decide whether those rights had been breached. He would be

> disappointed if the European Convention on Human Rights were to be routinely paraded in cases of this nature as make-weight grounds of appeal, or if there

---

[19] Lord Lester of Herne Hill and David Pannick, *Human Rights Law and Practice* (London, Butterworths, 1999) 73–76.

[20] Ch 4, pp 92–95; ch 6, pp 159–164.

[21] *Attorney-General v Guardian Newspapers (No 2)* [1990] 1 AC 109, 284–85 (Lord Goff); *Derbyshire CC v Times Newspapers Ltd* [1993] AC 534, 550–51 (Lord Keith of Kinkel); *R v Secretary of State for the Home Department ex p Simms* [2000] AC 115, 123–24 (Lord Steyn).

[22] *Sunday Times v UK* (1979) 2 EHRR 245; *Observer & Guardian v UK* (1992) 14 EHRR 153; *Tolstoy Miloslavsky v UK* (1995) 20 EHRR 442.

[23] [2000] 2 FCR 481; *The Times*, 22 June 2000.

were in every case to be extensive citation of authorities from the European Court of Human Rights, particularly where reliance was placed on cases pre-dating the 1989 Act.[24]

These comments suggested an unwilling judicial embrace of the Strasbourg jurisprudence,[25] coupled with a dangerous complacency over home-grown standards of justice, with a dash of mild Europhobia thrown in for good measure. The assumption that legislation already complies with the ECHR (so that courts need not look beyond it) had too often in the past proved to be unfounded.[26] Moreover, if this approach had been followed it would have contradicted HRA section 2(1), which stipulates that a court 'must' take Strasbourg decisions into account, albeit 'so far as, in the opinion of the court or tribunal, it is relevant to the proceedings.' This attempt to restrict citation of Strasbourg case law to post-1989 cases (that is, those post-dating the Children Act) flew in the face of the duty to take account of such jurisprudence *'whenever made or given.'*[27]

Fresh variations on the theme emerged after the Act's coming into operation. A restricted reading was given to section 2 when the Court of Appeal reviewed the infamous 'M25 murder' case.[28] The European Court of Human Rights had earlier held that the defendants' rights under Article 6 had been breached because of the failure to disclose at the trial that a key prosecution witness was a paid police informant.[29] The issue for the Court of Appeal was whether the conviction was unsafe.[30] Emphasising the weak obligation imposed by section 2(1), Lord Justice Mantell stressed that the duty under the HRA to 'take account' of the Strasbourg decision did not mean that the English court had 'to adopt' or 'to apply' it.[31]

Another understandable, but nevertheless questionable, approach was to treat the previous pronouncements of UK courts as binding where they had considered Convention case law, even where it was arguable that the earlier courts had misunderstood it. In a decision shortly before the Act came into force, the Divisional Court was faced with a Convention challenge to orders requiring the *Guardian* and *Observer* newspapers to hand over to the police letters received from the former MI5 officer David Shayler, concerning his allegations of a British plot to assassinate Colonel

---

[24] *Ibid.*

[25] A trend that one commentator has suggested has continued in the sphere of family law adjudication: S Harris-Short, 'Family Law and the Human Rights Act 1998: Judicial Restraint or Revolution?' in H Fenwick, G Phillipson and R Masterman (eds), *Judicial Reasoning under the UK Human Rights Act* (Cambridge, CUP, 2007).

[26] For details of the number of occasions on which, prior to the HRA coming into force, the UK had been found to have been in breach of the Convention see above, p 5.

[27] HRA s 2(1).

[28] *R v Davis (Michael George) (No 3)* [2001] 1 Cr App R 8, para 60.

[29] *Rowe and Davis v UK* (2000) 30 EHRR 1.

[30] Criminal Appeal Act 1968 s 2 (as amended by Criminal Appeal Act 1995).

[31] See p 193.

Gaddaffi.[32] It was argued that to force one of the journalists to do so would amount to a violation of the right not incriminate himself, since he was under investigation for a possible offence under the Official Secrets Act. Notwithstanding the 1997 European Court decision of *Saunders v UK*,[33] the Divisional Court regarded itself bound by decisions of the *English courts* on the meaning of the rule against self-incrimination, together with their interpretation of whether Article 6 was satisfied. Judge LJ said:

> [W]here a decision or group of decisions has been examined by the House of Lords or Court of Appeal, this court is bound by the reasoning of the superior courts in our jurisdiction. We are not permitted to re-examine decisions of the European Court to ascertain whether the conclusion of the House of Lords or the Court of Appeal may be inconsistent with those decisions, or susceptible to a continuing gloss.[34]

In related fashion, some judges sought to limit the application of Strasbourg decisions in contentious areas by making somewhat unconvincing attempts to 'distinguish' them. This is a technique that is rarely appropriate since the Strasbourg court does not regard itself as engaging in fact-finding. In *Ashworth Hospital v MGN Ltd*[35] the Court of Appeal cited again the discredited formula that there is no difference in principle between English law and Article 10 of the Convention. It then went on to distinguish a decision of the European Court of Human Rights in which it had been held that an order to disclose the identity of a whistle-blower violated Article 10,[36] before proceeding to make a similar order – in that instance that a newspaper should identify the source of stories concerning the health of the convicted murderer, Ian Brady.[37] Similarly, a ground breaking Strasbourg ruling with potentially wide application for undercover policing, *Teixeira de Castro v Portugal*,[38] was distinguished by two different benches, apparently fearful that it would introduce a defence of entrapment into English law.[39]

---

[32]   *R (Bright) v Central Criminal Court* [2001] 1 WLR 662.

[33]   (1997) 23 EHRR 313.

[34]   Above n 32, 682. Post-HRA, similar strictures seemingly apply not only where the appellate courts have *considered* the Strasbourg jurisprudence in question, but also where the Strasbourg jurisprudence has undergone subsequent development (see the discussion of *Price v Leeds City Council* [2006] UKHL 10 below pp 71–75). The door may remain open, however, for lower courts to revisit earlier decisions of higher courts where the Strasbourg case law has not previously been considered in the domestic context.

[35]   [2001] 1 WLR 515.

[36]   *Goodwin v UK* (1996) 22 EHRR 123.

[37]   *Ashworth Hospital v MGN Ltd* [2001] 1 WLR 515, 534–37 (Lord Phillips of Worth Maltravers MR).

[38]   (1998) 28 EHRR 101.

[39]   *Nottingham City Council v Amin* [2000] 1 WLR 1071, 1080–1 (Lord Bingham); *R v Shannon* [2001] 1 WLR 51, 69–70 (Potter LJ).

Overt negative reactions from the judiciary have been rare, but one example stands out. Outright hostility was manifested by one senior Scottish judge, Lord McCluskey, when he wrote in the *Scotland on Sunday* newspaper that the Act would be a 'field day for crackpots, a pain in the neck for judges and legislators and a goldmine for lawyers.'[40] The article went on specifically to discuss surveillance against drugs dealers and Article 8 – the very issue at stake in a case that he had heard only days before. The High Court of Justiciary held that his remarks would raise in an informed observer a reasonable apprehension of bias against the Convention and ordered that the appeal be heard by a different bench.[41]

In a sense the invocation of the doctrine of precedent and attempts to distinguish Strasbourg case law were reassuring: they indicate just how quickly most judges appear to have adjusted to the influx of a substantial new source of law into the legal system. Most Human Rights Act judgments are marked by engagement with the Strasbourg decisions at a detailed and sometimes extensive level.[42] This remarkable transformation of opinion writing in such a short period is no doubt due in large part to the training programme within the judiciary and to the presence on the bench of former advocates who have argued cases in Strasbourg.

CURTAILING JUDICIAL DISCRETION UNDER SECTION 2(1)HRA

As Tierney has observed:

the injunction contained in HRA section 2(1) that courts should take Strasbourg jurisprudence into account is a flexible adjudicatory device but one which inevitably creates an area of uncertainty for judges.[43]

This area of 'uncertainty' was criticised by the opposition during the debates on the Human Rights Bill, with the Conservatives arguing for an approach which would guarantee greater legal clarity and protect the domestic judge against accusations of unwarranted activism.[44] In fact the domestic courts' approach to the construction of s 2(1) has so far betrayed little of the progressive approach to the Convention jurisprudence that

---

[40] *Scotland on Sunday,* 6 February 2000.

[41] *Hoekstra, van Rijs et al v HM Advocate (No 2)* 2000 SLT 605. Lord McCluskey has been a long-term public opponent of incorporation, at least since his 1986 Reith Lectures: J H McCluskey, *Law, Justice and Democracy* (London, Sweet & Maxwell, 1987).

[42] See, eg, K Starmer, 'Two years of the Human Rights Act' [2003] *EHRLR* 14, 15–16; Department for Constitutional Affairs, *Review of the Implementation of the Human Rights Act* (July 2006), 11; and generally, M Amos, 'The Impact of the Human Rights Act on the United Kingdom's performance before the European Court of Human Rights [2007] *PL* 655.

[43] S Tierney, 'Devolution issues and s 2(1) of the Human Rights Act 1998' [2000] *EHRLR* 380, 392.

[44] See further pp 89–90.

caused such concern amongst the Conservative members prior to the HRA entering into force. The trend of judicial reasoning under section 2(1) has overwhelmingly been towards limiting this area of discretion. In the name of increasing legal certainty[45] and maintaining a consistent interpretation of the Convention throughout member states,[46] the House of Lords has developed a number of guiding principles under which Convention juris-prudence should be taken into account. While the combined effect of these principles has undoubtedly engineered a more predicable and consistent response to the Convention case law across the courts system, this may have come at a cost to applicants seeking to enforce their rights in domestic courts.

'Clear and Constant' Jurisprudence

Early attempts to give meaning the to s 2(1) duty sought to endorse an approach to the Strasbourg jurisprudence that would seek to identify the relevant principles inherent in the Convention as the correct persuasive authority. In the words of Sir Andrew Morritt VC in *Wallbank*, the task of the judges is

> not to cast around in the European Human Rights Reports like blackletter lawyers seeking clues. In the light of s 2(1) of the Human Rights Act 1998 it is to draw out the broad principles which animate the Convention.[47]

These sentiments were echoed by Lord Sutherland in *Clancy v Caird*:

> [D]ecisions [of the Strasbourg organs], however, are not to be treated in the same way as precedents in our own law. Insofar as principles can be extracted from these decisions, those are the principles which will have to be applied.[48]

The importance of the principles which underpin the Convention and its case law has been acknowledged in adjudication under the Act: Lord Bingham addressed the issue in *Amin*, while Lord Woolf in *R (Al-Hasan) v Secretary of State for the Home Department* remarked that it is 'the

---

[45] In *Kay and others v London Borough of Lambeth; Leeds City Council v Price* [2006] UKHL 10, para 43, Lord Bingham quoted Lord Hailsham's remarks in *Broome v Cassell and Co Ltd* [1972] AC 1027, 1054: 'In legal matters, some degree of certainty is at least as valuable as perfection.'

[46] See, eg, *R (Ullah) v Special Adjudicator; Do v Immigration Appeal Tribunal* [2004] UKHL 26, para 20; *R (S) v Chief Constable of South Yorkshire; R (Marper) v Chief Constable of South Yorkshire* [2004] UKHL 39, para 27; *Kay and others v London Borough of Lambeth; Leeds City Council v Price* [2006] UKHL 10, para 44; *Al-Skeini v Secretary of State for Defence* [2007] UKHL 26, para 105.

[47] *Aston Cantlow and Wilmcote with Billesley Parochial Church Council v Wallbank* [2002] Ch 51, 65.

[48] *Clancy v Caird* 2000 SLT 546, para 3 (Lord Sutherland).

principles which are relevant and important.'[49] And Lord Hope, writing extra-judicially, has observed that, although section 2(1) demands a certain 'respect for precedents' in the name of 'consistency', this must also allow for 'growth and development ... [A] strict application of the doctrine of precedent will be out of place in this field.'[50] These sentiments arguably sit uneasily with the emergent approach of the House of Lords to the implementation of Strasbourg authority.

From the earliest decisions to reach the House of Lords as a result of the HRA, the Law Lords have sought to bring structure to the domestic response to the Strasbourg case law. The Appellate Committee of the House of Lords has presented a clear line of authority on role of courts and tribunals under section 2(1) HRA,[51] originating in the reasoning of Lord Slynn of Hadley in *Alconbury*:

> Although the Human Rights Act 1998 does not provide that a national court is bound by these decisions it is obliged to take account of them so far as they are relevant. In the absence of special circumstances it seems to me that the court should follow any clear and constant jurisprudence of the European Court of Human Rights. If it does not do so there is at least a possibility that the case will go to that court which is likely in the ordinary case to follow its own constant jurisprudence.[52]

Lord Slynn's approach was subsequently endorsed by Lord Bingham in the *Anderson* case, where he stated:

> While the duty of the House under s 2(1) of the Human Rights Act 1998 is to take into account any judgment of the European Court, whose judgments are not strictly binding, the House will not without good reason depart from the principles laid down in a carefully considered judgment of the court sitting as a Grand Chamber.[53]

While there may arguably be more flexibility in the approach advocated by Lord Bingham – that Strasbourg 'principles' rather than 'jurisprudence' be

---

[49] *R (Al-Hasan) v Secretary of State for the Home Department* [2002] 1 WLR 545, 566.

[50] Lord Hope, 'The Human Rights Act 1998: The task of the judges' (1999) *Stat LR* 185, 192. On the issue of the effect of the Human Rights Act 1998 on the domestic doctrine of *stare decisis* see the decision of the House of Lords in *Kay v London Borough of Lambeth; Leeds City Council v Price* [2006] UKHL 10, paras 40–45, and the discussion below at pp 71–75.

[51] See, eg, *R (Anderson) v Secretary of State for the Home Department* [2002] UKHL 46, para 18; *R v Secretary of State for the Home Department ex p Amin* [2003] UKHL 51, para 44; *R (Ullah) v Special Adjudicator; Do v Immigration Appeal Tribunal* [2004] UKHL 26, para 20; *N v Secretary of State for the Home Department* [2005] UKHL 31, para 24.

[52] *R (Alconbury Developments Ltd) v Secretary of State for the Environment, Transport and the Regions* [2001] UKHL 23, para 26.

[53] *R (Anderson) v Secretary of State for the Home Department* [2002] UKHL 46, para 18.

followed[54] – there still remains the issue that the language used by both Lord Slynn and Lord Bingham hints at something stronger than the simple duty to 'take into account' Convention case law.[55] The injunction that 'clear and constant' jurisprudence be *followed* in the domestic setting seems to mirror the language of the European Court of Human Rights when dealing with the issue of departing from its own previous decisions. As the court stated in *Goodwin v United Kingdom*:

> While the court is not formally bound to follow its previous judgments, it is in the interests of legal certainty, foreseeability and equality before the law that it should not depart, without good reason, from precedents laid down in previous cases.[56]

The approach of the Strasbourg court is indicative of the fact that it has consistently stressed that the Convention is a living instrument which 'must be interpreted in the light of present-day conditions.'[57] As the European Court of Human Rights has noted:

> a failure by the Court to maintain a dynamic and evolutive approach would risk rendering it a bar to reform or improvement.[58]

For a domestic court to adopt similar grounds for following Strasbourg case law would distort the relationship between the domestic and Strasbourg institutions, the latter necessarily feeding off, inter alia, the decisions of the former in determining what those 'present day conditions' may be.

Departure from Strasbourg

During the parliamentary debates on the Human Rights Bill, Lord Irvine suggested that clause 2(1), as it then was, was designed to 'permit the United Kingdom courts to depart from Strasbourg where there was no precise ruling on a matter and a Commission opinion which does so had not taken into account subsequent Strasbourg case law.'[59] At report stage he added:

---

[54] It is interesting to note that s 4 of the Republic of Ireland's European Convention on Human Rights Act 2003 requires that 'a court shall, when interpreting and applying the Convention provisions, take due account of the *principles* laid down by those declarations, decisions, advisory opinions, opinions and judgments [of the Strasbourg bodies].' (emphasis added).'

[55] One of us has argued elsewhere that the injunction that 'clear and constant' jurisprudence should be 'followed' comes close to treating Strasbourg decisions as binding: R Masterman, 'Section 2(1) of the Human Rights Act 1998: Binding Domestic Courts to Strasbourg?' [2004] PL 725.

[56] *Goodwin v United Kingdom* (2002) 35 EHRR 18, para 74.

[57] *Tyrer v United Kingdom* (1979–80) 2 EHRR 1, para 31.

[58] *Stafford v United Kingdom* (2002) 35 EHRR 32, para 68.

[59] HL Debs, vol 583, col 514 (18 November 1997).

The Courts will often be faced with cases that involve factors perhaps specific to the United Kingdom which distinguish them from cases considered by the European Court ... it is important that our courts have the scope to apply that discretion so as to aid the development of human rights law.[60]

In the exercise of their discretion under section 2(1), it was hoped that domestic courts should 'be free to try to give a lead to Europe as well as to be led.'[61]

Early reluctance on the part of domestic courts either to invite Strasbourg to re-examine a point of law, or indeed to 'give a lead' to the Convention organs, can be illustrated by the decision of the Court of Appeal in *Anderson*.[62] *Anderson* concerned the entitlement of the Home Secretary to set minimum tariffs of imprisonment to be served by mandatory life prisoners, and preceded the hearing of the *Stafford*[63] case by the European Court of Human Rights, in the estimate of the Court of Appeal, by a year.[64] And in spite of the doubts in the Court of Appeal as to whether the then arrangements for the setting of tariffs would survive scrutiny by the Strasbourg court,[65] there was a marked reluctance to offer either an invitation to Strasbourg to reconsider its position or to provide a lead to the Convention organs: in the words of Simon Brown LJ (as he then was):

Where ... as here, the ECtHR itself is proposing to re-examine a particular line of cases, it would seem somewhat presumptuous for us, in effect, to pre-empt its decision.[66]

The Court of Appeal followed the approach advocated by the counsel for the Home Secretary – that the clear and constant jurisprudence of the European Court of Human Rights should be followed – while adopting an almost deferential attitude to the Strasbourg court, with Buxton LJ offering the following as justification for restraint:

where an international court has the specific task of interpreting an international instrument it brings to that task a range of knowledge and principle that a national court cannot aspire to.[67]

This rigid interpretation of section 2(1) is in stark contrast to the progressive approach to the Strasbourg jurisprudence seemingly envisaged by the Government during the parliamentary debates on the Human Rights

---

[60] HL Debs, vol 584, cols 1270–71 (19 January 1998).
[61] *Ibid.*
[62] *R (Anderson) v Secretary of State for the Home Department* [2001] EWCA Civ 1698.
[63] *Stafford v United Kingdom* (2002) 35 EHRR 32.
[64] *R (Anderson) v Secretary of State for the Home Department* [2001] EWCA Civ 1698, para 22.
[65] *Ibid,* para 66.
[66] *Ibid.*
[67] *Ibid,* para 91.

Bill, and arguably undermines the role of national authorities as the primary mechanism for securing the protections afforded by the Convention.

While it could be suggested that the phrase 'clear and constant' actually gives courts considerable scope to depart from Strasbourg case law, particularly in an area where that jurisprudence is rapidly developing,[68] the House of Lords decisions concerning section 2(1) specify narrow grounds on which such a departure might be justified.[69] In an article published before the HRA came into force, Lord Hoffmann cast doubt on the utility of a domestic court 'taking into account' a Strasbourg judgment in which the European Court of Human Rights had seriously misunderstood the relevant UK law, giving the example of *Osman v UK*[70] and its treatment of the duty of care under the English law of negligence.[71] In *R v Lyons (No 3)* Lord Hoffmann elaborated on this, after explicitly recognising that section 2(1) only obliged courts to 'take account' of the Convention jurisprudence, by saying that:

> [i]f, for example, an English court considers that the ECtHR has misunderstood or been misinformed about some aspect of English law, it may wish to give a judgment which invites the ECtHR to reconsider the question ... There is room for dialogue on such matters.[72]

The House of Lords has also, for example, indicated that it might not follow or adopt the reasoning of a European Court of Human Rights judgment on an issue on which that court had not 'receive[d] all the help which was needed to form a conclusion.'[73] A further indication of a situation where a United Kingdom court might legitimately depart from the 'clear and constant' jurisprudence of the European Court was given by Lord Hoffmann in *Alconbury*:

> The House [of Lords] is not bound by the decisions of the European Court and, if I thought that ... they compelled a conclusion fundamentally at odds with the

---

[68] Cf, eg, *Sheffield and Horsham v United Kingdom* (1999) 27 EHRR 163 with *Goodwin v United Kingdom* (2002) 35 EHRR 18.

[69] See: *R (Alconbury Developments Ltd) v Secretary of State for the Environment, Transport and the Regions* [2001] UKHL 23, para 26, where Lord Slynn referred to the 'sepcial circumstances' which would have to exist to justify a departure from 'clear' Strasbourg authority.

[70] (1998) 29 EHRR 245.

[71] Lord Hoffmann 'Human Rights and the House of Lords' (1999) 62(2) *MLR* 159, 162–64. See also: R Clayton 'Developing Principles for Human Rights' [2002] *EHRLR* 175, 178.

[72] *R v Lyons (No 3)* [2003] 1 AC 976, para 46.

[73] *R v Spear and Others* [2003] 1 AC 734, para 12 (Lord Bingham) (in which case the House of Lords chose not to follow the reasoning of the European Court of Human Rights in *Morris v UK* (2002) 34 EHRR 52).

distribution of powers under the British constitution, I would have considerable doubt as to whether they should be followed.[74]

In practice, these grounds on which departure from Strasbourg might be justified have been both narrowly drawn and infrequently used. In spite of occasional ackowledgements that 'the possibility of ... divergence is contemplated, implicitly at least, by the 1998 Act',[74a] the lack of meaningful examples of domestic courts departing from Strasbourg jurisprudence is such that, as one commentator has suggested, the very existence of grounds on which a departure might be justified should be doubted.[75]

The limiting principles described above should not rule out the possibility of providing for increased protection beyond that provided by Strasbourg through a removal of the margin of appreciation from the equation,[76] or by the development of a 'broadly consistent' domestic standard where the Convention decisions are few and inconsistent, or deal with the question of admissibility only.[77] In those circumstances a domestic court would arguably be forced to play a more creative role, with the principles that underpin the Convention elevated to a position of increased importance.[78] In the areas where the Strasbourg case law affords little or no direct guidance – either where the primary source of authority exists only in admissibility decisions,[79] or where the court has deferred to the judgment of national authorities[80] – the response of the domestic courts has been disappointing. As noted above, judgments under the HRA display a marked trend against attempting to disentangle the margin of appreciation aspects of Strasbourg decisions.[81] Similarly, one commentator has noted that where little guidance can be obtained from the Strasbourg case law there has been a worrying indication that domestic courts will treat the

---

[74] *R (Alconbury Developments Ltd) v Secretary of State for the Environment, Transport and the Regions* [2001] UKHL 23, para 76.

[74a] *R (on the application of Animal Defenders International) v Secretary of State for Culture, Media and Sport* [2008] UKHL 15, para 44 (Lord Scott).

[75] J Lewis, 'The European ceiling on human rights' [2007] *PL* 720, 730–31.

[76] Which *may* extend to the question of the scope of the primary right between 'different cultural, traditional and religious environments' (*Secretary of State for Work and Pensions v M* [2006] UKHL 11 (Lord Mance), paras 135–36).

[77] As in, eg, the case law on public protest, on which see: H Fenwick and G Phillipson, 'Public Protest, the Human Rights Act and Judicial Responses to Political Expression' [2000] *PL* 627, 640–41.

[78] H Fenwick and G Phillipson, 'Direct Action, Convention Values and the Human Rights Act' (2001) 21 *LS* 535, 564.

[79] *Ibid.*

[80] Strasbourg decisions on restrictions on freedom of expression on grounds of morality provide useful examples: *Handyside v United Kingdom* (1979–80) 1 EHRR 737; *Müller v Switzerland* (1991) 13 EHRR 212.

[81] pp 53–56.

issue as effectively non-justiciable,[82] effectively forcing the applicant to take their case to Strasbourg to seek a determination of their rights.

No Less, But No More Than the Convention Allows

A number of commentators have speculated that, in the appropriate case, the HRA sanctions a domestic court to provide for a more generous protection of the Convention rights than that afforded by Strasbourg.[83] A further related development in the construction of section 2(1) HRA has come as blow to those who saw in the scheme of the HRA the potential to provide the courts with a mandate to develop and expand on the Convention standards in the domestic context. A corollary of the precedent-like approach to the Strasbourg jurisprudence adopted by the House of Lords is the tendency towards regarding the Strasbourg standard as the aspiration rather than the foundation for the development of a domestic rights jurisprudence.[84] While this constrained approach has been recognised as one of the potential hazards of transposing an international treaty into a national 'Bill of Rights,' it also brings with it the potential both to frustrate the object of the ECHR itself – the 'further realisation' of the Convention rights – and of the HRA by running the risk of confining the domestic judiciary to a compatibility-only approach to the Convention rights. As Clapham has written:

> the problem is that judges or Governments may be tempted to point to such minimum standards as evidence of the limits of the human rights at stake. The challenge is to ensure that national courts treat the international human rights as a part of the national heritage and interpret them in the national context so as to give the appropriate maximum protection at the national level ... It is important

[82] J Lewis, 'The European Ceiling on Rights' [2007] *PL* 720, 732: 'Where there is little Strasbourg authority on the points, the courts have simply taken this to mean that it is a no-go area' (The example discussed by Lewis is of *R (Clift) v Secretary of State for the Home Department* [2006] UKHL 54; [2007] 1 AC 484). Although cf *R v Secretary of State for the Home Department ex p Limbuela* [2005] UKHL 66; [2006] 1 AC 396 where the 'only approximately relevant authority' was the admissibility decision *O'Rourke v UK*, ECtHR No 39022/97 (2003) discussed in C Warbrick, 'The European Convention on Human Rights and the Human Rights Act: the view from the outside' in Fenwick, Phillipson and Masterman, above n 25. See also the discussion of *Campbell v MGN*, below, pp 80–82.
[83] See, eg, HL Debs, vol 584, cols 1270–71 (19 January 1998) (Lord Irvine of Lairg); S Grosz, J Beatson and P Duffy, above n 7, 20–21; F Klug, 'A bill of rights: do we need one, or do we already have one?' [2007] *PL* 701. See also: R Dworkin, *A Bill of Rights for Britain* (London, Chatto and Windus, 1990), 21–23.
[84] For a more detailed examination see: R Masterman, 'Aspiration or Foundation? The Status of the Strasbourg Jurisprudence and the "Convention Rights" in domestic law', in Fenwick, Phillipson and Masterman, above n 25; J Lewis, above n 82.

that national courts have the autonomy to interpret the relevant international human rights so as to make them appropriate to the national culture.[85]

While it may be necessary in the interests of legal certainty to establish clear principles on which to base reliance on, or to distinguish (to use the language of precedent), the Strasbourg case law, it would seem to be counter to the scheme of the HRA and to the purpose of the ECHR to limit domestic courts to a precedent-like application of the Strasbourg jurisprudence. Nevertheless, Lord Bingham in *Attorney-General's Reference, No 4 of 2002*, has stated that not only should domestic courts retain a firm grounding in the Convention jurisprudence, but also that 'the United Kingdom Courts must take their lead from Strasbourg.'[86]

Domesticated Interpretations of 'the Convention Rights'

The decisions of the House of Lords in *R (Ullah) v Special Adjudicator*[87] and *R (S) v Chief Constable of South Yorkshire; R (Marper) v Chief Constable of South Yorkshire*[88] make explicit the link between section 2(1) HRA and the question of English courts providing for a domestic interpretation of one of the 'Convention rights.' These two decisions make the resounding point that a domestic court should not extend the protection offered to a Convention right through broadening the scope of the right in question unless clearly sanctioned to do so by Strasbourg. It is worth repeating the relevant extract of Lord Bingham's speech in *Ullah* in full to make evident the link with the interpretation of section 2(1) previously adopted by the House of Lords:

> While such case law is not strictly binding, it has been held that the courts should, in the absence of some special circumstances, follow any clear and constant jurisprudence of the Strasbourg court: *R (Alconbury Developments Ltd) v Secretary of State for the Environment, Transport and the Regions*.[89] This reflects the fact that the Convention is an international instrument, the correct interpretation of which can be authoritatively expounded only by the Strasbourg court. From this it follows that a national court subject to a duty such as that imposed by s 2 should not without strong reason dilute or weaken the effect of the Strasbourg case law. It is indeed unlawful under s 6 of the 1998 Act for a public authority, including a court, to act in a way which is incompatible with a Convention right. It is of course open to member states to provide for rights

---

[85] A Clapham, 'The European Convention on Human Rights in the British Courts: Problems Associated with the Incorporation of International Human Rights' in P Alston (ed), *Promoting Human Rights Through Bills of Rights* (Oxford, OUP, 1999) 134–35.
[86] *A-G's Reference, No 4 of 2002* [2004] UKHL 43, para 33. See also: *Douglas v Hello! Ltd* [2001] QB 967, 989 (Brooke LJ).
[87] [2004] UKHL 26.
[88] [2004] UKHL 39.
[89] [2001] UKHL 23.

more generous than those guaranteed by the Convention, but such provision should not be a product of interpretation of the Convention by national courts, since the meaning of the Convention should be uniform throughout the states party to it. The duty of national courts is to keep pace with the Strasbourg jurisprudence as it evolves over time: no more, but certainly no less.[90]

This analysis of the position of the Convention rights in domestic law leaves little scope for domestic court to expand the scope of the protection afforded to one of the Convention rights in domestic law. Lord Bingham's dictum endorses a minimalist interpretation of the HRA – reflecting the tension described by Clayton between the domestic court's acknowledgement of the 'constitutional status' of the HRA and charges of exceeding the legitimate judicial role.[91]

Even when confronted with Strasbourg authority, which the Law Lords have acknowledged 'is not in an altogether satisfactory state', 'lacks its customary clarity' and displays reasoning that has not been 'entirely convincing', the House has maintained its position.[92] In the words of Lord Hope in *N v Secretary of State for the Home Department*:

> Our task, then, is to analyse the jurisprudence of the Strasbourg court and, having done so and identified its limits, to apply it to the facts of this case ... It is not for us to search for a solution ... which is not to be found in the Strasbourg case law. It is for the Strasbourg court, not for us, to decide whether its case law is out of touch with modern conditions and to determine what further extensions, if any, are needed to the rights guaranteed by the Convention. We must take its case law as we find it, not as we would like it to be.[93]

This interpretation of the courts' role under the HRA also arguably further limits the potential for domestic courts to – in Lord Irvine's words – 'give a lead' to Strasbourg. The adoption of this position is clearly intended to guard against accusations of excessive activism or of acting without sufficient legal authority, but it also arguably adopts an overly deferential attitude to the judgments of an international court of review. What is clear is that in advising against both the dilution or the extension of the protections provided in the domestic context – in addition to specifying narrow grounds on which departure from 'clear and constant' jurisprudence might be justified – the House of Lords has reduced the scope of the discretion afforded on the face of section 2(1) to almost vanishing point.

---

[90]   *R (Ullah) v Special Adjudicator; Do v Immigration Appeal Tribunal* [2004] UKHL 26, para 20 (Lord Bingham).

[91]   R Clayton, 'Judicial Deference and "Democratic Dialogue": the legitimacy of judicial intervention under the Human Rights Act 1998' [2004] 33, 34. See further chs 4 and 5.

[92]   *N v Secretary of State for the Home Department* [2005] UKHL 31, paras 11, 14 (Lord Nicholls) and para 91 (Lord Browne of Eaton-under-Heywood).

[93]   *Ibid*, para 25. See also: *R (Clift) v Secretary of State for the Home Department* [2006] UKHL 54; [2007] 1 AC 484, para 49.

Discretion as to the 'Qualification' Analysis

Lord Bingham's dictum in *Ullah* was subsequently endorsed by Lords Steyn and Rodger in *Marper*, with Baroness Hale in that case adding that:

> we must interpret the Convention rights in a way which keeps pace with rather than leaps ahead of the Strasbourg jurisprudence as it evolves over time.[94]

The speech of Lord Steyn (with which Lords Rodger, Carswell and Browne were in agreement) does however endorse an interpretation of Lord Bingham's dictum which preserves an important area of discretion for the domestic judge. Lord Steyn held that when considering the question of the engagement of the primary right in question, the domestic judge should not broaden (or weaken) the Strasbourg interpretation of the right.[95] He went on to address the comments made in *Marper* by Lord Woolf CJ in the Court of Appeal, who had said:

> so there can be situations where the standards of respect for the rights of the individual in this jurisdiction are higher than those required by the Convention. There is nothing in the Convention setting a ceiling on the level of respect which a *jurisdiction* is entitled to extend to personal rights.[96]

Lord Woolf had gone on to indicate that the 'cultural traditions' of member states were to be relevant considerations when assessing the scope of the primary right in question. In this assertion he was supported by Sedley LJ.[97] Lord Steyn however, after endorsing the findings of the Senior Law Lord in *Ullah*, went on to observe:

> I do accept the when one moves on to consider the question of objective justification under Art 8(2) the cultural traditions in the United Kingdom are material. With great respect to Lord Woolf CJ the same is not true under Art 8(1) ... the question of whether the retention of fingerprints and [DNA] samples engages Art 8(1) should receive a uniform interpretation throughout member states, unaffected by different cultural traditions.[98]

In contrast to this, Lord Woolf had made no distinction between the powers of the respective branches of government in his assertion that there was no limit to the degree of respect that a 'jurisdiction' might afford a Convention right, leaving open the question of whether this might be

---

[94] *R (S) v Chief Constable of South Yorkshire; R (Marper) v Chief Constable of South Yorkshire* [2004] UKHL 39; [2004] 1 WLR 2196, paras 27 (Lord Steyn), 66 (Lord Rodger), 78 (Baroness Hale).

[95] *Ibid*, para 27.

[96] *R (S) v Chief Constable of South Yorkshire; R (Marper) v Chief Constable of South Yorkshire* [2002] 1 WLR 3223, para 34 (Lord Woolf) (emphasis added).

[97] *Ibid*, para 68 (Sedley LJ).

[98] *R (S) v Chief Constable of South Yorkshire; R (Marper) v Chief Constable of South Yorkshire* [2004] UKHL 39; [2004] 1 WLR 2196, para 27.

within the power of the courts if 'cultural traditions' so demanded. The House of Lords decisions in *Ullah* and *Marper* clearly indicate that – at least as far as the courts are concerned – a clear limit is imposed on the scope of the rights under the Convention by the judgments of the European Court of Human Rights. It is not therefore within the powers of a domestic court to extend the scope of a right in a direction not provided for by Strasbourg. The issue therefore becomes one of separation of powers: although it would remain within the power of the legislature to extend the protection offered to a certain right, this is not a liberty afforded to the courts under the HRA. Where domestic courts do retain a significant discretion to take into account local conditions – according to Lord Steyn in *Marper* – is in the determination of whether restricting the enjoyment of the right in question is justified in the circumstances of the case.

It is worth noting that this limitation on the powers of the courts under the HRA is what might be called a 'self-denying ordinance.' Looking back to the decision of the European Court of Human Rights in the *Handyside* case it seems that the Strasbourg institutions make no distinction between the respective competences of the branches of government within member states:

> *State authorities* are in principle in a better position than the international judge to give an opinion on the exact content of these requirements as well as on the 'necessity' of a 'restriction' or 'penalty' intended to meet them.[99]

As such – in the eyes of the Strasbourg institutions as in those of Lord Woolf – no distinction is made between the respective competences of member states arms of government:

> [t]here is nothing in the Convention setting a ceiling on the level of respect which a jurisdiction is entitled to extend to personal rights.'[100]

Indeed, as one former judge of the European Court of Human Rights has specifically noted, the role of the domestic judiciary under the Convention system

> goes further than seeing to it that the minimum standards in the ECHR are maintained. That is because the ECHR's injunction to further realise human rights and fundamental freedoms contained in the preamble is also addressed to domestic courts.[101]

---

[99] *Handyside v United Kingdom* (1979–1980) 1 EHRR 737, para 48.
[100] *R (S) v Chief Constable of South Yorkshire; R (Marper) v Chief Constable of South Yorkshire* [2002] 1 WLR 3223, para 34 (Lord Woolf) (emphasis added).
[101] Judge Sibrand Karel Martens, 'Incorporating the European Convention: the role of the judiciary' [1998] *EHRLR* 5, 14.

Yet, in the domestic context, the perceived limitations on the courts' role can be traced back to the traditional account of the separation of powers doctrine, in which

> Parliament has a legally unchallengeable right to make whatever laws it thinks right ... [t]he executive carries on the administration of the country ... [t]he courts interpret the laws, and see that they are obeyed.[102]

To extend the scope of one of the 'Convention rights' in the absence of Strasbourg authority would be to exceed the boundaries of the proper judicial role under the Act. This arguably restrictive interpretation of the judicial role under the HRA bears much in common with the courts' approach to section 3(1) HRA; in spite of the novel approach to interpretation which that provision allows,[103] and the considerable claims made of its potency,[104] parliamentary sovereignty continues to wield considerable sway.[105]

THE HRA AND *STARE DECISIS*

Section 2 HRA requires courts and tribunals to have regard to Convention decisions:

> *whenever made or given*, so far as, in the opinion of the court or tribunal, it is relevant to the proceedings in which that question has arisen.[106]

The Convention itself has no system of precedent.[107] The European Court of Human Rights has itself stated that the Convention is a living instrument so that the Court should be free to depart from its earlier decisions in the light of changing social conditions.[108] The implication is that interpretations by the domestic courts of Convention jurisprudence, even if correct when given, may be overtaken by later developments at Strasbourg. Consequently, domestic courts may be put in the position of re-interpreting legislation that has already been read at an earlier point to achieve compatibility. The combined nature of the duties *on all courts* under sections 2 and 3 HRA would suggest that Parliament intended this is to be

---

[102] *R v Secretary of State for the Home Department ex p Fire Brigades Union* [1995] 2 AC 513, 567 (Lord Mustill).

[103] *R v A (No 2)* [2002] 1 AC 45, 68 (Lord Steyn).

[104] See, eg, *R v A* above n 103, para 44; *Ghaidan v Godin-Mendoza* [2004] 2 AC 557; [2004] 3 All ER 411, para 44; G Phillipson, '(Mis-)Reading Section 3 of the Human Rights Act' (2003) 119 *LQR* 551.

[105] See ch 4.

[106] Emphasis added.

[107] However, the introduction of the Grand Chamber under the 11th Protocol reforms could be seen as moving in that direction.

[108] See, eg, *Tyrer v UK* (1978) 2 EHRR 1, para 31; *Cossey v UK* (1990) 13 EHRR 622, para 35.

the case without regard to whether the earlier domestic decision came from a higher court whose decisions are binding under the doctrine of precedent on the court now faced with the issue on the fresh occasion.[109] There is an admission in *Hansard* made during the Committee stage that suggests that the Government was alert to this issue.[110] Lord Hope, writing extra-judicially, also noted that 'a strict application of the principle of *stare decisis* will have to give way to a more creative, more relaxed approach to previous case law,'[111] adding that:

> respect for precedents must allow for growth and for development. So a strict application of the doctrine of precedent will be out of place in this field. The judges *at all levels* must be free to depart from decisions which are out of step with current trends and informed opinion – and precedents which were not informed by an application of the relevant Convention right will always have to be treated with caution. They may have to be disregarded as irrelevant.[112]

The scenario outlined came to fruition in *Price v Leeds City Council*[113] in which the House of Lords had to consider the effect on one of its own rulings (*Harrow London Borough Council v Qazi*[114]) of a later European Court of Human Rights decision (*Connors v UK*[115]). In *Qazi* a majority of the House had held that where under domestic legislation an occupier had no right to possession (a tenancy having previously been brought to an end by a valid notice served by his joint tenant) this was sufficient to satisfy Article 8(2), and the courts hearing a claim for a possession order against him need not consider his Convention rights. This ruling in itself was highly controversial in view of the position of the county court as a public authority under HRA section 6, although plainly it was much influenced by case-management concerns. In *Connors* the European Court of Human Rights held that the eviction of a family of gypsies from a local authority site by summary process following complaints made against them did not give sufficient opportunity to establish proper justification for the serious interference with his rights under Article 8, and consequently could not be regarded as justified by a 'pressing social need' or proportionate to the legitimate aim being pursued. The Court of Appeal in *Price* had concluded

---

[109]   L Lustgarten and I Leigh, 'Making Rights Real: The Courts, Remedies and the Human Rights Act' (1999) 58(3) *CLJ* 509, 510–12.

[110]   HC Debs, vol 313, col 405 (3 June 1998) (Geoff Hoon MP).

[111]   Lord Hope, 'The Human Rights Act 1998: The Task of the Judges' (1999) 20(3) *Stat LR* 185, 190.

[112]   *Ibid*, 192 (emphasis added).

[113]   *Kay and Others v Lambeth Borough Council; Price v Leeds City Council* [2006] UKHL 10.

[114]   [2004] 1 AC 983.

[115]   *Connors v United Kingdom* (2004) 40 EHRR 189; *Blecic v Croatia* (2004) 41 EHRR 185.

that *Connors* was unquestionably incompatible with *Qazi* but that since the latter was a decision of House of Lords it was bound to follow *Qazi*.[116]

Intervening in the House of Lords in *Price*, Liberty and JUSTICE had argued that the Court of Appeal was incorrect and that the later Strasbourg ruling should normally be followed by the lower court where four conditions were met:

1)   the Strasbourg ruling has been given since the domestic ruling on the point at issue,
2)   the Strasbourg ruling has established a clear and authoritative interpretation of Convention rights based (where applicable) on an accurate understanding of United Kingdom law,
3)   the Strasbourg ruling is necessarily inconsistent with the earlier domestic judicial decision, and
4)   the inconsistent domestic decision was or is not dictated by the terms of primary legislation, so as to fall within section 6(2) of the 1998 Act.[117]

These carefully measured criteria should have been sufficient to allay the fear of insubordinate and anarchic rulings by lower courts enticed by doubtful arguments about Strasbourg jurisprudence. However, the House of Lords came down on the side of legal certainty, arguably adopting an even more circumscribed approach than that advocated by any of the counsel in that case.[118] Prompted by the fact that amongst the Law Lords there were differing views in the House over whether *Connors* was inconsistent with *Qazi*, Lord Bingham adopted a cautious approach:

> The prospect arises of different county court and High Court judges, and even different divisions of the Court of Appeal, taking differing views of the same issue … certainty is best achieved by adhering, even in the Convention context, to our rules of precedent. It will of course be the duty of judges to review Convention arguments addressed to them, and if they consider a binding precedent to be, or possibly to be, inconsistent with Strasbourg authority, they may express their views and give leave to appeal, as the Court of Appeal did

---

[116]   *Leeds City Council v Price* [2005] 1 WLR 1825, para 26.
[117]   [2006] UKHL 10, para 41.
[118]   *Ibid.* The appellants argued that the domestic court 'might' depart from the higher domestic authority in the event of a 'very clear' inconsistency with a later Strasbourg decision. The respondent argued that a lower court 'may decline to follow binding domestic authority in the limited circumstances where it decides that the higher courts are bound to resile from that authority in the light of subsequent Strasbourg jurisprudence.' Counsel intervening on behalf of the Secretary of State advocated a 'relaxation' of the doctrine of precedent, arguing that 'a lower court should be entitled to depart from an otherwise binding domestic decision of the Strasbourg court on the same point. But the inconsistency must be clear. A mere tension or possible inconsistency would not entitle a lower court to depart from binding domestic precedent.'

here. Leap-frog appeals may be appropriate. In this way, in my opinion, they discharge their duty under the 1998 Act. But they should follow the binding precedent ...[119]

This aspect of the ruling clearly places a restrictive interpretation on the duty of the lower court under sections 2, 3 and 6 HRA. It must be open to question whether the statutory duty of that court not to *act* in a way incompatible with a person's Convention rights (section 6) is adequately discharged by hearing an argument that Convention jurisprudence is incompatible with domestic authority, concluding that is, but then ruling against the party raising the argument and suggesting an appeal. Apart from anything else there is the question of why a party invoking Convention rights in this situation must bear the burden, delay and cost of going to the higher court. *Price* is an unwelcome decision that runs directly counter to the scheme of Act: Parliament has clearly decreed, through applying sections 2, 3 and 6 on *all* courts, that they have the task of bringing rights home.

Moreover, when *Price* is taken together with *Ullah* (discussed above), there is a clear inconsistency. Lord Bingham justifies the 'no less/no more' doctrine on the basis that the Strasbourg court is authoritative source of determination of the meaning of Convention rights. Faced with the consequences of his own argument, in *Price*, his Lordship reverted to explaining that many Strasbourg decisions leave matters to the domestic courts under the margin of appreciation (and for this reason presumably those courts should be slow to find inconsistency with Strasbourg jurisprudence):

> Thus it is for national authorities, including national courts particularly, to decide in the first instance how the principles expounded in Strasbourg should be applied in the special context of national legislation, law, practice and social and other conditions. It is by the decisions of national courts that the domestic standard must be initially set, and to those decisions the ordinary rules of precedent should apply.[120]

If this is so, however, it plainly contradicts the 'no more' aspect of the *Ullah* doctrine. When the Strasbourg court invokes the margin of appreciation there is in truth no objection to a more expansive reading of 'Convention rights' by the domestic courts. It seems clear then, as suggested above, that the real objection to United Kingdom courts going beyond the minimum protection that the Convention requires is their fear

---

[119]   *Ibid*, para 43.
[120]   *Ibid*, para 44.

of being tarred judicial activists and legislators, rather than respect for the Strasbourg court.[121]

AUTHORITY FROM OTHER JURISDICTIONS

Additionally, the text of section 2(1) allows scope for – or at least does not expressly prohibit – the consideration of jurisprudence from other jurisdictions. For the domestic court, the utility of this legislative silence may have been, as Klug has noted, particularly evident where there is 'little or no steer from the Strasbourg organs.'[122] However, for some it had rather more depressing consequences; as Lord McCluskey lamented during the parliamentary debates on the Human Rights Bill:

> In future no lawyer will be able to advise a client on any matter which might involve a public authority without studying not just the European jurisprudence ... but also American case law, Canadian case law, and even Indian case law and Australian and New Zealand case law.[123]

Recourse to the authority of other jurisdictions was becoming commonplace in domestic courts prior to the coming into force of the HRA,[124] and that domestic courts have been willing to examine comparative jurisprudence has been evident from some of the earliest decisions taken under the HRA.[125] In *Brown v Stott*[126] for example, both Lord Bingham and Lord Hope of Craighead, quite apart from sophisticated engagement with the

---

[121] See also the difficulties experienced by lower courts attempting to reconcile the House of Lords decision in *Campbell v MGN* [2004] UKHL 22; [2004] 2 AC 457 with the more recent decision of the European Court of Human Rights in *Von Hannover v Germany* (2005) 40 EHRR 1. The latter case adopted a broader reading of 'private life' than that adopted by the House of Lords in *Campbell*, but a strict adherence to *Leeds City Council v Price* would hold that *Campbell* remains authoritative in the domestic sphere. See: *McKennit v Ash* [2005] EWHC 3003 (QB); *Murray v Express Newspapers Plc* [2007] EWHC 1908 (Ch); [2007] EMLR 22; and for discussion see: G Phillipson, 'The Common Law Privacy and the Convention' in Fenwick, Phillipson and Masterman, above n 25, 240–54.

[122] F Klug, 'The Human Rights Act 1998, *Pepper v Hart* and All That' [1999] *PL* 246, 251. For a particularly useful examination of the use of comparative jurisprudence in human rights adjudication see: C McCrudden, 'A Common Law of Human Rights? Transnational Judicial Conversations on Constitutional Rights' (2000) 20(4) *OJLS* 499.

[123] HL Debs, vol 582, col 1268 (3 November 1997). See also: Lord Lester of Herne Hill and Lydia Clapinska, 'Human Rights and the British Constitution', in J Jowell and D Oliver (eds), *The Changing Constitution* (5th ed) (Oxford, OUP, 2004) 83.

[124] See, eg, Lord Cooke, *Turning Points of the Common Law* (London, Sweet and Maxwell, 1997); Lord Cooke, 'The Road Ahead for the Common Law' (2004) 53 *ICLQ* 273; B Markesinis (ed), *The Gradual Convergence: Foreign Ideas, Foreign Influences and English Law on the eve of the 21st Century* (Oxford, Clarendon Press, 1994).

[125] See, eg, *Starrs v Ruxton* (2000) SLT 42; *Montgomery v HM Advocate* [2001] 2 WLR 779, 810 (PC).

[126] *Brown v Stott* [2003] 1 AC 681.

ECHR jurisprudence, went on an extensive comparative survey, reminiscent of the Canadian Supreme Court.[127] And in some cases the use of comparative materials has led to the adoption of legal tenets from without the Convention, or even European, traditions.

What is striking about the early experience of domestic courts' reference to comparative jurisprudence under the HRA, is that it was *not* restricted to those circumstances in which there was 'little or no steer' from the Strasbourg organs. In *Brown v Stott* for example, reference to the Canadian jurisprudence was not made as a consequence of the paucity of Strasbourg jurisprudence on self-incrimination,[128] but to offer a perspective from a comparable court in the national setting, as opposed to that of an international court of review. In one sense therefore, the English courts could be seen to be taking an activist approach: in placing increased reliance on comparative jurisprudence in human rights adjudication, even where their primary source, the Convention case law, has a wealth of 'relevant' jurisprudence available. In one sphere in particular, that of the protection of personal privacy under the common law doctrine of breach of confidence, the importation of a legal test for offensiveness from Australian law[129] appeared – at least until the House of Lords decision in *Campbell*[130] – 'to have had far more influence on the development of confidence as a privacy remedy than any principles derived from Article 8.'[131]

Comparative jurisprudence from those countries outside the Council of Europe is likely to offer little in terms of the strict question of judging the *compatibility* of a statutory provision with the Convention rights themselves; similarly it is unlikely to point to the direction in which the common law should be developed to ensure or maintain compatibility with the Convention rights.[132] But in an assessment of how other jurisdictions have dealt with similar limitations on rights or clashes between the individual and public interest comparative jurisprudence has proved useful to judges examining the method of adjudicating between competing interests. Equally useful for the process of assessing the legitimacy of a restriction in Convention terms has been the issue of alternative solutions or approaches adopted in comparable jurisdictions; the usefulness of this reasoning

---

[127]   *Ibid,* 704 and 724.

[128]   See, eg, *Funke v France* (1993) 16 EHRR 297, para 44; *Murray v UK* (1996) 22 EHRR 29, paras 44–45; *Saunders v UK* (1997) 23 EHRR 313, paras 67–76.

[129]   From the decision of the High Court of Australia in *Australian Broadcasting Corporation v Lenah Game Meats* [2001] HCA 63.

[130]   *Campbell v MGN Ltd* [2004] 2 AC 457.

[131]   G Phillipson, 'Transforming Breach of Confidence? Towards a Common Law Right of Privacy under the Human Rights Act' (2003) 65 *MLR* 726, 731.

[132]   An exception to this general point might be if the actual content of the Convention right was unclear.

technique was demonstrated as a part of the proportionality inquiry undertaken in *R v A*, where Lord Hope of Craighead analysed the approaches taken by rape-shield provisions in the United States (Michigan, New Jersey and California), Australia (New South Wales and Western Australia), Canada and Scotland.[133] Similarly in *R v Lambert*,[134] where Lord Steyn set down the 'eloquent' explanation of the presumption of innocence adopted by Sachs J in the South African Constitutional Court decision of *State v Coetzee*,[135] before endorsing the reasoning of Dickson CJC in the Supreme Court of Canada judgment in *R v Whyte*[136] regarding the proportionate nature of restrictions on that presumption.

It should not however be assumed that reference to comparative authority will be welcomed by the court: much will depend on the receptiveness of the judge or judges in question.[137] Equally, it is now clear that this 'constitutional borrowing' should be subject to those limitations which preserve the Convention jurisprudence as the domestic courts' primary source of authority in determining questions of rights. As early as *Brown v Stott*, Lord Hope urged caution in the use of comparative standards and in so doing drew attention to the need to maintain a common approach, noting that

> care needs to be taken in the context of the European Convention to ensure that the analysis by the Canadian courts proceeds upon the same principles as those which have been developed by the European Commission and the European Court.[138]

Lord Hope's concerns were echoed by Lord Bingham in *A-G's Reference No 4 of 2002*, with the requirement that domestic courts retain a firm grounding in the Convention jurisprudence made explicit: 'the United Kingdom Courts must take their lead from Strasbourg.'[139] A viewpoint repeated by the Senior Law Lord in *DPP v Sheldrake*:

> I do not think I should be justified in lengthening this opinion by a review of the cases relied on. Some caution is in any event called for in considering different

---

[133] *R v A* [2001] UKHL 25, paras 100–102. This case is also of interest due to the reliance placed in particular on two decisions of the Supreme Court of Canada – *R v Seaboyer* [1991] 2 SCR 577 and *R v Darrach* (2000) 191 DLR (4th) 539 – due to the similarity of the restrictions on admissible evidence in rape trials in place under the Canadian Criminal Code.

[134] *R v Lambert* [2001] UKHL 37.

[135] *Ibid*, para 34; *State v Coetzee* [1997] 2 LRC 593.

[136] *Ibid*, para 35; *R v Whyte* (1998) 51 DLR 4th 481.

[137] *R (the National Union of Journalists v Central Arbitration Committee* [2004] EWHC 2612, para 49 (Hodge J): 'the Canadian jurisprudence adds little to the interpretation in this case.'

[138] [2003] 1 AC 681, 724.

[139] *A-G's Reference, No 4 of 2002* [2004] UKHL 43, para 33. See also: *Douglas v Hello! Ltd* [2001] QB 967, 989 (Brooke LJ).

enactments decided under different constitutional arrangements. But, even more important, the United Kingdom courts must take their lead from Strasbourg.[140]

TOWARDS A MUNICIPAL RIGHTS JURISPRUDENCE?

The cumulative effect of the developments described above has been to severely curtail the discretion available to the domestic judge on the face of section 2(1). In the Court of Appeal decision in *Runa Begum v Tower Hamlets LBC*, Laws LJ addressed the role of the court under the HRA, stating:

> the court's task under the HRA ... is not simply to add on the Strasbourg learning to the corpus of English law, as if it were a compulsory adjunct taken from an alien source, but to develop a municipal law of human rights by the incremental method of the common law, case by case, taking account of the Strasbourg jurisprudence as s 2 HRA enjoins us to do.[141]

Returning to this theme in *R (ProLife Alliance) v British Broadcasting Corporation*,[142] concerning restrictions on political broadcasts made prior to a general election, Laws LJ stated that:

> The English court is not a Strasbourg surrogate ... our duty is to develop, by the common law's incremental method, a coherent and principled domestic law of human rights ... treating the ECHR text as a template for our own law runs the risk of an over-rigid approach.[143]

Yet, taken together, the effect of the principles of interpretation outlined above arguably cements the 'over-rigid approach' described by Laws LJ. This may be a movement towards a domesticated rights jurisprudence, but it is one which treats the Convention as the benchmark to be followed come what may, with the result that, as Lewis has argued, 'English human rights law finds itself to be nothing more than Strasbourg's shadow.'[144]

Perhaps most damaging to the potential for domestic courts to develop a distinctive municipal rights jurisprudence has been the adoption of the 'no less/no more' doctrine. Since that tenet of interpretation was first adopted by the House of Lords in *Ullah* it has become a mantra for the House of Lords in adjudication under the HRA.[145] In contrast to the grounds suggested by the courts on which 'departure' from Strasbourg might be

---

[140]   [2004] UKHL 42, para 33 (Lord Bingham of Cornhill).
[141]   *Runa Begum v Tower Hamlets London* [2002] 2 All ER 668, para 17.
[142]   *R (Pro-Life Alliance) v BBC* [2002] 2 All ER 756.
[143]   *Ibid*, paras 33, 34.
[144]   J Lewis, above n 82, 729–30.
[145]   See, eg, *R (Clift) v Secretary of State for the Home Department* [2006] UKHL 54; [2007] 1 AC 484, para 49; *M v Secretary of State for Work and Pensions* [2006] UKHL 11; [2006] 2 AC 91, para 129; *Huang v Secretary of State for the Home Department* [2007] UKHL 11; [2007] 2 AC 167, para 18; *Al-Skeini v Secretary of State for Defence* [2007]

legitimate, no such grounds appear to exist on which to afford a more generous definition to the scope of the primary right in the domestic context. Lord Brown has even considered a more emphatically worded direction to domestic tribunals, suggesting in *Al-Skeini* that Lord Bingham's 'no more, but certainly no less' could be refined to read 'no less, but certainly no more.'[146] Lord Brown continued:

> There seems to me, indeed, a greater danger in the national court construing the Convention too generously in favour of an applicant than in construing it too narrowly. In the former event the mistake will necessarily stand: the member state cannot itself go to Strasbourg to have it corrected; in the latter event, however, where the Convention rights have been denied by too narrow a construction, the aggrieved individual can have the decision corrected in Strasbourg.[147]

This approach is misjudged. First, and irrespective of the HRA, a judgment affording an applicant a more generous protection than that afforded by Strasbourg could always be overruled by Parliament; only in the event of an adverse judgment at Strasbourg would the legislature be under an obligation to respect the more generous interpretation of the right. Secondly, the very point of the HRA was to allow victims a remedy in domestic courts. It remains unclear why, in those (admittedly few) cases where the Strasbourg jurisprudence is unsatisfactory, unclear or otherwise silent, an applicant should be forced to take their case to the European Court of Human Rights for determination. By any reckoning, this offers an impoverished view of 'bringing rights home.'

THE EXCEPTIONS TO THE RULE

Looking beyond those cases in which a close focus has been given to the requirements of discharging the courts' obligations under section 2(1) HRA, a slightly different picture is beginning to emerge. One pertinent example can be found in the House of Lords decision in *R v Secretary of State for the Home Department ex p Limbuela*.[148] In that case the House of Lords had to adjudicate on the issue of whether the lack of support provided to 'late' asylum seekers as a result of the section 55 Nationality, Immigration and Asylum Act 2002 was in contravention of Article 3 of the Convention. In deciding that it was, at least one commentator has remarked that the House of Lords in *Limbuela*, 'broadened the scope of

---

UKHL 26, para 90; *R (on the application of Animal Defenders International) v Secretary of State for Culture, Media and Sport* [2008] UKHL 15, para 37.
[146] *Al-Skeini v Secretary of State for Defence* [2007] UKHL 26, para 106.
[147] *Ibid.*
[148] [2005] UKHL 66; [2006] 1 AC 396.

"inhuman and degrading treatment"' beyond that previously recognised at Strasbourg.[149] Had the 'no less/no more' doctrine been applied rigorously, then presumably the threshold at which Article 3 would be engaged should have been the same as – not broader than – that recognised by Strasbourg. Perhaps conscious of this, the requirements of section 2 HRA discussed above do not feature in the House of Lords decision.

The most obvious exceptions to the narrow section 2(1) principles outlined above can be seen in the development of the doctrine of breach of confidence following the coming into force of the HRA.[150] An early indication can be seen in the use of authority from outside the Convention system. As described above, the transformation of the breach of confidence doctrine under the HRA initially owed much to the decision of the High Court of Australia in *Australian Broadcasting Corporation v Lenah Game Meats*.[151] Had the restrictive approach to the reliance on comparative jurisprudence been uniformly applied since the coming into force of the HRA then the influence of that case may well have been less marked. What is striking about the effects of the *Lenah Game Meats* decision on the development of the breach of confidence doctrine is not that it was simply 'taken into account' by the Court of Appeal in *A v B plc*, *Campbell v MGN* and other early confidence cases,[152] but that a wealth of relevant Strasbourg authority on the scope of Article 8 was at the same time being ignored.[153] As Gavin Phillipson wrote in 2003:

> the principles deriving from Article 8 and its jurisprudence that *could* have provided useful guidance on issues such as the relative weight of different privacy interests are simply not figuring in the judgments, despite the fact that section 2 HRA requires courts to have regard to such decisions. No such jurisprudence is discussed or even mentioned in the Court of Appeal judgments in *A v B plc* and *Campbell*, or in *Theakston* and *Douglas II*.[154]

If this distinct lack of analysis of Article 8 principles is to be explained away on the basis of being early, tentative forays into the interplay between common law and Convention, then more recent cases might have been expected to have displayed the firm grounding in Strasbourg principle

---

[149]   J Lewis, above n 82, 736.

[150]   On which generally see: G Phillipson, 'Transforming breach of confidence: Towards a common law right to privacy under the Human Rights Act' (2003) 66 *MLR* 726; G Phillipson, 'The common law, privacy and the Convention' in Fenwick, Phillipson and Masterman, above n 25.

[151]   [2001] HCA 63.

[152]   See: *A v B plc* [2002] EWCA Civ 337; [2003] QB 195; *Campbell v MGN* [2002] EWCA Civ 1373; [2003] QB 633; *Theakston v MGN* [2002] EWHC 137 (QB); [2002] EMLR 22; *Douglas v Hello! Ltd (No 2)* [2003] EWCA Civ 139, [2003] EMLR 28.

[153]   See, eg: *Dudgeon v UK* (1981) 4 EHRR 149; *Z v Finland* (1998) 25 EHRR 371; *Lustig-Prean v UK* (2000) 29 EHRR 548; *Tammer v Estonia* (2003) 37 EHRR 43.

[154]   Phillipson, above n 150, 731.

demanded by *Ullah, N v Home Secretary* and the other cases described above. On the contrary however, the House of Lords decision in *Campbell v MGN* is perhaps the most striking exception to general principle that domestic courts 'must take their lead from Strasbourg.'[155]

Campbell is notable for the reason that the House of Lords resolved the question of the Convention imposing an obligation on the state to provide the individual with a remedy for the breach of Article 8 rights by private parties, in advance of a conclusive decision on point from the European Court of Human Rights.[156] While the decision of the European Court of Human Rights in *Peck v United Kingdom*[157] had concerned the interference with Article 8 rights by the state, the only approximately relevant decision on the particular horizontal application of Article 8 was in the form of the admissibility decision of *Spencer v United Kingdom*.[158] At the time the case of *Campbell* came before the House of Lords, the duty on the state to provide a remedy for the breach of Article 8 by private parties was a 'difficult question' to which 'Strasbourg case law provide[d] no definitive answer.'[159] Yet in *Campbell* the majority in the House of Lords felt able to conclusively find that Article 8 imposed an obligation on the state to resolve breaches of that Article by private parties, in this case the press. Again, the limiting principles outlined above are not mentioned in the Law Lords' decision.

The horizontal effect-specific aspects of this decision are returned to below,[160] but for present purposes *Campbell* marks an important step in creative reasoning under the HRA. While it is entirely arguable that *Campbell* is exactly the type of decision which Lord Irvine had in mind when he indicated that domestic courts should be able to 'give a lead' to Strasbourg, it is also goes against the grain of the restrictive readings of section 2(1) HRA outlined above. It is worth recalling at this stage the words of Lord Hope in *N v Secretary of State for the Home Department*:

> It is not for us to search for a solution ... which is not to be found in the Strasbourg case law.[161]

Campbell shows the House of Lords finding a solution which, while not strictly mandated by clear and consistent authority, was nevertheless later

---

[155] *A-G's Reference, No 4 of 2002* [2004] UKHL 43, para 33. See also *DPP v Sheldrake*, above n 140, para 33; *Douglas v Hello! Ltd*, above n 139, 989.

[156] Such a decision did not come from the European Court of Human Rights until *Von Hannover v Germany* (2005) 40 EHRR 1, handed down a month after the decision of the House of Lords in *Campbell v MGN*.

[157] *Peck v UK* (2003) 36 EHRR 41.

[158] *Spencer v UK* (1998) 25 EHRR CD105.

[159] G Phillipson, 'Judicial Reasoning in Breach of Confidence Cases under the Human Rights Act: Not taking privacy seriously?' [2003] *EHRLR* 54, 57.

[160] See ch 9.

[161] *N v Secretary of State for the Home Department* [2005] UKHL 31, para 25.

shown to be consistent with Strasbourg's developing approach.[162] *Campbell* demonstrates that, beyond those cases which strictly scrutinise the mechanical requirements of section 2(1), there are signs of an emerging – and progressive – rights jurisprudence which is not simply 'Strasbourg's shadow'[163] and which is arguably starting to 'make a distinctively British contribution to the development of the jurisprudence of human rights in Europe.'[164]

---

[162] As subsequently proven by *Von Hannover v Germany* (2005) 40 EHRR 1.

[163] J Lewis, above n 82.

[164] *Rights Brought Home: The Human Rights Bill*, Cm 3782 (October 1997), para 1.14. On the development of such a municipal jurisprudence, see R Masterman, 'Taking the Strasbourg Jurisprudence into account: Developing a "municipal law of human rights" under the Human Rights Act' (2005) 54 *ICLQ* 907, esp at 921–931. On the developing 'dialogue' between domestic courts and Strasbourg see ch 11, pp 294–295.

Chapter 4

The Courts (II): Interpretation and Its Limits

INTRODUCTION

Q UESTIONS SURROUNDING THE legitimate extent of the judicial role have long been the source of controversy. Concerns that unelected and unrepresentative judges are 'legislating' rather than interpreting the law or are interfering in matters of 'democratically-endorsed' government policy, have often been, and will continue to be, raised by academics and politicians alike.[1] The question is one of separation of power – of the appropriate constitutional role and division of functions between the executive, judicial and legislative branches of the United Kingdom government. This debate has been given a new dimension by the Human Rights Act 1998 (HRA), most obviously through the courts' exercise of their power under section 3(1) of that Act – the duty to interpret primary and secondary legislation to be, as far as possible, compatible with 'the Convention rights.'

Of course, there remains outright opposition to the transfer of 'political' power to the judicial branch brought about by the HRA.[2] Beyond this however, a strong assertion of a limited judicial role under the Act and an emphasis on the Act's democratic credentials have been key to the Act's acceptance by those previously hostile to the determination of questions of rights by the judicial branch.[3] Fundamental to this acceptance of the Act are sections 3 and 4 HRA: the former, suggesting that the judicial act remains an interpretative exercise rather than a legislative one; the latter, ensuring that the elected arms of the state are allowed the final say over issues of rights. As such, Ewing has written that the HRA has been viewed

---

[1] JAG Griffith, *The Politics of the Judiciary* (London, Fontana Press, 1991) chs 8, 9; R Stevens, *The English Judges* (Oxford, Hart Publishing, 2002) ch 5; A Bradley 'Judicial independence under attack' [2003] *PL* 397.

[2] KD Ewing, 'The Futility of the Human Rights Act' [2004] *PL* 829.

[3] Compare, eg, Professor Gearty's reservations over judicially enforceable Bills of Rights in KD Ewing and CA Gearty, *Freedom under Thatcher* (Oxford, Clarendon Press, 1990) and KD Ewing and CA Gearty, 'Rocky Foundations for Labour's New Rights' [1997] *EHRLR* 146 with his pro-HRA stance in CA Gearty, *Principles of Human Rights Adjudication* (Oxford, OUP, 2004).

as an '"ingenious compromise" between the "maximalists" and "minimal-ists", the former supporting a judicial power to invalidate legislation, as is the case in Canada,'[4] the latter opposed to any judicial power to make declarations in respect of the compatibility or validity of parliamentary legislation,[5] and endorsing a power of legislative construction only in respect of 'reasonable' interpretations.[6] While the choice between the interpretative obligation imposed by section 3 HRA and the declaration of incompatibility under section 4 undoubtedly falls well short of a power to strike down or invalidate legislation it *is* nevertheless clear that the Act has brought about a significant redistribution of governmental power. As Francesca Klug has noted:

> The courts are clearly given new powers of judicial review under the HRA that they did not have before. They can now review the decisions and actions of ministers and officials in substantive, human rights terms and they can even consider the compatibility of primary legislation with the Convention rights in the HRA, something they were effectively constitutionally barred from doing before.[7]

In this chapter we examine first the idea of the HRA as a 'constitutional' instrument, before exploring the limits of the courts' interpretative powers under section 3(1) HRA.

MAXIMALIST AND MINIMALIST PERSPECTIVES ON THE HUMAN RIGHTS ACT: A CONSTITUTIONAL OR INTERPRETATIVE MEASURE?

At the heart of the debate over judicially-enforced rights instruments lies the issue of legitimacy, and the question of whether disputes over rights should ultimately be determined by the elected and accountable legislative

---

[4] KD Ewing, 'The Human Rights Act and Parliamentary Democracy' (1999) 62 *MLR* 79, 79, quoting Lord Goodhart (HL Debs, vol 583, col 1112 (27 November 1997).

[5] A position Ewing appears to support: 'Parliament's position would have been stronger politically and constitutionally if incorporation of the ECHR had stopped short of giving the courts power to challenge primary legislation' (KD Ewing, 'The Human Rights Act and Parliamentary Democracy' (1999) 62 *MLR* 79, 99).

[6] On which see the comments of Lord Irvine of Lairg at HL Debs, vol 583, col 535 (18 November 1997). See also the comparable interpretative obligation in the New Zealand Bill of Rights Act 1990 s 6, which provides that 'Wherever an enactment can be given a meaning that is consistent with the rights and freedoms contained in this Bill of Rights, that meaning shall be preferred to any other meaning.' As Lord Cooke of Thorndon has noted, section 3(1) HRA is 'slightly more emphatic' ('The British Embracement of Human Rights' [1999] *EHRLR* 243, 249).

[7] F Klug, 'The Human Rights Act – A "Third Way" or "Third Wave" Bill of Rights' [2001] *EHRLR* 361, 370. Ewing has described the change brought about by the HRA as 'unquestionably the most significant formal redistribution of political power in this country since [the Parliament Act] 1911, and perhaps since [the Bill of Rights] 1688' ('The Human Rights Act and Parliamentary Democracy' (1999) 62 *MLR* 79, 79).

branch or by the unelected and unaccountable judicial branch. Those who characterise questions over human rights as the broad competing claims of political actors see the courts as being unsuitable arbiters: as Frankfurter J eloquently put it in *Dennis v United States*, courts

> are not designed to be a good reflex of a democratic society. Their judgment is best informed, and therefore most dependable, within narrow limits.[8]

Equally, the finality of decisions of the highest courts under many judicially enforced Bills of Rights is held to be objectionable as it results in the 'disenfranchize[ment of] the overwhelming majority of the population (in favour of a few select judges).'[9] Those who have questioned the appropriateness of the courts to resolve disputes over rights have however been countered by the assertion of more practical considerations, namely the 'wishful thinking' of those who felt that Parliament had the time, or inclination, to be a 'reliable guardian of human rights in practice.'[10]

The HRA in theory carefully treads between the extremes of political and judicial monopoly over rights by allowing a significant judicial check on executive and legislative action while preserving the appearance of parliamentary supremacy. Nevertheless, the debate continues over where the appropriate dividing line between legal and political power under the Act should lie in practice.

A Constitutional Measure – Our 'Bill of Rights'?

While the promise to 'incorporate' the European Convention on Human Rights had been a manifesto commitment of the incoming Labour administration in 1997, the HRA cannot be said enjoy the degree of popular support which accompanied the implementation of earlier Bills of Rights in Canada or South Africa.[11] Similarly, the HRA does not benefit from the entrenched status of those and other comparable rights instruments internationally; it is not insulated from the 'whims of temporary majorities.'[12]

---

[8]   *Dennis v United States* (1951) 341 US 494.

[9]   J Allan, 'Bills of Rights and Judicial Power – A Liberal's Quandary' (1996) 16(2) *OJLS* 337, 343. See also: J Allan, 'Portia, Bassanio or Dick the Butcher? Constraining Judges in the Twenty-First Century' (2006) *KCLJ* 1.

[10]   T Bingham, 'The European Convention on Human Rights: Time to Incorporate' (1993) 109 *LQR* 390, 392.

[11]   A number of contemporaneous domestic constitutional reforms – the Scotland Act 1998, Northern Ireland Act 1998 and Government of Wales Act 1998 – were implemented following their endorsement by referendum. As a result, Bogdanor has argued that they benefit from being entrenched in a political sense as a result, and could not be repealed without similar popular support (see: V Bogdanor, 'Devolution – the Constitutional Aspects' in Cambridge Centre for Public Law, *Constitutional Reform in the United Kingdom: Practice and Principles* (Oxford, Hart Publishing, 1998) 12, 13.

[12]   HC Debs, vol 225, col 1028 (27 May 1993) (Graham Allen MP).

In spite of frequently voiced views that the HRA is 'no ordinary law,'[13] or that it 'has a status rather different from, *and superior to*, that of most other legislation'[14] or that it is as a matter of fact 'our Bill of Rights,'[15] following the prolonged attacks on the Act which took place during 2006 and 2007, the HRA was exposed as resting on a precarious footing.[16]

The doctrine of parliamentary sovereignty prevents the formal entrenchment of the HRA in domestic law. However, the Diceyan conception of the doctrine – specifically that part which states that there can be no distinction between ordinary and constitutional statutes, as each can be repealed in the same manner as the other – no longer rings as true as it once might.[17] It can be said now with a degree of certainty that the HRA *is* no mere 'ordinary statute'; the common law has come to recognise that there exist 'constitutional statutes' which may only be repealed through the use of express words in primary legislation. The HRA is such a statute – a legislative measure which, as defined by Laws LJ in *Thoburn*, either:

(a) conditions the legal relationship between the citizen and the state in some general, overarching manner, or (b) enlarges or diminishes the scope of what we now regard as fundamental constitutional rights.[18]

And the Act's status as such has been endorsed in the House of Lords,[19] Judicial Committee of the Privy Council,[20] and Court of Appeal[21] in a number of cases subsequent to its coming into force. While it may be fair to suggest that a body of commentators believe that the HRA enjoys a constitutional status of sorts, it is unclear how in the abstract this translates into a tangible benefit for the victim of a purported infringement.

In consequence, it has been suggested that the constitutional nature of the Act sanctions the use of 'generous and purposive' interpretative techniques. In the sphere of rights adjudication it is argued that 'relatively strict methods of interpretation' may not be suitable, as 'constitutional adjudication needs to be approached generously in order to afford citizens the full measure of the protections of a Bill of Rights.'[22] For the domestic

---

[13]   HL Debs, vol 666, col 1350 (16 November 2004) (Lord Lester of Herne Hill).

[14]   D Feldman, 'The Human Rights Act and Constitutional Principles' (1999) 19 *LS* 165, 178 (emphasis added).

[15]   Lord Steyn, 'Democracy, the Rule of Law and the Role of Judges' [2006] *EHRLR* 243, 246.

[16]   See ch 1, pp 3–5.

[17]   On which, see: *R v Secretary of State for Transport ex p Factortame (No 2)* [1991] 1 AC 603; [1991] 1 All ER 70; *Thoburn v Sunderland City Council* [2003] QB 151, [2002] 4 All ER 156; and more recently *Jackson v Her Majesty's Attorney General* [2005] UKHL 56.

[18]   *Thoburn v Sunderland CC* [2003] QB 151, para 62.

[19]   *McCartan Turkington Breen v Times Newspapers* [2001] 2 AC 277, 297 (Lord Steyn).

[20]   *Brown v Stott* [2001] 2 WLR 817, 835 (Lord Bingham), 839 (Lord Steyn).

[21]   *R v Offen* [2001] 1 WLR 253, 276 (Lord Woolf).

[22]   Lord Steyn, 'The New Legal Landscape' [2000] *EHRLR* 549, 550.

judge, a convenient parallel is found in the jurisprudence of the Judicial Committee of the Privy Council.[23] In the famous decision in *Minister of Home Affairs v Fisher* Lord Wilberforce outlined the 'generous and purposive' method of interpretation that should be adopted when interpreting Bills of Rights; a judge should

> treat a constitutional instrument ... as ... *sui generis*, calling for principles of interpretation of its own, suitable to its character ... without necessary acceptance of all the presumptions that are relevant to legislation of private law.

He continued by noting that, while

> [r]espect must be paid to the language which has been used ... [i]t is quite consistent with this ... to take as a point for departure for the process of interpretation a recognition of the character and origin of the instrument, and to be guided by the principle of giving full recognition and effect to those fundamental rights and freedoms

given effect through the constitutional instrument in question.[24] In other words, the overarching interpretative presumption applicable to the HRA would be that of realising those rights which it gives 'further effect.'

In a number of early decisions under the HRA this 'generous and purposive' approach to the interpretation of its provisions was endorsed – *Kebilene*[25] and *Brown v Stott*[26] are two such examples. Judicial willingness to support such an approach gives force to the suggestion that the HRA has the potential to operate as the United Kingdom's Bill of Rights; as Geoffrey Marshall has outlined, the cases from which the 'generous and purposive' approach has been imported concern the interpretation of Constitutional Bills of Rights rather than parliamentary legislation.[27] For a

---

[23]   On which see KD Ewing, 'A Bill of Rights: Lessons from the Privy Council' in W Finnie, CMG Himsworth and N Walker (eds), *Edinburgh Essays in Public Law* (Edinburgh, Edinburgh University Press, 1991) 236–41. It is noteworthy that Professor Ewing's argument that the degree of deference afforded by that Court has blighted its rights jurisprudence is mirrored in his commentary on the Human Rights Act (see KD Ewing, 'The Futility of the Human Rights Act' [2004] *PL* 829).

[24]   *Minister of Home Affairs v Fisher* [1980] AC 319, 329.

[25]   *R v DPP ex p Kebilene* [2000] 2 AC 326, 375 (Lord Hope).

[26]   *Brown v Stott* [2003] 1 AC 691, 703 (Lord Bingham). It should be noted that there has been some disagreement over the appropriateness of giving the Convention rights themselves a 'generous' interpretation: see D Pannick 'Principles of interpretation of Convention rights under the Human Rights Act and the discretionary area of judgment' [1998] *PL* 545; cf RA Edwards, 'Generosity and the Human Rights Act: the right interpretation?' [1999] *PL* 400.

[27]   G Marshall, 'The Lynchpin of Parliamentary Intention: Lost, Stolen or Strained?' [2003] *PL* 236, 247. For that reason Marshall however, urged caution in applying a 'generous and purposive' approach to the interpretation of the HRA, describing the 'often-quoted rhetoric' as 'either empty or tendentious.'

system which is unaccustomed to 'constitutional adjudication' it is unsurprising however that an immediate and universal acceptance of such
methods of reasoning has not been forthcoming, writing in 2004, Richard
Clayton observed:

> [t]he English courts have not so far laid any particular emphasis on the
> importance of interpreting the [Human Rights] Act generously. In fact, there is
> an obvious tension between the courts giving effect to the HRA as a constitu-
> tional instrument and avoiding the charge of excessive judicial activism.[28]

Consequently, the case law on the HRA is littered with examples which
could be used as illustrations of a 'restrictive' interpretation of its terms.[29]
However, abstract arguments over the development of a 'generous and
purposive' approach to interpretation based on Privy Council jurisprudence sidestep the fact that the HRA brings with it its own novel approach
to interpretation. It is unsurprising therefore that the battleground over the
limits of interpretation under the HRA has revolved around section 3(1)
and that the tension described by Clayton is most apparent in the debates
over what Kavanagh has termed the 'elusive divide' between legitimate
judicial interpretation and illegitimate legislation under the HRA.[30]

Section 3(1) HRA

As is by now well known, the text of section 3(1) provides that 'so far as it
is possible to do so, primary legislation and subordinate legislation must be
read and given effect in a way which is compatible with the Convention
rights.' The reach of section 3(1), and the accompanying scope for judicial
discretion, is potentially enormous. In construing statutes and secondary
legislation, the use of section 3(1) is 'obligatory': it applies to statutory
wording whether clear or ambiguous.[31] Section 3(1) applies not only to
post-HRA legislation, but to primary and secondary measures 'whenever
enacted.'[32] It is the key provision behind Lord Hope's assertion that the

---

[28]   R Clayton, 'Judicial Deference and "Democratic Dialogue": the legitimacy of judicial
intervention under the Human Rights Act 1998' [2004] *PL* 33, 34.

[29]   See, eg, *R (Ullah) v Special Adjudicator; Do v Immigration Appeal Tribunal* [2004]
UKHL 26 and *Kay and Others v Lambeth Borough Council; Price v Leeds City Council*
[2006] UKHL 10 (both concerning s 2 HRA); *Bellinger v Bellinger* [2003] UKHL 21; [2003]
2 AC 467 (concerning s 3 HRA); *Poplar Housing and Regeneration Community Association
Ltd v Donoghue* [2002] QB 48; *YL v Birmingham City Council* [2007] UKHL 27 (both
concerning s 6 HRA); *R v Secretary of State for the Home Department ex p Greenfield* [2005]
UKHL 14 (concerning s 8 HRA).

[30]   A Kavanagh, 'The Elusive Divide between Interpretation and Legislation under the
Human Rights Act 1998' (2004) 24 *OJLS* 259.

[31]   *R v A*, below n 69, para 44 (Lord Steyn); *Re S*, below n 84, para 37 (Lord Nicholls).

[32]   HRA s 3(2)(a). It does not, however, appear to apply to the construction of the HRA
itself (*Al-Skeini v Secretary of State for Defence* [2007] UKHL 26, para 15) contrary to the

HRA will 'subject the entire legal system to a fundamental process of review and, where necessary, reform by the judiciary.'[33] The comments of Lord Woolf, in the *Poplar Housing* case, are instructive as to the alteration to the judicial inquiry which section 3(1) precipitates:

> When the court interprets legislation usually its primary task is to identify the intention of Parliament. Now, when section 3 applies, the courts have to adjust their traditional role in relation to interpretation so as to give effect to the direction contained in section 3. It is as though legislation which predates the Human Rights Act 1998 and conflicts with the Convention has to be treated as being subsequently amended to incorporate the language of section 3.[34]

While undoubtedly imposing a 'strong interpretative obligation',[35] the exercise sanctioned by section 3(1) is not without limits. Although a court 'must' attempt to find a Convention-compliant reading, it should only give effect to those which are 'possible.' In the event that a compatible reading is not possible, then the higher courts[36] are given discretion to make a declaration of incompatibility under section 4. The choice of whether to utilise the interpretative power of section 3, or to issue a declaration of incompatibility under section 4, reflects the balance struck by the HRA between elected and appointed governmental power. It is no surprise therefore, that delineating the boundaries of what may be possible under section 3(1) has been termed the most 'difficult' adjudicative task under the HRA.[37]

Balancing Judicial and Political Power

During the parliamentary debates, attempts were made to curtail the degree of discretion available to the domestic judge under the proposed Bill. Arguments were levelled that the failure to require the judiciary to be bound to follow decisions of the Strasbourg organs would cause the judges to be 'cast ... adrift from their international moorings' with the result that:

suggestions of at least one commentator (G Phillipson, '(Mis-)Reading Section 3 of the Human Rights Act' (2003) 119 *LQR* 551.

[33] *R v Director of Public Prosecutions ex p Kebiline* [2000] 2 AC 326, 374–75.

[34] *Poplar Housing and Regeneration Community Association Ltd v Donoghue* [2002] QB 48, 72.

[35] *R v Director of Public Prosecutions ex p Kebilene* [2000] 2 AC 326, 366.

[36] Under s 4(5) HRA, the Appellate Committee of the House of Lords, the Judicial Committee of the Privy Council, the High Court and Court of Appeal in England and Wales and in Northern Ireland, and in Scotland, the High Court of Justiciary (apart from when sitting as a trial court) and the Court of Session.

[37] *Poplar Housing and Regeneration Community Association Ltd v Donoghue* [2002] QB 48, 73.

the Bill is effectively a domestic Bill of Rights and not a proper incorporation of international rights. It means that the judges ... are not obliged to act on it and can go in whatever direction they wish.[38]

To attempt to address this, a Conservative amendment to replace the words 'must take into account' in Clause 2 with the words 'shall be bound by' was tabled – although subsequently withdrawn – in the House of Lords at Committee stage.[39] In a similar vein, a further amendment was tabled which would have had the effect of weakening the section 3(1) obligation by limiting the judiciary to interpretations which would be 'reasonable' as opposed to those which were 'possible.'[40] That amendment was similarly withdrawn, with the Lord Chancellor commenting that

the courts should apply the law and not make it and ... they should not be dragged into the area of opinion or into judgment of a political character.[41]

In contrast to the grand constitutional claims of some, therefore, more conservative arguments have been tabled that the HRA should only be a tool for the achievement of compatibility with the Convention rights, under which the scope for judicial discretion should be strictly circumscribed. One mechanism for curtailing judicial discretionary power under the Act (examined more fully in the preceding chapter) was to tie the development of a domestic rights jurisprudence tightly to the Strasbourg standard. In other words, the HRA should be seen as a tool enabling the domestic judiciary to better achieve compatibility with the State's obligations under international law; as Colin Warbrick has written:

[i]f the national courts use the Human Rights Act as though it were 'like' a bill of rights and move beyond what the Convention requires or allows, then they cut themselves free of all restraints.[42]

Constrained by the strict requirements of the Convention itself therefore, the endorsement of a limited judicial role under the Act safeguards against accusations of the judge 'govern[ing] society on the basis of his own

---

[38]   HL Debs, vol 583, col 514 (8 November 1997). See also HC Debs, vol 313, cols 397–98 (3 June 1998) (Edward Leigh MP). A number of commentators have also seen the ability of the domestic judiciary to depart from Strasbourg as being one of the characteristics of the HRA which most resembles a Bill of Rights: see F Klug, 'The Human Rights Act – A "Third Way" or "Third Wave" Bill of Rights' [2001] *EHRLR* 361, 370; D Bonner, H Fenwick, S Harris-Short, 'Judicial Approaches to the Human Rights Act' (2003) 52 *ICLQ* 549, 553.

[39]   HL Debs, vol 583, cols 511–515 (18 November 1997).

[40]   HL Debs, vol 583, cols 533–537 (18 November 1997).

[41]   HL Debs, vol 583, col 535 (18 November 1997).

[42]   C Warbrick, 'The European Convention on Human Rights and the Human Rights Act: The View from the Outside' in H Fenwick, G Phillipson and R Masterman (eds), *Judicial Reasoning under the UK Human Rights Act* (Cambridge, CUP, 2007) 56.

philosophy, his own biases, or his own worldview.'[43] As indicated in the previous chapter, and save for a number of select exceptions,[44] the courts have been hesitant to afford a more generous domestic protection than that strictly required by Strasbourg.

But in the scheme of the HRA, much rides on the interpretation of the word 'possible', and the approach to section 3 taken by the courts. If the section 3(1) obligation were to be relied on frequently, with an expansive reading given to what interpretations might be possible under that provision, then the neat balance between judicial and political power suggested on the face of the Act would be tipped in favour of the unelected and unaccountable judiciary. In its implementation, it has been noted that there is as much potential for the democratic will to be usurped through an activist use of section 3(1) as there is in any comparable power to invalidate legislation.[45] As Tom Campbell has argued therefore, while the 'general appearance of moderation and compromise that permeates the text and politics of the HRA' gives rise to a suspicion that the 'central provisions of the HRA appear quite weak … even innocuous' the framework of the HRA nevertheless gives the judiciary the tools to achieve the 'de facto full incorporation of the ECHR' into domestic law.[46] In other words, the HRA is a wolf masquerading as a sheep.

Readings of the Act were therefore proposed that would maximise its democratic credentials. In contrast to the suggestions of those Government ministers responsible for promoting the Human Rights Bill, a number of commentators endorsed the 'routine and unproblematic' use of declarations of incompatibility in favour of achieving compatibility via regular judicial interpretations.[47] Key here is section 4(6) HRA, which states that even in the event of a (non-binding) declaration of incompatibility being issued by one of the higher courts, the relevant 'incompatible' provision remains valid and enforceable.[48] Crucially, Parliament is not obliged to remedy the judicial determination of incompatibility. While commentators

---

[43] Justice Antonin Scalia, 'The Bill of Rights: Confirmation of Extent Freedoms or Invitation to Judicial Creation?' in G Huscroft and P Rishworth (eds), *Litigating Rights: Perspectives from Domestic and International Law* (Oxford, Hart Publishing, 2002) 23.

[44] See, eg, *Campbell v MGN* [2004] UKHL 22; *R v Secretary of State for the Home Department ex p Limbuela* [2005] UKHL 66; [2006] 1 AC 396 (both discussed above at pp 79–82).

[45] Lord Lester of Herne Hill, 'Developing constitutional principles of public law' [2001] *PL* 684, 691.

[46] T Campbell, 'Incorporation through Interpretation' in T Campbell, KD Ewing and A Tomkins, *Sceptical Essays on Human Rights* (Oxford, OUP, 2001) 80–81.

[47] *Ibid*, 99. See also: CA Gearty, Reconciling Parliamentary Democracy and Human Rights (2002) 118 *LQR* 248; G Marshall, 'The Lynchpin of Parliamentary Intention: Lost, Stolen or Strained?' [2003] *PL* 236.

[48] HRA Section 4(6) provides that: 'a declaration under this section … (a) does not affect the validity, continuing operation or enforcement of the provision in respect of which it is given; and (b) is not binding on the parties to the proceedings in which it is made.'

have acknowledged that the declaration by a higher court that a statutory provision is incompatible with the Convention rights will wield considerable political force,[49] it remains vital that the response, should there be one, from Parliament and the executive is a matter of choice and not of compulsion. Nevertheless, in the name of providing a remedy to the individual it is easy to see how the courts would be drawn to utilise section 3(1) above the declaration of incompatibility; it is the more immediate of the two options, while the 'weaker intervention'[50] of the section 4 declaration is reliant on the acquiescence of a compliant executive and Parliament to remedy the purported incompatibility. It is for this reason that Lord Steyn has observed that:

> rights could only effectively be brought home if section 3(1) was the prime remedial measure, and section 4 a measure of last resort.[51]

Deference to the Legislature

The general acceptance of a wide-ranging, and regularly used, power of interpretation under section 3(1) would also however require a sea-change in judicial attitudes. Judicial restraint has done much to shape the development of public law adjudication in the UK – most obviously through the *Wednesbury* unreasonableness standard of review.[52] The design of the HRA is not so radical as to exchange parliamentary supremacy for judicial supremacy; in failing to create a power of judicial strike-down and in upholding the primacy of Parliament even in the event of a declaration of incompatibility, the Act makes explicit provision for a degree of deference to the elected arms of the state. The concept of deference has added a further layer of complexity to the judicial task under the Act, and has unsurprisingly provoked the publication of a raft of work on the degree of latitude (if any) which the courts should afford the elected arms of the state, and the intensity of review which will follow.[53]

---

[49] See, eg, HC Debs, vol 307, col 780 (16 February 1998); HL Debs, vol 582, col 1231 (3 November 1997); KD Ewing, 'The Human Rights Act and Parliamentary Democracy' (1999) 62 *MLR* 79, 99.

[50] A Young, 'A Peculiarly British Protection of Human Rights?' (2005) 68 *MLR* 858, 862.

[51] *Ghaidan v Godin-Mendoza* [2004] UKHL 30, [2004] 2 AC 557, para 46.

[52] *Associated Provincial Picture Houses Ltd v Wednesbury Corporation* [1948] 1 KB 223.

[53] For a sample of the literature, see: Lord Steyn: 'Deference: A Tangled Story' [2005] *PL* 346; J Jowell, 'Judicial Deference: servility, civility or institutional capacity?' [2004] *PL* 592; R Edwards, 'Judicial Deference under the Human Rights Act' 65(6) *MLR* 859; F Klug, 'Judicial Deference under the Human Rights Act' [2003] *EHRLR* 125; T Hickman, 'Constitutional Dialogue, Constitutional Theories and the Human Rights Act 1998' [2005] *PL* 306; C O'Cinneide, 'Democracy and Rights: New Directions in the Human Rights Era' [2004] 57 *Current Legal Problems*; D Nicol, 'The Human Rights Act and the politicians'

As the will of Parliament is respected in the design of the Act itself, one school advances the view that there is no further need for a 'discretionary area of judgment'[54] to be afforded to the legislative enactments of Parliament.[55] Francesca Klug has argued for this reason that there is

> no need for judges, legal practitioners or academics to develop complex theories of judicial deference if the scheme of the Act is properly appreciated and appropriately applied.[56]

TRS Allan has further suggested that the development of a doctrine of deference contains the potential to undermine the independence and impartiality of the judicial branch:

> A judge who allows his own view on the merits of any aspect of the case to be displaced by the contrary view of public officials – bowing to their greater expertise or experience or democratic credentials – forfeits the neutrality that underpins the legitimacy of constitutional adjudication.[57]

From the earliest decisions under the HRA, however, it has been evident that 'national courts may accord to the decisions of national legislatures some deference *where the context justifies it.*'[58] And, on occasion, the courts have shown a marked reluctance to rigorously scrutinise legislative schemes for Convention compatibility – almost to the extent of suggesting that, as Parliament may have indicated in a legislative scheme where the balance should lie, the courts have no further scrutiny role to perform.[59] This may, at least in part, be attributable to traditional judicial reluctance to engage in review of the merits of governmental actions based on a hierarchical conception of the separation of powers.[60] But while Dicey undoubtedly continues to wield considerable influence, there is clear tension here with the role of the courts as prescribed by the HRA; as Jowell

---

(2004) 24(3) *LS* 451; D Nicol, 'Are Convention rights a no-go zone for Parliament?' [2002] *PL* 438. See further ch 6, pp 159–164.

[54] Lord Lester of Herne Hill and David Pannick, *Human Rights Law and Practice* (London, Butterworths, 1999) 73–6.

[55] F Klug, 'Judicial Deference under the Human Rights Act' [2003] *EHRLR* 125.

[56] *Ibid*, 125.

[57] TRS Allan, 'Human Rights And Judicial Review: A Critique of "Due Deference"' [2006] *CLJ* 671, 676.

[58] *Brown v Stott* [2003] 1 AC 681, 711 (emphasis supplied).

[59] See, eg, *R (Prolife Alliance) v BBC* [2004] 1 AC 185. The view persists among some commentators that excessive deference has effectively neutered the HRA's ability to effectively protect individual rights (see KD Ewing, 'The Futility of the Human Rights Act [2004] *PL* 829, 843. Cf A Lester, 'The Utility of the Human Rights Act: a reply to Keith Ewing' [2005] *PL* 249).

[60] See, eg, Lord Mustill's comments in *R v Secretary of State for the Home Department ex p Fire Brigades Union* [1995] 2 AC 513, 567: 'Parliament has the legally unchallengeable right to make whatever law it thinks right. The executive carries on the administration of the country in accordance with the powers conferred on it be law. The courts interpret the laws, and see that they are obeyed.' See ch 5, pp 121–130.

has written, in enacting the HRA, Parliament has entrusted the courts with the task of 'delineating the boundaries of a rights-based democracy.'[61] This jurisdiction, whatever the degree of latitude afforded to the primary decision-maker, is not one which the courts can 'abdicate.'[62] More realistic therefore is the view put forward by Lord Woolf in *R v Lambert*:

> The courts ... are entitled to and should, as a matter of constitutional principle pay a degree of deference to the view of Parliament as to what is in the interest of the public generally when upholding the rights of the individual under the Convention. The courts are required to balance the competing interests involved.[63]

In the sphere of the interpretation of legislation under the HRA, it is perhaps unsurprising that there has been recognition that 'greater deference is to be paid to an Act of Parliament than to a decision of the executive or a subordinate measure'[64] as the former has the 'imprimatur of democratic approval.'[65] But this 'direct deference' is not however, a one-size-fits-all concession to the view of Parliament as expressed in legislation; the degree of deference to which a statute may be subject is a variable standard:

> When carrying out their assigned task [under the Human Rights Act] the courts will accord to Parliament and ministers, as the primary decision-makers, an appropriate degree of latitude. The latitude will vary according to the subject matter under consideration, the importance of the human right in question, and the extent of the encroachment on that right.[66]

While the scheme of the Act ensures that no piece of parliamentary legislation may be excluded from HRA review, the intensity of that review

---

[61]   J Jowell, 'Judicial Deference: Servility, Civility or Institutional Capacity?' [2003] *PL* 592, 597. See also the comments of Lord Bingham in *A v Secretary of State for the Home Department* [2004] UKHL 56; [2005] 2 AC 68, para 42.

[62]   *International Transport Roth GmbH v Secretary of State for the Home Department* [2003] QB 728, para 27 (Simon Brown LJ).

[63]   *R v Lambert* [2002] QB 1112, para 16. In addition, in *Wilson v First County Trust (No 2)* [2001] EWCA Civ 633; [2002] QB 74 the Court of Appeal accepted the need for deference to the legislature in matters of social policy but continued (at para 33): 'unless deference is to be equated with unquestioning acceptance, the argument ... recognises ... the need for the court to identify the particular issue of social policy which the legislature or the executive thought it necessary to address, and the thinking which led to that issue being dealt with in the way that it was. It is one thing to accept the need to defer to an opinion which can be seen to be the product of reasoned consideration based on policy; it is quite another thing to be required to accept, without question, an opinion for which no reason of policy is advanced.'

[64]   *International Transport Roth GmbH v Secretary of State for the Home Department* [2002] 3 WLR 344, 376–8.

[65]   *Huang v Secretary of State for the Home Department* [2007] UKHL 11, para 17.

[66]   *A and others v Secretary of State for the Home Department* [2004] UKHL 56, para 80 (Lord Nicholls). See also eg, *R (Mahmood) v Secretary of State for the Home Department* [2001] 1 WLR 840, para 18; *R v Secretary of State for the Home Department ex p Daly* [2001] UKHL 26, para 32.

may well vary from case to case. In the sphere of resource allocation or of national security it might have been expected – based on prior experience – that the courts would afford the legislature a wide margin of discretion, while in cases concerning criminal procedure a more robust intervention might be expected. Equally, significantly less latitude should be afforded to the legislature in cases concerning absolute rights than when the decision-maker is entitled to a view as to where the public interest should lie. In practice, such aspects of legislative choice have not been considered in neat isolation from each other; the degree of respect which the courts afford legislative choices is inherent in the judicial task under section 3(1).

THE LIMITS OF INTERPRETATION UNDER SECTION 3(1)

The 'Radical' Approach to Interpretation

Initial signs were of a cautious approach to the interpretative powers of section 3(1), with a number of early decisions leading to declarations of incompatibility in preference to judicial interpretation of the provision at issue.[67] The Court of Appeal decision in *R v Offen* however pointed towards a much broader approach to section 3(1),[68] with the expansive reach of that provision seemingly confirmed by the most significant of the early judicial explorations of the potential of section 3(1), the House of Lords decision in *R v A (No 2)*.[69]

R v A concerned the construction of section 41 Youth Justice and Criminal Evidence Act 1999, a provision designed to prevent the submission of evidence based on the complainant's previous sexual history in rape proceedings except in closely defined circumstances. The Law Lords' concern over the provision – which Lord Slynn referred to as 'disproportionately restrictive'[70] – was that the blanket exclusion of such materials could preclude the submission of evidence which would guarantee the defendant's right to a fair trial under Article 6 ECHR. Lords Slynn, Steyn, Clyde and Hutton all were of the view that beyond this concern lay the potential for the application of section 41 to lead to a prima facie

---

[67] See, eg, *R v Secretary of State for the Environment, Transport and the Regions ex p Holding and Barnes plc* [2001] HRLR 2 (subsequently overturned by the House of Lords: [2003] 2 AC 295); *R (H) v Mental Health Review Tribunal, North and East London Region* [2001] 3 WLR 512; *Wilson v First County Trust (No 2)* [2001] 3 WLR 42.
[68] *R v Offen* [2001] 1 WLR 253 (CA). Discussed below at pp 197–198.
[69] *R v A (No 2)* [2002] 1 AC 45; [2001] 3 All ER 1.
[70] *Ibid*, para 13

incompatibility with Article 6(1) ECHR.[71] The key question for the Law Lords was whether the remedy of such an 'incompatibility' would be 'possible' under section 3(1).

The decision in *R v A* – that section 3(1) could be used to remedy the perceived incompatibility – was that of a unanimous Appellate Committee. But the differences in approach evident between Lord Steyn and Lord Hope are worthy of some consideration. The reading of section 3(1) adopted by Lord Steyn in *R v A* was expansive – and in fact has been described as 'far-fetched' and 'judicial overkill' by one commentator.[72] Lord Steyn stated that the provision 'goes much further' than ordinary methods of interpretation – specifically referring to contextual and purposive interpretations – and noted that section 3(1) may allow a court to adopt a reading of a statutory provision which 'linguistically may appear strained.'[73] Vitally, he also noted that section 3(1) will not only allow the 'reading down' of statutory language – the avoidance of incompatibility through adoption of a narrow or slightly altered reading of the provision – 'but also the implication of provisions' – that is, the more controversial technique of 'reading in'.

Crucial to this expansive view of section 3(1) was Lord Steyn's assertion that the declaration of incompatibility should be a 'measure of last resort', which, 'must be avoided unless it is plainly impossible to do so.'[74] In fact, Lord Steyn went on to suggest that the *only* circumstance in which it would be necessary for the court to issue a declaration under section 4 HRA, would be where there was a 'clear limitation on Convention rights ... stated in terms' in the statutory provision in question.[75] As such, aside from cases of an express contradiction in terms, *all* other prima facie conflicts between the Convention and statute law could be remedied by way of the section 3(1) power either by way of 'reading down' or 'reading in'.

By contrast, Lord Hope's speech sounded a note of caution, reminding the court that section 3(1) HRA does not allow the judges to act as legislators.[76] While acknowledging that the rule is a powerful one, Lord Hope added that it is nevertheless 'only a rule of interpretation.'[77] Judges,

---

[71]   *Ibid*, paras 10, 43, 136 and 161 respectively. Lord Hope, on the other hand, felt that 'it has not been shown that ... the provisions of section 41 which are relevant to the respondent's case are incompatible with his Convention right to a fair trial' (para 106).

[72]   D Nicol, 'Statutory Interpretation and Human Rights after *Anderson*' [2004] *PL* 274, 276 and 280. For a summary of other criticisms of the decision, see A Kavanagh, 'Unlocking the Human Rights Act: The "Radical" Approach to Section 3(1) Revisited' [2005] *EHRLR* 259, 259–60.

[73]   *R v A (No 2)*, above n 69, para 44.

[74]   *Ibid*, para 44

[75]   *Ibid*.

[76]   *Ibid*, para 108.

[77]   *Ibid*.

he said, should not in effect legislate, compatibility must be 'possible' by way of interpretation, and interpretation will not be possible if:

> the legislation contains provisions which expressly contradict the meaning which the enactment would have to be given to make it compatible.[78]

In the context of section 41 therefore, Lord Hope felt that what was 'possible' would be constrained by the intentions of the Parliament passing the provision in question; to adopt an interpretation – such as that suggested by Lord Steyn – 'would not be possible, without contradicting the plain intention of Parliament.'[79] As Lord Hope noted,

> the whole point of the section ... was to address the mischief which was thought to have arisen due to the width of the discretion which had previously been given to the trial judge.[80]

In other words, such use of section 3(1) would bring back the possibility for mischief which Parliament had sought specifically to avoid.

The approach of Lord Steyn in *R v A* appeared to confine the declaration of incompatibility to all but the most manifest and express inconsistencies between domestic statutes and the Convention Rights, and made the claim that section 3(1) was undoubtedly what Lord Steyn later referred to as the 'prime remedial measure' of the HRA.[81] While this consequence may be read to have been within the intentions of the framers of the HRA,[82] *R v A* and *R v Offen*[82a] equally appeared to herald a movement away from the dialogical model of interpretation under the HRA which 'would lead to more rather than fewer such declarations'[83] towards a virtual judicial monopoly over the interpretation of the Convention rights.

Imposing Limitations on Section 3(1)?

Far from embracing the bold vision of section 3(1) endorsed by *R v A*, in subsequent cases the House of Lords appeared more concerned with what could *not* be done using s 3(1). In a judgment handed down just one week after the decision of the House of Lords in *R v A*, the Court of Appeal in

---

[78] *Ibid.*
[79] *Ibid*, para 109.
[80] *Ibid.*
[81] *Ghaidan v Godin-Mendoza* [2004] UKHL 30, [2004] 2 AC 557, paras 46, 50.
[82] HL Debs, vol 582, col 1231 (3 November 1997) (Lord Irvine of Lairg).
[82a] [2001] 1 WLR 253 (discussed at pp 197–198).
[83] CA Gearty, 'Reconciling Parliamentary Democracy and Human Rights' (2002) 118 *LQR* 248, 250.

Re S; Re W[84] arguably went one step further by making 'two major adjustments and innovations in the construction and application of the Children Act' 1989 in the name of achieving compatibility with Article 8 ECHR.[85] The first of these adjustments was to allow the trial judge a wider margin of discretion over whether to award an interim or final care order. The second – and, in the words of Lord Nicholls in the House of Lords, the 'more radical' – was to set down a new scheme of 'starred' care plans, under which a court would be able to supervise the achievement of the plan's aims. The Court of Appeal had – by 'reading into' the statute a system of starred care plans – in effect created a new supervisory jurisdiction. In doing this, as if to exaggerate the method employed to achieve this change, Nicol notes, the Court of Appeal did not even refer explicitly to section 3(1).[86]

In the view of the Lord Nicholls – with whose speech the remaining Law Lords agreed – not only was this innovation 'radical', but it was also the polar opposite of parliamentary intent as evidenced in the Children Act 1989:

> where a care order is made the responsibility for the child's care is with the [local] authority rather than the court. The court retains no supervisory role ... That was the intention of Parliament.[87]

In interpreting the Children Act in this way, Lord Nicholls noted that the Court of Appeal had departed from a 'cardinal principle' of that Act.[88] Purporting to attribute to a statutory provision

> a meaning which departs substantially from a fundamental feature of an Act of Parliament is likely to have crossed the boundary between interpretation and amendment.[89]

However, as Lord Nicholls observed, this boundary could be crossed in cases other than those where an express limitation in terms was stated on the face of the Act.[90] Additionally, therefore, the Court of Appeal had strayed from legitimate interpretation into the realms of legislative amendment for the reason that the decision of the Court of Appeal would have had 'important practical repercussions which the court is not equipped to evaluate':[91]

---

[84]   *Re S (Children) (Care Order: Implementation of Care Plan); Re W (Children) (Care Order: Adequacy of Care Plan)* [2001] EWCA Civ 757; [2001] 2 FLR 582.

[85]   *Re S (Children) (Care Order: Implementation of Care Plan); Re W (Children) (Care Order: Adequacy of Care Plan)* [2002] UKHL 10; [2002] 2 AC 291, para 1.

[86]   D Nicol, 'Statutory interpretation and Human Rights After *Anderson*' [2004] PL 274, 276.

[87]   *Re S*, above n 84, para 25.

[88]   Lord Nicholls repeatedly uses this phrase, at paras 23, 27, 28, and 42.

[89]   *Re S*, above n 84, para 40 (Lord Nicholls).

[90]   *Ibid*, para 40.

[91]   *Ibid.*

The starring system would not come free from additional administrative work and expense. It would be likely to have a material effect on authorities' allocation of scarce financial and other resources. This in turn would affect authorities' discharge of their responsibilities to other children. Moreover, the need to produce a formal report whenever a care plan is significantly departed from, and then await the outcome of any subsequent court proceedings, would affect the whole manner in which authorities discharge, and are able to discharge, their parental responsibilities.[92]

The judicial use of section 3(1) would therefore also be limited should the consequences of any such interpretation impact on the responsibilities of other branches of government, particularly where public spending considerations would be affected. The concern of the Lords in *Re S* was not only that the interpretation be possible, but also that it could be given effect in the way envisaged by section 3(1).[93] For the House of Lords in *Re S* therefore, a possible interpretation under section 3(1) would not only be ruled out by an express limitation on a Convention right on the face of the Act, but would also cross the constitutional line into illegitimate amendment if the interpretation were to depart from a 'cardinal principle' of the Act at issue, or if the repercussions of the interpretation would require the intervention of the elected branches of government. Lord Nicholls was careful to acknowledge that, even with such limitations, section 3(1) retained the capability to provoke disagreement, noting that '[w]hat one person regards as sensible, if robust, interpretation, another regards as impermissibly creative';[94] an acknowledgment – if one were needed – that in the already controversial sphere of contestable rights the judges were never going to be able to please all of the people all of the time.

R (Anderson) v Secretary of State for the Home Department[95] also appeared to confirm that the clear intent of Parliament as expressed in statutory language could act as a bar to the use of section 3(1).[96] *Anderson* concerned a challenge to the power of the Home Secretary – provided for explicitly by section 29 of the Crime (Sentences) Act 1997 – to determine the minimum tariff to be served by adult prisoners convicted of murder,

---

[92] *Ibid*, para 43.

[93] This is echoed in the views of Stanley Burnton J in *R (D) v Secretary of State for the Home Department* [2003] 1 WLR 1315, 1327: 'It seems to me that in deciding whether an alternative interpretation of legislation is "possible", the court must take account of the practical and negative consequences of that alternative interpretation.'

[94] *Re S*, above n 84, para 40.

[95] *R (Anderson) v Secretary of State for the Home Department* [2002] UKHL 46; [2003] 1 AC 837.

[96] See also: *A (FC and others) v Secretary of State for the Home Department* [2004] UKHL 56. See also the comments of Lord Hope in *R v Lambert* [2002] 2 AC 545; [2001] 3 All ER 577: '[s 3(1)] does not give power to the judges to overrule decisions which the language of the statute shows have been taken on the very point at issue by the "legislator"' (para 79).

and the date of their eligibility for release on license. The challenge arose out of judicial review proceedings in respect of the Home Secretary's decision to increase Anderson's 15 year tariff, as recommended by both the trial judge and Lord Chief Justice, to 20 years. Anderson argued that the ability of the Home Secretary to determine the minimum period to be served prior to becoming eligible to be released on licence was in breach of Article 6(1) ECHR as the Home Secretary was exercising a sentencing function and could not be said to be an 'independent and impartial tribunal' in the determination of criminal charges against the individual.

The unanimous House of Lords – comprising seven Lords of Appeal in Ordinary – held that a declaration of incompatibility be issued on the grounds that it would be impossible to read section 29 as allowing the Home Secretary no discretion over the effective length of time to be served by mandatory life prisoners following a conviction for murder. For Lord Bingham, the judicial act under section 3(1) must remain an exercise of 'interpretation': to use that section to attribute a meaning to a legislative provision:

> quite different from that which Parliament intended ... would go well beyond any interpretative process sanctioned by section 3 of the 1998 Act.[97]

To qualify the specific power conferred on the Home Secretary by the provision through the use of section 3(1) would 'not be judicial interpretation but judicial vandalism.'[98] For Lord Steyn, curtailing that Home Secretary's power under section 29 to achieve Convention-compatibility would amount to 'interpolation inconsistent with ... plain legislative intent.'[99] Accordingly:

> section 3(1) is not available where the suggested interpretation is contrary to express statutory words or is by implication necessarily contradicted by the statute.[100]

That the use of section 3 may also be precluded on grounds of constitutional competence was seemingly displayed in the case of *Bellinger v Bellinger*.[101] Under section 11(c) Matrimonial Causes Act 1973, parties to a marriage must be 'respectively male and female'. Mrs Bellinger – a post-operative male to female transsexual – sought a declaration that the provision was incompatible with Articles 8 and 12 ECHR. The Court of Appeal had held by two to one that section 11(c) could not be interpreted using section 3(1) to give effect to Mrs Bellinger's Convention Rights. In the House of Lords, in the light of clear – but certainly not constant –

[97]   *Anderson*, above n 95, para 30 (Lord Bingham).
[98]   *Ibid.*
[99]   *Ibid*, para 59.
[100] *Ibid.*
[101] *Bellinger v Bellinger* [2003] UKHL 21; [2003] 2 AC 467.

authority from the European Court of Human Rights in the decision in *Goodwin v United Kingdom*[102] the court unanimously endorsed the making of a declaration of incompatibility.

The decision of the House of Lords in *Bellinger* contains remarkably little discussion of the potential to use section 3 in the circumstances – as Lord Hope notes, quite simply, section 11(c) Matrimonial Causes Act 1973 is 'not capable of being given the extended meaning' of the sort which had been sought by Mrs Bellinger.[103] In linguistic terms at least, however, it is at least arguable that giving an extended definition to the word 'female' in *Bellinger* would have required significantly less interpretative latitude than required in either *Offen* or in *R v A*. However, for the House of Lords in *Bellinger* – building on the decision in *Re S; Re W* – the isolated nature of the linguistic interpretation was not their sole concern:

> the recognition of gender re-assignment for the purposes of marriage is part of a wider problem which should be considered as a whole and not dealt with in piecemeal fashion. There should be a clear, coherent policy. The decision regarding recognition of gender reassignment for the purpose of marriage cannot sensibly be made in isolation from a decision on the like problem in other areas where a distinction is drawn between people on the basis of gender.[104]

While the linguistic change may have been 'possible' in the sense envisaged by section 3(1), addressing the wider ramifications of such an interpretation was – in the House of Lords' view – well beyond the constitutional competence of the courts. As with *Re S; Re W*, the court in *Bellinger* was not competent to make the wholesale changes required to provide Mrs Bellinger with the remedy she desired. In consequence, Parliament, and not the courts, should be the appropriate author of whatever steps were necessary to achieve compatibility in this sphere.

Bellinger should not, however, be taken simply as a case illustrating the institutional modesty of the House of Lords. A number of developments post-*Goodwin* informed the decision of the Law Lords. First, steps had been taken in Whitehall to begin examining the implications of *Goodwin*. Secondly – and perhaps most pertinently – the Government had subsequently announced the imminent publication of draft legislation concerning the legal recognition of acquired gender. Thirdly, counsel for the Lord Chancellor conceded that *Goodwin* had effectively rendered section 11(c) Matrimonial Causes Act 1973 incompatible with Articles 8 and 12.[105] The

---

[102] (2002) 35 EHRR 18.

[103] *Bellinger*, above n 101, para 56. Lord Hobhouse added, that to interpret the provision in the way suggested by Mrs Bellinger 'would ... not be an exercise in interpretation, however robust. It would be a legislative exercise of amendment making a legislative choice as to what precise amendment was appropriate' (para 78).

[104] *Bellinger*, above n 101, para 45.

[105] *Ibid*, paras 25–7.

elected branches had effectively declared ownership of this specific issue *and* the wider legislative reform necessary to achieve broader compatibility in the sphere of acquired gender recognition.[106]

Commentators have differed in their assessment of the cumulative effect of this line of cases. Nicol, for one, has argued that *Re S*, *Anderson* and *Bellinger* point to a retreat from Lord Steyn's 'activist' position in *R v A* and embrace the more restrained construction put forward by Lord Hope in that decision. Nicol suggests that the post-*R v A* cases clearly reject 'the notion that "interpretations" could conflict with clear statutory words' – as *R v A* had arguably suggested – thereby endorsing parliamentary sovereignty above the Convention, 'as the country's supreme constitutional doctrine.'[107] Kavanagh on the other hand suggests that *R v A* should be looked at in the context of its subject matter, suggesting that as fair trial rights are within the constitutional competence of the judiciary – in contrast to social policy, or resource decisions – the House of Lords was entitled to adopt a more 'radical' approach, and may do so again should an appropriate case arise.[108] Kavanagh further argued that:

> cases such as *Re S*, *Bellinger* and *Anderson* are not authority for the proposition that judges will never or should never adopt a strained interpretation under s. 3. Nor do they demonstrate that it is preferable as a general matter to issue a declaration of incompatibility under s. 4. Rather, they show that if a proposed interpretation under s. 3 requires radical reform of a statute, which goes beyond the type of reform that can be achieved successfully by judicial rectification in the context of that individual case, the courts will be reluctant to adopt such an interpretation.[109]

Subsequent developments show that Kavanagh provides the more realistic assessment of the emerging practice under section 3(1). The contextual approach to interpretation is key to understanding the differing outcomes of *Bellinger v Bellinger* and the leading case which followed, *Ghaidan v Godin-Mendoza*. *Ghaidan* reached the House of Lords following a Court of Appeal decision criticised for abandoning 'the kind of rigorous analysis of pertinent authority which might sensibly be regarded as an essential attribute of legitimising innovative judicial law-making in the domestic context.'[110] However, if commentators were hoping for what could be

---

[106] For a strong critique of the House of Lords decision in *Bellinger v Bellinger*, see G Phillipson, 'Deference, Discretion and Democracy in the Human Rights Act Era' (2007) *Current Legal Problems* 40.

[107] D Nicol 'Statutory Interpretation and Human Rights after *Anderson*' [2004] *PL* 274, 280.

[108] A Kavanagh 'Statutory interpretation and human rights after *Anderson*: A more contextual approach' [2004] *PL* 537.

[109] *Ibid*, 545.

[110] I Loveland, 'Making it up as they go along? The Court of Appeal on same sex spouses and succession rights to tenancies' [2003] *PL* 222, 235.

construed as a further curtailment of the radical potential of section 3, they were to be disappointed.

Ghaidan v Godin-Mendoza

Ghaidan v Godin-Mendoza is now the leading House of Lords decision on section 3(1) HRA.[111] At issue in *Ghaidan* were the succession rights to a protected tenancy under the Rent Act 1977 following the death of the original tenant. Under the provisions of the Rent Act a person who had lived with the original tenant 'as his husband or wife' would succeed to a statutory tenancy, while a family member residing with the original tenant may have been entitled to succeed to a less favourable 'assured' tenancy. The respondent, Mendoza, was the surviving partner of the original tenant, with whom he had been in 'a stable and monogamous homosexual relationship'. Mendoza argued – citing Article 8 read with Article 14 – that the phrase 'living with the original tenant as his husband or wife' in the Rent Act 1977 should be interpreted under section 3(1) so as to include same-sex partners, thus allowing him to succeed to the statutory tenancy. Against this backdrop, Harris-Short has commented that *Ghaidan* was 'a quite extraordinary example of judicial innovation on an issue raising difficult and complex issues of public policy.'[112]

The House of Lords held by four to one that it was possible to interpret the provision in the way suggested by Mendoza. The leading speech of Lord Nicholls can be seen as an attempt to reconcile the radical and restrained approaches of Lord Steyn and Lord Hope first seen in *R v A*, but one which in so doing leaves the domestic judge with a considerable degree of linguistic and interpretative freedom.

In Lord Nicholls' view, the only express limitation on the courts' role under section 3(1) comes from the word 'possible.'[113] There are however, two further implied limitations on the exercise of the interpretative function. First, the interpretation adopted should not 'adopt a meaning inconsistent with a fundamental feature of legislation.'[114] Thus the court is required to make an assessment of whether the interpretation proposed goes 'with the grain of the legislation.'[115] Building on the position of Lord Hope in *R v A*, parliamentary intent therefore remains relevant to the judgment over the possibility of interpretations under section 3(1). Lord Rodger acknowledged that the importation of terms into a statutory

---

[111]   *Ghaidan v Godin-Mendoza* [2004] 2 AC 557, [2004] 3 All ER 411.
[112]   S Harris-Short, 'Family Law and the Human Rights Act 1998: Judicial Restraint or Revolution?' in Fenwick, Phillipson and Masterman, above n 42.
[113]   *Ghaidan*, above n 111, para 32.
[114]   *Ibid*, para 33.
[115]   *Ibid*. See also Lord Rodger of Earlsferry at para 121.

provision to achieve compatibility may result in the appearance that a court has 'amended' the provision in question. However, so long as the 'court implies words that are consistent with the scheme of the legislation but necessary to make it compatible' then to do so would remain an act of interpretation – the task with which the judges have been entrusted under the HRA by Parliament.[116] However, reading in words which are inconsistent with the 'scheme of the legislation or with its essential principles' cannot be regarded as an act of interpretation, and as such, would 'fall on the wrong side of the boundary between interpretation and amendment of the statute.'[117]

Secondly, Lord Nicholls stated that Parliament cannot 'have intended that section 3 should require courts to make decisions for which they are not equipped'.[118] In addition therefore, the court is required to make an assessment of whether – for one reason or another – Parliament is better placed than the courts to remedy the incompatibility claimed. As this is reliant on the presumption that there will necessarily be areas of the law in which the courts – as well as Parliament – will be competent to make decisions and remedy incompatibilities, this surely challenges the view of a general and overriding trend in favour of the issue of declarations of incompatibility.

Within the judge-defined confines of these express and implied limitations, the judiciary retains a wide discretion which may be shaped by the ability of the court to provide the remedy sought in the circumstances of the case. Lord Nicholls accepted that Parliament – through the enactment of section 3(1) HRA – intended that courts should be able to 'modify the meaning, and hence the effect, of primary and secondary legislation'[119] Tackling the supposed constraints of statutory language, his Lordship noted that the courts should have regard, not only to the statutory language in question but also to the 'concept expressed in that language.'[120] He continued along the now familiar lines that section 3(1) applies, not only to ambiguous language, but to all statutory provisions,[121] and further noted that section 3(1) might require a court to depart from the unambiguous wording of a statute in order to achieve compatibility.[122] Lord Nicholls argued that if this is accepted – in other words if it can be accepted that unambiguous words can be 'interpreted' in order to achieve compatibility – then:

---

[116]   *Ibid*, para 121. See also Lord Steyn at para 40.
[117]   *Ibid*.
[118]   *Ibid*, para 33.
[119]   *Ibid*, para 32.
[120]   *Ibid*, para 31.
[121]   *Ibid*, para 29.
[122]   Cf the position of Nicol outlined above, n 107.

it becomes impossible to suppose that Parliament intended that the operation of section 3 should depend critically upon the particular form of words adopted by the parliamentary draftsman.[123]

This point is echoed by Lord Rodger in the other substantial majority speech in *Ghaidan* where he argues that significant linguistic amendments can be judicially imposed:

> if the implication of a dozen words leaves the essential principles and scope of the legislation intact but allows it to be read in a way which is compatible with Convention rights, the implication is a legitimate exercise of the powers conferred by section 3(1).[124]

In enacting section 3(1) HRA, he argued:

> Parliament was not out to devise an entertaining parlour game for lawyers, but, so far as possible, to make legislation operate compatible with Convention rights. This means concentrating on matters of substance, rather than matters of mere language.[125]

If by 'concentrating on matters of substance' Lord Rodger is alluding to a pervasive interpretative obligation to realise the 'Convention rights' in domestic law, then *Ghaidan* may well be viewed as a positive step for those concerned with bringing rights home, as well as having enhanced the radical potential of section 3. Indeed, for Lord Steyn, the abandonment of overly literal techniques of interpretation was key to the implementation of the 'core remedial purpose of section 3(1),'[126] which was to impose 'a strong rebuttable presumption in favour of an interpretation consistent with Convention rights.'[127] In other words, if it is within the competence of the court to provide the remedy sought by the individual through interpreting the provision(s) in question in a manner compatible with the Convention rights, then – unless compelling reasons can be put forward to the contrary – the court is under a duty to do just that.

Ghaidan also however, illustrates that the prioritisation of the Convention rights may well come at a cost. The linguistic constraints imposed by the specific language adopted by the Parliament responsible for the provision under scrutiny would appear – on this reading of section 3(1) – to be few. Arguably therefore, for the radical approach to section 3 to retain its legitimacy, any such interpretation should be founded on a detailed analysis of the concept being enacted. The House of Lords

---

[123] *Ghaidan*, above n 111, para 31.
[124] *Ibid*, para 122. See also the more recent judgment of Simon J in *R v Holding* [2006] 1 WLR 1040, para 47: 'the precise form of words read in for the purpose of section 3 is of no significance.'
[125] *Ibid*, para 123.
[126] *Ibid*, para 49.
[127] *Ibid*, para 50

decision in *Ghaidan* is arguably lacking in this respect; as Harris-Short has observed by way of contrast, in determining the purpose of an 'almost identical' statutory provision in *M v H*, the Canadian Supreme Court 'made extensive and detailed reference to the original parliamentary debates, a wide range of socio-economic research, statistical evidence and academic critique ... In comparison the evidential basis on which the Court of Appeal and House of Lords rejected the social policy objectives of the Rent Act 1977 was feeble.'[128] While few would cast doubt on the outcome in *Ghaidan*, the process adopted may well be open to question.[129]

WHAT IS POSSIBLE UNDER THE HUMAN RIGHTS ACT?

Taken as a whole, the decision in *Ghaidan* might be read as adding further dimensions to the 'radical' approach to section 3(1). Clearly, in denying that the language adopted by Parliament is determinative, the decision allows for a wide linguistic freedom in the use of section 3(1). However, for Lord Millett in dissent, the specific wording chosen by Parliament retained considerable force. Lord Millett agreed with the majority on the issue of the prima facie incompatibility between the provisions of the Rent Act 1977 and Article 8 read with Article 14. He was not however, able to agree that the solution should be found in the use of section 3(1) HRA. In contrast to the views of the majority, Lord Millett held that the linguistic change required to remedy the problem was not 'possible' under the guise of interpretation under section 3(1).[130] Lord Millett concluded that the relevant provision of the Rent Act was firmly wedded to the idea that the relationship recognised should be between the gender-specific terms 'husband and wife'. Two reasons were given as to why the section 3(1) intervention would not be the appropriate response. First, as Parliament had not chosen a form of words which would recognise same-sex relationships, to adopt a reading which would alter this would therefore depart from a 'fundamental feature of the legislation.'[131] Secondly, his Lordship concluded that the subject matter of the dispute fell more readily within the area of parliamentary, rather than judicial, expertise: 'all these questions

---

[128]   S Harris-Short, above n 112, 320.

[129]   For criticism of this approach – for the reasons that it 'endangers both legal certainty and the constitutional legitimacy of the method' – see: Jan Van Zyl Smit, 'The New Purposive Interpretation of statutes: Section 3 HRA after *Ghaidan v Godin-Mendoza*' (2007) 70(2) *MLR* 294. See also R Wintemute, 'The Human Rights Act's First Five Years: Too strong, too weak, or just right?' (2006) 17 *KCLJ* 209, 214–15. See also ch 9, pp 252–257.

[130]   *Ghaidan*, above n 111, para 82.

[131]   *Ibid*, paras 83–95.

are essentially questions of social policy which should be left to Parliament.'[132] Even if an interpretation had been 'possible' in linguistic terms, to Lord Millett's eyes, Parliament, not the courts, should be the appropriate author of the amendment. While *Ghaidan* confirms that the courts should consider the intention of Parliament in enacting the disputed provision, the legislative framework within which that provision exists, and whether the courts are the appropriate engineers of any amendment necessary in the name of achieving compatibility, Lord Millett's dissent illustrates that there remains significant potential for judicial disagreement over all of these issues.

For the majority in *Ghaidan* however, the remedial capacity of section 3(1) was key. As Kavanagh has argued, the remedial nature of section 3(1) will come to the fore where a 'declaration of incompatibility would be unable to provide a remedy for the individual litigant, or where the court feels that a section 4 declaration is unlikely to result in legal change.'[133] Such was the situation in *Ghaidan*. In contrast to *Bellinger*, in which the ramifications of a section 3(1) interpretation would have been beyond the powers of the courts to remedy, the use of section 3(1) in *Ghaidan* offered the most appropriate solution to the discrete problem before the court, and provided Mendoza with an effective remedy.[134]

What is clear from the case law to date is that the extent of what is 'possible' under section 3(1) may differ from case to case; although trite, as Lord Steyn observed in *ex p Daly*, 'in law context is everything.'[135] It is uncontroversial that section 3(1) requires an analysis of the Convention's requirements, and then of the 'compatibility' of the domestic provision with those requirements. Subject to a prima facie finding of an incompatibility, there follows an analysis of whether the achievement of reading and giving effect to the provision through process of interpretation is 'possible.' The nature of the 'interpretation' which is 'possible' will be a question of degree and context. Compatibility may well be achieved as much through interpreting the 'natural meaning of the words' as through the implication of words or provisions.[136] In such cases it may remain reasonable to say that the judicial act under section 3(1) remains one of 'interpretation' as opposed to 'legislation.' But in those cases in which a linguistically strained interpretation is adopted or which pursue an interpretation that arguably departs from the intent of the legislature in enacting the provision,

---

[132] *Ibid*, para 99.

[133] A Kavanagh, 'Choosing between sections 3 and 4 of the Human Rights Act 1998: Judicial reasoning after *Ghaidan v Mendoza*' in Fenwick, Phillipson and Masterman, above n 42, 128.

[134] Cf G Phillipson, 'Deference, Discretion and Democracy in the Human Rights Era' (2007) *Current Legal Problems* 40, 63–8.

[135] *R v Secretary of State for the Home Department ex p Daly* [2001] 2 AC 532, para 28.

[136] As in, eg, *Culnane v Morris* [2006] 1 WLR 2880.

continuing to describe the judicial exercise as 'interpretation' does not arguably reflect the realities of possibility under the HRA. As through their use of section 3(1) of the Act the courts are now able to – and openly acknowledge that they may – 'modify the meaning, and hence the effect, of primary and secondary legislation,'[137] it is perhaps no longer sustainable (if it ever was)[138] to talk of the rudimentary division between 'interpretation' and 'legislation.'[139]

Following from this, the rhetorical adherence to the demands of parliamentary sovereignty that peppers the case law on HRA sections 3 and 4 may also be open to question.[140] Lord Hope's speech in *Lambert* provides an example:

> Section 3(1) preserves the sovereignty of Parliament. It does not give power to the judges to overrule decisions which the language of the statute shows have been taken on the very point at issue by the legislator ... [T]he interpretation of a statute by reading words in to give effect to the presumed intention must always be distinguished carefully from amendment. Amendment is a legislative act. It is an exercise which must be reserved to Parliament.[141]

Some would no doubt find it difficult to reconcile this view with the reality of the decisions the Court of Appeal in *Offen* or of the House of Lords in *R v A*, both of which – on Lord Hope's analysis – could be more readily described as acts of amendment than acts of interpretation. Even in spite of the arguably more restrained approaches to section 3(1) evident in *Re S; Re W*, *Anderson* and *Bellinger*, following *Ghaidan*, it is doubtful whether Nicol's assertion that the case law on section 3(1) endorses parliamentary sovereignty, above the Convention, 'as the country's supreme constitutional doctrine'[142] can be stated so confidently and without qualification.[143]

---

[137]   *Ghaidan*, above n 111, para 32.
[138]   Lord Reid, 'The Judge as Law Maker' (1972) 12 *Journal of the Society of Public Teachers of Law* 22.
[139]   Recognising this, Kavanagh, has argued that 'the activity of interpretation involves, rather than eschews, judicial law-making' ('The Elusive Divide between interpretation and legislation under the Human Rights Act' (2004) 24 *OJLS* 259, 261), while Young has written of *Ghaidan* as an example of 'acceptable judicial legislation' ('*Ghaidan v Godin-Mendoza*: Avoiding the Deference Trap' [2005] *PL* 23, 27).
[140]   See, eg, *R v Director of Public Prosecutions ex p Kebilene* [2000] 2 AC 326, 367; *R v Lambert* [2002] 2 AC 545, para 79; *Re S (Children) (Care Order: Implementation of Care Plan); Re W (Children) (Care Order: Adequacy of Care Plan)* [2002] UKHL 10; [2002] 2 AC 291, para 39; *A and others v Secretary of State for the Home Department* [2004] UKHL 56, para 220.
[141]   *Lambert*, above n 140, paras 79 and 81.
[142]   D Nicol 'Statutory Interpretation and Human Rights after *Anderson*' [2004] *PL* 274, 280. Cf A Kavanagh 'Statutory interpretation and human rights after *Anderson*: A more contextual approach' [2004] *PL* 537.
[143]   See also the various suggested limitations on the doctrine contained in the case of *Jackson v Her Majesty's Attorney General* [2005] UKHL 56; [2006] 1 AC 262.

With this in mind it is perhaps equally unhelpful to talk of what is or is not 'possible' under the HRA in abstract terms.[144] The limits of the possible are not only context-dependent but the existing case law shows that 'possibility' may be gauged according to different criteria dependant on that context. Thus possibility may be assessed 'inter alia' linguistically, practically, legally or constitutionally. For instance, while it may be possible to effectively 'disembowel' a statutory provision in an area of the law which is 'at the centre of the adjudicative function',[145] a relatively minor linguistic change in an area of social policy with broad legislative ramifications may not be possible under section 3(1).[146] While a reading or interpretation under section 3(1) might in certain circumstances be precluded on the grounds of supposed parliamentary intent or language,[147] in others the arguable intent of Parliament might well be sidestepped in favour of a 'strained' interpretation,[148] while parliamentary language, following *Ghaidan*, might well be disregarded as being non-determinative whether clear or otherwise. In short, a generous interpretation of section 3(1) has been adopted, allowing the domestic judge a wide margin of discretion in the context of the individual case.

In addition, the judiciary retains a wide discretion over the implied restrictions on the use of section 3. What does appear to be clear is that courts should not, to use Lord Nicholl's phrase from *Ghaidan*, 'adopt a meaning inconsistent with a fundamental feature of the legislation' under scrutiny. However, as demonstrated by *Ghaidan*, ascertaining the purpose of the provision or statute in question appears to be a task for legalistic judicial analysis alone. Similarly, the choice of whether to afford a degree of deference to the view of the legislator is not subject to hard and fast rules, with a number of interventionist decisions coming in areas which, prior to the coming into force of the HRA, might traditionally have provoked a less robust response from the courts.[149]

---

[144] As Aileen Kavanagh has written: 'Statutory interpretation is not carried out in the abstract or for the pure intellectual satisfaction of discerning the meaning of unclear statutory provisions. Rather, it is carried out in order to reach a conclusion on the legal dispute before them. Judicial interpretations are instrumental to legal outcomes.' ('Choosing between sections 3 and 4 of the Human Rights Act 1998: Judicial reasoning after *Ghaidan v Mendoza*' in Fenwick, Phillipson and Masterman, above n 42, 128).

[145] CA Gearty, *Principles of Human Rights Adjudication* (Oxford, OUP, 2004) 77.

[146] See, eg, *Bellinger v Bellinger* [2003] UKHL 21.

[147] See, eg, *Anderson*, above n 95; *Re S*, above, n 84.

[148] See, eg, *R v A*, above n 69; *Lambert*, above n 140.

[149] See, eg, *A and others v Secretary of State for the Home Department* [2004] UKHL 56 (although cf *Secretary of State for the Home Department ex p Rehman* [2001] UKHL 47, discussed in ch 6, pp 206–207); *Ghaidan v Godin-Mendoza* [2004] 2 AC 557; [2004] 3 All ER 411.

To counter concerns that the judicial exercise under section 3 is becoming a 'semantic lottery'[150] there are however, indications that the judiciary have not lost sight of the purpose behind enacting the HRA, and that of enacting section 3: to 'so far as it is possible to do so', interpret and give effect to legislation in a Convention-compatible manner. As Lord Bingham explained in *Sheldrake*:

> In explaining why a Convention-compliant interpretation may not be possible, members of the committee used differing expressions: such an interpretation would be incompatible with the underlying thrust of the legislation, or would not go with the grain of it, or would call for legislative deliberation, or would change the substance of a provision completely, or would remove its pith and substance, or would violate a cardinal principle of the legislation ... All of these expressions, as I respectfully think, yield valuable insights, but none of them should be allowed to supplant the simple test enacted in the Act: 'So far as it is possible to do so ...'[151]

For that reason, the House of Lords has consistently 'declined to try to formulate precise rules' on the application of section 3(1).[152] In stark contrast to the prevailing approach to section 2(1) HRA, the courts' interpretative powers under section 3(1) appear not to be curtailed by limiting principles of general application. The case law on section 3(1) preserves the discretion evident on the face of the Act, advocating neither a general preference for the use of either the interpretative powers of the courts, nor the declaration of incompatibility. For Lord Steyn in *Ghaidan*, the failure of the courts to establish a general preference toward the use of the section 3(1) power pointed to the development of the law having taken a 'wrong turning'.[153] However, to establish a virtual judicial monopoly over questions of rights would compromise the balance between the branches of government at the heart of the Act. As Gavin Phillipson has argued, the HRA – and section 3 in particular – 'allows for a degree of judicial choice, between the use of the Act's pro-rights and pro-majoritarian aspects.'[154] It is to the latter that we now turn.

---

[150] *Ghaidan v Godin-Mendoza* [2004] 2 AC 557; [2004] 3 All ER 411, para 31 (Lord Nicholls).

[151] *A-G's Reference No 4 of 2002; Sheldrake v Director of Public Prosecutions* [2004] UKHL 43, para 28 (Lord Bingham).

[152] *Ibid.*

[153] *Ghaidan*, above n 111, para 39.

[154] G Phillipson, 'Deference, Discretion and Democracy in the Human Rights Era' (2007) *Current Legal Problems* 40, 76.

Chapter 5

The Co-operative Constitution?

INTRODUCTION

A S OUTLINED ABOVE, the Human Rights Act 1998 (HRA) model avoids making the judges the final arbiters of Convention rights issues in the UK. In those cases where a judicial interpretation is not possible, and a declaration of incompatibility is issued, Parliament remains competent either to respond by amending the incompatibility or choosing not to do so. While the Government saw the HRA project as engendering a culture of rights across the entire public service,[1] the interplay between the use of sections 3 and 4 HRA provides perhaps the most obvious indicator of the state of this 'co-operative' constitutional measure.

The brief history of the HRA shows that neither section 3 nor section 4 has found itself in the position of becoming the pre-eminent judicial response to disputed issues of interpretation.[2] While the intentions of the Government may well have been that the vast majority of interpretative questions could be resolved through use of the courts' interpretative powers,[3] the number of declarations of incompatibility that have been issued have ensured that section 3(1) is yet to be irreversibly confirmed as the Act's 'prime remedial provision'.[4] And while the use of the declaration of incompatibility has been arguably 'more frequent than the Government expected'[5] neither is it yet regarded as the 'routine and unproblematic'[6] response to disputed interpretations as hoped for by the rights sceptics.

The discretionary power of the 'higher courts'[7] to issue declarations of incompatibility is the feature of the HRA that gives it 'its unique character

---

[1] Ch 1, pp 16–18.
[2] See: Department of Constitutional Affairs, *Review of the Implementation of the Human Rights Act* (July 2006) 4.
[3] Ch 1, pp 19–20.
[4] *Ghaidan v Godin-Mendoza* [2004] UKHL 30; [2004] 2 AC 557, para 46 (Lord Steyn).
[5] R Singh, 'The Declaration of Incompatibility' [2002] *JR* 237, 238.
[6] T Campbell, 'Incorporation through Interpretation' in T Campbell, KD Ewing and A Tomkins, *Sceptical Essays on Human Rights* (Oxford, OUP, 2001) 99.
[7] Under section 4(5) HRA, the Appellate Committee of the House of Lords, the Judicial Committee of the Privy Council, the High Court and Court of Appeal in England and Wales

as a participatory human rights instrument, setting it apart from earlier Bills of Rights based on a judicial interpretative monopoly.'[8] The declaration of incompatibility facility is also central to the idea of the HRA as a collaborative exercise involving all three branches of government in the protection of the Convention rights.[9] Equally, it is key to an understanding of the HRA as an instrument of rights protection designed to be in keeping, rather than at odds, with our predominantly political constitution.[10] As Francesca Klug has written:

> [The HRA] is informed by a view of human rights that acknowledges that they are not always, or even usually, absolute but derive from political struggle and thrive on political argument. The purpose of the dialogue model is to keep the idea and dynamic of human rights alive, rather than close down the debate about them and hive them off to a rarefied court.[11]

Hence, under the HRA model, the courts may declare a statute to be incompatible with the Convention rights, but they may not strike it down or otherwise contest its legality. For Professor Gearty, this rejection of the 'orthodox precedents' of other Bills of Rights represents the 'genius' of the HRA model.[12] However, as a result of this compromise between legal and political authority, the remedial capacity of the declaration of incompatibility mechanism has been questioned by a number of commentators. The declaration of incompatibility has been described as 'undeniably weak in theory'[13] as such a declaration has no binding or coercive effect: under section 4(6) a declaration of incompatibility is neither binding on the parties to the case, nor on the Government. David Feldman has written that:

> The declaration of incompatibility is really an admission that the court is unable to provide an effective remedy for a violation of a Convention right, because of primary legislation. It is more a recognition of the legislative supremacy of Parliament than a real part of the courts' remedial armoury.[14]

---

and in Northern Ireland, and in Scotland, the High Court of Justiciary (apart from when sitting as a trial court) and the Court of Session.

[8]   D Nicol, 'Gender Reassignment and the Transformation of the Human Rights Act' (2004) 120 *LQR* 194, 198.

[9]   Ch 1, pp 16–18.

[10]   On which see: JAG Griffith, 'The Political Constitution' (1979) 42 *MLR* 1.

[11]   F Klug, 'The long road to human rights compliance' (2006) 57(1) *Northern Ireland Legal Quarterly* 186, 201.

[12]   C Gearty, *Can Human Rights Survive?* (Cambridge, CUP, 2006) 94–98. Gearty writes (at 95) that the HRA 'deliberately undermines its own authority, inviting the political back in to control the legal at just the moment when the supremacy of the legal discourse seems assured.'

[13]   R Wintemute, 'The Human Rights Act's First Five Years: Too Strong, Too Weak, Or Just Right?' (2006) *KCLJ* 209, 215.

[14]   D Feldman (ed), *English Public Law* (Oxford, OUP, 2004) 979.

While Tom Hickman has noted that:

> section 4, unlike section 3, decouples rights from remedy. Whilst section 3 allows relief to the applicant and those similarly situated, section 4 leaves the legislative provision in place, with its pernicious effects continuing to apply to those subject to it.[15]

As one of us has written elsewhere, the declaration of incompatibility is therefore something of a 'booby prize' in remedial terms for the otherwise successful litigant.[16]

The inevitable conclusion of there being no legal obligation to either respond to, or act to remedy, a declared incompatibility is that there may be circumstances in which the Government may chose not to amend or repeal the legislation at issue.[17] During the debates on the Human Rights Bill as much was made clear by Jack Straw MP. Despite indicating that he thought it likely that section 4 declarations would be accepted and remedied in the 'overwhelming majority of cases' the then Home Secretary was careful to remind Parliament that under the provisions of the Bill and subsequent Act

> [i]t is possible that the Judicial Committee of the House of Lords could make a declaration that ... Ministers propose, and Parliament accepts, should not be accepted.[18]

Mr Straw had in mind a decision which would cause 'very great controversy', giving the example of a hypothetical situation in which the Law Lords declared the UK's abortion regime to be incompatible with the Convention.[19]

In practice however, the Government has not to date ignored any of the declarations of incompatibility issued. At the time of writing, 24 declarations of incompatibility have been issued by the Higher Courts under the

[15] T Hickman, 'Constitutional Dialogue, Constitutional Theories and the Human Rights Act' [2005] *PL* 306, 327.

[16] I Leigh, 'The UK's Human Rights Act 1998: An Early Assessment' in G Huscroft and P Rishworth (eds), *Litigating Rights: Perspectives from Domestic and International Law* (Oxford, Hart Publishing, 2002) 324.

[17] See also the provisions of the more recently enacted Victorian Charter of Human Rights and Responsibilities Act 2006, which, although they do not oblige the government to remedy the noted incompatibility following a 'declaration of inconsistent interpretation' (s 36), also ensure that a formal response is provided by the responsible Minister (s 37).

[18] HC Debs, vol 317, col 1301 (21 October 1998). These comments were echoed in the House of Lords by Lord Irvine, who said that 'we expect that the government and Parliament will in all cases almost certainly be prompted to change the law following a declaration of incompatibility' (HL Debs, vol 583, col 1139 (27 November 1997)). See also the White Paper, *Rights Brought Home: The Human Rights Bill*, Cm 3782 (1997), 'A declatation [of incompatibility] ... will almost certainly prompt the Government and Parliament to change the law' (para 2.10).

[19] *Ibid.*

HRA. Of those 24, 15 remained final,[20] seven were overturned on appeal,[21] with a further two remaining subject to appeal.[22] Most famous perhaps, have been those issued in respect of the Government's anti-terrorist measures, although declarations of incompatibility have been made across a wide range of areas including mental health, asylum policy, sexual offences, social security and housing.

---

[20] *R (H) v Mental Health Tribunal for the North and East London Region and the Secretary of State for Health* [2001] EWCA Civ 415 (Mental Health Act 1983 ss 72 and 73 declared incompatible with Art 5(1) and (4); legislation amended by the Mental Health Act 1983 (Remedial) Order 2001 SI 2001/3712; *McR's Application for Judicial Review* [2003] NI 1 (s 62 of the Offences Against the Person Act 1861 declared incompatible with Art 8; repealed by Sexual Offences Act 2003, ss 139, 140, Sch 6 para 4, Sch 7); *International Transport Roth GmbH v Secretary of State for the Home Department* [2002] EWCA 158 (Immigration and Asylum Act 1999 Pt II declared incompatible with Art 6 and Art 1 of Protocol 1; amended by Nationality, Immigration and Asylum Act 2002 s 125, Sch 8); *R (Anderson) v Secretary of State for the Home Department* [2002] UKHL 46 (Crime (Sentences) Act 1997 s 29 declared incompatible with Art 6; repealed by Criminal Justice Act 2003 ss 303(b)(i), 332, Sch 37, Pt 8, with further provision for sentencing made in Ch 7 thereof and Schs 21 and 22 thereto); *R v Secretary of State for the Home Department ex p D* [2002] EWHC 2805 (Mental Health Act 1983 s 74 declared incompatible with Art 5(4); amended by Criminal Justice Act 2003 s 295); *Blood and Tarbuck v Secretary of State for Health* (unreported) (Human Fertilisation and Embryology Act 1990 s 28(6)(b) declared incompatible with Art 8 read with Art 14; amended by the Human Fertilisation and Embryology (Deceased Fathers) Act 2003); *Bellinger v Bellinger* [2003] UKHL 21 (Matrimonial Causes Act 1973 s 11(c) declared incompatible with Arts 8 and 12; remedied by the Gender Recognition Act 2004); *R (M) v Secretary of State for Health* [2003] EWHC 1094 (Mental Health Act 1983 ss 28 and 29 declared incompatible with Art 8; remedied by Mental Health Act 2007 ss 23–26); *R (Hooper and others) v Secretary of State for Work and Pensions* [2003] EWCA Civ 875 (Social Security Contributions and Benefit Act 1992 ss 36 and 37 declared incompatible with Art 8 read with Art 14 and Art 1 of the First Protocol; amended by Welfare Reform and Pensions Act 1999 s 54(1) (which came into force in April 2001)); *R (Wilkinson) v Inland Revenue Commissioners* [2003] EWCA Civ 814 (Corporation Taxes Act 1988 s 262 declared incompatible with Art 1 of the First Protocol read with Art 14; amended by Finance Act 1999 ss 34(1), 139, Sch 20); *A and others v Secretary of State for the Home Department* [2004] UKHL 56 (Anti-Terrorism, Crime and Security Act 2001 s 23 declared incompatible with Art 5 read with Art 14; repealed by the Prevention of Terrorism Act 2005); *R (Morris) v Westminster City Council and the First Secretary of State* [2005] EWCA Civ 1184 and *R (Gabaj) v First Secretary of State* (unreported) (both cases made a declaration of incompatibility in respect of Housing Act 1996 s 185 with Art 14; the Government is in the process of consulting on the appropriate response); *R (Clift) v Secretary of State for the Home Department; Secretary of State for the Home Department v Hindawi and another* [2006] UKHL 54 (Criminal Justice Act 1991 ss 46(1) and 50(2) declared incompatible with Art 14 read with Art 5; provisions had been repealed by the Criminal Justice Act 2003, with further amendments designed to be implemented under the Criminal Justice and Immigration Bill 2007 currently before Parliament); *Smith v Scott* [2007] CSIH 9 (Representation of the People Act 1938 s 3(1) declared incompatible with Art 3 of the First Protocol; the Government is currently consulting on how to remedy the incompatibility).

[21] *R (Alconbury Developments Ltd) v Secretary of State for the Environment, Transport and the Regions* [2001] HRLR 2 (overturned by the House of Lords [2001] UKHL 23; *Wilson v First County Trust Ltd (No 2)* [2001] EWCA Civ 633 (overturned by House of Lords [2003] UKHL 40); *Matthews v Ministry of Defence* [2002] EWHC 13 (overturned by the Court of Appeal; upheld by House of Lords [2003] UKHL 4); *R (Uttley) v Secretary of State for the Home Department* [2003] EWHC 950 (overturned by House of Lords [2004] UKHL 38); *R (MH) v Secretary of State for Health* [2004] EWCA Civ 1609 (overturned by

In this chapter we begin by examining what have been labelled the 'dialogical' aspects of the HRA, in particular the issue of, and Governmental responses to, declarations of incompatibility. Then, we look at the broader nature of the 'functional partnership between the courts, government and Parliament'[23] asking how, and to what degree, the separation of powers has been altered by the coming into force of the HRA.

PROMOTING DIALOGUE THROUGH DECLARATIONS OF INCOMPATIBILITY?

The ability of UK courts to hand 'incompatible' legislation back to Parliament finds parallels in the 'democratic dialogue' justificatory theory first advanced by Hogg and Bushell in the context of the Canadian Charter; that a court's power to review legislation on human rights grounds contributed a particular perspective to a broader debate over the legitimate exercise of state power vis-à-vis individual rights which would *not* be brought into the public domain were the courts not possessed of the power of judicial review and the legislature retained the sole authority of decisions of individual liberty.[24] As Hogg and Bushell observe:

> Where a judicial decision is open to legislative reversal, modification or avoidance, then it is meaningful to regard the relationship between the court and the competent legislative body as a dialogue ... the judicial decision causes a public debate in which the *Charter* values play a more prominent role than they would if there had been no judicial decision. The legislative body is in a position to devise a response that is properly respectful of the *Charter* values that have

House of Lords [2005] UKHL 60); *Re MB* [2006] EWHC 100 (Admin) (overturned by the Court of Appeal; upheld by the House of Lords [2007] UKHL 46); *R (Wright) v Secretary of State for Health and Secretary of State for Education and Skills* [2006] EWHC 2886 (Admin) (overturned by Court of Appeal [2007] EWCA Civ 999.

[22] *R (Baiai and others) v Secretary of State for the Home Department* [2006] EWHC 823 (Admin) (unsuccessfully appealed to the Court of Appeal; Government has been granted permission for a partial appeal to the House of Lords); *Nasseri v Secretary of State for the Home Department* [2007] EWHC 1548 (Admin) (the Government intends to appeal against the judgment).

[23] D Nicol, 'Gender Reassignment and the Transformation of the Human Rights Act' (2004) 120 *LQR* 194, 197.

[24] P Hogg and A Bushell, 'The *Charter* Dialogue between Courts and Legislatures (Or perhaps the *Charter of Rights* isn't Such a Bad Thing After All' (1997) 35 *Osgoode Hall Law Journal* 75. See further: CP Manfredi and JB Kelly, 'Six degrees of dialogue: a response to Hogg and Bushell' (1999) 37 *Osgoode Hall Law Journal* 513; K Roach, Constitutional and common law dialogues between the Supreme Court and Canadian Legislatures' (2001) 80 *Canadian Bar Review* 481; J Debeljak, 'Rights protection without judicial supremacy: a review of the Canadian and British models of Bills of Rights' (2002) 26 *Melbourne University Law Review* 285; LB Tremblay, 'The legitimacy of judicial review: the limits of dialogue between courts and legislatures' (2005) 3 *International Journal of Constitutional Law* 617.

been identified by the Court, but which accomplishes the social and economic objectives that the judicial decision has impeded.[25]

One essential precursor to the 'dialogue' is that the judgment of the court not be final – the elected arms of the state must be able to respond. This justificatory theory is not readily applicable to systems of de facto judicial supremacy, as

> the dialogue that culminates in a democratic decision can only take place if the judicial decision ... can be reversed, modified, or avoided in the ordinary legislative process.[26]

There is a clear correlation with the available options under the HRA; whether the section 3(1) interpretative obligation be invoked, or a declaration of incompatibility issued, the elected Parliament is in a position to respond and is not bound in either instance to adhere to the findings of the court. This latter point should not be understated; in *either* circumstance Parliament has the ability to respond. Adoption of a section 3(1) interpretation does not therefore rule out the possibility of future parliamentary or governmental input.[27] Indeed, as we have seen, the HRA model opens up channels of 'dialogue' beyond those envisaged as between Parliament and the courts. First, the executive and Parliament must consider the Convention compatibility of proposed legislation: under section 19 the Convention aspects of all new legislation becomes a required topic of parliamentary debate. Beyond this, the Joint Committee on Human Rights has established for itself a more detailed legislative scrutiny role.[28] In the context of adjudication, if a court is considering the issue of a declaration of incompatibility, the Crown is to be given notice and may intervene should it choose to do so.[29] It is these participatory elements of the system of rights protection afforded under the HRA which has seen Klug describe it as a 'third wave' bill of rights.[30]

---

[25]   *Ibid*, 79–80.

[26]   *Ibid*.

[27]   Although contrast the view of Campbell, who argues that Parliament may well be reluctant to challenge the interpretative judgment of the courts, and may – in effect – defer to it: 'the right of judges to interpret the law is as politically entrenched as the right of Parliament to make law. Interpretation is almost universally seen as the prerogative of the courts because it is part of adjudication, and that is taken to be their exclusive function. It is therefore not only politically difficult but also constitutionally questionable for parliaments to reject a court's particular interpretations or even question a court's interpretative methods. Judicial power that is built on the right to interpret is therefore not vulnerable to democratic pressures, although this could change as the public becomes aware of the nature of human rights interpretation.' (T Campbell, 'Incorporation through Interpretation' in Campbell, Ewing and Tomkins, n 6 above, 87).

[28]   Ch 2, pp 28–42.

[29]   HRA s 5.

[30]   F Klug, 'The Human Rights Act – a "Third Way" or "Third Wave" Bill of Rights?' [2001] *EHRLR* 361.

From the perspectives of the framers of the Act, these inter-institutional relationships were crucial to the success of the Act in creating a culture of human rights. As Jack Straw indicated during the parliamentary debates, a 'serious dialogue ... about the operation and developments of the rights in the Bill' would be the 'only way in which we can ensure the legislation is a living development that assists our citizens.'[31] As described above, the early signs from the senior judiciary were of a hesitance to label decision-making under the Act as a part of a 'dialogue.'[32] And if the Government had aspired to an ongoing dialogue with the judiciary in an informal sense, it soon became clear that the judiciary did not share their aspirations. When in 2005 the then Home Secretary Charles Clark indicated in an interview in the *New Statesman* that he had become 'frustrated at the inability to have general conversations ... with the law lords', adding that, 'some dialogue between the senior judiciary and the executive would be beneficial,'[33] Lord Steyn's response was terse:

> Mr Clark apparently fails to understand that the Law Lords and Cabinet ministers are not on the same side ... A cosy relationship between Ministers and Law Lords would be a worrying development.[34]

Any such 'dialogue' between the judiciary and the executive branch on the HRA would be confined to that which took place within the formal decision-making processes of the courtroom and Parliament.

The notion that the HRA gives rise to a formal 'dialogue' between the three branches of government has gained some currency since the coming into force of the Act.[35] Yet the dialogue metaphor has also been criticised for its imprecision and for having the potential to relegate judicial decisions to the status of mere advisory opinions in a broader debate on the protection of the Convention rights.[36] Nevertheless, it provides an appropriate encapsulation of the exchange of institutional perspectives allowed for by the HRA provided that acknowledgement is made of the

---

[31] HC Debs, vol 314, col 1141 (24 June 1998).

[32] Ch 1, pp 17–18.

[33] Quoted in Lord Steyn, 'Democracy, the Rule of Law and the role of the judges' [2006] *EHRLR* 243, 248.

[34] *Ibid.* Lord Phillips, the Lord Chief Justice, shared Lord Steyn's concerns, stating in a lecture in February 2007 that 'judges must be particularly careful not even to appear to be colluding with the executive when they are likely later to have to adjudicate on challenges of action taken by the executive' (<http://www.judiciary.gov.uk/docs/speeches/lcj260207.pdf> accessed 18 May 2008).

[35] See, eg, K Starmer, 'Two years of the Human Rights Act' [2003] *EHRLR* 14; R Clayton, 'Judicial Deference and "democratic dialogue": the legitimacy of judicial intervention under the Human Rights Act 1998' [2004] *PL* 33; Klug, above, n 30; Hickman, above n 15.

[36] See, respectively, C O'Cinneide, 'Democracy, Rights and the Constitution – New Directions in the Human Rights era' (2004) 57 *Current Legal Problems* 175, 205; T Hickman, 'Constitutional dialogue, constitutional theories and the Human Rights Act' [2005] *PL* 306, 309–310.

role of courts and legislatures within the Convention system as a whole. While the HRA itself outlines the specific role of the courts, the executive and Parliament in protecting rights domestically, the Convention itself further delineates the powers of the three arms of government. First, whatever contribution to a 'dialogue' is made by the domestic institutions occurs largely within the confines of interpretations of 'the Convention rights'[37] and the Strasbourg case law which gives meaning to those rights.[38] This is particularly the case when considering interpretational and definitional questions, as distinct from questions surrounding the proportionality of a given measure. Secondly, even if the doctrine of parliamentary sovereignty has survived the passing of the HRA unscathed, the ultimate meaning of those 'Convention rights' is not an area in which the authority of Parliament is insulated from future challenge at Strasbourg. As the House of Lords has reminded us – even if national authorities seek to expand on, or interpret, the Convention's provisions – the Convention remains, 'an international instrument, the correct interpretation of which can be authoritatively expounded only by the Strasbourg court.'[39] To present the HRA as offering an opportunity for blue-sky thinking on rights generally is to misconstrue the nature of the HRA, and the position of national authorities under the Convention.[40]

Perhaps more pertinently, the idea of a dialogue suggests an exchange of views, yet the governmental responses to those declarations of incompatibility issued under the Act have uniformly endorsed and implemented the judicial readings of compatibility put forward. If this is a dialogue at all, it is one in which the judicial voice is beginning to be heard the loudest.

RESPONDING TO INCOMPATIBILTY

While it is acknowledged that the elected branches retain the power to refuse to accept a declaration of incompatibility, their practice has, to date, not given rise to any examples of their so doing. As described above, at the time of writing, each of the judicially made declarations that remained in force following the appeal process has been responded to in a positive

---

[37] HRA s 1(1). See also the directions in the key provisions of the HRA that the court should seek readings of compatibility that are compliant with the Convention rights (s 3(1)) and should determine the legality of public authority activity also by reference to those Convention rights (s 6(1)).

[38] Under the HRA's directions to 'take into account' that jurisprudence (s 2(1)).

[39] *R (Ullah) v Special Adjudicator; Do v Immigration Appeal Tribunal* [2004] UKHL 26, para 20 (Lord Bingham).

[40] Nicol, for one, alludes favourably to the 'potential for unrestrained debate' that the HRA could foster (D Nicol, 'Law and Politics after the Human Rights Act' [2006] *PL* 722, 748). For a response to Professor Nicol's article see: T Hickman, 'The Courts and politics after the Human Rights Act: a comment' [2008] *PL* 84.

manner by the legislative and executive branches. In each instance, the executive and/or Parliament has either endorsed the reading of incompatibility put forward by the courts and acted appropriately to remedy it, or has indicated that a response to do so would be forthcoming.

Of the 24 declarations of incompatibility made in total, 15 survived to merit a governmental response. On becoming final, the remedial order mechanism laid down in section 10 HRA would in theory come into play, allowing the responsible Minister the power to amend the legislation in question to remedy the incompatibility by way of a statutory instrument.[41] In fact, of those 15, only one incompatibility has been remedied using the remedial order procedure.[42] Aside from those declarations to which the Government is still formulating a formal response,[43] the remainder have been remedied by primary legislation. In response to the declarations issued in *Anderson* and *Bellinger v Bellinger*,[44] for example, Parliament remedied the incompatibility by through the Criminal Justice Act 2003 and Gender Recognition Act 2004 respectively. Perhaps the only example of an ongoing 'dialogue' – in which the Government's response to a declaration of incompatibility has itself come before the courts – can be seen in the discussion of anti-terrorist measures which follows below.[45]

That the formal response to the issue of declarations of incompatibility has largely come through primary legislation should offer a degree of comfort to those who are sceptical of the anti-democratic tendencies of the HRA, given the potential for the section 10 remedial order process to bypass detailed parliamentary scrutiny.[46] However, in the scheme of governmental responses to those declarations of incompatibility issued to date, to emphasise the use of primary legislative – as opposed to remedial – powers as tools of remedying incompatibilities detracts attention from a more pressing issue for those who are sceptical of judicial power under the HRA; the failure of the elected branches to challenge, or otherwise refuse to endorse, a judicial reading of compatibility. We do not suggest that what

---

[41] HRA s 10.

[42] *R (H) v Mental Health Review Tribunal for the North and East London Region and the Secretary of State for Health* [2001] EWCA Civ 415.

[43] *R (Morris) v Westminster City Council and First Secretary of State* [2005] EWCA Civ 1184; *R (Gabaj) v First Secretary of State* (unreported); *Smith v Scott* [2007] CSIH 9.

[44] Ch 4, pp 99–102.

[45] Ch 8.

[46] HRA s 10, Sch 2. Under normal circumstances, under Sch 2, paras 2(a), 3, the remedial order would be laid before Parliament for 60 days before coming into effect, allowing time for representations to be made to the responsible Minister. The order would only come into effect after a second period of 60 days had passed and the amendment endorsed by Parliamentary resolution. In 'urgent' cases however, remedial orders may be made without prior Parliamentary approval under Sch 2, paras 2(b), 4, with any representations made to the Minister having to come after the order's coming into effect. 'Urgency' is, of course, a matter of ministerial viewpoint.

has taken place is the crystallisation of an effective constitutional convention to the effect that the elected branches will as a matter of practice accept declarations of incompatibility. Yet the available evidence surely demonstrates the political potency of a judicial statement of incompatibility – especially so in those areas of the law where the courts are portrayed as being at odds with Parliament, or more realistically, with the executive.[47]

During the parliamentary debates, Lord Borrie predicted that in the HRA era:

> the political reality will be that, while historically the courts have sought to carry out the will of Parliament, in the field of human rights Parliament will carry out the will of the courts.[48]

While it may be going to far to portray the emerging practice under the HRA as establishing a *de facto* judicial supremacy over the domestic interpretation of the Convention rights, it would also underplay the political significance of declarations of incompatibility to describe the judicial contribution to the rights debate in the United Kingdom as the actions of a 'privileged political pressure group'.[49]

The practice, to date, of the acceptance and remedy of judicially-declared incompatibilities by the elected branches has not however, been sufficient to convince the European Court of Human Rights that a declaration of incompatibility amounts to an effective remedy for the purposes of Article 13 ECHR. In *Burden and Burden v United Kingdom*, the European Court of Human Rights held that the declaration of incompatibility did not amount to an effective remedy because it did not place the relevant minister under a legal obligation to amend the provision at issue.[50] The court held that the practice of remedying the incompatibility based on the courts' declarations did not provide sufficient certainty for the recipient of the declaration. The European Court did recognise however, that this position may change over time:

> It is possible that at some future date evidence of a long-standing and established practice of ministers giving effect to the courts' declarations of incompatibility

---

[47] In particular in the sphere of counter-terrorist measures (on which see ch 8). Although admittedly to a lesser degree in those cases where the Government had already indicated that a response would be forthcoming (see eg, *Bellinger v Bellinger*, pp 100–103 above).

[48] HL Debs, vol 582, col 1275 (3 November 1997).

[49] T Hickman, 'The courts and politics after the Human Rights Act: a comment' [2008] *PL* 84, 100 (the phrase is used to describe the role of the courts under Professor Nicol's proposed dialogical model: n 40 above).

[50] *Burden and Burden v UK* (2007) 44 EHRR 51, para 39.

might be sufficient to persuade the Court of the effectiveness of the procedure. At the present time, however, there is insufficient material on which to base such a finding.[51]

The Parliamentary Joint Committee on Human Rights has argued for the Government to adopt a 'much clearer policy on systematically responding to declarations of incompatibility' which would be capable of providing the evidence of a 'convention' of acceptance of such declarations.[52] As indicated above, it is unlikely that the past examples of adherence to judicial declarations could be described as conventional in the constitutional sense; the experience of declarations of incompatibility being accepted by the elected branches can only be descriptive of a practice, rather than normative. In addition, it is clear for some that the crystallisation of such a constitutional convention would be destructive of the worth of the Act altogether. As Tom Campbell has argued, should a legislative response to a declaration of incompatibility endorsing the courts' reading of Convention-compliance become a matter of routine then the HRA will have lost its democratic credentials and the courts would have acquired a *de facto* power to invalidate primary legislation.[53] While such a practice would arguably satisfy the European Court of Human Rights, and would be undoubtedly strengthen the remedial structure put in place by the HRA, it would also amount to a further (and arguably unacceptable) extension of judicial power, at Parliament's expense.

In the next part of this chapter we take a step back to look to examine the division of governmental power under the HRA, challenging the Government's submission that the separation of powers remains largely unaffected by the implementation of its system of rights protection.[54]

THE SEPARATION OF POWERS AFTER THE HUMAN RIGHTS ACT

The extent to which the constitution of the United Kingdom embraces, or eschews, the separation of powers doctrine has long been a source of controversy.[55] In spite of the many exceptions to any strict understanding

---

[51] *Ibid.*

[52] Joint Committee on Human Rights, *Monitoring the Government's Response to Court judgments finding breaches of human rights*, 2006–2007 (HC 728), paras 109–21.

[53] T Campbell, 'Incorporation through interpretation', n 6 above.

[54] Jack Straw MP, n 60 below; Lord Irvine of Lairg, n 59 below: Lord Irvine, 'Activism and restraint: human rights and the interpretative process' [1999] *EHRLR* 350, 366.

[55] Contrast eg, *Dupont Steel v Sirs* [1980] 1 All ER 529, 540 (Lord Diplock); *R v Secretary of State for the Home Department ex p Fire Brigades Union* [1995] 2 AC 513, 567 (Lord Mustill) with SA de Smith, 'The Separation of Powers in New Dress' (1966) 12 *McGill LJ* 491; O Hood Phillips, 'A Constitutional Myth: Separation of Powers' (1977) 93 *LQR* 11.

of that doctrine that have historically existed in our constitutional arrangements,[56] it has been said that a rudimentary separation of functions can be said to exist.[57] Thus Lord Mustill was famously able to note in the *Fire Brigades Union* case that:

> It is a feature of the peculiarly British conception of the separation of powers that Parliament, the executive and the courts have each their distinct and largely exclusive domain. Parliament has a legally unchallengeable right to make whatever laws it thinks right. The executive carries on the administration of the country in accordance with the powers conferred on it by law. The courts interpret the laws, and see that they are obeyed.[58]

This definition of the separation of power in the United Kingdom owes far more to the residue of governmental power as left behind by the parliamentary sovereignty doctrine than to any considered division of competence between the three arms of government. It is parliamentary sovereignty disguised as separation of powers theory; the separation of powers doctrine in the United Kingdom is both defined and delimited by the of parliamentary sovereignty. From that perspective, much, we were told, would remain the same following the implementation of the HRA. The HRA was described by the Lord Chancellor during the parliamentary debates as having been 'carefully drafted and designed to respect our traditional understanding of the separation of powers.'[59] Reduced to its bare minimum, this can be taken to mean that under the provisions of the HRA, the courts are not empowered to strike down, invalidate, or otherwise disapply Acts of the Sovereign Legislature. As Jack Straw MP further outlined during the parliamentary debates:

> The sovereignty of Parliament must be paramount. By that, I mean that Parliament must be competent to make any law on any matter of its choosing. In enacting legislation, Parliament is making decisions about important matters of public policy. The authority to make those decisions derives from a democratic mandate. Members of this place possess such a mandate because they are elected, accountable and representative ... To allow the courts to set aside Acts of Parliament would confer on the judiciary a power that it does not possess, and which would draw it into conflict with Parliament.[60]

---

[56] Eg, the historic ability of the Lord Chancellor to exercise executive, legislative and judicial functions (see, eg, *DPP v Jones* [1999] 2 AC 240, and generally D Woodhouse, *The Office of Lord Chancellor* (Oxford, Hart Publishing, 2001)). See now the Constitutional Reform Act 2005.

[57] E Barendt, 'Separation of Powers and Constitutional Government' [1995] *PL* 592, 601.

[58] *R v Secretary of State for the Home Department ex p Fire Brigades Union* [1995] 2 AC 513, 567 (Lord Mustill).

[59] HL Debs, vol 582, col 1228 (3 November 1997).

[60] HC Debs, vol 306, col 772 (16 February 1998).

Described as such, the scheme established by the HRA is one which upholds the traditional conception of the separation of executive, legislative and judicial power. Parliament makes the laws and the courts interpret them, becomes Parliament makes the laws and the judiciary are empowered to interpret them – 'so far as is possible' – to be compatible with the Convention rights. On such an analysis, the role of the courts is purely interpretative, and it is clear that pre-HRA conceptions of the limitations of judicial power continue to resonate.[61] As described above, the reluctance of the courts to act in a way which might be seen to usurp the legislative function persists following the implementation of the HRA.[62] On this reading of the Act therefore, Parliament's role as sovereign legislature is preserved through the fact that any declaration made under section 4 'does not affect the validity, continuing operation or enforcement of the provision in respect of which it is given.'[63] The Westminster Parliament – the representative body – is given the final word. As such, the short-lived Department for Constitutional Affairs issued the claim in its 2006 review of the Act that:

> arguments that the Human Rights Act has significantly altered the constitutional balance between Parliament, the executive and the judiciary have ... been considerably exaggerated.[64]

This, we argue, represents only one side of the coin.

The Influence of the Convention Case Law

First, the influence of the jurisprudence of the European Court of Human Rights brings with it a strong adherence to constitutional values.[65] While the European Court of Human Rights has consistently stated that the Convention does not demand the maintenance of any 'theoretical constitutional concepts as such',[66] the notion of the separation of executive,

---

[61] Ch 4, p 108.

[62] See, eg, *Re S (Children) (Care Order: Implementation of Care Plan); Re W (Children) (Care Order: Adequacy of Care Plan)* [2002] UKHL 10; [2002] 2 AC 291; *R (Anderson) v Secretary of State for the Home Department* [2002] UKHL 46; [2003] 1 AC 837; *R (Ullah) v Special Adjudicator; Do v Immigration Appeal Tribunal* [2004] UKHL 26.

[63] Section 3(2)(b).

[64] Department of Constitutional Affairs, *Review of the Implementation of the Human Rights Act* (July 2006) 4.

[65] Most obviously, its commitment to the rule of law: 'The Convention uses the words "law" and "lawful" 39 times. The preamble refers to the "common heritage of ... the rule of law" which the States parties share, and which the court has described as "one of the fundamental principles of a democratic society, [which] is inherent in all the Arts of the Convention"': S Grosz, J Beatson and P Duffy, *Human Rights: The 1998 Act and the European Convention* (London, Sweet and Maxwell, 2000) 169.

[66] *McGonnell v UK* (2000) 30 EHRR 289, para 51.

legislative and judicial power can be said to have achieved a certain prominence in the case law of the Strasbourg court: the 'growing importance' of the doctrine was noted in *Stafford v United Kingdom*,[67] while in *Benjamin and Wilson v United Kingdom* the principle was referred to as 'fundamental.'[68] In addition, the separation of judicial and executive power has been acknowledged as a 'legitimate aim' to be pursued by domestic authorities.[69] In domestic courts, these developments have not gone unnoticed. In *R (Anderson) v Secretary of State for the Home Department*, Lord Bingham observed that the European Court of Human Rights had been correct to:

> describe the complete functional separation of the judiciary from the executive as 'fundamental' since the rule of law depends on it,[70]

with Lord Hutton adding that such a separation is an 'essential part of a democracy.'[71] Such was the emphasis placed on the importance of the separation of powers doctrine in *Anderson* that one commentator has speculated that the judgment may be 'a starting point for building a separation of powers jurisprudence which, although rooted in Article 6, extends beyond the existing objective and subjective tests for independence and impartiality.'[72] A stand-alone separation of powers jurisprudence is yet to be realised in domestic law, but the influence of Article 6 of the Convention has had obvious repercussions for the division of governmental power in the United Kingdom, most strikingly in the area of procedural fairness[73] and in the consequential institutional reforms in respect of the office of Lord Chancellor and establishment of a Supreme Court.[74]

---

[67]   *Stafford v UK* (2002) 35 EHRR 32, para 78.
[68]   *Benjamin and Wilson v UK* (2003) 36 EHRR 1, para 36.
[69]   *A v UK* (2003) 36 EHRR 51, para 77.
[70]   *R v Secretary of State for the Home Department ex p Anderson* [2003] 1 AC 837, 882.
[71]   *Ibid*, 899.
[72]   M Amos, '*R v Secretary of State for the Home Department ex p Anderson* – Ending the Home Secretary's Sentencing Role' (2004) 67(1) *MLR* 108, 123.
[73]   See, eg, *Davidson v Scottish Ministers (No 2)* [2004] UKHL 34 (on which see: R Masterman, 'Determinative in the Abstract? Article 6(1) and the separation of powers' [2005] *EHRLR* 628); *R (Brooke) v Parole Board* [2007] EWHC 2036 (Admin).
[74]   On which, see, Constitutional Reform Act 2005; and generally: A Le Sueur, 'Judicial power in the changing constitution' in J Jowell and D Oliver (eds), *The Changing Constitution* (5th ed) (Oxford, OUP, 2004); R Masterman, above n 73; R Masterman, 'A Supreme Court for the United Kingdom: two steps forward, but one step back on judicial independence' [2004] *PL* 48; Lord Windlesham, 'The Constitutional Reform Act 2005: ministers, judges and constitutional change: part I' [2005] *PL* 806; Lord Windlesham, 'The Constitutional Reform Act 2005: the politics of constitutional reform: part II' [2006] *PL* 35.

Enhanced Accountability

If the separation of power is to provide anything meaningful for a system of governance, it is certainly not that each branch of government undertake its own function completely independently of the other branches. Discussing Montesquieu in *The Federalist* papers, James Madison wrote that the separation of powers doctrine did not mean that each department of government 'ought to have no *partial agency* in, or no *control* over, the acts of each other.'[75] It is in the realm of checks and balances that the immediate impact of the HRA is most obvious – it provides a statutory footing on which executive action can be checked on human rights grounds. This alone clearly amounts to a significant extension of judicial power beyond the confines of the *Wednesbury*-based judicial review jurisdiction.[76]

The structure of the HRA envisages a specific role for courts, legislature and executive. The Act avoids judicial supremacy, but equally allows for circumstances in which the parliamentary determination of questions of rights may be subject to judicial refinement with a view to achieving compatibility with the Convention.[77] It is easy therefore to see why the Government in 1998 described the HRA project as a co-operative exercise between courts, executive and Parliament. The role of the courts is to police the exercise of public authority activity on Convention grounds, and to interpret and give effect to legislation in a Convention-friendly manner, so far as that is possible. As we saw in chapter 2, the role of the elected branches and political process in upholding rights remains as important as that of the courts:

> Judicial recognition and assertion of the human rights defined in the Convention is not a substitute for the processes democratic government but a complement to them.[78]

The executive finds itself bound to act compatibly with the Convention Rights under section 6 HRA, is required to gauge the compatibility of its legislative proposals,[79] and is given specific discretionary powers to be used in the event of a finding of incompatibility.[80] While Parliament is given an

---

[75] *The Federalist*, No XLVII (emphasis in the original).

[76] Ch 6.

[77] Cf the arrangements under the Scotland Act 1998, Northern Ireland Act 1998 and Government of Wales Act 1998 where actions of the representative bodies established under those Acts must be compatible with the Convention Rights to remain intra vires (see ch 2, pp 43–48).

[78] *Brown v Stott* [2003] 1 AC 681, 703 (Lord Bingham).

[79] HRA s 19.

[80] HRA s 10.

enhanced role in scrutinising legislation, both within the debating chambers and in the Joint Committee on Human Rights, and in holding the executive to account for its decisions and policies. Given the fact that both Parliament and the executive have their own specific role to play under the Act, it becomes more realistic to reassess *governmental*, not simply judicial, power in the light of the HRA.

In legislative and executive terms, the cumulative effect of this scheme is an explicit place for the debate of Convention rights prior to, and during, the formal legislative process. As we have seen, the integration of rights discourse into the political process has been only a qualified success. While the 'indefatigable'[81] Joint Committee on Human Rights has rightly been praised for the range and depth of its work, the executive dominance of the House of Commons continues to distort the practical implementation of the Government's collaborative scheme. Meanwhile, the seeming consensus on preserving the status quo in respect of the powers of the Upper House[82] means that the occasional willingness of the House of Lords to carefully examine the human rights implications of proposed legislation will continue to be hampered by their lack of meaningful powers of veto or delay.[83]

While it is fair then to talk of a model of 'politicised rights' protection in the parliamentary sense, prior to the implementation of the Act there were fears that the courts too would be drawn into making decisions for which the courts were not the appropriate forum for resolution or debate.[84]

Blurring Boundaries

The institutional framework implemented under the HRA has contributed to a re-alignment of the separation of powers doctrine which appears to

---

[81] F Klug, 'The long road to human rights compliance' (2006) 57(1) *Northern Ireland Legal Quarterly* 186, 200.

[82] See Joint Committee on Conventions, *Conventions of the UK Parliament*, 2005–2006 (HL 265-I; HC 1212-I). The Committee did however acknowledge the claim to more extensive powers which the House of Lords would have were to be composed by way of election. An elected Upper House became a step closer to reality following a House of Commons vote in its favour on 7 March 2007 (the Commons had been allowed a free vote on composition in response to the Government White Paper, *The House of Lords: Reform*, 2007 (Cm 7027)).

[83] We say 'occasional' as the House of Lords record in respect of human rights issues is far from unblemished. Contrast the House of Lords' rigorous analysis and amendment of, eg, the Police and Criminal Evidence Bill 1984 and Anti-Terrorism, Crime and Security Bill 2001 with its less rights-friendly treatment of the Sexual Offences (Amendment) Bills 1998 and 1999. See generally: D Feldman, 'Parliamentary scrutiny of legislation and human rights' [2002] *PL* 323.

[84] See, eg, Lord Devlin, 'Judges and Lawmakers' (1976) 39 *MLR* 1; Lord McCluskey, *Law, Justice and Democracy* (London, Sweet and Maxwell, 1987); N Lyell, 'Whither Strasbourg? Why Britain should think long and hard before incorporating the European Convention on Human Rights' [1997] *EHRLR* 132.

suggest that – to paraphrase Lord Mustill – while the executive, the legislature and the courts might have each their own distinct domain, the three may not be as exclusive as was once thought. As has been noted above, critics of judicially-enforced Bills of Rights raise the issue of the transfer of power from the political arms of the state to the unrepresentative and unelected judges as evidence of the undesirability (and counter-majoritarian nature) of such instruments. Rights are – for the most part – contestable and therefore more appropriately resolved in the open debate of the political arena than through narrow legalistic argument in the courtroom. The categorisation of rights as questions of law as opposed to politics remains a matter of controversy, even under the balanced scheme imposed by the HRA.

The endeavours of the judiciary to find the correct balance can be seen in their attempts to expound coherent principles of deference. As Simon Brown LJ (as he then was) noted in *International Transport Roth*:

> Constitutional dangers exist no less in too little judicial activism as in too much. There are limits to the legitimacy of executive or legislative decision-making, just as there are to decision-making by the courts.[85]

The difficulties of the courts in so doing are perhaps most emphatically displayed by the stark difference between the approaches of the Court of Appeal and the House of Lords in the *ProLife Alliance* case. The former was an uncompromising assertion of the courts' role as 'constitutional guardian of freedom of political debate' and 'trustees of our democracy's framework' in the run-up to a general election.[86] The latter demonstrated the reluctance of the court to displace the determination of the public interest as determined by the legislature regardless of the Convention issues raised, and was reminiscent of the lightest of touch *Wednesbury* review.[87] As will be seen, it is hoped that the decision of the House of Lords in *Huang* heralds a more consistent and rigorous standard of review.[88]

The exclusivity of Parliament's role as legislator has also been called into question following implementation of the HRA. As a result of the 'broad and ample style'[89] of rights instruments generally, Lord Irvine wrote that the HRA would 'necessarily leave the judges with a significant margin of

---

[85] *International Transport Roth GmbH v Secretary of State for the Home Department* [2002] EWCA Civ 158; [2003] QB 728, para 54.

[86] *R (Pro-Life Alliance) v BBC* [2002] 3 WLR 1080, para 36.

[87] *R (Pro-Life Alliance) v BBC* [2003] UKHL 23; [2004] 1 AC 185.

[88] *Huang v Secretary of State for the Home Department* [2007] UKHL 11; [2007] 2 AC 167. On which see ch 6, pp 165–166.

[89] *Minister of Home Affairs v Fisher* [1980] AC 319, 328 (Lord Wilberforce).

interpretative autonomy.'[90] Alongside the caution of the frequent remind-ers of the limitations of the section 3(1) obligation, we have also seen statements which confirm the quite radical potential of that provision. As Lord Nicholls stated in *Re S; Re W*:

> Section 3(1) ... is a powerful tool whose use is obligatory. It is not an optional canon of construction. Nor is its use dependent on the existence of ambiguity. Further the section applies retrospectively. So far as it is possible to do so primary legislation 'must be read and given effect' to in a way which is compatible with Convention rights. This is forthright, uncompromising lan-guage.[91]

And as Lord Hope – who notably advocated a more restrained interpreta-tive technique in *R v A (No 2)* – was nevertheless able to say in *ex p Kebilene* that the HRA will provoke a 'fundamental process of review and, where necessary, *reform by the judiciary.*'[92]

It is perhaps no surprise that two of the most striking deployments of this new interpretative latitude have come in cases which directly impact on the perceived expertise of the judiciary. The decisions of the Court of Appeal in *R v Offen*, and the House of Lords in *R v A* demonstrate that 'in the criminal field, the courts will intervene unhesitatingly if they take the view that a judicial discretion is being circumscribed on unpersuasive grounds.'[93] That 'activist' interpretative techniques should be utilised in the sphere of criminal justice is perhaps unsurprising; in the realm of criminal procedure and process, arguments that the courts are usurping the author-ity of the elected branches are far less persuasive. However, *Ghaidan v Godin-Mendoza* has not only demonstrated the ability of the judiciary to exercise their significant interpretative power in the arena of social policy, but also shown how easily the constraints of parliamentary language can be jettisoned while they do so.

The common law myth that judges do not make law was effectively dispelled by Lord Reid and others many years ago.[94] Yet the HRA has given rise to a new variation on an old theme – that in interpreting the statutes under the HRA, the judges should not cross the line between interpretation and amendment. Recognising this, Kavanagh, has argued that 'the activity of interpretation involves, rather than eschews, *judicial*

---

[90] Lord Irvine, 'Activism and Restraint: Human Rights and the interpretative process' in *Human Rights, Constitutional Law and the Development of the English Legal System* (Oxford, Hart Publishing, 2003) 64.

[91] *Re S (Children) (Care Order: Implementation of Care Plan); Re W (Children) (Care Order: Adequacy of Care Plan)* [2002] 2 AC 291, para 37 (Lord Nicholls).

[92] [2000] 2 AC 326, 375 (emphasis added).

[93] R Clayton, 'The Limits of what's Possible: Statutory Construction under the Human Rights Act' [2002] *EHRLR* 559, 560.

[94] Lord Reid, 'The Judge as Law Maker' (1972) 12 *Journal of the Society of Public Teachers of Law* 22. See also: Lord Lester, 'English Judges as Law Makers' [1993] *PL* 269.

law-making,'[95] while Young has written of *Ghaidan* as an example of 'acceptable judicial legislation.'[96] The reality of judicial power under the HRA as evidenced in cases such as *R v A* and *Ghaidan* makes it increasingly difficult to sustain the once unqualified truth that Parliament continues to exercise unfettered legislative discretion.

CONCLUSION: THE CO-OPERATIVE CONSTITUTION?

Lord Irvine of Lairg QC said in a public lecture at Durham University in 2002 that, '[the HRA] has breathed new life into the relationship between Parliament, Government and the judiciary.' Optimistically, he continued:

> that all three are working together to ensure that a culture of respect for human rights becomes embedded across the whole of our society.[97]

The separation of powers has undoubtedly been revitalised by the passing and implementation of the HRA. Specifically, the Act has undeniably redefined the judicial role; and in so doing has altered the balance of power between judiciary, legislature and executive as it is traditionally understood. Yet, as evidenced above, many facets of judicial reasoning under the HRA display an adherence to a conception of the separation of powers which does not reflect the new legal realities.

The successes of the Act as a co-operative measure are, however, open to question. While the history of governmental and parliamentary responses to declarations of incompatibility strengthens the position of the HRA as a remedial instrument, by 2008 the Government's promise to 'bring rights home' under the HRA seems increasingly hollow, with the Act regularly portrayed as giving rise to more conflict than co-operation.[98] In constitutional terms, there is tension between the aspirations of this third-wave Bill of Rights and the practical realities of our unreformed, executive dominated Parliament. While the minimalist approach adopted by the courts to the scope of the Convention rights in domestic law reflects a desire to sustain legal certainty, it arguably sits uneasily with the HRA's status as a constitutional instrument, and with the intentions of the Strasbourg institutions that states authorities be the primary mechanism for realising the Convention rights. And while there is seeming acknowledgement that

---

[95] A Kavangh, 'The Elusive Divide between interpretation and legislation under the Human Rights Act' (2004) 24 *OJLS* 259, 261.

[96] A Young, '*Ghaidan v Godin-Mendoza*: Avoiding the Deference Trap' [2005] *PL* 23, 27.

[97] Lord Irvine of Lairg, 'The Impact of the Human Rights Act: Parliament, the Courts and the Executive', in *Human Rights, Constitutional Law and the Development of the English Legal System* (Oxford, Hart Publishing, 2003) 132.

[98] For an overview see: H Fenwick, G Phillipson and R Masterman, 'The Human Rights Act in contemporary context' in H Fenwick, G Phillipson and R Masterman (eds), *Judicial Reasoning under the UK Human Rights Act* (Cambridge, CUP, 2007).

the constitutional status of the HRA demands that the courts adopt a 'generous and purposive' interpretation so that individuals can benefit from the full effect of the rights it confers,[99] the interpretative demands of section 3(1) are placing increasing strain on the pretence of parliamentary sovereignty. In other words, the balance between elected and judicial power has not been the only constitutional tension highlighted by the implementation of HRA.

---

[99] For discussion see: R Masterman, 'Taking the Strasbourg Jurisprudence into Account: Developing a "Municipal Law of Human Rights" under the Human Rights Act' (2005) 54 *ICLQ* 907, 913–915.

Part II

Domestic Remedies for Violations of Convention Rights

Chapter 6

Public Law Remedies: the Scope and Standard of Judicial Review Under the HRA

INTRODUCTION

T
HE OBJECTIVE OF this chapter is to examine the range and depth of review in public law under section 6 in order to establish the impact of the Human Rights Act 1998 (HRA). In the absence of a Bill of Rights providing a judicial power to strike down conflicting legislation, judicial review of administrative action inevitably bears the brunt of the strain of protecting individuals from official violations of their human rights. Prior to the coming into force of the Act there was some debate as to whether it would cause a shift in the standard of review with abandonment of judicial deference to the executive.[1]

The drafting section 6 of the Act encourages such speculation. This appears to make breach of Convention rights by a public authority a distinct new ground of illegality, with the consequence that the courts would become concerned with the merits and effects of the decision, rather than the process by which it was reached. Judicial deference to the executive could only be maintained so far as the Convention permitted limitations to rights under the so-called proportionality doctrine. As we shall see, on the whole, the courts have so far adopted a less radical position which while it has involved a general intensification of the standard of review in human rights cases, and the more so where unqualified rights (such as those under Articles 2 and 3) are involved nevertheless falls short of review of the merits as such.

A second battleground concerns which bodies are subject to the section 6 duty as 'public authorities'. It was inevitable that attempts to broaden the reach of human rights protection would focus in part on casting the

---

[1] Lord Irving of Lairg, 'The Development of Human Rights in Britain under an Incorporated Convention on Human Rights' [1998] *PL* 221, 232ff; D Pannick, 'Comment: Principles of Interpretation of Convention Rights under the Human Rights Act and the Discretionary Area of Judgment' [1998] *PL* 545; The Hon Sir John Laws, 'The Limitations of Human Rights' [1998] *PL* 254.

definition of public authorities beyond core state entities. Attention has focused especially on the position of providers delivering public services under contractual arrangements and on the voluntary sector. Here the position is complex. It by no means follows that human rights protection can be maximised by simply catching more entities within the 'public authority' net, since private and not-for-profit sector bodies have human rights of their own to be considered, and the courts have wisely resisted demands to extend the Act to them.

The account that follows deals first with the position before the HRA and with the implications of the ECHR for judicial review. It then deals with the controversy of which bodies section 6 applies to before turning to the standard of review. The range of possible arguments are first discussed, followed by consideration of seminal rulings that intensify the standard of review in response to the HRA and through the doctrine of proportionality. The capacity of proportionality to justify a more deferential approach is also explored. Finally, the question of whether review has gone far enough to satisfy Strasbourg is tackled.

PRIOR TO THE HUMAN RIGHTS ACT

English administrative law had, prior to the HRA, failed to develop effective protection for human rights against incursions by public officials and authorities. Much of the blame for the parlous defence of civil liberties and human rights can be attributed to the judges' sentimental attachment to the *Wednesbury* test as the appropriate standard for reviewing official action. Under this test action was only reviewable if it was so unreasonable that no reasonable decision-maker would have taken it.[2] Long-criticised for its circularity, imprecision and excessive deference to the executive, *Wednesbury* nevertheless continues to hold considerable sway.[3]

Its influence can be seen clearly in *Brind*, in which, a mere 15 years ago, the House of Lords ruled that the Home Secretary was not legally obliged to consider the Convention right of freedom of expression when imposing restrictions on television and radio interviews with people connected with a terrorist organisation.[4] Their Lordships considered that to hold otherwise would amount to what they described as 'back door' incorporation of the Convention and that they should not rush in where (at that time) Parliament had chosen not to. The Convention's relevance was limited to instances of statutory ambiguity – something which in the circumstances of the case (concerning a very wide power to give 'directions' to broadcasters)

---

[2] *Associated Picture Houses v Wednesbury Corporation* [1948] 1 KB 223.
[3] Andrew Le Sueur, 'The Rise and Ruin of Unreasonableness' [2005] *Judicial Review* 32.
[4] *R v Secretary of State for the Home Department ex p Brind* [1991] 1 AC 696 (HL).

their Lordships were reluctant to find. At the same time the House affirmed that proportionality was not part of United Kingdom law and that the broadcasting ban was not open to challenge on conventional grounds for irrationality.

Nevertheless, very belatedly, in the interval between *Brind* and the implementation of the HRA a number of judicial techniques were developed which demonstrated greater sensitivity to rights. Where the decision-maker claimed to have considered the Convention the courts would examine whether he or she had done so correctly.[5] The *Wednesbury* test was modified by the requirement that courts subject administrative decisions with human rights implications to 'anxious scrutiny' or 'most rigorous examination'.[6] Later decisions, notably the litigation in which gay and lesbian service personnel challenged the reasonableness of their discharge from the armed forces, have confirmed that the greater the human rights dimensions of a case the closer the attention the courts will give to the legality of the official decision[7] – described in places as 'substantial objective justification'.[8] Hence, by the time the HRA came into force *Wednesbury* had become in effect a variable standard: the more fundamental the right interfered with, the greater the need for justification.

Despite that, as *Smith* itself shows, before the HRA the judges regarded themselves (if reluctantly) to be restricted to secondary review of administrative discretion. Even in the period immediately prior to the Act entering into force there was a continuing reticence to develop administrative law doctrine. In *Kebilene* the High Court declined to follow the lead of the Australian courts[9] and develop the doctrine of legitimate expectations so as to impose on a prosecutor a duty to exercise the discretion not to bring a prosecution in a prospective defendant's favour where a violation of Convention rights might result if there was a conviction.[10]

In terms of the European Convention the pressure to expand judicial review has come from two distinct sources. The first is concern over whether judicial review is an effective domestic remedy for the purpose of Article 13 of the Convention. This is a question that, strictly, arises irrespective of the HRA. The decision in *Smith and Grady v UK* (the sequel to the domestic litigation in *Smith*) that judicial review had failed to

---

[5] *R v Secretary of State for the Home Department ex p Launder* (1997) 1 WLR 839, 867 (Lord Hope of Craighead).
[6] *R v Home Secretary ex p Bugdaycay* [1987] 1 All ER 940, 952; and see Lord Templeman (at 956), referring to 'a special responsibility' on the court.
[7] *Smith v MOD* [1996] QB 517, 554, 563, 564–5; *R v Secretary of State for Home Department ex p Leech* [1994] QB 198.
[8] *Smith v MOD* [1996] QB 517, 554; *R v Lord Saville of Newdigate ex p A* (2000) 1 WLR 1855, 1866–67; and *Launder*, 867.
[9] *Minister for Immigration and Ethnic Affairs v Teoh* (1995) 128 ALR 353, 365.
[10] *R v DPP ex p Kebilene* [1999] 4 ALL ER 801, 811 (Lord Bingham). The legitimate expectation point was dropped on appeal.

amount to an effective remedy had already demonstrated the need for domestic courts to make review more intensive. As is well known, the European Court found that the domestic courts had set the irrationality threshold so high

> that it effectively excluded any consideration by the domestic courts of the question of whether the interference with the applicants' rights answered a pressing social need or was proportionate to the national security and public order aims pursued.[11]

The Court's ruling stood in contrast to some of its earlier judgments that domestic judicial review satisfied Article 13.[12] Together, with the (then imminent) implementation of the HRA, the judgment prompted a domestic reappraisal of whether even 'anxious scrutiny' went far enough. Even if there had been no HRA, however, the ruling in *Smith and Grady* that judicial review was deficient would still have required the domestic courts to develop the grounds of review to satisfy Article 13 in human rights cases.

The second expansionary pressure arises from Article 6 – the right to a fair hearing before an independent and impartial tribunal in determination of criminal charges or civil rights or obligations. Here the picture has been mixed. In some areas of domestic administrative law the influence of Article 6 has been to require reconsideration of long-established standards, for example, a re-working of the 'real danger' test in bias into one of 'real possibility'.[13] It strengthens the trend towards an emerging duty to give reasons for decisions[14], although the courts have yet to find that the effect of the HRA is to create a general duty[15], and the common law will already require reasons in situations where under Article 6 where the Strasbourg court would not consider there was a civil right or obligation.[16] However, in other fields arguments based on Article 6 have yet to reach their full potential: for example, the Court of Appeal has found no apparent bias or violation of Article 6 where a member of a Mental Health Review Tribunal was employed by the same Health Trust that ran the hospital where the applicant was detained.[17]

---

[11] *Smith and Grady v UK* (2000) 29 EHRR 413, para 138.

[12] Notably *Soering v UK* (1989) EHRR 439 and *Vilvarajah v UK* (1991) 14 EHRR 248.

[13] See *Porter v Magill* [2002] AC 357.

[14] *Stefan v General Medical Council* [1999] 1 WLR 1293, 1301 (Lord Clyde). In a number of cases after implementation of the HRA Art 6 has been cited in support of the duty to give reasons: *R v Crown Court at Canterbury ex p Howson-Ball* [2001] Env LR 36; *Anya v University of Oxford* [2001] EWCA Civ 405 [2001] ELR 711, at [12].

[15] *Gupta v General Medical Council* [2001] UKPC 61; [2002] 1 WLR 1691; *Moran v DPP* [2002] EWHC 89 (Admin).

[16] *R (Wooler) v Fegetter* [2002] EWCA Civ 554; [2003] QB 219 (Sedley LJ), at [46].

[17] *R (PD) v West Midlands and North West Mental Health Review Tribunal* [2004] EWCA Civ 311. Contrast *R (Brooke) v Parole Board* [2007] EWHC 2036 (Admin) in which the parole board was found to lack the required independence and impartiality.

Article 6 also has implications for the remedies available in judicial review. In *Kingsley v UK*[18] the Strasbourg court held that Article 6 had been violated by the process under which the Gaming Board had denied the applicant a licence, when the High Court had quashed an initial determination by the Board and remitted it to the Board to re-determine.[19] This aspect of the procedure is a routine feature of administrative law and follows from the fact that the court is a forum for review, not appeal. Nevertheless, the European Court held that Kingsley was denied a fair hearing by an impartial tribunal since the body to which his case was returned was identical in composition to the one which had already found against him. *Kingsley* has, however, yet to make any discernible impact on domestic law and has been cited only occasionally by domestic courts and then in support of the proposition that where a court is able to quash a flawed decision and remit it back to an unbiased decision-maker Article 6 is satisfied.

More attention has been paid, however, to the issue of whether judicial review is capable of correcting deficiencies in administrative processes for determining a person's 'civil rights' that lack the necessary quality of independence and impartiality required under Article 6. The Strasbourg court has stated in *Albert and Le Compte v Belgium* that trial by an independent and impartial tribunal requires that

> either the jurisdictional organs themselves comply with the requirements of article 6(1), or they do not so comply but are subject to subsequent control by a judicial body that has full jurisdiction and does provide the guarantees of article 6(1).[20]

In a series of cases, but especially two prominent House of Lords decisions[21], the issue has been whether domestic courts have 'full jurisdiction' and whether the scope of judicial review is adequate to meet this standard.

Spanning these concerns, the central issue in debate concerning the standard of review after the HRA has been how to reconcile the more demanding standards of the ECHR where the proportionality test applies within the tradition in English administrative law of deference to the executive. Proportionality had been mooted as an emerging standard of

---

[18] *Kingsley v UK* (2000) 29 EHRR 493; see I Leigh, 'Bias, Necessity and the Convention' [2002] *Public Law* 407–414.

[19] See also *Tsfayo v UK (Application no 60860/00)*, European Court of Human Rights, 14 November 2006.

[20] 5 EHRR 533, para 29.

[21] *R (Alconbury Developments Ltd.) v Secretary of State for the Environment, Transport and Regions* [2001] 2 WLR 1389; *Begum (Runa) v Tower Hamlets LBC* [2003] UKHL 5; [2003] 2 WLR 388.

judicial review as far back as the GCHQ decision.[22] However, Lord Lowry identified the dangers in *Brind* when he stated that to adopt proportionality would leave very little space between conventional judicial review doctrine, emphasizing the supervisory nature of the court's task, and the forbidden approach of appellate review.

As we shall see this conundrum has largely framed the post-HRA debate over the standard of review among academics and in the courts themselves. First, however, we turn to the question of which bodies should be bound by the Act.

THE RANGE OF REVIEW

Section 6 of the HRA of the makes it unlawful for a 'public authority' to act in a way that is incompatible with a person's Convention rights. The question of what constitutes a 'public authority' is obviously of crucial importance in determining the breadth of the application of this duty and, conversely, the protection given by it to individuals. A number of entities straddle the public/private frontier, such as privatised utilities or charities performing functions for the benefit of the public or in receipt of state funding. As might be expected a number of human rights enthusiasts argue for a wide interpretation of 'public authority' so as to maximise the field of application of the Act. We shall contend, however, that this strategy is ambiguous in terms of human rights protection. A more sophisticated appreciation of what protecting rights involves leads, we shall argue, to a more nuanced approach to defining 'public authorities' subject to section 6.

The definition of public authorities was one issue that was discussed extensively in the parliamentary debates on the Act.[23] The failure to resolve it decisively in Parliament has led to a series of challenges in the courts about whether the Act applies to particular types of bodies.

The government's intention was that there should be two categories of 'public authorities' under section 6[24]: bodies which are for all purposes within the reach of the section (described in later cases as 'core' public authorities); and those which are covered only for limited areas of their work ('hybrid authorities'). The latter category − 'any person, certain of whose functions are functions of a public nature' (s 6(3)(c)) − does not fall under the section 'in relation to a particular act', 'if the nature of the act is

---

[22] *Council of Civil Service Unions v Minister for the Civil Service* [1985] AC 374, 410 (Lord Diplock).
[23] Eg, *HL Debs*, vol 594 cols 1231 ff, 16 November 1997; HL Debs, 24 November 1997, cols 758 ff; HC Debs, 16 February 1998, cols 780 ff, vol 306.
[24] HL Debs, 3 November 1997, vol. 301 col. 1232 (Lord Irvine); HC Debs, 17 June 1998, vol. 314 cols 406 ff (Jack Straw MP).

private' (s 6(5)).[25] The Act gives no further elucidation of public functions or private acts and, regrettably, the Government repeatedly refused to amend the legislation to delineate either category more clearly.

Clarity could have been brought either by listing the relevant bodies or the relevant criteria to be considered by the courts in drawing the public/private divide. A list would have needed frequent amendment, but this approach has the great virtue of deliberate consideration and certainty. Judicial tests in this area, on the other hand, tend to be indistinct and to develop incrementally – leaving charitable bodies especially vulnerable to costly litigation over whether the HRA should apply to them. The practical difficulties in compiling such a list are greatly over-stated. In a comparable legislative reform – the Freedom of Information Act 2000 – ministers opted for a comprehensive list of which bodies were subject to the new duties[26] and there are other examples of the same approach.[27]

By choosing not to list 'hybrid' public authorities under the HRA the Government was virtually inviting a sequel to the litigation over the public/private boundary which had dominated judicial review for the previous two decades.[28] The Home Secretary stated that the problem had been given careful scrutiny in Cabinet Committee and that the decision was a calculated one, with the intention of leaving the matter to the courts, in the expectation that the judicial review case law on 'public functions' would be used – (which he described as 'reasonably clear').[29] However, this last assertion was decidedly dubious at the time because of notorious inconsistencies in the then existing judicial review case law.[30] As we shall see, the confusion has only been compounded by post-HRA developments. In an early sign of the problems ahead the Lord Chancellor changed his

[25] Cf New Zealand Bill of Rights Act 1990 s 3, referring to: 'any person or body in performance of any public function, power, or duty conferred or imposed on that person or body by or pursuant to law'. Held in *R v H* [1994] 2 NZLR 143, 147–148 (Richardson J) to apply to an informer who supplies information to the police repeatedly and at their instigation about his employer: employee's actions had the status 'governmental action' which were, therefore, subject to s 21 of the Bill of Rights Act (preventing unreasonable search and seizure).

[26] Freedom of Information Act 2000 Sch 1. In *YL v Birmingham CC* [2007] UKHL 27, [106], Lord Mance used the absence of private care providers from the 2000 Act's list and the distinction under that Act between bodies designated because of their public functions and bodies providing functions under a contract with a public authority (s 5) as a supporting reason why private care providers acting under contract should not be treated as public authorities under the HRA.

[27] See House of Commons (Disqualification) Act 1975 Sch 1; Parliamentary Commissioner Act 1967 Sch 2; the Cabinet Office also has a comprehensive listing of public bodies to which ministers make appointments.

[28] D Oliver, *Common Law Values and the Public-Private Divide* (London, Butterworths, 1999).

[29] HC Deb, vol 314, col 409–10 (17 June 1998).

[30] Contrast *R v Panel on Takeovers and Mergers ex p Datafin* [1987] QB. 815 with *R v Disciplinary Committee of the Jockey Club ex p Aga Khan* [1993] 2 All ER. 853.

mind during the parliamentary debates over whether the Press Complaints Commission would be treated as a public authority.[31]

As so often in real life, the inevitable happened. A series of cases before the courts have produced an inconsistent set of standards over which bodies the Act applies to and in respect of what functions. The Law Society and the Solicitors' Disciplinary Tribunal were held to be public authorities[32] but Lloyds of London was held not to be.[33] A housing association was held to be a public authority[34], as were the managers of a private psychiatric hospital accepting referrals from health authorities[35], but a charitable foundation offering residential care was held not to be.[36] A private company that had been set up by the council under statutory authority was held to be a public authority[37], particularly since the company had stepped into the shoes of the council and the council given assistance to the company. On the other hand, a statutory body of the established church (the parochial church council) has been held not to be a public authority.[38]

Even the apparently straightforward question of whether a body is a 'core' public authority has proved difficult at times. In the *Wallbank* case[39] the Court of Appeal held that a Parochial Church Council of the Church of England was a core public authority. The Court referred to the 'unique status'[40] of the Church of England in law, and the special position within it of the PCC. The PCC was a body corporate under statutory powers (a

---

[31]   He initially advised that the PCC would not be a public authority but later revised that opinion: *The Times*, 2 Dec, 1997. The Home Secretary expressed the considered view that the PCC would be public authority: HC Debs, vol 314, col. s 414 (17 June 1998). See also *R v Press Complaints Commission ex p Stewart-Brady*, *The Times* 18 November, 1996, CA. Post-HRA it has been left open whether the PCC is a public authority under the Act: *R (Ford) v PCC*, 31 July 2001 (unreported).

[32]   *Pine v Law Society* [2001] EWCA Civ 1574; [2002] UKHRR 81.

[33]   *R (West) v Lloyd's of London* [2004] EWCA Civ 506; [2004] 3 All ER 251.

[34]   *Poplar Housing and Regeneration Community Association Limited v Donoghue* [2001] EWCA Civ 595; [2001] 3 WLR 183.

[35]   *R (A) v Partnerships in Care Ltd* [2002] EWHC 529 (Admin) [2002] 1 WLR 2610.

[36]   *R v Leonard Cheshire Foundation & anr ex p Heather* [2002] EWCA Civ 366.

[37]   *Hampshire County Council v Graham Beer (T/A Hammer Trout Farm)* [2003] EWCA Civ 1056; [2004] 1 WLR 233.

[38]   *Aston Cantlow and Wilmcote with Billesley Parochial Church Council v Wallbank* [2003] UKHL 37; [2003] 3 WLR 283

[39]   [2001] 3 WLR 1323. The case involved a challenge to the liability of a 'lay rector' at common law to pay for repairs to the chancel of the Parish Church: an obscure duty arising from the status of glebe lands. The Court of Appeal found that enforcement of this liability would infringe the defendants' right to the peaceful enjoyment of their possessions, contrary to Art 1 of the First Protocol to the ECHR, and, because it singled out for liability the owners of what was once glebe land, in violation of Art 14. See I Leigh, 'Freedom of Religion: Public/Private, Rights/Wrongs' in M Hill (ed), *Religious Liberty and Human Rights* (Cardiff, University of Wales Press, 2002) ch 6, 149–152; D Oliver, Chancel Repairs and the Human Rights Act' (2001) *PL* 651.

[40]   *Ibid*, 1331 (para 31); and see *Marshall v Graham* [1907] 2 KB 112, 226.

'measure'), exercised by the Assembly of the Church of England.[41] Two aspects stood out: the PCC 'possesses powers which private individuals do not possess to determine how others should act'[42] and 'it is created and empowered by law'.[43]

This conclusion contradicted, however, the Home Secretary's statement in Parliament during debates on the Bill that some functions of a Parochial Church Council were private in nature[44], which presupposed that, at the most, the PCC was a *hybrid* rather than a core public authority. Moreover, the Court of Appeal's ruling contradicted Convention jurisprudence to the effect that even Established churches were non-governmental in nature (and so were capable of bringing a Convention complaint[45]). Consequently the decision was given in apparent neglect of the possible position of the Church as a Convention 'victim', with what Lord Nicholls subsequently described the 'extraordinary conclusion'[46] of depriving the PCC of its collective right of freedom of religion.

The House of Lords, much exercised by the argument that a core public authority could not enjoy Convention rights,[47] reversed this finding.[48] Several of their Lordships attempted to bridge the gap between the domestic statutory test and the Convention[49] by eliding 'public' functions with 'governmental' functions.[50] Lord Nicholls cited government departments, local authorities, the police and the armed forces as examples of core public authorities. He pointed to a number of distinguishing characteristics:

[41] *Ibid*, 1331–2 (para 32), referring to the Parochial Church Councils (Powers) Measure 1956 (as amended) s 3, made under the Church of England Assembly (Powers) Act 1919.

[42] The emphasis on distinctive legal powers mirrored the test of an 'emanation of the state' for the purposes of identifying which bodies are bound by European directives: *Foster v British Gas* [1990] 3 All ER 897, ECJ. Applied by the Court of Appeal in *National Union of Teachers and Others v Governing Body of St Mary's Church of England Junior School* [1997] 3 CMLR 630 to rule that a Church of England school which had voluntary aided status was an emanation of the State.

[43] *Ibid*, 1333, paras 34 and 35.

[44] HC Debs, col. 1015, 20 May 1998, The Court of Appeal refused to consider the Parliamentary debates under the rule in *Pepper v Hart*, claiming that the expression 'public authority' was not ambiguous or obscure: 1331 (para 29).

[45] *Holy Monasteries v Greece* (1995) 20 EHRR 1; *Hauanemi v Sweden* (1996) 22 EHRR CD 155.

[46] *Wallbank* [2003] UKHL 37; [2004] 1 AC 546, para 15.

[47] And see: H Davies, 'Public Authorities as "Victims" under the Human Rights Act' (2005) 64 *CLJ* 315.

[48] *Wallbank* [2003] UKHL 37; [2004] 1 AC 546. See further 00 below.

[49] Art 34 allows 'non-governmental' organisations to complain under the Convention machinery as victims. See further: *Holy Monasteries v Greece* (1995) 20 EHRR 1; *Affaire Radio France v France*, E Ct HR, App No 53984/00 (discussed by H Quane, The Strasbourg Jurisprudence and the Meaning of a "Public Authority" under the Human Rights Act' [2006] *PL* 106 at 117 ff.).

[50] *Wallbank*, para 10 (Lord Nicholls), para 159 (Lord Rodgers), and para 47 (Lord Hope, 'governmental organisations').

the possession of special powers, democratic accountability, public funding in whole or in part, an obligation to act only in the public interest, and a statutory constitution.[51]

That the Church of England exercised *some* governmental functions (for example running church schools, and conducting marriage services) did not give it in general the character of a governmental organisation.[52] As Lord Hope pointed out it was not part of government and the State had not surrendered or delegated to the Church any of its powers.[53] In addition to finding that the PCC was not a core public authority, a majority of their Lordships found, that in enforcing liability for chancel repairs on a landowner, the Parochial Church Council was not exercising a public function and so was not, in this respect, acting as a 'hybrid' public authority either.[54]

Across the cases as a whole the courts have proposed a variety of tests for identifying a public authority. These include the extent to which in carrying out the function in question the body is publicly funded, exercising statutory powers, taking the place of central or local government, or providing a public service.[55] On closer scrutiny, however, none of these is a bright line. 'Providing a public service' is obviously circular. Public funding will often be question of degree and can range from situations where a small level of grant funding is state-provided to those where all but a small portion of the body's funds come from public sources. Whether a body 'stands in the shoes' of government may be clear where an activity has been privatised (ie transferred from public to private control) but much less so in the case of self-regulation where professional standards have been imposed by a disciplinary body, for example, to assuage demands for legislative intervention in the public interest. Even statutory recognition can be variable where a body is *licensed* to conduct the function in question or where statute parallels a power that could be created by private agreement. Judges have been forced to admit that there is 'no single test'[56] and that what is at stake is a 'combination of factors ... the decision is very much one of fact and degree'.[57]

The relevance of Convention jurisprudence to the issue is problematic.[58] The Government rejected an amendment designed to replicate the Strasbourg jurisprudence in determining which bodies the Convention should

---

[51] *Wallbank*, para 7. And see Lord Hobhouse, para 86, arguing that the PCC acted in sectional rather than the public interest.

[52] *Wallbank*, para 3.

[53] *Wallbank* para 62

[54] Lord Scott dissenting.

[55] *Wallbank*, para 12 (Lord Nicholls).

[56] *Wallbank*, para 11 (Lord Nicholls).

[57] *Poplar Housing*, paras 65–66.

[58] H Quane, op. cit..

apply to.[59] This would have applied the test adopted under the Convention itself ie section 6 would only have applied if the UK would have been liable for the action of the body concerned if a complaint were made in Strasbourg.[60] Consequently, there would have been no risk of a gap emerging between Strasbourg and HRA liability: the reach of section 6 would have adjusted automatically with developments in the Strasbourg jurisprudence.[61] Moreover, there would have been symmetry with the position of applicants, who may only apply if they would qualify as victims under the Convention machinery.[62] So far as the courts are concerned, formally decisions on the scope of 'non-governmental' organisations are *not* within the scope of the duty to 'take account' (HRA section 2) since Article 34 is not among the 'Convention rights' incorporated. However, that did not prevent their Lordships in *Wallbank* from referring to it and it is arguable that there is a extant common law duty to adhere to the Convention in instances of statutory ambiguity, irrespective of the HRA.[63] In practice the House of Lords in *Wallbank* achieved the same effect and closed the door on the possibility that the domestic courts would give an extended reading to 'public authority' so as to include what Strasbourg would treat as non-governmental bodies under Article 34. The same concerns influenced the majority of the House in *YL v Birmingham CC*.

In an analysis of the Convention jurisprudence Helen Quane has concluded that the European Court of Human Rights tends

> to focus on the status of the body, its rights/powers, the nature of its functions, the context in which it performs them and whether it is subject to state supervision.[64]

---

[59] HC Debs, vol 314, cols 419 ff. (17 June 1998).

[60] The expression 'public authority' appears only in Art 8(2) of the Convention, but the issue of which bodies a state should be liable for has been raised in other contexts; see, eg, *Costello-Roberts v UK* (1993) 19 EHRR 112, under Art 3, 8 and Protocol 1, Art 2; and *Appleby v UK* (2003) 37 EHRR 38 (rejecting an argument under Art 10). In *YL v Birmingham CC* [2007] UKHL 27 Lord Mance distilled two relevant principles from the Strasbourg jurisprudence: 'First, the State may in some circumstances be responsible for failure to take positive steps to regulate or control the activities of private persons where there will otherwise be a direct and immediate adverse impact on a person's Convention protected interests. Second, the State may in some circumstances remain responsible for the conduct of private law institutions to which it has delegated state powers. The case law does not always distinguish clearly between these principles, (para 92).

[61] If the HRA merely applied to bodies whose actions attracted Convention liability, there would, however, be a significant difference as a result of incorporation- instead of the vicarious liability of the government in a distant international tribunal, public authorities themselves would be liable for breach of Convention rights and for payment of compensation.

[62] S 7, discussed below.

[63] *R v Secretary of State for the Home Department ex p Brind* [1991] 1 AC 696 (HL) requires that statutory ambiguity (here, concerning the meaning of 'public authority' in HRA s 6) should be resolved in a Convention-friendly manner.

[64] Quane, op. cit., 121.

Institutional autonomy from the state has tended to outweigh the presence of state funding or public law status as a factor in weighing against a finding of governmental status. However, as with the domestic law, no one test predominates.

Identifying a 'public authority', it seems, is much like elephant-spotting: you know one when you see it. This confusion has led to calls for early clarification from the Joint Parliamentary Committee on Human Rights.[65] Their report on public authorities and the academic discussion of the judicial decisions suggests that are two distinct issues of principle that merit discussion: privatisation or contracting-out and the position of the voluntary sector. We consider each briefly in turn.

Privatisation

The failure of multi-national companies to observe human rights norms is a prevalent theme in much writing about globalisation. In the same way in more small-scale debates about privatisation workers and service users are often depicted as losing hard-won rights to capitalists intent on achieving ruthless economies. In this context the application of the HRA (or its extension) to former public utilities or services assumes political importance as a means of providing a safety net of public service standards.

It is against that ideological background that Jack Straw's claim, made as Home Secretary, that the Act extended the reach of human rights protection beyond a minimal notion of the state should be taken.[66] The White Paper had referred only by way of example 'to the extent that they are exercising public functions, companies responsible for areas of activity which were previously within the public sector, such as the privatised utilities'.[67] In Parliamentary debates some examples were given by the Home Secretary of potential hybrid authorities exercising mixed public and private functions: the Royal National Lifeboat Institute (charitable work private), Railtrack plc (commercial contracts private), Group 4 plc (private company, but acting as a public authority when running prison), the City Takeover and Mergers Panel and the General Medical Council (professional regulatory functions public) and the British Board of Film Classification.[68]

As this list makes clear there is wide variety of situations in which non-government organisations may exercise public functions, ranging from instances where a private company delivers services or functions under

[65] The Joint HR Committee report, *The Meaning of Public Authority under the Human Rights Act* (2003–04), HL 39/ HC 382.
[66] HC Debs, vol 314, col. 406 (17 June 1998).
[67] *Rights Brought Home*, para 2.2.
[68] HC Debs, vol 314, cols 407–413 (17 June 1998).

contract for which the government is responsible (contracting out) to instances where the state has co-opted or recognised the work of professional regulatory or charitable bodies. A great deal of later confusion has resulted from failing to delineate these different categories more clearly.

So far as contracting out is concerned, the Government clearly intended that the HRA would apply. Otherwise, as critics point out, the force of Act could be diluted by privatisation.[69] It is misleading, however, to suggest that the effect of contracting out is to *evade* liability under section 6, since core public authorities would remain liable so far as public functions are concerned (ie statutory responsibilities) despite the chosen method of discharging the function through a commercial arrangement. For example, the responsibilities of the Prison Service to prisoners in its care remain irrespective of whether a prison is operated by a private company and the company's actions may be imputed to the Prison Service as its agent.[70] In such situations a prudent public authority will impose as a condition on contractors to ensure human rights compliance. This procedure, however, would leave the service user whose rights are to be protected as a stranger to the arrangement, effectively barred under the doctrine of privity of contract from enforcing their human rights directly against the contractor responsible for service delivery. The only remedy would be to bring proceedings against the statutory authority for the failings of its contractor. Nevertheless, the service user should not be disadvantaged as a result except in the sense that the legal responsibilities may be opaque at first sight.[71]

The House of Lords faced a number of these issues in an appeal raising the question of whether the HRA applied to a private residential care home housing an 84-year old woman with Alzheimer's disease under an arrangement with the local council. In *YL v Birmingham CC* the House held by a majority that a private care home in which the appellant was placed under arrangements with a local authority was not performing functions of a public nature and consequently was not a hybrid public authority under the HRA.[72] The majority stressed that the company was a private, profit-making entity that made contractual arrangements both with private paying

---

[69] For a straightforward example see: *Marcic v Thames Water Utilities Ltd* [2001] 3 All ER 698 (privatised water company a public body). For further discussion of the issue: K Markus [2003] *EHRLR* 92; M Sunkin, 'Pushing Forward the Frontiers of Human Rights Protection: The Meaning of Public Authority under the Human Rights Act' [2004] *PL* 643; P Craig, 'Contracting Out, the Human Rights Act and the Scope of Judicial Review' (2002) 118 *LQR* 551.

[70] For a somewhat unsatisfactory rejection of a comparable argument in relation to a residential care home acting on behalf of a local authority: *R v Servite Houses and LB of Wandsworth Council ex p Goldsmith and Chatting* (2000) 2 LGR 997 (discussed by Craig, op. cit., at 561 ff.).

[71] Cf Lord Neuberger in *YL v Birmingham CC* [2007] UKHL 27, para 149.

[72] [2007] UKHL 27, Lords Scott, Mance and Neuberger; Lord Bingham and Baroness Hale dissenting.

residents and with the council in the case of publicly-funded residents. To apply the HRA to the latter group would be to create an anomaly: those paying for themselves in a private home would have fewer rights than residents in the same home accommodated at public expense.[73] For Lord Bingham and Lady Hale, dissenting, it was the state's assumption of responsibility for vulnerable people under the National Assistance Act 1948 that was decisive. The precise way in which that responsibility was discharged – whether by providing the care itself or arranging it through a private provider (as in this case) – was immaterial. The Parliamentary Joint Committee on Human Rights agreed with the dissenting opinions and has welcomed a ministerial commitment to extend the Act to private care homes.[74]

Where it might seem more plausible to argue that 'contracting out' avoids HRA claims is in the case of functions that would be treated as private in nature. Core public authorities are bound by section 6(1) the Act in respect of all functions whereas hybrid authorities will not be bound as regards their private functions. Consequently, if such an activity is transferred from a core public authority the Act will no longer apply.[75] In these instances there would be *notional* human rights liability when they are performed by 'core' public authorities but none in the hands of contractors. The phrase 'notional liability' is used deliberately, however: in many instances there would be no HRA remedy in fact because, on closer examination, no enforceable Convention rights arise even against a core public authority. This is so, for example, with state employees, who, having freely chosen their employment, can rarely invoke the Convention against their employers.[76]

In these cases nothing of substance is lost by denying such claim at an earlier stage because of the absence of a public authority. Quite the reverse: a great deal of time and effort is saved by avoiding the near-theological debates about the nature of a non-governmental body as a prelude to the relatively straightforward dismissal of a Convention rights claim.

In a slightly different context the *Poplar Housing Association* case[77] illustrates the point graphically: it is clear that a tenant who faces eviction

---

[73]   Lord Mance (para 117), Lord Neuberger (para 151).

[74]   *Eighteenth Report for 2006–7, The Human Rights of Older People in Healthcare*, HL 156-I/ HC 378-I, paras 159–161.

[75]   Note, however the comments of Lord Scott in *YL v Birmingham CC* [2007] UKHL 27 (at para 30) that this 'proves too much': 'If every contracting out by a local authority of a function that the local authority could, in exercise of a statutory power or the discharge of a statutory duty, have carried out itself, turns the contractor into a hybrid public authority for section 6(3)(b) purposes, where does this end? Is a contractor engaged by a local authority to provide lifeguard personnel at the municipal swimming pool a section 6(3)(b) public authority?'.

[76]   Eg, *Kalaç v Turkey* (1997) 27 EHRR 522; *Ahmed v UK* (2000) 29 EHRR 1.

[77]   140 above.

for non-payment of rent will be unable to successfully invoke the Article 8 right to respect for his home against his landlord.[78] Knowing that, there was little to gain from extended legal argument about whether the Housing Association in question was a public authority (the Court of Appeal held that it was but went on dismiss the Article 8 claim). This is precisely the type of unnecessary and costly litigation that was foreseeable and avoidable had section 6 been drafted better.

The Voluntary Sector

In situations in which not-for-profit bodies are enmeshed in a system of social welfare provision together with public bodies, more complex issues arise. This is typically the case in fields such as residential care for the vulnerable or elderly, childcare, adoption and fostering, social housing and so on. The policy argument for treating such bodies as public authorities rests in part on *equality*: the rights of a person using a service under public control may otherwise vary according to whether the provider is a voluntary body or a state one.

The Joint Parliamentary Committee on Human Rights has advanced a similar argument in suggesting that where the state has 'assumed responsibility' for an area of policy that the bodies concerned with delivery should be treated as public authorities under section 6.[79] While this gives a satisfying rationale for including professional and sporting self-regulatory associations, the argument is less convincing in the case of voluntary service providers.

In their case it is misleading to characterise any such differences as 'evading' the HRA. In some instances these voluntary bodies have been continuously involved in providing social welfare services before the state assumed *any role* in the field. Frequently voluntary bodies operated historically with a particular religious or social ethos. It is for discussion whether the price of assisting the state in the modern era within a varied economy of care should be human rights compliance. The very notion of civil society implies a degree of freedom for such groups to take their own distinctive approaches. While this could be recognised by reconciling their own rights under the Convention (including under Article 11 of the European Convention)[80] with those of service users[81], it is more straightforward to follow the Strasbourg approach and treat voluntary bodies as

---

[78] Even were Art 8 to apply protection of the landlord's interests will obviously fall under Art 8(2).

[79] Cf Lord Bingham and Lady Hale, dissenting, in *YL v Birmingham CC*.

[80] See, eg, the High Court ruling that Art 11 included the right of the RSPCA to refuse membership to potential applicants who the society thought might damage its objectives (including those seeking to reverse its stance against hunting with dogs) and that such

not subject to the Convention in the first place, because of their non-governmental status.

If, as will often be the case, the Convention would not apply according to the Strasbourg jurisprudence, far from 'evading' liability, to bring these bodies under the Act would be to *extend* it. Is this not, however, precisely the type of far-sighted application of human rights in which British judges should give the lead?[82] Not necessarily: the difficulty is that to bring non-state bodies within the Convention framework may risk re-balancing their rights in a way that diminishes their independence and distinctiveness and assimilates them to the position of state actors. This is because the limitations to rights under which any such balancing would take place (typically Articles. 8 (2), 9(2), 10(2) and 11(2)) have been framed with classic state actors in mind.

The debate about the reach of section 6 exposes several underlying issues about human rights and the state. As Quane argues:

> an over-inclusive approach (to 'public authorities') risks giving horizontal effect to the HRA and undermining the legitimacy and moral authority inherent in human rights claims, while an under-inclusive approach risks undermining the effective implementation of Act.[83]

Those who argue for an extended approach point to the fragmented nature of modern governance and the effect of privatisation in particular.[84] Some, however, would clearly go further and regard voluntary sector providers of social services as exercising a form of power over vulnerable people who have effectively no choice but to use their services.[85]

On the other, hand, advocates of a narrower approach do so within a liberal understanding that limiting the concept of the state allows space for the private sphere and for civil society.[86] This does not imply a human-rights-free zone. Rather it is a recognition that many of the virtues of

---

applicants had no countervailing right of freedom of expression which demanded admittance: *RSPCA v A-G and others*, [2001] ALL ER (D) 188, Lightman J.

[81]   Cf Baroness Hale at [74] in *YL v Birmingham CC.*

[82]   63ff. above.

[83]   H Quane, 'The Strasbourg Jurisprudence and the Meaning of a 'Public Authority' under the Human Rights Act' [2006] *PL* 106.

[84]   In a second report on the meaning of a public authority, the JCHR, frustrated at the lack of progress in clarifying the issue through litigation, has proposed that Parliament pass a brief interpretative provision. This would make clear that: 'a function of a public nature includes a function performed pursuant to a contract or other arrangement with a public authority which is under a duty to perform the function.' See Parliamentary Joint Committee on Human Rights, *The Meaning of Public Authority Under the Human Rights Act, Ninth Report for 2006–07*, HL 77/HC 410, para 150.

[85]   M Sunkin, Pushing Forward the Frontiers of Human Rights Protection: The Meaning of Public Authority under the Human Rights Act' [2004] *PL* 643, 652.

[86]   Professor Dawn Oliver argues for a minimal test of whether a function is public – whether it involves the exercise of coercive power or special authority that would otherwise

private and voluntary sectors depend on recognising *their own* rights to be free of the State. In part this independence is conceived in legally expressible human rights, notably freedom of association, of religion, thought and belief and of speech. When these are taken into consideration it becomes clear that to advance the human rights of service recipients will often be to deny other human rights of private and voluntary sector bodies. On this view human rights protection is not an unqualified good that is maximised by spreading it as far and wide as possible, thus broadening the definition of a public authority. Rather, it has an *optimum* level, inherent in the Convention's origins as a system of protection against the state. To speak of human rights against non-state bodies risks seriously devaluing the currency or, to switch metaphors, spreading the jam too thinly.

Leaving the question of which bodies the Act should apply to we return now to the question of *how* it should apply.

THE STANDARD OF REVIEW: PARAMETERS OF THE DEBATE

Controversy over the appropriate standard of review under the HRA has presented a variety of possible approaches. At the one pole it is clear that the courts have manifestly *not* treated the HRA as a constitutional springboard from which to launch into 'merits review'. That remains the 'forbidden' appellate or substitutionary method.[87] The explanation for this diffidence does *not* lie with the text of the Act itself, which is enigmatic:

6 (1) It is unlawful for a public authority to act in a way which is incompatible with one or more of the Convention rights.

(2) Subsection (1) does not apply to an act if –

(a) as the result of one or more provisions of primary legislation, the authority could not have acted differently; or

(b) in the case of one or more provisions of, or made under, primary legislation which cannot be read or given effect in a way which is compatible with the Convention rights, the, the authority was acting so as to give effect to or enforce those provisions.

The White Paper gave no clue as to the Government's intentions concerning the standard of review[88] and, strikingly, there has been virtually no parliamentary or judicial analysis or commentary of the text, before or since enactment.

be unlawful at common law: D Oliver, 'Functions of a Public Nature under the Human Rights Act' [2004] *PL* 329, 345.

[87] *R v Secretary of State for the Home Department ex p Brind* [1991] 1 AC 696, 767 (Lord Lowry).

[88] *Rights Brought Home* Cm 3782 (1997) paras 2.2–2.6 are silent on the issue.

This apparently leaves the door open to a court that wished to resort to 'hard-edged' review. Several arguments could justify such an approach.[89] A court could emphasise the surprisingly strong wording of section 6(1) and treat it as a duty on public authorities not to breach a person's Convention rights, unless compelled to do so by primary legislation. Such an approach would treat the Act as differentiating sharply between deference to Parliament (which is explicitly maintained by section 6(2)) in contrast to the treatment of the executive. The Act would then be treated as a legislative mandate to abandon judicial deference to the executive, which could only then be maintained so far as the Convention itself permitted limitations to rights under the proportionality doctrine in the case of qualified rights.[90] Support for this viewpoint comes from the text of section 6 itself: which makes it *unlawful* for a public authority to *act* in contravention of a person's Convention rights. Elsewhere Lord Bingham has remarked that the HRA 'gives the courts a very specific, wholly democratic, mandate'.[91]

Further support comes from the architecture of the Act, which applies the same provision (section 6(1)) to both courts and the executive as different types of 'public authority', without making any differentiation in the standard to be applied. This can be seen to call into question the distinction between appeal and review. Since there would be no question of 'deference' to a lower court that acted contrary to section 6[92], it can be argued that an equally rigorous approach should be applied when the actions of other public bodies are under review under section 6.

Such arguments have drawn only occasional support from the judiciary in the first few years' operation of the Act. As we shall see, isolated dicta can be cited in which judges treat the Act as expanding review for error of law or refer to proportionality as a question of law. Remarkably – and in almost exact reprise of the parliamentary debates – when the courts have scrutinised section 6(1) it has been to consider the definition of a public authority.[93] With one exception they have shown studied disinterest in the remainder of the wording. In practice the section 6(1) standard has been treated as requiring no elucidation and few judgments engage in any analysis of whether the text of the Act has any bearing on the standard of review.

---

[89] See further: I Leigh, 'Taking Rights Proportionately: Judicial Review, the Human Rights Act and Strasbourg' [2002] *PL* 265–287.

[90] M Taggart, 'Tugging on Superman's Cape: Lessons from Experience with the New Zealand Bill of Rights Act 1990' in The University of Cambridge Centre for Public Law, *Constitutional Reform in the United Kingdom: Practice and Principles* (Oxford, Hart Publishing, 1998) 85, 92 .

[91] *A v Secretary of State for the Home Department* [2005] AC 68, at para 42.

[92] *A-G's Reference No 2 of 2001* [2003] UKHL 68, 'I cannot accept that it can ever be proper for a court … to act in a manner which a statute (here, section 6 of the Human Rights Act) declares to be unlawful' (Lord Bingham of Cornhill), at [30].

[93] 140 ff above.

A rare exception occurs in the dissenting speech of Lord Hope in *Attorney-General's Reference No 2 of 2001*[94]. There he points to the differences between the Scotland Act 1998 which makes violation of Convention rights by members of the executive (including prosecutors) a *vires* question, and the HRA, which uses the term 'unlawful'.[95] The crucial difference in his lordship's view is twofold. First, under section 6 'the act is unlawful only against the victim' and not 'all the world'. Secondly, there is no *entitlement* to a remedy: under section 8(1) the court may grant such relief or remedy within its powers as it considers just and appropriate. 'Unless the act (or proposed act) is 'unlawful' the court has no jurisdiction under the Act to provide a remedy'[96] but there is not an automatic remedy for each unlawful act. This reasoning makes a good deal of sense in relation to central government, where the powers are not in total derived from statute in the same way as the Scottish executive. However, other public authorities, notably local authorities, are fully creatures of statute. It is doubtful whether the discretionary nature of public law remedies[97] generally dilutes the standard of review in their case[98] and, if not, it begs the question why unlawfulness under the HRA should be regarded as exceptional.

Lord Hope's comments apart, the prevailing judicial silence on this issue is curious and appears to indicate a strong judicial consensus that the Act was not intended to usher in 'merits review'.

If section 6 has not be seen as requiring radical change in the standard of review, it is true, on the other hand, that the conservative position that it requires no change has drawn little support. According to this view the common law had already made the necessary adjustments in advance of the HRA coming into force – the 'anxious scrutiny' or modified *Wednesbury* test acting as a form of innoculation against the Convention virus. Some judges in early decisions emphasised the continuity with pre-HRA review by declaiming that *Wednesbury* and proportionality required fundamentally the same standard of review and that therefore continued deference to the executive was required.[99] The continuity argument involved a rose-tinted view of *Wednesbury* (the European Court of Human Rights had flatly contradicted it by its *Smith and Grady* judgment[100]) and since the House of Lords' decision in *Daly*[101] it is no longer heard.[102] It is

---

[94] [2003] UKHL 68, at paras 73–79. We are grateful to Aidan O'Neill QC for drawing this to our attention. See however, Lord Bingham of Cornhill, at para 30.

[95] *Ibid*, Para 58 and see his speech in *Dyer v Watson* [2002] 3 WLR 1488, 1523, at para 111.

[96] *Ibid*, Para 54.

[97] Remedies are discretionary under the Supreme Court Act s 31(1) also.

[98] I Leigh, *Law, Politics and Local Democracy* (Oxford, OUP, 2000) ch 2.

[99] *R v Secretary of State for the Home Department ex p Isiko, The Times*, 20 February 2001 (Schiemann LJ).

[100] Cf Lord Cooke of Thorndon in *Daly* at para 32.

[101] Discussed in the next section.

clear, however, that the persistence of this mode of thought underlies *Wednesbury*-like formulations of the standard of HRA review that nevertheless surface regularly in the cases.

This has especially been marked in relation to the 'fair balance' test:

> the Court must decide whether a fair balance was struck between the demands of the general interest of the community and the requirements of the protection of the individual's fundamental rights.[103]

The judgment of Moses J in *Ismet Ala v Secretary of State for the Home Department*[104] illustrates how the 'fair balance' test can be used to allow *Wednesbury* to re-enter at the back door[105] by treating the two as virtually indistinguishable. In *Ismet Ala* an ethnic Albanian from Kosovo who had illegally entered the country in 1997 but subsequently married a British citizen, applied for judicial review of the Secretary of State's certification that his human rights claim was manifestly unfounded. He contended that his removal would be disproportionate and an infringement of his rights under Article 8, arguing that no reasonable decision-maker would have concluded that his appeal was bound to fail, and that delay had frustrated his chances of being granted refugee status under the policies prevailing at that time. The application was granted. On appeal, Moses J concluded, in language highly reminiscent of *Wednesbury,* that the adjudicator's task was to decide whether the Secretary of State had 'struck a fair balance between the need for effective immigration control and the claimant's rights under Article 8' or whether minister's decision was 'outwith the range of reasonable responses'.[106] A similar approach in *M v Croatia*[107], where Ouseley J had said the test was whether 'the disproportion is so great that no reasonable Secretary of State could remove [an immigrant] in those

---

[102]   In non-HRA cases the courts continue to use *Wednesbury (eg R (Jones) v Mansfield DC* [2003] EWCA Civ 1408) and the Court of Appeal has held that, although it had difficulty in seeing the justification for retaining the test, only the House of Lords can pronounce it dead: *Association of British Civilian Internees Far Eastern Region v Secretary of State for Defence* [2003] EWCA Civ 473; [2003] 3 WLR 80, [34] (Dyson LJ).

[103]   Dyson LJ in R (*Samaroo) v Secretary of State for the Home Department* [2001] EWCA Civ 1149; (2001) UKHRR 1622 (deciding that deportation would not violate Art 8). The test is taken from *Sporring v Sweden* [1982] 5 EHRR 35, para 69.

[104]   [2003] EWHC 521.

[105]   Cf I Leigh, 'Taking Rights Proportionately: Judicial Review, the Human Rights Act and Strasbourg' [2002] *PL* 265, 276–77.

[106]   *Edore v Secretary of State for the Home Department* [2003] EWCA Civ 716 [44] (Simon Brown LJ): '[T]he mere fact that an alternative but favourable decision could reasonably have been reached will not lead to the conclusion that the decision maker has acted in breach of the claimant's human rights. Such a breach will only occur where the decision is outwith the range of reasonable responses to the question as to where a fair balance lies between the conflicting interests.'

[107]   [2004] INLR 327.

circumstances' and the Secretary of State's own practice should be examined to determine the range of reasonable responses, was subsequently found to be incorrect by the House of Lords in *Huang*.[108]

DISTINGUISHING PROPORTIONALITY FROM *WEDNESBURY*[109]

There is an inherent contradiction between such pronouncements and the dominant post-HRA approach to the standard to review, formulated by Lord Steyn in his speech in *ex p Daly*.[110] There the House of Lords was concerned with the applicability of proportionality in assessing the legality of the policy for searching prisoners' cells. This required staff to examine the prisoner's possessions, including legally privileged correspondence (which was not, however, normally to be read) in his or her absence. Applying the common law of fundamental rights, their Lordships found the policy to be unlawful. However they also concluded, that the same result would also be reached under the HRA applying the Convention.

Lord Steyn, was careful to distinguish proportionality from the modified *Wednesbury* approach and therefore sought to clarify the 'material difference' between the two.[111] The criteria for proportionality were, he argued, 'more precise and more sophisticated'[112] in three respects. It required

> the reviewing court to assess the balance which the decision maker has struck, not merely whether it was within the range of rational or reasonable decisions

and 'may require attention to be directed to the relative weight accorded to interests and considerations.' The third difference concerned the process of reasoning. Taking Article 8 as an example, this required the court to engage with 'the twin requirements that the limitation of the right was necessary in a democratic society, in the sense of meeting a pressing social need, and the question whether the interference was really proportionate to the legitimate aim being pursued'[113], rather than the threshold question for 'anxious scrutiny'. Although using either approach the outcomes would often be the same, sometimes a different conclusion would follow under

---

[108] *Huang v Secretary of State for the Home Department* [2007] UKHL 11; [2007] 2 AC 167.

[109] Mark Elliott, 'Scrutiny of executive Decisions under the HRA 1998: Exactly How Anxious?' [2001] 6 *JR* 166; Andrew Sharland 'The Role of Proportionality in Judicial Review' [1997] JR 81; R Clayton 'Proportionality and the Human Rights Act 1998: Implications for Substantive Review' [2002] *JR* 124; R Clayton 'Regaining a Sense of Proportion: The Human Rights Act and the Proportionality Principle' (2001) 5 EHRLR 504; J Rivers, 'Proportionality and Variable Intensity of Review' (2006) 65 (1) *CLJ*, 174.

[110] *R (Daly) v Secretary of State for the Home Department* [2001] 2 WLR 1622.

[111] Para 26 ff.

[112] Para 27.

[113] Para 27.

proportionality and it was 'therefore important that cases involving Convention rights must be analysed in the correct way'.[114]

While there is no doubt that these comments of Lord Steyn's have emerged as the dominant approach to post-HRA judicial review, there is considerable uncertainty over what they require in any particular context. It is no exaggeration to say that proportionality has attracted widespread support as a legal test largely *because* it can be used with equal force by those wishing to maintain the tradition of deference to the executive *and* by advocates of more intensive review.

On the one hand, Lord Steyn was at pains to point out that proportionality did not equate to merits review. This was in keeping with an emerging academic and professional consensus that the HRA would maintain broad continuity with the tradition of deference. The tasks of judges and administrators would remain distinct. One the other hand, however, his Lordship cited an article by Professor Jeffrey Jowell, which argued that while the Act would not bring about merits review as such, it nevertheless (together with common law decisions on fundamental rights) pointed towards the development of 'constitutional review', requiring judges to justify their decisions in terms of the necessary qualities of a democratic society.[115]

THE NEW APPROACH IN PRACTICE

Substantial Evidence

Traditionally the courts have seen their role within judicial review as secondary, with the consequence that evidential or factual questions are for the 'primary decision-maker' (the public body subject to review) and not for them. In *Daly*, however, Lord Bingham noted the new approach required under the HRA:

> Now ... domestic courts must *themselves* form a judgment whether a convention right has been breached (*conducting such inquiry as is necessary to form that judgment*) and, so far as permissible under the Act, grant an effective remedy.[116]

---

[114] Para 28.
[115] J Jowell, 'Beyond the Rule of Law: Towards Constitutional Judicial Review' [2000] *PL* 671, 682.
[116] *R (Daly) v Secretary of State for the Home Department* [2001] 2 WLR 1622, para 23 (emphasis added).

This passage may imply that this new exercise for the courts requires corresponding changes in *how* they evaluate the effects of the policies and actions of public authorities.[117]

There were some examples of this general approach in relation to qualified rights in early HRA litigation referring to the need for 'objective' or 'substantial' justification for interference with Convention rights[118] but they were quickly over-shadowed as the *Daly* approach became dominant. The clearest instances of this approach, however, are likely to be where the Convention rights are unqualified.[119] In these instances it would be expected that the courts would ask themselves the undiluted question whether the public authority has contravened the applicant's Convention rights in fact.[120] Although some commentators have sought to minimise the difference between the unqualified and qualified Convention rights in this regard[121], the courts can be seen, post-HRA, to be sensitive to the different role that they play in cases of unqualified rights.

The strongest statements to date have come in a decision concerning the need for forcible medical treatment of a medical patient. In *R (Wilkinson) v Broadmoor Special Hospital Authority and others*[122] the Court of Appeal held that it was entitled to reach its own view as to the merits of the medical decision and whether it infringed the patient's human rights.[123] As Simon Brown LJ stated 'the court must inevitably now reach its own view' both of whether the patient was capable of consenting and of whether the proposed treatment would violate Convention rights under Articless 2 or 3, or, in so far as Article 8 was relevant, whether it would be a necessary

---

[117] For discussion of possible procedural changes that may be required see: Leigh and Lustgarten, 'Making Rights Real' 523–6.

[118] *R v Secretary of State for the Home Department ex p Javed and others*, *The Times*, 9 February 2000, affirmed on appeal on different grounds (*Regina (Javed) v Secretary of State for the Home Department and Another* [2001] 3 WLR 323 (CA)); *Farrakhan v SSHD* [2001] EWHC Admin 781 (Turner J) (overturned on appeal *R (Farrakhan) v SSHD* [2002] QB 1391); *R (Mahmood) v Secretary of State for the Home Department*, [2001] 1 WLR 840 (CA), 857 (Lord Phillips MR).

[119] See: Lord Hope in *R v DPP ex p Kebilene* [2000] 2 AC 326, referring to the discretionary area of judgment, at [80].

[120] See: I Leigh, 'Taking Rights Proportionately: Judicial Review, the Human Rights Act and Strasbourg' [2002] PL 265, 282 ff; P Craig, *Administrative Law* (4th ed) (London, Sweet & Maxwell, 1999) 561, arguing that 'primarily responsibility' lies with the courts, entailing 'substitution of judgment' over the content of Convention rights and where rights are unqualified.

[121] S Attrill, 'Keeping the Executive in the Picture: a reply to Professor Leigh' [2003] PL 41.

[122] [2002] 1WLR 419 (CA).

[123] Note that in *R (Bloggs 61) v Secretary of State for the Home Department* [2003] EWCA Civ 686, [2003] 1 WLR 2724, Keene LJ (at para 81) regarded *R v Lord Saville ex p B (No 2)* [2000] 1 WLR 1855 as an instance in which the Court of Appeal itself considered directly the various factors relevant to the degree of risk to which the soldiers in question would be exposed, though without expressly deciding whether it should be making a primary judgment of the issue.

and proportionate restriction.[124] The judgment also demonstrates the need for a new procedural approach. The hospital authority failed in its argument that cross-examination was not permitted because the action had been brought by judicial review. To order that appropriate that medical witnesses attend and be cross-examined would also satisfy Article 6 of the Convention. Hale LJ took the view:

> Super-*Wednesbury* is not enough. The appellant is entitled to a proper hearing, *on the merits*, of whether the statutory grounds for imposing this treatment upon him against his will are made out.[125]

Wilkinson was applied, but in some respects restricted, in later Court of Appeal decisions on forcible medical treatment.[126]

It is apparent, however, that there remains some judicial reluctance to treat review of alleged breaches of unqualified rights as merits review in fact where no deference is appropriate.[127] In *Bloggs 61* a prisoner whom the Prison Service had decided to transfer from protected witness accommodation back to the general prison population unsuccessfully argued that that to do so would breach his right to life under Article 2 because of the danger of reprisals from his former associates.[128] The Court of Appeal held, in the words of Auld LJ, that:

> despite the fundamental and unqualified nature of the right to life, it is still appropriate to show *some* deference to and/or to recognise the special competence of the Prison Service in making a decision going to the safety of an inmate's life.[129]

Under this approach there is a spectrum of intensity of review, with unqualified rights at the more intense end, rather than a total difference in approach to qualified rights cases.

---

[124] [2002] 1WLR 419, [26], [24]–[25] (CA).

[125] Para 83 (emphasis added).

[126] In *R (N) v Dr M* [2002] EWCA Civ 1789 [2003] 1 WLR 562 Dyson LJ pointed out that judges were free when appropriate to determine the facts for themselves in such cases without oral evidence (which 'should not often be necessary') and added that 'it should not be overlooked that the court's role is essentially one of review', para 39. See also *CF v SSHD* [2004] EWHC 111 (F); [2004] 1 FCR 577, paras 217–18.

[127] Andrew Le Sueur, 'The Rise and Ruin of Unreasonableness' [2005] *JR* 32 cites (at n 18) the comments of Munby J in *R (IR) v Shetty* [2003] EWHC 3022; and *Claire F v Secretary of State for the Home Department* [2004] EWHC 111.

[128] *R (Bloggs 61) v Secretary of State for the Home Department* [2003] EWCA Civ 686, [2003] 1 WLR 2724.

[129] Para 65. Cf Keene LJ paras 79–81, who argued that even if the court were to make the 'primary judgment' in unqualified rights cases it would nevertheless have to attach 'considerable weight' to professional opinion so that there might not be much difference in practice between primary and secondary review. See also Keene LJ's comments in H Fenwick, G Phillipson and R Masterman (eds) *Judicial Reasoning Under the UK Human Rights Act* (Cambridge, CUP, 2007) ch 8.

There does seem to be a difference in approach between differently constituted benches in the Court of Appeal here. Applying the *Bloggs 61* approach in *Willkinson* would have required the court to 'attach considerable weight' to the medical opinion, rather than ordering cross-examination. To have adopted the *Wilkinson* approach in *Bloggs*, however, would have taken the court into evaluating for itself the risk to the prisoner by way of evidence. It is noteworthy perhaps that the European Court of Human Rights in *HL v UK*[130] has cited *Wilkinson* as evidence that the UK courts now engage in stricter scrutiny than prior to the Act. If it turns out not to be the dominant approach after all the result is likely to be further excursions to Strasbourg invoking Article 13.

Treating Proportionality as a Question of Law

Section 6 of the HRA supports an alternative to the line of argument that a court should assess for itself whether the decision of the public authority breaches a person's Convention rights. The language suggests that every statutory and common law discretion of a public authority must now be read subject to a limitation that the authority cannot, in the absence of clear legislation compelling it to do so, act in contravention of a person's 'Convention rights'. Section 6(1) therefore could be said to create a new form of over-arching illegality[131] in the sense that Lord Diplock used that term in the GCHQ case: 'the decision-maker must correctly understand the law that regulates his decision-making power and give effect to it'.[132] This approach has received support from Lord Phillips MR in *R (Q) v Secretary of State for the Home Department*, where he stated that 'since the coming into effect of the Human Rights Act 1998, errors of law have included failures by the State to act compatibly with the Convention.'[133]

The implication would be to treat Convention challenges as 'hard-edged' questions on review. Whereas, prior to the HRA, proportionality had fallen to be considered as an adjunct to the common law grounds for review of discretion, now it could be said to be standing on its own feet. That was the approach taken in an early case. In *B v Secretary of State for the Home Department*[134] the Court of Appeal quashed the decision to deport an Italian national, following his convictions for gross indecency and indecent assault and the service of a five-year term of imprisonment, finding the

---

[130] *HL v UK*, Appl No 45508/99, 5 October 2004 [Section IV], para 139 (concerning the lawfulness of the detention of a mental health patient under Art 5(4)).
[131] Cf P Craig, Administrative Law (4th ed) (London, Sweet & Maxwell, 1999) 546, 556–7.
[132] *CCSU v Minister for the Civil Service* [1985] AC 374, 410–11.
[133] [2003] 2 All ER 903, [112].
[134] *B v Secretary of State for the Home Department* [2000] Imm AR 478.

deportation to be a disproportionate interference with B's right of free movement as an EU national and his right to family life under Article 8 (he had lived for most of his life in the UK). Simon Brown LJ stated that the exercise was 'both different from and more onerous' than the *Wednesbury* approach – no longer limited to irrationality review, the court should be prepared to substitute its own decision for the IAT's.[135] Later judgments applied a different approach[136], however, and the same judge had second thoughts in a later deportation case decided under the revised statutory framework.[137]

Some support to the proportionality as law argument is also derived from the *Belmarsh* detainees case. A majority of the House of Lords found that the measures providing for detention without trial of foreign nationals under the Anti-Terrorism Crime and Security Act 2001 violated the Convention.[138] Hence the derogation entered under Article 15 of the Convention and by an order under the HRA were not operative. With that hurdle removed there was a clear violation of Article 5, since the detention was neither prior deportation nor trial: rather, it was as an alternative to both. The House issued a quashing order in respect of the Human Rights Act 1998 (Designated Derogation) Order 2001 and a declaration of incompatibility finding section 23 of the 2001 Act incompatible with Articles 5 and 14 insofar as it was disproportionate and discriminated on grounds of nationality.[139] In at least some of their Lordships' speeches the decision can be seen as a prominent example of treating proportionality (here, the issue of whether measures were *strictly required* by the exigencies of the situation) as a question of law. This is clear from Lord Bingham's rejection of the Attorney-General's argument that this was a constitutional 'no-go zone' for the courts:

> The Attorney General is fully entitled to insist on the proper limits of judicial authority, but he is wrong to stigmatise judicial decision-making as in some way undemocratic. .... The 1998 Act gives the courts a very specific, wholly democratic, mandate.[140]

---

[135] *Ibid*, para 47.

[136] *R (Mahmood) v Secretary of State for the Home Department* [2001] 1 WLR 840; *R (Isiko) v Secretary of State for the Home Department (C/2000/2939) and Samaroo and Sezek v Secretary of State for the Home Department* [2001] UKHRR 1150.

[137] *Edore v The Secretary of State for the Home Department* [2003] EWCA Civ 716, stating that in view of the intervening decisions it would now be 'unhelpful' to characterise the question of proportionality as one of law. Note that *Edore* was held by the House of Lords on *Huang v Secretary of State for the Home Department* [2007] UKHL 11 to be incorrectly decided.

[138] *A (FC and Others) v Secretary of State for the Home Department* [2004] UKHL 56, See further 00.

[139] *Ibid*, para 73.

[140] *Ibid*, para 42.

At a later point, criticising the Court of Appeal's refusal to intervene because of reluctance to upset the first instance determination (by SIAC), his lordship argued from the European's Court of Human Rights's approach that 'the greater intensity of review now required in determining questions of proportionality' was a matter of law and that the lower courts had therefore 'erred *in law*'. [141]

RE-ASSERTING DEFERENCE IN JUDICIAL REVIEW

Lord Steyn's twin concerns in *Daly* of setting out a more intensive test than *Wednesbury* (commending 'something close to an autonomous merits decision') but abjuring merits review are plainly in tension.[142] It no surprise then that subsequent decisions have tended to favour one aspect over the other, rather than keeping them perfectly aligned. In this section we discuss three specific ways in which the courts have nevertheless justified a more deferential approach, post-*Daly*. These are through use of the fact-finding/policy distinction in relation to Article 6; 'indirect deference' to Parliament; and use of the different stages of proportionality analysis.

The Policy/Fact-finding Distinction Under Article 6

As we saw earlier, the Strasbourg case law allows that deficiencies in administrative process affecting a person's, civil rights and obligations under Article 6 can be corrected if there is access to a court of 'full jurisdiction'. In practice 'full jurisdiction' has been interpreted by the domestic courts under the HRA primarily to resist efforts at widening judicial review.

In the *Alconbury* litigation[143] the question was whether the availability of judicial review was a sufficient safeguard to rescue the planning, highways and compulsory purchase processes from an apparent lack of independence for the purpose of Article 6. The House of Lords applied the 'full jurisdiction' test and found, in contrast to the Divisional Court, that overall the procedures under the legislation were compatible with Article

---

[141] *Ibid*, para 44, emphasis added; and cf Lord Hope (para 131); Lord Rodger (paras 173–74). Some caution is necessary, however. Lord Nicholls and Lord Hope in particular seemed to approach the proportionality question as requiring close scrutiny but as a soft-edged issue nonetheless: [80]–[81] and [108] respectively.

[142] *Huang v Secretary of State for the Home Department* [2007] UKHL 11, [49].

[143] *R (Alconbury Developments Ltd.) v Secretary of State for the Environment, Transport and Regions*, [2001] 2 WLR 1389.

6.[144] The House's own understanding was based on a close reading of the development of the Article 6 jurisprudence in general[145] and a group of cases in which the UK planning regime had been challenged in particular.[146] Lord Slynn concluded that these decisions reflected a difference in role between elected ministers and unelected judges so that a rehearing on an application by an appeal on the merits was not required; it was enough that there should be 'sufficient review of the legality of the decisions and of the procedures followed'.[147] Lord Hoffmann opined that a requirement for judicial review of policy decisions of elected ministers would:

> be profoundly undemocratic. The HRA 1998 was no doubt intended to strengthen the rule of law but not to inaugurate the rule of lawyers.[148]

This approach was further applied in *Begum (Runa) v Tower Hamlets LBC*[149] where the issues before the House of Lords were whether a reviewing officer (who was an officer of the Housing Authority responsible for the decision being reviewed under the Housing Act 1996) constituted an independent and impartial tribunal and, if not, whether the county court, to which an appeal lay on a question of law, possessed 'full jurisdiction' so as to comply with Article 6(1). Assuming for the purpose of argument that a civil right within Article 6 was at issue, Lord Hoffmann found that the same factors which must be considering in applying the rule of law – 'democratic accountability, efficient administration and the sovereignty of Parliament' – were recognised in the Strasbourg jurisprudence so that 'an English lawyer can view with equanimity the extension of the scope of art. 6'.[150] In *Begum*, therefore, the House of Lords accepted that, provided the overall procedure was lawful and fair, it was open to Parliament to choose on economic grounds to deal with resolving disputes through an adjudicating officer who was not independent,[151] subject to the safeguard of review by the county court.

The European Court of Human Rights, however, has taken a more restricted approach. In a similar case involving review of housing benefit by a review committee containing five councillors from the decision-making council (thus, not an independent and impartial tribunal) it found

---

[144]   Lord Slynn, at [54]; Lord Nolan, at [58] Lord Hoffmann, at para 136; Lord Clyde, at [160]; Lord Hutton, at [196] and [197].

[145]   See the speeches of Lord Hoffmann at [84] ff. and Lord Clyde at [154] especially.

[146]   *ISKCON v UK* Application No 20490/92, 8 March 1994; *Bryan v UK* (1995) 21 EHRR 342; *Varey v UK* Application No 26662/95, 27 October 1999; *Chapman v UK*, Application No 27238/95 (unreported) 18 January; 2001 (Grand Chamber of the European Court of Human Rights).

[147]   Para 9. See also Lords Nolan and Hoffmann at paras 61 and 84 respectively.

[148]   Para 129.

[149]   [2003] UKHL 5; [2003] 2 WLR 388.

[150]   Para 35.

[151]   Para 46.

that there was a violation of Article 6.[152] The problem was that the review board's lack of independence was not corrected, because the High Court on judicial review did not have 'full jurisdiction' to substitute its own view for factual errors of the Board.[153] As in the *Kingsley* case[154], it seems that UK courts have too readily assumed that familiar domestic practices meet the Article 6 standard. The decision in *Tsafyo* does not wholly invalidate the House of Lords' approach in *Alconbury* and *Begum*, but it does cut it back to genuine matters of policy.[155]

'Indirect' Deference to Parliament

In a well-known passage in his dissenting judgment in *Roth*[156] Laws LJ gave perhaps the most sophisticated account to date of the application of judicial deference, setting out four principles.[157] It is the first of these that is especially relevant here:

> greater deference is to be paid to an Act of Parliament than to a decision of the executive or subordinate measure ... Where the decision-maker is not Parliament, but a minister or other public or governmental authority exercising power conferred by Parliament, a degree of deference will be due on democratic grounds: the decision-maker is Parliament's delegate.[158]

Deference is usually referred to in the context of respect for Parliament, and deference to primary legislation is both in-built in scheme of the HRA and in continuity with the tradition of parliamentary sovereignty.[159] We

---

[152] *Tsafyo v UK* (App No 60860/00), European Court of Human Rights, 14 November 2006.

[153] Although the Strasbourg court recognised that exercises of 'professional knowledge or experience and the exercise of administrative discretion pursuant to wider policy aims' would be different, here the key question was a straightforward factual one- whether the applicant had 'good cause' for delay in applying for benefit.

[154] 137 above.

[155] See especially *Tsafyo v UK*, para 46.

[156] *International Transport Roth GmbH and others v Secretary of State for the Home Department* [2002] EWCA Civ 158; [2003] QB 728.

[157] See further Sir David Keene 'Principles of deference under the Human Rights Act', in H Fenwick, G Phillipson and R Masterman (eds), *Judicial Reasoning Under the UK Human Rights Act* (Cambridge, CUP, 2007).

[158] *International Transport Roth GMBB v Secretary of State for the Home Department* [2003] QB 728, 765–767.

[159] See generally: R Edwards, 'Judicial Deference under the Human Rights Act' (2002) 65 *MLR* 859; J Jowell, 'Judicial Deference and Human Rights: A Question of Competence' in P Craig and R Rawlings (eds), *Law and Administration in Europe* (Oxford, 2003); J Jowell, 'Judicial deference, Servility, Civility or Institutional Capacity' [2003] *PL* 592; R Clayton, 'Judicial Deference and Democratic Dialogue: the legitimacy of judicial intervention under the Human Rights Act 1998' [2004] *PL* 33; K Ewing, 'The Futility of the Human Rights Act' [2004] *PL* 829; Lord Steyn, 'Deference: A Tangled Story' [2005] *PL* 346; F Klug, 'Judicial Deference under the Human Rights Act' [2003] *EHRLR* 125.

could call this 'direct deference'. This, however, is quite different to deference to *the executive*. In the quotation above Laws LJ speaks of ministers or other public or governmental authorities exercising power conferred by Parliament and acting as 'Parliament's delegate'.[160] This can be termed 'indirect deference'.

Indirect deference is difficult to justify from the plain wording of HRA section 6, despite the well-known dicta that the courts should defer to democratically elected bodies.[161] As we have seen, the wording of section 6(2) requires deference only where a public authority is *compelled* to act in contravention of a person's Convention rights by primary legislation, or secondary legislation required to be in that form because of an obligation in primary legislation. This suggests that the courts would be more likely to defer where an executive policy decision has an explicit legislative basis, as opposed to where a broad discretion is granted by Parliament. This would also be consistent with common law presumptions about fundamental rights, which are to be over-ridden only by the clearest of words.[162]

Despite these powerful objections, one judicial strategy has been to justify deference by reference to parliamentary sovereignty, even where the power granted by Parliament to the executive is *discretionary*. Two examples of 'indirect deference' in operation can be given.

In *Farrakhan*[163] the Court of Appeal declined to intervene in the Home Secretary's refusal of entry. Giving the judgment of the court Lord Phillips MR referred to the exclusion of a right of appeal against the Secretary of State's decision to exclude a person on the grounds that it was conducive to the public good (section 60(9) Immigration and Asylum Act 1999). Far from that leading to the need for added judicial scrutiny of the power: 'the effect of the legislative scheme is legitimately to require the court to confer a wide margin of discretion upon the minister'.[164]

Perhaps the most striking example of 'indirect deference' in operation, however, concerns another public authority, rather than an elected organ of government – the House of Lords' judgment in *ProLife Alliance*.[165] That decision – and especially the difference between it and the Court of Appeal's approach– is revealing. The BBC is an unelected body and so no question of deference arose directly. The Court of Appeal found that the

---

[160] Note, however, the alternative approach of Lord Walker of Gestingthorpe who in *Pro-Life Alliance* (at [137]) who described responsibility for the alleged infringement of human rights as shared between Parliament and the executive decision-maker (citing Andrew Geddis [2002] *PL* 615, 620–3).

[161] *Kebilene v DPP* [2000] 2 AC 326, 381 (Lord Hope); *Brown v Stott* [2001] 2 WLR 817, 834–5 and 842.

[162] *R v Lord Chancellor ex p Witham* [1998] QB 575; *R v Secretary of State for the Home Department ex p Simms* [2000] AC 115.

[163] n 118 above.

[164] [2002] QB 1391, at [74].

[165] *R (ProLife Alliance) v BBC* [2002] 3 WLR 1080.

BBC's decision to refuse to screen an election broadcast showing film footage of the destruction of foetuses on grounds of taste and decency violated Article 10. Free speech by a political party at election time had to prevail, save in wholly exceptional circumstances. The majority of the House of Lords, on the other hand, found that the Court of Appeal had addressed the wrong question, and had carried out its own balancing exercise, when Parliament had already decided that the balance lay in favour of restrictions.[166]

To finesse the issue as a question of the broadcasters' *duty* in this way is, frankly, unpersuasive. This is because, despite the apparently strong mandatory words used in the statute, the determination of what is contrary to good taste and decency is largely a matter of judgment in the hands of broadcasters, and this must vary according to context. What *ProLife Alliance* demonstrates, then, is the ease with which a discretionary judgment can be presented as a matter of duty, where Parliament is taken to have foreclosed the options open to the decision-maker. This strategy raises the stakes – the issue is not the judgment of the BBC but of Parliament – and invokes Laws LJ's parliamentary 'delegate' argument.

Whether the 'indirect deference' approach is itself compatible with the Convention is questionable. Although the European Court of Human Rights has treated democracy as one of the foundation stones of the Convention system, it by no means follows that routine deference is due either to legislative or to elected executive bodies. The commitment to democracy has to be considered in the context of the counter-majoritarian nature of Convention rights. It cannot be sufficient to override Convention rights merely to appeal to electoral accountability. Otherwise, the status of unqualified and non-derogable rights would be fatally undermined and the careful restrictions on limitations of qualified rights would be by-passed.

Differential Stages to Proportionality: Prisoners and Deportation Cases

Another way in which the courts have ruled that some issues are in effect not open to scrutiny is in applying the structure of the proportionality test. In cases involving prisoners and deportees certain restrictions on rights have been said to *flow axiomatically* from deportation or imprisonment. The courts see themselves as debarred from interfering with these aspects since to do so would fundamentally change the nature of the punishment. Effectively this rules out one limb of proportionality analysis: whether the infringement of the right is no more than necessary in order to achieve a

---

[166] See especially Lord Nicholls, at para 12 and Lord Hoffmann, at para 77. Lord Scott dissented, finding that the rejection of the programme was not necessary in a democratic society.

legitimate aim. While claiming to apply the first limb, the courts appear to be easily satisfied that it has been met.[167] A candid admission to this effect was made by Elias J in *R (Hirst) v Secretary of State for the Home Department*[168] who stated, in considering the Prison Service's policy of denying prisoners permission to call the media except in exceptional circumstances:

> where the right is removed as the deliberate and considered response to the need to provide an effective penal policy, there is in truth no room for the court to apply the principle of minimum response.[169]

Consequently, analysis focuses primarily on the narrow second-stage question of whether the impact on the applicant's human rights is excessive or disproportionate.[170] The failure to explore this issue is disappointing: by contrast Canadian courts applying section 1 of the Charter routinely consider the practice in other countries at this point, rather than merely accepting that to interfere would to alter the nature of the deliberate and considered choice of the executive.[171] Moreover, deference re-enters in even this slimmed-down proportionality analysis at the second stage.

This 'inherent restriction' approach is more perhaps easily defensible where Parliament has expressly decreed in legislation that imprisonment shall operate to deprive inmates of certain rights, for example, the right to vote, as in *Pearson*.[172] In such cases there can said to be a clear and democratic choice (although as the Court of Human Rights has noted that is no guarantee that it is a *considered* choice[173]). However, in other cases the challenge is to a discretionary decision of the executive which impacts upon the applicant's Convention rights and which is not required by primary legislation, for example, to restrict prisoners' access to journalists or not to make available IVF treatment.[174] In these instances the finding that the restriction is 'inherent' seems more questionable.

---

[167] See, eg, the acceptance with little analysis of the need to deport to foreigners convicted of drugs offences at conclusion of their sentence, considered under Art 8(2): *R (Samaroo) v SSHD* [2001] EWCA Civ 1139 (2001) UKHRR 1622.

[168] [2002] 1 WLR 2929.

[169] *Ibid*, at para 33.

[170] *Samaroo*, above, paras 19–20 (Dyson LJ).

[171] See, eg, *Dagenais v CBC* [1994] 3 SCR 835; *RJR MacDonald v Canada Attorney-General* [1995] 3 SCR 199.

[172] *R (Pearson) v Secretary of State for the Home Department* [2001] EWCH Admin 239, finding no violation of Convention rights on grounds of deference.

[173] The Court of Human Rights held that the disenfranchisement of convicted prisoners violated Art 3 of Protocol 1. There was, the court found, no evidence that Parliament had ever sought to weigh the competing interests or to assess the proportionality of the ban as it affected convicted prisoners: *Hirst v UK (No 2)* Application 74025/01, 30 March 2004 (para 51); affirmed, by the European Court of Human Rights (Grand Chamber), 6 October 2005.

[174] *R (Mellor) v Secretary of State for the Home Department* [2001] 3 WLR 533.

TAKING STOCK

Revitalising Daly

Each of the more deferential strategies just discussed appears to cut-back to some extent from the promise of a more intense standard of review foreshadowed in 2001 in *Daly*. It is noteworthy that the House of Lords itself has recently (March 2007) revisited the question of the standard of review in an attempt to provide further clarification.

In *Huang v Secretary of State for the Home Department*[175] the Law Lords gave an important ruling concerning the intensity of review required of the Asylum and Immigration Tribunal – the statutory immigration appellate authority for immigration decisions by the Secretary of State – when dealing with human rights arguments. In practice a high proportion of judicial review applications arise in this field. Lower courts had regarded the Tribunal's role as a restricted one, limited to considering whether the Secretary of State misdirected himself, acted irrationally or was guilty of procedural impropriety.[176] Their Lordships held, however, that this was incorrect. Where it was alleged that the decision would constitute a disproportionate interference with the right to respect for private and family life under Article 8 ECHR, the immigration judges should decide themselves on the facts whether the decision was compatible with Convention rights, ie whether it constitutes a proportionate interference with family life.

The intriguing question concerning this judgment is whether it is of more general significance and heralds a new more intensive approach to review. When *Huang* was in the Court of Appeal Laws LJ used the occasion to produce a wide-ranging re-working of the standard of review that distinguished between the deference due on policy questions and on other issues under proportionality.[177] The House of Lords took a much narrower and

---

[175] [2007] UKHL 11.

[176] *Edore v Secretary of State for the Home Department* [2003] 1 WLR 2979, [2003] EWCA Civ 716 and *M (Croatia) v SSHD* [2004] UKIAT 24, [2004] INLR 327 which were ruled in *Huang* to be incorrectly decided (*Huang v Secretary of State for the Home Department* [2007] UKHL 11, paras 11–12).

[177] [2005] EWCA Civ 105; [2005] 3 WLR 488. See Laws LJ's comments on deference (para 60). 'The adjudicator's decision of the question whether the case is truly exceptional is entirely his own. He *does* defer to the Rules; for this approach recognises that the balance struck by the Rules will generally dispose of proportionality issues arising under Art 8; but they are not exhaustive of all cases. There will be a residue of truly exceptional instances. The argument involves a variant on the two-stage approach to proportionality, since it distinguishes between the adjudicator's and the court's role in relation to 'policy' decisions (in effect falling within the routine category here) and those where there is role for autonomous adjudication. Within the policy realm the courts should recognise that 'principle and practicality alike militate in favour of an approach in which the court's role is closer to review

more direct approach to reach the same conclusion, since it was able to declare earlier Court of Appeal authority misconceived. As a result it is unclear how much if anything of the Court of Appeal's reasoning is extant.

Lord Steyn's dictum from *Daly* pointing out that there is no shift to merits review under the HRA is explained in *Huang* as a bar on the primary review by the courts of *policy*.[178] This opens the possibility that there could and should be primary review of factual determinations. Their Lordships read the immigration legislation 'purposively and in context'[179] as requiring primary review by the appellate immigration authority in this case. Although limited in *Huang* to the legislation in question, arguably the reasoning could equally be applied more widely – review of facts where necessary to protect Convention rights can be seen as an imperative under Article 6.[180] While this may disturb the legislative allocation of competences under numerous administrative schemes it cannot be regarded as undermining democratic governance such that deference forbids it. On the contrary, fact-finding is a core judicial function, although outside the traditional bounds of judicial review. In the case of unqualified rights this bridge has already been crossed.[181] It remains to be seen whether *Huang* foreshadows a new intensity of review more generally.

The Strasbourg Reaction

The question remains of what Strasbourg will ultimately make of the development of judicial review post-HRA. There, the post-*Smith and Grady* picture is suggestive rather than conclusive.

In two Strasbourg judgments the domestic proceedings were taken to be adequate:[182] *Smith and Grady* was treated by the European Court as turning on the limited nature of domestic proceedings where national security was involved. In other cases, however, the Court has found a

---

than appeal' [53]. However, even in the policy realm more is now required than the *Wednesbury* approach – the government must provide 'substantial reasoned justification'. Moreover, (para 54): '*Wednesbury* review consigned the relative weight to be given to any relevant factor to the discretion of the decision maker. In the new world, *the decision maker* is obliged to accord decisive weight to the requirements of pressing social need and proportionality.' (emphasis added). Failure to do so could invite judicial scrutiny, as in *Daly* itself. For cases not involving policy, however, the principle of respect for the democratic powers of the state simply did not apply.

[178] *Huang v Secretary of State for the Home Department* [2007] UKHL 11, para 13. In the policy realm, however, the standard of review under the Convention is nevertheless more intensive than under *Wednesbury*, although falling short of merits review.

[179] *Ibid*, para 11, referring to Immigration and Asylum Act 1999 s 65(1).

[180] See also *Tsfayo v UK* (Application no 60860/00), ECHR, 14 November 2006.

[181] *R (Wilkinson) v Broadmoor Special Hospital Authority and others* [2002] 1WLR 419 (CA); 155–56 above.

[182] *Bensaid v UK* (2001) 33 EHRR 10, esp paras 53–58 (involving removal of an illegal immigrant); *Hilal v UK* (2001) 33 EHRR 2, esp paras 75–79 (refusal of asylum).

violation of Article 13. In *Hatton v United Kingdom*[183] the defect was the inability of the national courts to consider whether an alleged increase in night flights at Heathrow was a justified limitation under Article 8. In *HL v UK* the Strasbourg court held that 'anxious scrutiny' was inadequate in that it did not allow the court to reach own determination of the lawfulness of the detention of mentally ill person, in violation of Article 5(4).[184] The domestic proceedings in each ante-dated the HRA but the European Court accepted that the HRA had intensified judicial review[185]. In *HL* the Court referred to the *Wilkinson* decision to buttress its conclusion that the 'Super-Wednesbury' test applicable at the time did not satisfy Article 5(4).[186]

In *Peck v UK*[187] the relevant issue under Article 13 was that Peck had unsuccessfully argued in judicial review proceedings that a local authority's decision to disclose footage of him taken from CCTV which had then been broadcast on television was irrational. In terms identical to *Smith and Grady* the European Court found that Article 13 had been breached. The government had cited *Alconbury*, especially Lord Slynn's comments about proportionality. The Strasbourg court pointed out that *Alconbury* post-dated the coming into force of the HRA (whereas the domestic proceedings pre-dated it) and that the government had accepted that Lord Slynn's comments were obiter. It continued:

> In any event, the Government does not suggest that this comment is demonstrative of the full application by domestic courts of the proportionality principle in considering, in the judicial review context, cases such as the present.[188]

Taken in the context of a breach of Article 13 this can be regarded as a hint that domestic courts could go further. However, neither *HL* nor *Peck* is conclusive and it seems that we will have to wait for a case in which the domestic proceedings occurred after the commencement of the HRA[189] to be certain whether judicial review has now gone far enough for Strasbourg.

---

[183] *Hatton v UK* (2003) 37 EHRR 28, paras 131–142.

[184] *HL v UK,* Application no. 45508/9, European Court of Human Rights, 5 October 2004. The domestic proceedings were *R v Bournewood Community and Mental Health NHS Trust ex p L* [1999] AC 458, HL.

[185] *Ibid,* para 141.

[186] *HL v UK,* paras 138–140.

[187] *Peck v UK* (2003) 36 EHRR 41.

[188] Para 106.

[189] The *Alconbury* case itself went to the European Court of Human Rights but resulted only in admissibility decision: *Holding and Barnes plc v UK*, Application no 2352/02, 12 March 2002 (declared inadmissible).

CONCLUSION

It is already clear that one impact of the HRA upon administrative law has been to accelerate a pre-existing tendency to treat review as context-specific. Lord Steyn's enigmatic comment in *Daly* that '[I]n law context is everything' is emblematic.[190] Consequently the standard of review now appears as a spectrum of different standards applicable to different questions. In this respect domestic review in the UK has moved significantly towards a conscious recognition of a range of standards as has occurred in other countries. In Canada, for example, applying what is termed a 'pragmatic and functional' approach, review ranges from 'correctness' to 'patent unreasonableness'.[191] Four factors especially are considered in determining the appropriate standard of review in a given context: the presence or absence of privative clauses, whether the question is within the expertise of the respondent, the purpose of the Act and the provision in question and whether a question of law or of fact is involved.[192] In the UK's case the scale has not been articulated so clearly by the courts. There is at this point much complexity (some points on the range of options have scales within them also) and is still some dispute over where particular issues are to be placed on the range.

Prior to the HRA it was commonplace to talk of 'hard-edged' and 'soft-edged' review. In the former category the archetype was 'precedent fact' and questions of law. The exercise of discretion *Wednesbury* was the archetypical soft-edged question. 'Anxious scrutiny' occupied the middle ground and discretionary decisions involving allocation of public resources or socio-economic policy were softest of all. It is clear that after the HRA the hard-edged/soft-edged metaphor is insufficiently nuanced, although judges and commentators have struggled to find an accurate alternative vocabulary that does not have misleading connotations.[193]

On any measure, however, the HRA has clearly moved consideration of human rights questions towards the more intense or detailed end of the range. However, plainly not all rights are alike and the situations in which they might be limited varies enormously. Unqualified rights attract more intense scrutiny than qualified rights. It could be expected also that some potential limitations on qualified rights (for example protection of national security) would be treated much more generously than others (for example

---

[190]   *R v Secretary of State for the Home Department ex p Daly* [2001] 2 AC 532, para 28.
[191]   *Pushpanathan v Minister of Citizenship and Immigration* [1998] 1 SCR 982; *Baker v Canada* [1999] 2 SCR 817; *Suresh v Canada (Minister of Citizenship and Immigration)* [2002] 1 SCR 3. See further, D Dzyenhaus (ed), *The Unity of Public Law* (Oxford, Hart Publishing, 2004).
[192]   *Pushpanathan* paras 29–38.
[193]   The debate about 'deference' being in point.

prevention or detection of crime) according to the perceived familiarity or competence of the courts.

Murray Hunt has written perceptively that public law's 'big task for the next few years' will be to give practical effect to the difference between proportionality and 'full merits review' without forfeiting the insight that proportionality requires a new and highly structured approach to adjudication which subjects justification for decisions to rigorous scrutiny to determine their legality.[194] This has been a live issue since the seminal judgment in *Daly* in 2001 and remains to some extent unresolved, as the occasional lapses into *Wednesbury*-like reasoning and other deferential techniques described above show. Several senior judges have indicated their belief that the law is likely to remain in flux for some time as the battle these approaches continues and that the present position may simply be a staging post.[195]

Reviewing the judgments given since 2000, it is striking that, while counsel and judges have repeatedly succumbed to the fascination of exploring what constitutes a 'public authority', they have shown a remarkable lack of curiosity over the remaining words in section 6(1) of the HRA. The issue has been systematically ignored and perhaps because of a strong consensus that the Act was not intended to introduce merits review. Nevertheless, within a system which supposedly defers to parliamentary sovereignty the wholesale failure to explore the parameters of the words that Parliament has chosen to express itself in an admittedly constitutional measure[196] is remarkable and suggests a very high degree of collegial thinking. The law awaits an authoritative ruling that integrates and ranks the various tests on the standard of review.

---

[194] M Hunt, 'Sovereignty's Blight: Why Contemporary Public Law Needs the Concept of 'Due Deference', in N Bamforth and P Leyland (eds), *Public Law in a Multi-Layered Constitution* (Oxford, Hart Publishing, 2003) 342.

[195] See: Lord Walker in *Pro-Life Alliance* at para 138: 'this is an area in which our jurisprudence is still developing'; Auld LJ and Keene LJ in *Bloggs 61*.

[196] *McCartan Turkington Breen v Times Newspapers Ltd* [2001] 2 AC 277, 297 (Lord Steyn); *Thoburn v Sunderland City Council* [2002] EWHC 195 (Admin) [2003] QB 151, paras 62–64 (Laws LJ).

Chapter 7

Human Rights and the Criminal Trial

INTRODUCTION

WHERE A PERSON stands to be investigated, arrested, put on trial and deprived of their liberty we are dealing with a core area of state activity in which risks to human rights arise. There are dangers of abuse of police or prosecutorial discretion and of miscarriages of justice. Sadly, the recent history of English criminal justice is marred by prominent examples of such miscarriages where people wrongly convicted and imprisoned have been released after the belated admission of systemic failures by the police, the prosecution or the courts.[1] Major attempts have been made over recent decades to address some of the causes, with the introduction of a balanced system of regulated but effective police powers in the Police and Criminal Evidence Act 1984[2] and of an independent Crown Prosecution Service.[3] However new sources of injustice have come to light, especially disclosure of unused prosecution material.[4] Moreover, since the major reforms of 1984 there has been a steady stream of controversial criminal justice measures nearly all limiting some aspect of a suspect's or defendant's rights.[5]

It was therefore to be expected that a large number of Human Rights Act 1998 (HRA) challenges would arise in criminal trials, with some re-balancing of the rights of defendants and of police powers. This is a field in which a number of detailed specific rights apply under the Convention, especially concerning the deprivation of liberty (Article 5) and the right to a

---

[1] C Walker and K Starmer (eds), *Miscarriages of Justice: A Review of Justice in Error* (London, Blackstone Press, 1999).

[2] M Zander, *The Police and Criminal Evidence Act 1984* (5th ed) (London, Sweet & Maxwell, 2005).

[3] Prosecution of Offences Act 1985.

[4] This is a significant pressure point in view of the reliance on informants in the new era of intelligence-led policing.

[5] Eg, permitting the drawing of adverse inferences from a suspect's silence (Criminal Justice and Public Order Act 1994, ss 34, 36 and 37); extending the powers of arrest of the police (Serious Organised Crime and Police Act 2005, s 110); introducing compulsory pre-trial disclosure by the defendant (Criminal Procedure and Investigations Act 1996, s 5).

fair trial (Article 6) but also as regards retrospective offences and penalties (Article 7). Moreover, experience from other countries – particularly in Canada following the introduction of the Charter of Rights in 1984 – suggested that the infusion of human rights law would have a major impact on criminal procedure and criminal trials.

An important sources of duties in a criminal trial stems from the status of the trial court as a public authority under section 6 HRA; the same is true of the Crown Prosecution Service and other prosecutors, the police, probation and prison services. Moreover, the duty not to act in contravention of a person's Convention rights applies not only to the rights of defendants but also of those of victims[6] and witnesses.[7] Wherever a court, the police or the prosecution has a procedural, evidential, or remedial discretion, whether under common law or statute, a decision about how to use the discretion could fall under section 6. Convention rights are therefore relevant to a number of decisions affecting a person's liberties in the course of criminal proceedings, quite apart from the substantive law to be applied. These include, for example: extensions of detention in police custody, delay before prosecution, decisions to prosecute, the adjournment of proceedings, the grant of legal aid, imposition of bail conditions, orders relating to pre-trial disclosure, the imposition of publication restrictions or bans, the treatment of vulnerable or protected witnesses, the mandatory or discretionary exclusion of evidence (under Police and Criminal Evidence Act sections 76 and 78)[8], evidential inferences from silence, and the effect of conditions imposed on community sentences such as probation, community service orders, curfews and tagging orders.

The potential scope of inquiry is therefore vast and this chapter is necessarily more selective.[9] We focus here on how UK courts have defined the scope of the relevant rights through the definition of a 'criminal charge' and on the effect of Convention rights on substantive criminal law, ie instances in which it is claimed that the scope of an offence is inconsistent with or needs to be narrowed in the light of a Convention right. Discussion then moves to the potential impact upon the gathering and the treatment at trial of evidence and the consequences for an appeal where there has been a breach of Convention rights in a criminal trial. Finally some of the major challenges to sentencing powers that have arisen under the HRA are considered.

---

[6] See especially *R v A (No 2)* [2001] UKHL 25; [2002] 1 AC 45 (the rape shield case, discussed at 95–97 above).

[7] *Van Colle v Chief Constable of Hertfordshire* [2007] EWCA Civ 325.

[8] 184 below.

[9] For a more comprehensive survey see B Emerson and A Ashworth, *Human Rights and Criminal Justice* (London, 2001).

THE SCOPE OF PROTECTION: THE MEANING OF 'CRIMINAL CHARGE'

The issue of what constitutes a 'criminal charge' is important because the concept carries with it significant human rights safeguards for the individual who is the target of the process. These include the right to a fair trial within a reasonable time before an impartial tribunal[10], the presumption of innocence,[11] and the procedural rights listed in Article 6(3). The latter are the rights to be informed of the charges; to adequate time and facilities for the preparation of a defence; to defend oneself in person or by a lawyer of one's choice; to free legal assistance for those of insufficient means where interests of justice require; to examine or cross-examine witnesses; and to an interpreter.

The risk is that these protections will be by-passed or undermined if domestic courts take an overly-restrictive approach towards the concept of a 'criminal charge'. Government policy which is consciously intended to streamline the administration of justice or to divert matters from disposal in court because of the delays and costs involved raises precisely this difficulty. Examples are anti-social behaviour orders,[12] and on-the-spot fines (penalty notices for disorder).[13] Although measures of this type may not involve arrest or the formality of a court appearance, they may, nevertheless, have a significant impact on the individual's freedom of movement, leisure time, character, reputation, employment opportunities or property. In the case of the control orders introduced by the Prevention of Terrorism Act 2005 the government's motivation was different: that criminal proceedings would either be undesirable because 'intelligence' would not satisfy the criminal burden of proof or because a conviction could only be obtained at the cost of revealing material about the methods and sources of the security and intelligence agencies in a way that would harm national security. In practice the courts have treated some controls orders as involving a deprivation of liberty under Article 5 and therefore attracting the guarantees of that provision.[14] In other cases the range of sentences has been extended in novel ways – for example, by provisionally anticipating conviction (as with confiscation and freezing orders)[15] – or by administrative techniques that may be invoked by a relevant conviction and also by lesser conduct leading to a caution, such as use of the sex offenders register[16] and football banning orders.[17]

---

[10] Art 6(1) ECHR.
[11] Art 6(2).
[12] Crime and Disorder Act 1998 s 1.
[13] Criminal Justice and Police Act 2001 Pt 1.
[14] 216–217 below.
[15] Drug Trafficking Offences Act 1994 and subsequent legislation.
[16] Sex Offenders Act 1997, Pt 1; Sexual Offences Act 2003 Pt 2.
[17] Football Spectators Act 1989 s 14(b).

The Strasbourg court has developed a sophisticated approach to determining where the protections of Article 6 apply.[18] The domestic classification of a legal process is the starting point. If domestic law regards a matter as criminal in nature this is likely to be end of the inquiry also. Where a matter is treated as civil or administrative in domestic law, however, the Court is prepared to go beyond the domestic classification in order to consider the nature of the offence and the severity of the punishment.[19] Under the first of these criteria the court considers such factors as whether the legal rule in question is generally binding, how it is enforced, whether any sanction is dependent on culpability, whether the purpose is to punish or deter, and refers for the purpose of comparison to the position in other states within the Convention system. As regards severity of the punishment, the court considers the potential rather than the actual penalty: the imposition of imprisonment is usually treated as an indicator of that a charge is 'criminal' unless it is very minor and a fine that is intended to deter or punish or which can result in imprisonment in default will have the same implication. Other processes that can result in imprisonment in default may be regarded as criminal also: for example, the imposition of a confiscation order under the Drugs Trafficking Offences Act 1994.[20]

It is noticeable, however, that in applying this jurisprudence locally the UK courts have been reluctant to find that procedures that might be thought of as alternatives to the criminal justice system proper are 'criminal charges' Anti-social behaviour orders have been held not to be criminal charges.[21] Nor are sex offender orders,[22] nor football banning orders.[23] Where a suspect is warned and placed on the sex offenders register the House of Lords found there was no criminal charge since there was no intention to prosecute and the register was not 'public'.[24] Even where a determination may result in a defendant released on licence returning to prison the courts have found that Article 6 does not apply, since recall, following a decision of the Parole Board, is not regarded as a punishment as such.[25] Preliminary proceedings to determine a defendant's fitness to plead (by reason of insanity) have been held not to be within the scope of a criminal charge either.[26]

---

[18]   P van Dijk, F van Hoof, A van Rijn, and L Zwaak, *Theory and Practice of the European Convention on Human Rights* (4th ed) (Antwerp, Intersentia, 2006) 539–557.

[19]   *Engel v Netherlands* (1979–80) 1 EHRR 647, para 82.

[20]   *Welch v UK* (1995) 20 EHRR 247.

[21]   *R v Manchester Crown Court ex p McCann* (2002) UKHL 39, [2003] 1 AC 787.

[22]   *B v Chief Constable of Avon and Somerset Constabulary* [2001] 1 WLR 340; *Jones v Greater Manchester Police Authority* [2002] ACD 4.

[23]   *Gough v Chief Constable of Derbyshire* [2002] QB 1213.

[24]   *R (R) v Durham Constabulary* [2005] UKHL 21.

[25]   *R v Parole Board ex p Smith (No 2)* [2005] UKHL 4; [2005] 1 WLR 350.

[26]   *R v H* [2003] 1 WLR 411, HL; see also *Antoine v UK* ECtHR, 13 May 2003.

From this catalogue it can be seen that the UK have courts have approached the definition of a 'criminal charge' in a consistently restrictive way. The consequence has been to minimise the application of the HRA in a key field. To be fair, however, the UK courts are not alone in taking an instrumental approach towards the concept of a criminal charge. Some inconsistency can also be laid also at the door of the European Court of Human Rights. Lord Justice Sedley has pointed to a string of inconsistent judgments from the Strasbourg court distinguishing between criminal and regulatory proceedings, seemingly designed to escape the implications of its own previous rulings on protections under Article 6.[27]

SUBSTANTIVE OFFENCES AND ARTICLE 6

Perhaps the most obvious way in which human rights and criminal law may clash is where the conduct for which a person is liable to be prosecuted is protected by their human rights. In the past, for example, the European Court of Human Rights has found that liability to prosecution for homosexual acts in private in Northern Ireland[28] and in liability where more than two consenting men are engaged in homosexual intercourse in private breach the Convention.[29] In similar vein the European Court and Commission have considered but rejected challenges to the restriction of the common law defence of marital rape, for convictions for blasphemy and for obscenity.[30] As these instances demonstrate in practice applications to Strasbourg have served as a safety valve in the case of offences, often of some antiquity, that may be felt to be out of step with changing social mores, or which have become morally controversial. Following the introduction of the HRA, UK courts are now bound to consider these arguments in a way that would not have applied previously.

Several examples have arisen of such challenges although the courts have been reluctant so far to uphold them. In *R v Taylor*[31] the Court of Appeal rejected the defendant's argument that his conviction under the Misuse of Drugs Act 1971 for supply of cannabis violated his right under Article 9 to manifest his religion as a Rastafarian (he was arrested by police as he was entering a Rastafarian temple). Although, the court found that religious liberty was engaged, it found also – arguably, with far too little serious

---

[27] Lord Justice Sedley, 'Wringing Out the Fault: Self-Incrimination in the 21st Century' (2001) 52 *NILQ* 107, 124, citing decisions on criminal penalties for breach of injunctions, prisoners' rights, and extradition.

[28] *Dudgeon v UK* (1981) 4 EHRR 149.

[29] *ADT v UK* Appl No 0035765 (ECHR, 31 July, 2000).

[30] Respectively *SW v UK* (1995) 21 EHRR 363 (no breach of Art 7); *Gay News and Lemon v UK* (1983) 5 EHRR 123 (no breach of Art 10); *Handyside v UK* (1976) 1 EHRR 737 (no breach of Art 10).

[31] [2001] EWCA Crim 2263.

attempt at analysis – that the restriction was justified.[32] Similarly judges have refused to read into the offence of possession of a controlled drug a human-rights based defence of necessity.[33] In *R v Shayler* the House of Lords rejected the claim of a former MI5 officer that his conviction under the Official Secrets Act 1989 violated Article 10.[34] He had claimed that the absence from the legislation of a defence for disclosures in the public interest was inconsistent with the Strasbourg jurisprudence on freedom of expression. However their Lordships held that the other opportunities (which he had not used) to air his concerns about alleged MI5 illegality and incompetence meant that the limitation on his right of free speech could be considered no more than was necessary in a democratic society.

Where an inconsistency between the terms of an offence and a Convention right is found the court's first avenue will be, if possible, to read the offence more narrowly using the section 3 duty. If the defendant's conduct falls within the narrower ambit of the offence then the HRA will be of no use to her. Thus in *Connolly v DPP*[35] the Divisional Court read section 1 Malicious Communications Act 1998 so as to confine liability to circumstances falling within Article 10(2), but this did not avail the defendants, who were found to have been justifiably convicted when sending photos of aborted foetuses to a pharmacist who prescribed the morning after pill. Where an inconsistency between the terms of the offence and a Convention right cannot be so resolved, the court may issue a declaration of incompatibility but, again, this will do nothing to prevent a conviction.[36]

Attempts to use the courts to forestall anticipated prosecutions in order to claim the protection of the Convention have also failed in two instances. In *R (Pretty) v DPP*[37] the applicant who suffered from incurable motor neurone disease claimed inter alia that the offence of assisted suicide under section 2 of the Suicide Act 1961 for which her husband stood to be prosecuted if he helped her to take her life violated her rights under Articles 2, 3, 8, 9 and 14 of the Convention. The House of Lords rejected the argument that there was in effect a right to die, which the state was obliged to recognise in this way, as did the European Court of Human

---

[32] Contrast the detailed consideration given to the same question by the Constitutional Court of South Africa in *Prince v President Cape Law Society* 2002 (2) SA 794; see further R Ahdar and I Leigh, *Religious Freedom in the Liberal State* (Oxford, OUP, 2005) 170–173.

[33] *R v Altham* [2006] 1 WLR 3287 (no Art 3-based defence for use of cannabis in pain relief); cf *R v Quayle* [2005] 1 WLR 3642 re Art 8.

[34] [2002] UKHL 11.

[35] [2007] EWHC 237 (Admin). A comparable effect has been achieved by the House of Lords as regards the common law offence of public nuisance. In *R v Rimmington* [2005] UKHL 63 their Lordships rejected an argument that the offence was too vague to comply with Art 7. They nevertheless narrowed its ambit by holding a line of modern cases on malicious letter campaigns to be wrongly decided with the result that the defendants were acquitted.

[36] See further 111–21.

[37] [2001] UKHL 61; [2002] 1 AC 800.

Rights.[38] At the other end of the scale altogether were the contrived proceedings in *R (Rusbridger) v Attorney-General.*[39] There the House of Lords found that, in modern times, Treason Felony Act 1843 section 3 could not be used to prosecute in the case of newspaper articles in the *Guardian* advocating the abolition of the monarchy and the creation of a republic, since to do so would interfere with freedom of expression. However, since the articles had been published without hindrance and that there was no serious likelihood of prosecution the challenge was entirely hypothetical: there had been no chilling effect that warranted allowing the proceedings for a declaration of incompatibility to continue.

The Lords' findings in *Rusbridger* apparently acknowledge a twilight zone of law that is unrepealed but which cannot be enforced without breaching the Convention. Some defendants indeed have extrapolated from the duty on the police and the prosecution section 6 under HRA not to violate a person's Convention rights that side challenges (or satellite litigation) can be made to prevent a prosecution continuing. Two examples in which prosecutions have been found on the facts to violate Conventions rights appear to suggest that this course is an option. In *Percy v DPP*[40] the High Court quashed a conviction under section 5 of the Public Order Act 1986 (insulting behaviour likely to cause a breach of the peace) for the defendant's act of burning a US flag outside a military base. The court found that the magistrates had wrongly failed to consider whether punishment was necessary and proportionate. In *Dehal v CPS*[41] the High Court found that a prosecution should not have been brought for public order offences arising from an abusive poster placed on the notice-board of a Sikh temple following an internal dispute. In a brief judgment Moses J stated:

> What was needed was not merely a conclusion, namely that the prosecution was a proportionate response, but a careful analysis of the reasons why it was necessary to being a criminal prosecution at all. In order to justify one of the essential foundations of democratic society the prosecution must demonstrate that it is being brought in pursuit of a legitimate aim, namely the protection of society against violence and that a criminal prosecution is the only method necessary to achieve that aim.[42]

In fact each of these appeals was brought by case stated after *conviction.* Nevertheless, the language suggesting that a prosecution may be attacked in this way creates conceptual difficulties. If it refers to the potential for a defendant to assert his or her Convention rights by pre-emptive strike

---

[38] *Pretty v UK* (2002) 35 EHRR 1.
[39] [2003]UKHL 38; [2003] 3 WLR 232.
[40] [2001] EWHC Admin 1125.
[41] [2005] EWHC 2154.
[42] *Ibid*, para 9.

rather than waiting for trial there is less difficulty.[43] If, however, it is taken to mean that the decision to prosecute can be challenged on Convention grounds over and above whether the offence in question is Convention compatible[44] (which of course itself includes whether an over-broad offence can be read down), then this would be a novel development. It could be argued in favour of allowing such challenges that this is consistent with the fact-centred approach of the European Court of Human Rights.

However, applying section 6 in this way to the prosecuting authorities runs counter to the scheme of sections 3 and 4 HRA, at least where statutory offences are concerned. These provisions suggest that a court should, first, read down the wording of an offence to achieve compatibility and, secondly, if that is not possible, issue a declaration of incompatibility. In the first scenario the defendant whose actions are protected by the Convention must be *acquitted*, since, in the light of the read-down offence, there is no liability. In the second the defendant must be *convicted* since section 4 makes clear that a declaration of incompatibility does not affect the validity of the law in question. There is no space here for the third option of suggesting that an offence cannot be *enforced* on Convention grounds in some situations. If there were a third option, the next logical step would be to attack prosecutions for offences previously declared incompatible under section 4 or by the European Court of Human Rights where no remedial order has been made, at which point the conflict with section 4 would become transparent. Judicial language suggesting a third option is best treated therefore as referring only to the point at which the defendant can assert her Convention rights and to the issues that must be considered by the prosecution and trial court at different stages in the proceedings.

REVERSE ONUS OF PROOF AND THE PRESUMPTION OF INNNOCENCE

English law has long treasured the presumption of innocence, famously described by Viscount Sankey in *Woolmington v DPP* as 'one golden thread' running throughout the web of criminal law.[45] This speech acknowledged, however, the possibility of statutory exceptions. Prior to the

---

[43] See also the comments of Waller LJ in *Blum v DPP, CPS and SSHD* [2006] Admin 3029, [27], explaining *Percy* and *Dehal* as confined to the reasonableness test under the Public Order Act 1986 s 4.

[44] See S Turenne, 'The Compatibility of Criminal Liability with Freedom of Expression' (2007) *Crim LR* 866, 881 who concludes that the prosecution must be shown to be necessary as a distinct element over and above whether legislation is compatible.

[45] [1935] AC 462, 421–2, HL.

HRA[46] the Court of Appeal had recognised that exemptions, exceptions and provisos to criminal offences could therefore place the burden on the accused to demonstrate that he fell within them,[47] although in 1987 the House of Lords adopted a restricted approach to such provisions.[48] A key distinction is between the transfer to a defendant of an evidential burden (ie, responsibility to raise a reasonable doubt concerning some element of the offence) and a provision that requires a defendant to establish some element to a higher standard ie one of probability (a so-called 'legal' or 'persuasive' burden). Significantly, the courts had declined prior to the HRA to interpret reverse onus provisions as imposing only an evidential burden on the accused (this approach was rejected by the House of Lords in *Hunt* in 1987).

Under Article 6(2) of the Convention, 'everyone charged with a criminal offence shall be presumed innocent until proved guilty according to law'. This article has given rise to repeated litigation concerning statutory offences which place the burden on the *defendant* to establish that some element of the offence does not apply. An example would be a requirement to prove that that she was unaware of prohibited items found in her possession. The Convention jurisprudence permits reverse burdens of proof provided that *overall* the burden lies on the prosecution to establish guilt. Reverse burdens must, however, be within 'reasonable limits' in order to comply with Article 6(2).[49] Only in the case of a legal or persuasive reverse burden, however, is it necessary to consider whether the reverse burden is within reasonable limits: evidential burdens are taken to conform to Article 6.2.

Applying these principles, the UK courts have used section 3 HRA to read down statutory provisions that appeared to create a legal reverse onus of proof so that they were treated as imposing only an evidential burden. This is how the House of Lords in *Lambert* treated provisions in the Misuse of Drugs Act 1971 section 28(2), (3), allowing a defence if the defendant proved that he neither believed nor suspected nor had any reason to suspect that the substance found in his possession was a controlled drug.[50] To read the provision literally (ie as creating a legal reverse onus) would allow the defendant to be convicted notwithstanding the jury's reasonable doubts about his belief, contrary to the presumption of innocence. However, under the provision *read down* once the defendant raised a reasonable doubt concerning his knowledge, burden would then

[46] See P Roberts and A Zuckerman, *Criminal Evidence* (2nd ed) (Oxford, OUP, 2004) 377–381.

[47] *R v Edwards* [1974] 1 QB 27, CA.

[48] *R v Hunt* [1987] AC 352.

[49] *Salabiaku v France* (1988) 13 EHRR 379, para 28 .See also *Radio France v France* [2004] EHRLR 460.

[50] *R v Lambert* [2002] UKHL 37; [2002] 2 AC 545 (Lord Hutton dissenting).

shift to the prosecution to establish beyond reasonable doubt his knowledge of the drug.[51] The outcome in *Lambert* was a striking use of the section 3 interpretive duty that, as the majority, acknowledged was contrary to the ordinary meaning of the provisions and the hitherto accepted understanding of their effect.

Subsequently this approach has been applied to the reverse burden on the defendants concerning the following: proving that he had joined an organisation proscribed under the Terrorist Act 2000 before proscription or that he had not take part in its activities since proscription,[52] to fraudulent disposal of property under the Insolvency Act 1986,[53] and to making damaging disclosure of information concerned with defence or international relations under sections 2 or 3 of the Official Secrets Act 1989.[54]

On the other hand, the *Salabiaku* 'reasonable limits' exception has also been applied by the House of Lords. In *R v Johnstone* their Lordships upheld the compatibility with Article 6(2) of a provision placing on the defendant the burden of showing that he believed on reasonable grounds that the use of a sign was not an infringement of a registered trade mark (Trade Marks Act 1994, section 92(5)).[55] Lord Nicholls indicated that various factors had to be considered in determining whether a particular provision struck a fair balance between society's and the defendant's interests: more serious punishments following conviction required more compelling justification for legal reverse burdens, the extent and nature of the factual matters to be proved by the defendant, and their importance relative to those to be shown by the prosecution.[56] In this instance the need to combat the international trade in counterfeit goods, the awareness of traders of the risks of piracy and the difficulties of investigating international supply chains and the difficulty of the prosecution's task in such cases justified the reverse onus. Given the importance and difficulty of combating counterfeiting, and given the comparative ease with which an accused can raise an issue about his honesty, overall it is fair and reasonable to require a trader, should need arise, to prove on the balance of probability that he honestly and reasonably believed the goods were genuine.[57]

---

[51]   See Lord Slynn at para 17; Lord Steyn at para 42; Lord Hope at paras 90–91; and Lord Clyde at para 157.

[52]   *Sheldrake v DPP; A-G's Reference (No 4 of 2002)* [2005] 1 AC 264, HL.

[53]   *R v Edwards* [2004] CR App R 27, CA. In the same appeal, however, a different provision of the same Act (s 353) was found to impose a legal burden of proof on the defendant.

[54]   *R v Keogh* [2007] 1 WLR 1500.

[55]   *R v Johnstone* [2003] UKHL 28 [2003] 1 WLR 1738. The defendant was however acquitted because of a misdirection by the trial judge.

[56]   Para 50.

[57]   Para 53.

On a number of other occasions such challenges to reverse onus provisions have likewise failed; for example, proving good reason or lawful excuse for having a pocket knife in a public place,[58] and proving that excess alcohol was consumed by a driver after ceasing driving.[59]

Returning to the issue for a fourth time in three years[60] in *R v Sheldrake*[61] their Lordships denied any inconsistency between the *Lambert* and *Johnstone* approaches and all but rebuked the Court of Appeal for having the temerity to suggest that there was.[62] At the end of this frenzied period of litigation the advice to lower courts was entirely prosaic: that each provision imposing a reverse onus had to be considered in context and with consideration for the facts and circumstances of the case.

Commentators have rightly complained that the failure of the domestic courts to articulate clear principles has led not merely to inconsistencies over which reverse onus provisions are read down and which are found to pass scrutiny under Article 6(2) but is itself likely to encourage 'a blizzard of single instances' as these many provisions are tested one by one in the courts.[63]

EVIDENCE OBTAINED IN VIOLATION OF CONVENTION RIGHTS

Why This Is an Issue of Remedies

In many countries it is taken for granted that where fundamental rights have been violated in the way that evidence has been collected by the police or prosecuting authorities the appropriate judicial response is to prevent it being given in evidence at trial. The United States courts, for example, in early 20th century decisions concerning unreasonable searches (contrary to

---

[58]   Criminal Justice Act 1988, s 139 (4)-(5), *L v DPP* [2002] 1 CR App R 32; *R v Matthews* [2003] 3 WLR 693.

[59]   Road Traffic Act 1988, s 15(3), *R v Drummond* [2002] CR App R 25.

[60]   The first occasion was *R v DPP ex p Kebilene* [2000] 2 AC 326 in which their Lordships reversed the Divisional Court's ruling that the Director of Public Prosecution was bound by the Convention prior to the commencement of the Human Rights Act. In view of this finding the comments of their Lordships concerning the reverse onus in Prevention of Terrorism (Temporary Provisions) Act 1989 s 16A were *obiter*.

[61]   [2004] UKHL 43 [2005] 1 AC 264, HL. The Court of Appeal had earlier applied the *Lambert* approach to treat the provision in question (the Road Traffic Act 1988 s 50) as imposing an evidential burden: *Sheldrake v DPP* [2004] QB 487.

[62]   In *A-G's Reference (No 1 of 2004)* [2004] EWCA Crim 1025, 2 CR App R 27, most unusually, a five-judge Court of Appeal was convened. Lord Woolf CJ's attempt at distilling 10 propositions from the prior case law to guide future courts was not welcomed by the House of Lords in *Sheldrake*: see esp Lord Bingham at paras 30–32. See further P Roberts, 'Criminal Procedure, the Presumption of Evidence and Judicial Reasoning under the Human Rights Act' in H Fenwick, G Phillipson and R .Masterman (eds), *Judicial Reasoning under the UK Human Rights Act* (Cambridge, CUP, 2007).

[63]   Roberts and Zuckerman, op. cit., 383.

the Fourth Amendment to the Constitution) specifically rejected the idea that exclusion was too drastic an outcome where the unconstitutionally-obtained evidence was probative. Rather, the Supreme Court held that exclusion flowed from the breach of constitutional rights and 'those rights would be further infringed if the evidence was allowed to be used'.[64] Likewise, in New Zealand the courts initially responded to the Bill of Rights Act by adopting a prima facie exclusion rule. As Richardson J put it in a 1993 decision ruling a confession to be inadmissible, exclusion is required to *affirmatively protect* fundamental rights and freedoms. Otherwise, in his words, a statement of fundamental rights would be a 'hollow shell' and an 'elaborate charade'.[65] Cooke P was dismissive in the same case of the prosecution contention that the court should merely consider the Bill of Rights violation as a relevant factor affecting admissibility. He robustly characterised this as 'diluting the Bill of Rights Act by metaphysical distinctions'.[66] Subsequent decisions in New Zealand have, however, diluted the protection.[67] The Supreme Court of Canada has referred to the *further disrepute* to the administration of justice if evidence obtained by a Constitutional violation is admitted, either by depriving the defendant of a fair hearing or condoning unacceptable conduct by the prosecutorial or investigatory authorities.[68]

As these examples show, exclusion of evidence is thought of in at least some common law legal systems as a natural remedy for violation of constitutional or human rights. This is not to say that exclusion of unconstitutional evidence is automatic in all cases: in the US, Canada and New Zealand the law has developed in a way that takes account of a variety of factors and, on occasion, allows unconstitutionally obtained

---

[64] *Dodge v United States* 272 US 530 (1926) at 532. See also *Weeks v United States* 232 US 383 (1914).

[65] *R v Goodwin* [1993] 2 NZLR 153, 191, NZCA.

[66] *Goodwin*, 171.

[67] Later decisions adopt a balancing approach under which the court determines whether exclusion of the evidence would be a proportionate remedial response to the Bill of Rights violation, having regard to the facts of the particular case: *R v Shaheed* [2002] 2 NZLR 377; *R v Williams* [2007] NZCA 52. See further: R Mahoney, 'Abolition of New Zealand's Prima Facie Exclusionary Rule', [2003] *Crim LR* 607; S Optican and P Sankoff, 'The New Exclusionary Rule: A Preliminary Assessment of *R v Shaheed*' (2003) *NZL Rev.* 1. Legislation has in effect codified this approach: Evidence Act (NZ) 2006, s 30; and see Law Commission, *Evidence: Evidence Code and Commentary* (Report 55, vol 2, Wellington, 1999).

[68] *R v Collins* (1987) 38 DLR (4th) 508, 523 (Lamer J). The Charter of Rights introduced a form of modified exclusionary rule into the law for the first time in 1984. Section 24(2) of Charter provides that: 'where a court concludes that evidence was obtained in a manner that infringed or denied any rights or freedoms guaranteed by the Charter, the evidence shall be excluded if it is established that, having regard to all the circumstances, of the admission of it in the proceedings would bring the administration of justice into disrepute'. See P Hogg, *Constitutional Law of Canada* (5th ed) Scarborough ON, Carswell, 2006) paras 41.3 ff.

evidence to be admitted exceptionally.[69] Moreover, reference is sometimes made not only to the protection of constitutional rights but also to the overlapping concerns of deterring unconstitutional police behaviour by removing any incentive, and to protecting the administration of justice. Nevertheless, the starting point is one that acknowledges the importance of fundamental rights and that exclusion of evidence is an appropriate remedy when they are violated.

In contrast, the traditional approach of the UK courts has been Nelsonian – that is to turn a blind eye to all but the most egregious examples[70] of official malpractice in obtaining evidence. Elaborate explanations have grown up for why a policy of selective myopia is not merely defensible but even desirable.[71] Foremost is the argument that a criminal trial is not the place to discipline state officials such as police officers. Rather, the sole purpose is to determine the guilt of the defendant and for this purpose it is the cogency of the evidence and not its provenance that is crucial. As Lord Diplock put it in the leading case of *Sang* in 1979:

> However much the judge may dislike the way in which a particular piece of evidence was obtained before proceedings commenced it is no part of his judicial function to exclude it for that reason[72]

According to this view police malpractice is a separate issue to be pursued in disciplinary proceedings, or perhaps a civil action against the police. This approach undoubtedly has the advantage that the defendant is not in effect rewarded because of factors unrelated to his or her guilt, although doubts remain about the effectiveness of civil actions against the police and of police disciplinary proceedings. Moreover arguably there is a measure of inconsistency in allowing one branch of the state (the courts) to utilise material derived from illegal action by another branch (the police).

The position is not an absolutist one, however. Confessions have always been treated separately: voluntariness was the key criterion and not reliability as such, and this is now reflected in the onus of proof that the prosecution must discharge before such statements may be admitted under

---

[69] In the US later judgments have, placed less reliance on repairing the violations of the defendant's constitutional rights than on deterring unconstitutional behaviour by removing any incentives for official misconduct: *Elkins v United States,* 364 US 206 (1960); *Mapp v Ohio,* 367 US 643; *Miranda v Arizona* (1966) 384 US 436; *US v Leon* 486 US 897, 906 (1983) (Justice White).

[70] See 221–25 below for discussion of evidence obtained by torture. In cases of severe prosecution misconduct abuse of process could also lead to the dismissal of the prosecution: *R v Horseferry Magistrates Court ex p Bennett* [1994] 1AC 42; *R v Mullen* [2000] QB 520.

[71] For reviews of the arguments see: A Ashworth, 'Excluding Evidence as Protecting Rights', [1977] *Crim LR* 723.

[72] *R v Sang* [1979] 2 All ER 1222, 1230; cf. Lord Scarman at *Ibid.,* 1245. In Scotland a different approach, that of balancing the defendant's interests against the state's applied: *Lawrie v Muir* (1950) SLT 371.

the Police and Criminal Evidence Act 1984.[73] Section 78 of the same Act gives a more general discretion to judges to exclude evidence where, having regard to the manner in which it was obtained, its admission would have a prejudicial effect on the fairness of the trial.[74] However, section 78 is not to be used as a disciplinary measure either, as the Court of Appeal made clear in the 1998 case of *Chalkley*, since the emphasis is on fairness to the defendant, rather than on disapproval of illegality by the prosecution.[75] Fairness has been taken to refer primarily to the trial process rather than the investigation. Furthermore in a limited category of cases under the abuse of process doctrine applies if the conduct of the prosecution is so egregious that in conscience that the case should not be allowed to continue.[76]

Prior to the HRA, Convention-based arguments for excluding evidence had, however, made no headway against the general approach. In the well-known decision of *Khan* in 1996 the House of Lords held that tape recordings obtained through a an illegally placed listening device were admissible.[77] Their Lordships upheld the trial judge's decision not to exclude the tapes under his discretion under section 78. An argument that since there had almost certainly been a breach of Article 8 of the Convention this should lead to exclusion of the tapes, failed.

The Convention Position

The European Convention does not require the exclusion of evidence either for illegality or violation of Convention rights. In *Schenk v Switzerland*[78] court ruled that the admission of evidence obtained by a breach of Convention rights does not itself render the trial unfair in violation of Article 6.[79] When *Khan* went before the European Court of Human Rights it confirmed that there had been a breach of Article 8 because of the

---

[73]   S 76.

[74]   See D Ormerod and D Birch, 'The Evolution of the Discretionary Exclusion of Evidence', [2004] *Crim LR* 767, concluding (at 779): 'twenty years after enactment, s 78 remains firmly anchored in the reliability (relevant evidence) rather than rights-based principle'.

[75]   *R v Chalkley; R v Jeffries* [1998] 2 All ER 155, 180 (Auld LJ).

[76]   The leading examples are two cases in which defendants appeared in court after the authorities had colluded in them being brought to the country forcibly without the benefit of extradition proceedings: both were struck out as an abuse of process: *R v Horseferry Magistrates Court ex p Bennett* [1994] 1 AC 42; *R v Mullen* [1999] 2 Cr App R 143.

[77]   *R v Khan* [1997] AC 558.

[78]   (1988) 13 EHRR 242.

[79]   And see Lord Nolan [1997] AC at 581 and Lord Nicholls of Birkinhead at 583.

absence of legal authority for the surveillance.[80] However, it reaffirmed its earlier stance in *Schenk* and dismissed the claim that Article 6 had been violated.[81]

Despite the unhelpful Strasbourg jurisprudence there are good reasons why the issue should not be regarded as closed to the domestic courts. The first is the nature of the Strasbourg jurisprudence on the treatment of evidence by domestic courts in criminal cases. Both *Schenk* and *Khan* were decided at the Convention level under the 'margin of appreciation'.[82] The law of evidence is an area in which the European Court has repeatedly refused to intervene with the decisions of national courts, except in extreme cases. In *Khan v UK* the Court explained that it was not for it to determine in principle which types of evidence should be admissible; rather, its concern under Article 6 was with the fairness of the proceedings as a whole.[83] There is no European evidential norm – although some decisions of the Court are fractionally more interventionist than the overall trend.[84] Given the range of very different forms of criminal process across Europe the Strasbourg position is completely understandable, but it certainly does not prevent domestic courts giving additional protections beyond the minimal levels at which Article 6 is breached. Arguably, however, the court's approach goes further than necessary to respect the margin: it would be possible to state as a minimum that evidence (in whatever form) that breaches a Convention right should not be permitted, without prescribing a common approach to divergent systems of evidence. Dissenting judgments both in *Khan* and in the later case of *PG v UK* stressed the connection between the notion of fairness of the trial under Article 6 and breaches of the law.[85]

Moreover, evidence obtained from torture or inhuman or degrading treatment (ie in violation of Article 3, rather than Article 8) has been

---

[80] *Khan v UK* (2001) 31 EHRR 45.

[81] Cf *Perry v UK* (2004) 39 EHRR 3 in which the European Court of Human Rights found that covert surveillance at a police station breached Art 8 (not necessary in a democratic society) but not Art 6. In the domestic proceedings the court found that there was no breach of Art 6 or 8: *R v Perry*, The Times, 28 April 2000.

[82] 53ff. above.

[83] Para 34.

[84] See *Barbera, Messegue and Jabardo v Spain* (1989) 11 EHRR 360, holding that the court can review the whole treatment of the evidence by the domestic judge. In *Saidi v France* (1994) 17 EHRR 251, para, 43 it was said that the Court's role was to determine 'whether the proceedings in their entirety, including the way in which the evidence was taken, were fair'. In *Van Mechelen v Netherlands* (1998) 25 EHRR 647 the court found a breach of Art 6 because there was no evidence that the domestic court had correctly weighed the prejudice to the defence in allowing cross-examination of anonymous witnesses via a video link which did not allow observation of demeanour. And see *Teixeira de Castro v Portugal* (1999) 28 EHRR 101 (below).

[85] Partly Concurring, Partly Dissenting Opinion of Judge Loucaides in *Khan v UK*; cf Judge Tulkens in *PG and JH v UK* (2001) Application no 44787/98.

treated by the court as excluded, despite its probative value. Thus, when in a drugs prosecution a German court admitted in evidence a bag of drugs that the defendant had been made to regurgitate by the forcible administration of an emetic under medical supervision, this rendered the whole trial unfair.[86]

Exceptionally, however, the Strasbourg Court has been prepared to assess the weight of evidence before the domestic trial court,[87] for example if unfair or arbitrary conclusions have been drawn from the evidence.

These are limited, if important, incursions on the general principle. As we have argued in chapter 3, Strasbourg rulings on Article 6 are not a bar to the UK courts giving additional human rights protection and adopting a more stringent approach to evidence obtained in violation of a Convention right. Nothing in the Strasbourg approach compels UK courts to exclude evidence obtained in violation of the Convention, but nothing stands in the way of them doing so either.

How a Maximalist Position Could Be Argued

There are good reasons why the HRA should in time lead to a re-appraisal. Under section 6, the police clearly have a duty to comply with the Convention in their dealings with suspects. Parliament has therefore put human rights considerations centre stage in the criminal justice process. Consequently, the police are unmistakably on notice that they must satisfy the Convention or face legal action, although the anticipated enforcement of section 6 is by judicial review or civil litigation rather than exclusion of evidence. Like the judiciary, the police have been exposed to extensive training on the HRA. It is therefore harder than before incorporation to argue that a decision to exclude evidence bears the character of tripping up an honest but perhaps, over-enthusiastic, piece of detection.

Moreover, during debates on the HRA a Home Office minister suggested exclusion of evidence under section 78 could be one means of granting a remedy: section 8 of the HRA (referring to 'such relief or remedy as it considers just and appropriate') allows a court to exclude evidence as a remedy for breach of Convention rights.[88] In any event the interpretive obligation under section 3 also applies to statutory provisions governing evidence, such section 78. As Sir Richard May points out (writing extra-judicially) the Court of Human Rights treats the Convention system

---

[86] *Jalloh v German* Appl 54810/00 11 July 2006 E Ct HR, (suspect restrained by four police officers and made to regurgitate a swallowed bag of drugs through the forcible (medically supervised) administration of an emetic).

[87] *Barbera, Messegue and Jabardo v Spain* (1989) 11 EHRR 360.

[88] Lord Williams of Mostyn, HL Debs, vol 582, col 1311 (3 November, 1997).

as subsidiary to national systems for rights protection and the domestic courts' responsibilities must be read in that light.[89]

If the domestic judiciary were to use the HRA to reappraise their traditional attitude to improperly obtained evidence this would be a way of marking the fundamental nature of Convention rights. Arguably breach of a Convention right *should* be treated differently to other forms of official illegality as a further sign of the 'constitutional' status of the HRA.[90] There is a parallel with the case for heightened intensity of review under judicial review where violations of human rights are concerned.[91]

On the other hand, there are potential difficulties in giving a distinctive domestic effect to Convention rights in this way. A distinction between breaches of the Convention and other illegality is problematic because in practice HRA section 3 is likely to set the context for arguments about illegality under other statutory provisions also. Moreover, the use of Convention jurisprudence might be unprincipled: the Strasbourg approach to Article 8 for example has been developed in isolation from Article 6 and it is arguable that the boundaries of protection for private life under Article 8(2) might have been drawn elsewhere had violation of the right entailed exclusion of evidence at a criminal trial. The domestic court could overcome some of these pitfalls by differentiating between and within Convention rights in assessing the evidential impact of illegality, although there are some disadvantages to such an approach also.[92]

What Has Happened Under the HRA

What is striking about the situation following the HRA taking effect is the consistent attitude of the domestic courts that no changes to the existing position are required. Shortly after the Act came into force, the House of Lords in *R v P* affirmed the view that, where breaches of Article 8 were involved, providing an effective remedy was 'outside the scope of the

---

[89] R May, *Criminal Evidence* (4th ed) (London, Sweet & Maxwell, 1999) 360.

[90] 130 above.

[91] 149ff. above.

[92] In an appeal from Jamaica, *Allie Mohammed v The State.* 1999] 2 WLR 552, the Privy Council rejected either automatic exclusion or even a presumption of exclusion for unconstitutionally obtained evidence. Rather, in the words of Lord Steyn, denial of the constitutional right had to be balanced against the gravity of the offence and the interest to the community in securing the evidence. In view of the absence of deliberate abuse by the police, the confession need not be excluded. In the case of the second constitutional question – this was fundamental – it was inconceivable that a conviction could stand where there had not been a fair trial. This approach, however, has the unfortunate effect of creating a judicial ranking of fundamental rights, whereas it should be axiomatic that all constitutional rights are of fundamental importance, since that is why they have been given this special status in the first place. The absence of deliberate misconduct in denial of the right to see a lawyer is, from this perspective, beside the point.

criminal trial' and therefore the exclusion of evidence was not required.[93] In another decision the House refused to use the HRA to introduce a 'fruit of the poisoned tree' exclusionary rule when it held that evidence later obtained as a result of the unlawful retention of a suspect's DNA samples by the police need not be ruled inadmissible to comply with Articles 8 or 6.[94] These decisions by the highest court, given within weeks of the commencement of Act, effectively smothered at birth any hope that the Convention might be used to re-balance this aspect of the criminal justice process.[95]

There are two clear reasons for the failure to re-evaluate the law post-incorporation, both involving the domestic courts' interpretation of Convention jurisprudence. So far as section 78 is concerned, domestic judges have laid stress upon pronouncements from the European Court of Human Rights that the *discretion* to exclude is the domestic remedy for breaches of Article 6. They have therefore specifically ruled out the adoption of an exclusionary rule by reinterpretation of section 78 under the HRA.[96] In *Mason*, where there was an admitted breach of Article 8 from bugging of a police cell without legal authority, Lord Woolf LCJ stated that:

> The language of s 78(1) has been given a generous application by the courts and this has enabled the European Court of Human Rights to regard it as providing a significant protection to an accused person.[97]

The second recurring reason concerns the handling of allegations that a defendant has been entrapped by the police. In *Teixeira de Castro v Portugal*[98] the European Court of Human Rights had held that the admission of evidence in a drugs case by a national court from police officers who were agents provocateurs violated Article 6. The UK courts have, however, given a restricted reading to *Teixiera*, so minimising the need to exclude tainted evidence under Article 6 in the first place. In a

---

[93]　*R v P* [2001] 2 WLR 463, 475 (Lord Hobhouse). The House of Lords affirmed pre-HRA authority that interception material obtained abroad could be lawfully admitted in an English trial, although had it been obtained in England it would have legally barred.

[94]　*A-G's Reference No 3 of 1999* [2001] 2 AC 91. Section 64 of the Police and Criminal Evidence Act 1984 was subsequently amended to allow the police to retain DNA samples despite the acquittal of the person from whom they were taken, and in *R v Chief Constable of South Yorkshire ex p Marper* [2004] UKHL 39 the House of Lords held that this provision was compatible with Arts 8 and 14.

[95]　For other examples of courts holding that evidence may be admitted despite breaches of Art 8: *R v Loveridge* [2001] 2 Cr App R 29; *R v Mason* [2002] Cr App R 38. See, however, *R v Grant* [2005] 2 Cr App R 29 staying proceedings where the police had conducted surveillance in breach of Art 8 with the intention of obtaining access to privileged communications between the defendant and his lawyer.

[96]　*R v Hardy and Hardy* [2003] Cr. App R 30, para 18 (Rose LJ).

[97]　*R v Mason and others* [2002] EWCA Crim 385, [49].

[98]　(1999) 28 EHRR 101.

decision given just over a week after the coming into force of the HRA the Court of Appeal upheld the conviction of John James Shannon, who had (somewhat improbably) been enticed into supplying drugs by a News of the World journalist disguised as a Arab sheikh.[99] The Court reaffirmed the principle that there was no defence of entrapment in English law, and that under section 78 it had to consider the effect of allowing in the evidence on the procedural fairness of the proceedings. The defendant's argument that earlier English authorities[100] had been overtaken by *Teixiera* and that a fresh approach was now required was rejected. Similarly, in November 1999 a Divisional Court which included Lord Bingham CJ ruled that neither the Strasbourg case law nor section 78 obliged a court to rule out evidence obtained by police officers who had participated in the commission of a crime.[101] Lord Bingham held that the stipendiary magistrate had incorrectly treated the officers as agents provocateurs and that *Teixeira* was distinguished by aggravating factors which were not present in the English proceedings[102] (indeed, could not have been under English rules of evidence), such as the absence of judicial supervision of the investigation. This position was confirmed by the House of Lords in *R v Loosely*[103] in which Lords Bingham, Lord Hoffmann and Lord Hutton[104] held that English law on entrapment was compatible with Article 6 (rejecting an argument that *Teixiera* will treat the police as breaching Article 6 unless they act entirely passively).[105]

Conclusion

Human-rights violations in the gathering of evidence appear at first sight to present the courts with a stark choice between either upholding a suspect's rights and punishing police abuse by excluding the evidence, or, alternatively, admitting telling evidence and, thereby, condoning malpractice. In cases of organised crime and terrorism especially one can readily

---

[99] *R v Shannon* [2001] 1 Cr App R 168.
[100] *R v Smurthwaite* [1994] 1 All ER 898; *R v Chalkley* [1998] QB 848.
[101] *Nottingham CC v Amin* [2000] 2 All ER 946.
[102] *Ibid*, 953.
[103] *R v Looseley; A-G's Reference (No 3 of 2000)* [2001] UKHL 53 [2001] 1 WLR 2060. In the second of these conjoined appeals however, the House of Lords upheld the trial judge's ruling that repeated attempts (15 in all) by undercover police officers to obtain drugs from the defendant before he succumbed should lead to a stay of proceedings as an abuse of process. See further, P Roberts and A Zuckerman, *Criminal Evidence* (2nd ed) (Oxford, OUP, 2004) 178–181.
[104] *Looseley*, paras 30, 71 and 109 respectively.
[105] The European Commission of Human Rights itself distinguished *Teixiera* in a case in which the undercover police officers were not instigators of the offence: *Shahzad v UK* [1998] EHLR 210.

understand the courts' reluctance to exclude such evidence, especially if the consequence is that the defendant will walk free.

It can be argued, however, that judges bear some responsibility for encouraging the police to work inside the boundaries of legality, rather than straddling the edge. Lord Scarman was perhaps referring to this, albeit indirectly, when in *Sang* he stated:

> The judge's control of the criminal process begins and ends with the trial, though his influence may extend beyond its beginning and conclusion.[106]

This responsibility requires a preparedness to exclude evidence when the line has been crossed. When that happens a costly and time-consuming investigation may well come to naught. It is tempting, but misleading, in these situations for the police to blame devious 'fat cat' defence lawyers and for the tabloid newspapers to paint the HRA as a villains' charter. It should be recognised, however, that in the modern era of intelligence-led policing choices of investigative methods are the product of calculated decisions (in which the Crown Prosecution Service may have been consulted in advance) about how evidence should be amassed. In reality, then, the responsibility when improperly obtained evidence is adduced at trial often lies in the way an investigation was planned or controlled.

The ultimate danger of ignoring official malpractice in favour of short-term pragmatic considerations is that in the long-term there will be a corrosion of the fundamental values that give society and those acting in its name the right to investigate, to try and to punish lawlessness. The disappointing use of the HRA in this field to date has done little to protect those values.

APPEALS

Unsafe/Unfair

The question of whether a convicted defendant should be acquitted because of a technical or procedural error by the prosecution or the trial judge has a substantial history in English law.[107] Particularly where legal defects in a trial with otherwise clearly incriminating evidence are concerned, the issue may involve an apparent conflict between the rule of law and commonsense. To acquit on a 'technicality' – to use the journalese – may bring the criminal justice system into disrepute and produce a substantial injustice. For this reason the law has long provided other

---

[106] [1979] 2 All ER 1222, 1246.
[107] For a recent summary: J Spencer, 'Quashing Convictions for Procedural Irregularities' (2007) *Crim LR* 835.

options: to convict notwithstanding, and the possibility of ordering a retrial. Other cases may, however, involve serious prosecution misconduct or errors so egregious as to call the reliability of the conviction into doubt. The current law addresses this variety of situations through a single test to be applied by an appellate court – whether the conviction is unsafe.[108]

In considering where to place breaches of the defendant's Convention rights on the scale outlined one might intuitively argue that they should always register at the more serious end, since they involve breach of a fundamental right, rather than some other legal requirement. As we have seen, however, when discussing evidence, Strasbourg itself does not take such a clear approach: there is no requirement that evidence obtained in violation of a Convention right must be excluded by a trial court and no automatic breach of Article 6 (the right to fair trial) if it is admitted.

A European Court of Human Rights ruling that a particular conviction has involved a violation of a person's Convention rights does not by itself have any effect on a conviction by the UK courts. Strasbourg, may of course, order compensation to be paid and, in practice, where successful applicants are still in custody or detention they have often been released immediately following the ECHR judgment. Whether the Court of Appeal should then set aside the conviction as unsafe is a separate issue.

In *R v Lyons*[109] the House of Lords found that a conviction should not be quashed despite the fact that it was based partially on evidence which the European Court of Human Rights had found violated Article 6.[110] Strictly, the HRA was irrelevant to the issue since the conviction pre-dated commencement. Nevertheless, the issue is substantially the same as that arising under the Act. Here the unfairness derived directly from a statutory provision expressly providing that answers obtained by company inspectors undue legal compulsion could be given in evidence.[111] In view of that, the House of Lords declined to find that the conviction was unsafe. In theory, the same issue could arise under the HRA if the domestic courts were to find a statutory rule governing evidence at the trial to be incompatible with the Convention and make a declaration under section 4 of the Act. In *Lyons* there was a second relevant objection based on the dualist approach to commitments under international treaties that characterises UK law. As Lord Hoffmann put it forcefully:

---

[108]   Criminal Appeal Act 1968 s 2 (as amended by Criminal Appeal Act 1995).
[109]   *R v Lyons* [2002] UKHL 44 [2003] 1 AC 976
[110]   *Lyons v UK* (2003) 37 EHRR CD 183. See also *Saunders v UK* (1997) 23 EHRR 313.
[111]   Companies Act 1985 s 434(5). In *Staines v Morrissey* (1997)2 Cr App R 426, 440–44 it had been held that evidence obtained a under a similar provision (Financial Services Act 1986 s 177(6)) should not be declared inadmissible in the absence of legislation to implement the ruling in *Saunders*. For powerful critique of *Saunders* see Lord Justice Sedley, 'Wringing Out the Fault: Self-Incrimination in the 21st Century' (2001) 52 *NILQ* 107.

[T]he Convention is an international treaty and the ECtHR is an international court with jurisdiction under international law to interpret and apply it. But the question of whether the appellants' convictions were unsafe is a matter of English law. And it is firmly established that international treaties do not form part of English law and that English courts have no jurisdiction to interpret or apply them. ... Parliament may pass a law which mirrors the terms of the treaty and in that sense incorporates the treaty into English law. But even then, the metaphor of incorporation may be misleading. It is not the treaty but the statute which forms part of English law. And English courts will not (unless the statute expressly so provides) be bound to give effect to interpretations of the treaty by an international court, even though the United Kingdom is bound by international law to do so. Of course there is a strong presumption in favour of interpreting English law (whether common law or statute) in a way which does not place the United Kingdom in breach of an international obligation... The sovereign legislator in the United Kingdom is Parliament. If Parliament has plainly laid down the law, it is the duty of the courts to apply it, whether that would involve the Crown in breach of an international treaty or not.[112]

Their Lordships therefore rejected the argument that they should give effect to the obligation to make just satisfaction for breach of the defendant's conviction rights by quashing the conviction.

The European Court has tended when considering breaches of Article 6 to view the domestic legal system as a whole. Thus, if defects in the original trial have been corrected by an appellate court, there is no breach of Article 6.[113] With the incorporation of the Convention the issue of how to transpose this aspect of Art 6 jurisprudence was problematic.[114] Under the section 6 HRA each court (including the trial court) is a public authority and is obliged not to violate a person's Convention rights. One domestic rendering of Article 6 therefore could have been that, wherever an appellate court found that the trial by the lower court had violated Article 6 the appeal should be allowed. Instead in *R v Craven*[115] the Court of Appeal chose to mimic the Strasbourg effect in *Edwards* and to hold that in a case where the prosecution had failed to disclose evidence this could be corrected on appeal by the higher court considering whether the evidence could have affected the jury's verdict.

---

[112]   Paras 27–28.
[113]   Eg, *Edwards v UK* 5 EHRR 417. Other Strasbourg decisions suggest, however, that on occasion an appellate court may be unable to correct defects (eg, if it cannot determine the effect of a proper direction from the trial judge over the defendant's silence when questioned on the jury: *Condron v UK* (2001) 31 EHRR 313).
[114]   Cf the discussion of judicial review; 159–61.
[115]   [2001] Cr App R 12, CA.

Turning to the effect of a breach of Article 6, the post-HRA case law reveals a variety of judicial perspectives.[116] An absolutist position of regarding all reaches of Article 6 as rendering the trial unsafe has been taken by some judges. In *A (No 2)* Lord Steyn stated that the right to a fair trial was absolute so that a conviction obtained in breach of the right must be quashed.[117]

On the other hand other judges do not regard such breaches as automatically rendering the conviction unsafe. This became clear in the so-called 'M25 murder' case. The Court of Human Rights held in March 2000 that the defendants' rights under Article 6 had been breached because of the failure to disclose at the trial that a key prosecution witness was a registered (ie paid) police informant.[118] Significantly, the European Court found that in this instance the failure had not been redeemed by the earlier proceedings in the Court of Appeal.[119] The question for the Court of Appeal following the Strasbourg ruling was whether therefore the conviction was unsafe.[120] Despite finding that it was, the court added its own unique and unnecessary rider: that this did not amount to a finding of innocence. Lord Justice Mantell developed a distinction between the fairness of the trial and the safety of a conviction. His Lordship stressed that the duty under the HRA to 'take account' of the Strasbourg decision did not mean that the English court had 'to adopt' or 'to apply' it. He obviously had in mind that the UK courts might on some future occasion treat as safe a conviction obtained in a trial which had been found to be unfair. One can perhaps detect in this decision a whiff of judicial impatience at the meddling of the Strasbourg judges in proceedings that had satisfied the standard of English justice.[121] It is certainly symptomatic of a minimalist approach to incorporation of the Convention that significantly devalues Article 6.

Between these two positions stands *R v Togher*, decided a few weeks later, in which the Lord Chief Justice stated that it was 'almost inevitable' that unfairness at the trial would make the conviction unsafe and that it would be 'most unfortunate' if the approach of the European Court and the English courts differed unless it was requirement of legislation.[122] Although the 'almost inevitable' aspect of the judgment is a welcome

---

[116] I Dennis, 'Fair Trials and Safe Convictions', [2003] *Current Legal Problems* 211; N Taylor and D Ormerod, 'Mind the Gaps: Safeness, Fairness and Moral Legitimacy', [2004] *Crim LR* 266.
[117] [2002] 1 AC 45, [38]. Cf. Lord Bingham in *R v Forbes* [2001] 1 AC 473, [24].
[118] *Rowe and Davis v UK* (2000) 30 EHRR 573.
[119] *R v Davies, Rowe and Johnson* [1993] 1 WLR 613.
[120] *R v Davis, Rowe and Johnson (No 3)* [2001] Cr App R 8.
[121] Earlier the Court of Appeal had upheld the use of public interest immunity certificates for the rehearing: *R v Davies, Rowe and Johnson (No 2)* [2001] Cr App R 115.
[122] *R v Togher* [2001] 3 All ER 463.

endorsement of the primacy of Article 6, the test has been criticised for providing no guidance to subsequent courts in how to draw the (albeit exceptional) line.[123]

Domestic courts can also be criticised for failing to articulate a clear rationale and test for distinguishing between unsafeness and unfairness. On the one hand, in *R v Lewis* the Court of Appeal found a conviction to be safe notwithstanding the European Court of Human Rights earlier ruling that the defendant's Article 6 rights had been breached by the judge's denial of his application for disclosure of material that might have made good his defence of entrapment.[124] On the other hand, in *R v Allen*[125] the defendant's conviction for murder and conspiracy to rob was quashed after the European Court of Human Rights had found that the actions of a 'cell informer' had denied his right not to incriminate himself, contrary to Article 6.[126]

The reason why no simple solution is appealing to the unsafe/unsafe conundrum is the variety of factors that may give rise to breach of Article 6. These range from deliberate police or prosecution wrongdoing at the investigation stage to an honest misdirection by the trial judge. While examples of deliberate wrongdoing will satisfy the standard for abuse of process and will always make a conviction unsafe[127] in other instances, the Strasbourg Court itself recognises that a breach of Article 6 need not always result in the conviction being quashed.

Commentators have made various suggestions for reconciling any apparent contradictions. Professor Ian Dennis has argued in defence of maintaining the distinction, proposing that in instances where the unfairness does not affect the safety of the conviction that a 'declaration of violation' (ie a bare finding by the appellate court without quashing the conviction) is sufficient remedy.[128] Other solutions also focus on acknowledging the unfairness without quashing the conviction. The existing caselaw gives some support to reducing a defendant's sentence a remedy for breach of Article 6.[129] Others have proposed that payment of damages to the defendant while upholding the conviction might be appropriate,[130] although the predictable tabloid and public reaction to a judge who

---

[123] See especially Taylor and Ormerod, op. cit..
[124] *R v Lewis* [2005] Crim LR 796.
[125] [2004] EWCA Crim 2236; [2005] *Crim LR* 716.
[126] *Allen v UK* (2003) 36 EHRR 12.
[127] Tayor and Ormerod, op. cit.
[128] Dennis, op. cit., 236; see also Rose LJ in *R v Botmeh and Alami* [2002] 1 Cr App R 345, 356.
[129] B Emerson and A Ashworth, *Human Rights and Criminal Justice* (London, 2001) para 17–34.
[130] Emerson and Ashworth, *Human Rights and Criminal Justice*, para 17–33.

sentenced a defendant to prison *and* awarded him damages would surely have a chilling effect.

Retrospective Effect

One early but predictable question arising in relation to criminal appeals was that of retrospectivity: whether the HRA should be applied to prosecutions tried before the October 2000 commencement date but where the appeal was heard after the Act came into force. The combined effect of sections 7 and 22 was that a person could rely on his Convention rights against a public authority whenever the act in question took place (ie regardless of whether it was before or after commencement), but that the Act could only be used offensively to sue a public authority from commencement. This policy was intelligible: a public authority after all chooses whether or not to bring proceedings but has no choice about being sued. The complication, however, was that courts and tribunals are also 'public authorities' under section 6 of the Act, so that if a person could invoke Convention rights before them irrespective of the date of the act in question then the HRA would necessarily apply to courts hearing appeals.

This was an obvious difficulty and widely foreseen by practitioners when the Act was under discussion. In the absence of a much clearer commencement provision ruling out this argument the assumption was that Parliament intended the Act to be applied to appeals heard after October 2000. It came as a surprise therefore when the House of Lords in *R v Lambert*[131] reached the opposite conclusion, applying a presumption against retrospectivity to hold that a defendant could not use the HRA to challenge a pre-commencement decision by a court which was lawful when it was made. It did so by a process of unpersuasive reasoning which depended upon distinguishing the appeal court from other public authorities: the court did not 'bring or instigate' proceedings in hearing an appeal after October 2000. This ruling certainly succeeded in closing the doors to a large number of appeals against otherwise unimpeachable convictions (like *Lambert* itself).

However, difficulties with this line of reasoning were overlooked.[132] It proved *too much* since all prosecutions (not just appeals) would be captured by the same line of argument, so that, if correct, the Act would not apply to them at all! In fact all matters within the courts' jurisdiction could be said to arise as a matter of duty at the instigation of others, so

---

[131] [2002] 2 AC 545.

[132] D Beyveld, R Kirkham and D Townend, 'Which Presumption? A Critique of the House of Lords Reasoning on Retrospectivity and the Human Rights Act' (2002) *LS* 185; for a more sympathetic treatment: C Gearty, *Principles of Human Rights Adjudication* (Oxford, OUP, 2004), 169–171.

that the inclusion of courts as public authorities would be rendered virtually meaningless. By the time, a few months later, that the House of Lords admitted the glaring error in *Lambert* it was too late to undo it without causing chaos and further inconsistency. In *Kansal (No 2)*[133] the House therefore followed *Lambert* for reasons of certainty, notwithstanding that a majority of their Lordships now believed it to be wrongly decided.

SENTENCING

In contrast to the relative lack of impact of the HRA upon substantive criminal law, procedure and evidence, the effect upon sentencing and punishment of convicted offenders has been more marked. Challenges have taken two main forms: to limitations on judicial discretion in sentencing, whether by the involvement of the executive or through mandatory sentences imposed by statute and, secondly, to changes imposed through legislation in the status and significance of earlier convictions. Before we examine the impact of the HRA upon these fields some background is necessary.

The sentencing of convicted offenders is a uniquely practical test-bed for the constitutional separation of powers: the prevailing norm within the UK tradition has been for the maximum applicable sentence to be stipulated by statute and for the trial judge to determine up to that maximum the precise sentence in the light of the circumstances of the offence and the offender's history and situation. No one rationale for punishment prevails,[134] but, broadly speaking, the statutory maximum embodies a retributivist approach in reflecting society's view of the gravity of offences of a particular type, whereas the judge's discretion allows not only for more precise calibration of the individual circumstances of this offence in comparison to similar ones, but also for other factors, including deterrence and possible rehabilitation of the offender, to be taken into account. This, however, is highly simplified outline since Parliament has in most circumstances entrusted the courts with a range of sentencing options (including community sentences) from which to choose.

The executive's part in the process has traditionally come once the sentence (especially in the case of prison sentences) is being served, through the discretionary early release of prisoners deemed no longer to pose a risk or to have been sufficiently rehabilitated. In the case of prisoners serving

---

[133]   *R v Kansal (No 2)* [2002] 2 AC 69.

[134]   Criminal Justice Act 2003 s 143 requires a court to consider the following purposes: '(a) the punishment of offenders, (b) the reduction of crime (including its reduction by deterrence), (c) the reform and rehabilitation of offenders, (d) the protection of the public, and (e) the making of reparation by offenders to persons affected by their offences.'

fixed or indeterminate sentences – mainly murderers, where the only punishment a court can give is life imprisonment – executive discretion loomed particularly large in determining the actual sentence served. Although much decision-making had in practice been delegated to the independent Parole Board, nevertheless there remained the significant risk that Home Secretaries, with whom the ultimate decision lay, could be influenced by political or popular pressures, especially in the cases of notorious offenders.

As will be clear, the sentencing system is a complex and finely balanced one. Nevertheless, two significant sources of tension are virtually institutionalised in these arrangements. On the one hand, for decades the press and politicians have reacted to sentences that they perceive to be lenient in the light of the statutory maximum. One response has been to curtail judicial sentencing discretion. The judiciary, on the other hand, regard with suspicion not just these incursions that prevent them tailoring sentences to the particulars of the offence and the offender, but also more generally the executive involvement in criminal justice, an area they see as their own special reserve.

By the mid-1990s and in particular under the overlapping terms of office of Michael Howard as Home Secretary and Lord Taylor as Lord Chief Justice, simmering discontent boiled over into open public conflict over government plans to introduce mandatory life sentences for offenders convicted of a second serious offence.[135] Following an unprecedented but unsuccessful campaign of opposition by the senior judiciary the proposals were enacted in the Crime (Sentences) Act 1997. The Act made only minor concession to judicial concerns by allowing a court not to impose the mandatory life sentence. It was a requirement of section 2 of the 1997 Act that persons convicted of a 'second serious offence'[136] should serve a mandatory life sentence of imprisonment and courts would only be entitled not to impose such a sentence where they could demonstrate that there were 'exceptional circumstances' relating to either of the offences which would 'justify its not doing so'. Case law in the period before the HRA quickly established that this gave little leeway to judges.[137]

Nevertheless, following the introduction of the HRA the issue was dramatically reconsidered under section 3(1) in *R v Offen*.[138] The Court of Appeal was concerned that, given the 'restrictive' approach to the interpretation of the phrase 'exceptional circumstances', it was possible that the section could be applied in an 'arbitrary and disproportionate' manner in

---

[135] I Loveland, 'War Against the Judges' (1997) 68 *Pol Q* 162.
[136] 'Serious offences' were defined in Crime (Sentences) Act 1997 s 2(5)–(7).
[137] *R v Kelly (Edward)* [2000] QB 198.
[138] *R v Offen* [2001] 1 WLR 253 (CA).

contravention of Article 5, and possibly Article 3, of the Convention.[139] Giving the judgment of the Court, Lord Woolf said very little about the scope or requirements of section 3(1) HRA, disarmingly stating that:

> [t]he consequence of section 3 is that legislation which affects human rights is required to be construed in a manner which conforms with the Convention wherever this is possible.[140]

Flowing from this, the Court of Appeal felt able to suggest that, 'section 2 of the 1997 Act will not contravene Convention rights if courts apply the section so that it does not result in offenders being sentenced to life imprisonment when they do not constitute a significant risk to the public.'[141]

This reading was a considerable liberalisation of the approach to be taken to the provision in question. As Professor Conor Gearty has commented:

> however it is dressed up or explained away, the *Offen* case has effectively disembowelled a particularly savage legislative intervention', so that, 'even opponents of judicial activism find themselves applauding the result while diverting their eyes from how it was brought about.[142]

Lord Woolf however, downplayed the significance of the interpretation adopted, stating that under its terms:

> the 1997 Act will still give effect to the intention of Parliament. It will do so, however, in a more just, less arbitrary and more proportionate manner.[143]

In view of the history of this contentious provision Gearty's assessment is to be preferred: in this instance we have a concrete example of a judicial rearguard action to recapture through 'interpretation' ground that had been lost in the political conflict over sentencing.

Equally significantly, although more predictable in the light of Strasbourg rulings on the meaning of Article 6, the HRA has hastened the expulsion of the Home Secretary from active decision-making over the release of life prisoners.[144] The system of indeterminate life sentences belonged to a different era. In the 1960s when capital punishment in Britain was replaced with mandatory life sentences, giving the power of review to a minister seemed to be a natural extension of the Home Secretary's role in considering the prerogative of mercy. Nearly 40 years

---

[139] *Ibid*, paras 95–96.
[140] *R v Offen* [2001] 1 WLR 253, para 92.
[141] *Ibid*, para 97.
[142] C A Gearty, *Principles of Human Rights Adjudication* (Oxford, OUP, 2004) 77.
[143] *R v Offen* [2001] 1 WLR 253, para 99.
[144] See also N Padfield, *Beyond the Tariff: Human Rights and the Release of Life Sentence Prisoners* (Devon, Willan Publishing, 2002).

later, however, it appeared to violate an important principle: that sentences should be determined by an independent officer and not a politician, who may be too sensitive to public and tabloid opinion. The ECHR does not oppose indeterminate sentences as such: it is independence in the review process that is scrutinised under Article 6.

The Home Secretary's role in discretionary life sentences for convictions other than murder had already been reduced to a purely formal one following Strasbourg challenges[145] and the system of detention of youth offenders 'at Her Majesty's pleasure' had likewise been reformed following European Court of Human Rights rulings.[146] The final step – long-predicted – came following *Anderson* in 2002.[147] At the time, section 29 Crime (Sentences) Act 1997 allowed for the Secretary of State to release a discretionary life prisoner if so recommended by the Parole Board (which could only act if he referred the case or a class of cases to it), after consultation with the Lord Chief Justice together with the trial judge (if available). Under this regime the Home Secretary set the 'tariff sentence' to be served by the prisoner, although he usually did so in accordance with advice submitted by the trial judge and the Lord Chief Justice. However the European Court of Human Rights had concluded that:

> the continuing role of the Secretary of State in fixing the tariff and in deciding on a prisoner's release following its expiry, has become increasingly difficult to reconcile with the notion of separation of powers between the executive and the judiciary, a notion which has assumed growing importance in the case law of the Court.[148]

The House of Lords found that the Home Secretary's role under section 29 violated Article 6, since setting the tariff was effectively setting the punishment for the offence and therefore issued a declaration of incompatibility. When it came there was little fanfare or indignation from ministers. They had already anticipated the ruling[149] and legislation to repeal ministerial involvement in the process quickly followed on.[150] The House of Lords had hammered home the final nail in a coffin lid secured by previous Strasbourg rulings.[151]

---

[145] *Weeks v UK* (1987) 10 EHRR 293; *Thynne, Wilson and Gunnell v UK* (1990) 13 EHRR 666; *Practice Statement (Crime: Life Sentences)* [2002] 1 WLR 1789.

[146] Especially *V v UK* (1999) 30 EHRR 121. See also *Practice Statement (Juveniles: Murder Tariff)* [2000] 1 WLR 1655.

[147] *R (Anderson) v SSHD* [2002] UKHL 46; [2003] 1 AC 837; see 63 above.

[148] *Stafford v UK* (2002) 35 EHRR 32, para 78; see also *Benjamin and Wilson v UK* (2003) 36 EHRR 1.

[149] See the interim measures described by Lord Steyn at para 45 in *Anderson*.

[150] Criminal Justice Act 2003 Sch 37 Pt 8

[151] The House of Lords has also determined that statutory provisions relating to the determination of tariffs by judges (*R (Hammond) v Home Secretary* [2006] 1 AC 603) are incompatible with the European Convention on Human Rights. In contrast, the regime

CONCLUSION

In its 2006 survey of developments under the HRA the Department for Constitutional Affairs concluded that the Act had 'no significant impact on criminal law or on the Government's ability to fight crime'.[152] This is an accurate confirmation of the relative lack of impact of the Act in the criminal justice sphere. Although, as explained in the introduction, one would expect the opposite, only a handful of successful HRA arguments have prevailed in criminal cases, for example, in relation to some reverse burdens and executive involvement in sentencing. Some other major opportunities to develop the law (notably in relation to evidence obtained in violation of Convention rights) have been ducked by the courts altogether. The restricted reading given to the meaning of a 'criminal charge' and the maintenance of a distinction between an unsafe conviction and an unfair trial have further restricted the potential impact of Convention rights. The tabloid myth of the Act as villain's charter has remained exactly that. At the same time, however, a number of arguably more meritorious human rights claims have also been denied a remedy as a result of the UK courts' conservative approach.

relating to young offenders held 'At Her Majesty's Pleasure' was compatible; *R (Smith) v Home Secretary* [2006] 1 AC 159.

[152] Department of Constitutional Affairs, *Review of the Implementation of the Human Rights Act* (London, 2006) 10.

Chapter 8

Human Rights and Counter-Terrorism Measures

HISTORICAL BACKGROUND

IT IS AN obvious but easily overlooked point that, for the United Kingdom, human rights concerns over anti-terrorist powers did not begin with the response to the attacks of 9/11. The UK's experience in dealing with a disaffected group of its citizens within its own borders over some 30 or more years beforehand undoubtedly shaped its legislative responses to 9/11 in several respects, as we shall see below. Northern Ireland also provides other cautionary lessons. The process of exceptional powers becoming accepted into the mainstream legal process through familiarity is a clear risk.[1] Derogations from the international human rights standards (the European Convention on Human Rights) applied to Northern Ireland from 1957 until 2001 (when they were overtaken by the post-9/11 measures) with the exception of a short interval between 1984–88.

Certainly, reflecting on that earlier period, neither domestic legislators nor judges presented any substantial obstacle to the steady erosion of civil liberties.[2] Successive governments obtained renewal of emergency legislation regularly, from the pub bombings in 1974 that were the precursor to the Prevention of Terrorism (Temporary Provisions) Act 1974, up until its permanent replacement by the Terrorism Act 2000.[3] Even before 1974 in Northern Ireland itself the disastrous policy of internment had been implemented.[4] In the face of clear and detailed legislation, domestic judges

---

[1] Provisions allowing for adverse comment on a defendant's silence and allowing for the compulsory taking of body samples, for example, were first introduced in UK law as counter-terrorist measures before being extended more generally.

[2] K Ewing and C Gearty, *Freedom under Thatcher: Civil Liberties in Modern Britain* (Oxford, Clarendon Press, 1990) ch 7.

[3] C Walker, *The Prevention of Terrorism in British Law* (2nd ed) (Manchester, Manchester University Press, 1992); On the 2000 Act: H Fenwick *Civil Liberties, New Labour, Freedom and the Human Rights Act* (London, Longman, 2000) 72ff.

[4] Emergency Provisions (Northern Ireland) Acts 1973–1998; R J Spjut, 'Internment and Detention Without Trial in Northern Ireland 1971–1975: Ministerial Policy and Practice' (1986) 49 *MLR*. 712 .

were relatively powerless. Moreover, when it lay within their power to develop the law to protect human rights against incursion in the name of fighting terrorism they showed little inclination. At a moment when the Troubles were relatively calm the House of Lords in the *Brind* case declined to intervene to hold remarkable powers over broadcasters to be irrational, disproportionate, or, indeed, an infringement of human rights at all (since ministers did not need even to consider the ECHR).[5]

Against this background the central question to be considered, then, in this chapter is what difference, if any, the Human Rights Act 1998 (HRA) has made in the new emergency that has applied since the attacks on 9/11.

Formerly, violations of international human rights law resulting from counter-terrorism measures would have been pursued solely (and invariably after considerable delay) before the European Court of Human Rights. This happened, for example, with the Northern Ireland army interrogation case[6], with the 'Death on the Rock' killings in Gibraltar[7], and in challenges to the powers of detention before charge under anti-terrorist legislation.[8] The desire to avoid the international embarrassment of condemnation before the Strasbourg court in high-profile cases like these was one incentive towards incorporation of the Convention.

In the new environment both Parliament and government vet legislative proposals for Convention compatibility.[9] Domestic courts have an obligation to interpret statutory powers as far as possible in a way that conforms to the European Convention on Human Rights and, where this is impossible to achieve, may give a declaration of incompatibility.[10] Public authorities such as the police, prosecutors and the security services are under a duty not to violate a person's Convention rights (regardless of their citizenship). Have these new responsibilities produced a markedly different response than those during the thirty years of the Northern Ireland conflict?

9/11, PARLIAMENT AND THE 2001 ACT

The government's commitment to respect for human rights was given an early test after 11 September 2001. Although a comprehensive code of measures covering international terrorism – the Terrorism Act 2000 – had

---

[5] *R v Secretary of State for the Home Department ex p Brind* [1991] 1 AC 696, concerning ministerial directions prohibiting the broadcasting of interviews with persons from terrorist-connected organisations.
  [6] *Ireland v UK* (1978) 2 EHRR 25.
  [7] *McCann v UK* (1995) 21 EHRR 97.
  [8] *Brogan v UK* (1988) 11 EHRR 117.
  [9] See the discussion of HRA s 19: ch 2 above.
  [10] Ch 5 above.

only recently been put on the statute book and had been intended as a standing codification of law on the subject, the government was quick to propose a raft of further measures in the Anti-Terrorism Crime and Security Act 2001.[11]

The Terrorism Act 2000 had been passed following the review of the need for a continuation of anti-terrorism legislation by Lord Lloyd of Berwick[12] in the light of the Northern Ireland peace process. It was accepted that there was a case for standing anti-terrorist powers to replace the succession of temporary revisions of the previous quarter-century. Powers that had been incrementally introduced in response to the Northern Ireland troubles, such as extended detention before charge of terrorist suspects, proscription of terrorist organisations and measures against fundraising and information-gathering for terrorist purposes, were now applied to international terrorism. Significantly, the power of internment had been allowed first to lapse and then had been formally removed from the statute book,[13] and was not re-introduced despite the worst atrocity of the Troubles: the murder of 29 people at Omagh in August 1998.

Despite this very recent wholesale reform of the legislation, the government responded to 9/11 with a fresh series of measures. Early signs of ministers' thinking came in a speech in October 2001 to the Labour Party Conference by the Home Secretary, David Blunkett.[14] The speech was significant as much for its hostile tone – in one passage the Home Secretary denigrated 'airy fairy' civil libertarians – as for its proposals. The latter included three especially controversial ideas guaranteed to disquiet anyone with the slightest libertarian instincts, whether vague or specific. These were: that the penalties for bombing hoaxing should be increased, and with retrospective effect; the creation of a new offence of incitement to religious hatred; and a power to detain indefinitely non-British citizens who were deemed to be a security threat but who could not, for their own safety, be deported to a safe country. These proposals struck at the foundations of the democratic values of the rule of law (notably aversion to retrospective legislation and detention without trial) and freedom of expression which, it was claimed, were under threat from Al-Qaeda.

---

[11] See L Freedman (ed) *Superterrorism: Policy Responses* (Oxford, Wiley-Blackwell, 2002). For analysis of the legal implications, see: D Bonner, 'Managing Terrorism While Respecting Human Rights? European Aspects of the Anti-Terrorism Crime and Security Act 2001 (2002) 8 *European Public Law* 497; H Fenwick 'The Anti-Terrorism, Crime and Security Act 2001: A Proportionate Response to September 11?' [2002] 65 *MLR* 724; A Tomkins, 'Legislating Against Terror: the Anti-Terrorism, Crime and Security Act 2001 [2002] *PL* 106; D Bonner, *Executive Measures, Terrorism and National Security* (Aldershot, Ashgate, 2007) Pt III.

[12] *Inquiry into Legislation Against Terrorism*, Cm 3420 (1996).

[13] Northern Ireland (Emergency Provisions) Act 1998.

[14] <http://news.bbc.co.uk/1/hi/in_depth/uk_politics/2001/conferences_2001/labour/1564434.stm> accessed 18 May 2008.

In order to implement the detention scheme it was necessary for a derogation to be entered under the European Convention on Human Rights. This course had only been followed twice before, on both occasions in response to events in Northern Ireland. It is reserved, in the words of Article 15 of the Convention, for 'time of war or other public emergency threatening the life of the nation'. The derogation was made in November 2001, as is required under the ECHR, by a letter to the Secretary General of the Council of Europe. This referred to a grave domestic public emergency arising from the attacks in New York and Washington, the presence in the UK of foreign nationals who were a threat to national security and to pronouncements from the UN Security Council. It provided for limited suspension of Article 5 of the Convention, a step which is necessary since the Convention permits detention only for limited purposes including prior to trial and deportation, neither of which would be applicable in this instance. The lodging of a derogation does not, however, foreclose judicial review of whether it is 'strictly necessary'.[15] As we shall see, the validity of the derogation was tested in the courts. However, an opportunity for political scrutiny of the derogation also arose because of the domestic requirement (under section 14 of the HRA) to lay subordinate legislation giving notice of the derogation in order to qualify the definition of 'Convention Rights' applicable in UK courts and tribunals. The Human Rights Act (Designated Derogation) Order 2001 was laid before Parliament on 12 November 2001.[16] Paradoxically, the entering of the derogation enabled the Home Secretary to sign the certificate required under section 19 of the HRA, stating that the Anti-Terrorism Crime and Security Bill was compatible with the Convention Rights. Although legally correct, the reasoning suggests a high expectation of tokenism in the scrutiny given by Parliament.

The 2001 Act contained a range of measures directed not only at terrorism but also the support of terrorism. These included powers to freeze the assets of terrorist groups and of individuals posing a threat to the UK or its nationals, increased duties of disclosure on financial institutions and enhanced supervision of bureaux de change, an easing of restrictions on the sharing of information by the security and intelligence agencies, law enforcement agencies and customs, greater access to information held by air and freight carriers, a code of practice relating to retention of communications data, tighter controls over material usable in the making of chemical biological or nuclear weapons, new offences of hoaxing

---

[15] See the judgments of the European Court of Human Rights in *Lawless v Ireland* (1961) EHRR 15; *The First Greek Case* (1969) 12 YB Eur Conv HR 1; *Brannigan and McBride v UK* (1993) 17 EHRR 553; *Aksoy v Turkey* (1996) 23 EHRR 553.

[16] SI 2001/3644.

concerning noxious substances, and extended powers for the police to photograph, search and examine persons to establish their identity.

A number of other controversial proposals were modified during the parliamentary discussions on the Bill, due to the efforts of the Joint Parliamentary Committee on Human Rights[17] and to the House of Lords. The proposal to increase retrospectively the penalties for bomb-hoaxing was withdrawn. In addition, reflecting a widespread campaign in the media from prominent broadcasters and comedians and by religious groups, the Lords deleted a proposed new hate speech law, creating an offence of incitement to religious hatred.[18] This proposal, and that relating to retaining communications, was seen as an attempt by ministers to use the opportunity of an international crisis to legislate on matters considerably wider than terrorism while the political climate made opposition minimal. Several important amendments were incorporated thanks to the Upper House: a 'sunset clause' requiring the detention power to lapse after 15 months unless renewed (Anti-Terrorism Crime and Security Act 2001 s 29), review of the legislation[19], limitation on widely drawn powers to introduce new criminal offences by delegated legislation to implement European Union 'Third Pillar' measures[20] (both of these changes had been recommended by the Home Affairs Select Committee[21]), and restrictions on the powers to share information among government agencies.

By far the most controversial power in the 2001 Act, however, was contained in Pt IV, providing for indefinite detention without trial – a power traditionally reserved for wartime.[22] Although, mindful of the Northern Ireland experience, the government avoided referring to 'internment', the consequence was the same: a power of indefinite detention without trial for foreign nationals whom the Home Secretary certified as suspected terrorist suspects and who could not be deported because of fear of persecution. A right of appeal lay to the Special Immigration Appeals Commission (SIAC), which would determine, based on all of the available information, whether there were reasonable grounds for the detention. In hearings before SIAC, material could be withheld from the detainee on

---

[17] *Second Report of the Joint Committee*, 37 HC 372 (2001–02); *Fifth Report of the Joint Committee*, HL 51, HC 420 (2001–02).

[18] In a considerably modified form the proposal was eventually passed at the third attempt in the Racial and Religious Hatred Act 2006: I Hare, 'Crosses, Crescents and Sacred Cows: Criminalising Incitement to Religious Hatred' [2006] *PL* 520–37; R Ahdar and I Leigh, *Religious Freedom in the Liberal State* (Oxford, OUP, 2005) ch 12; H Fenwick and G Phillipson, *Media Freedom and the Human Rights Act* (London, LexisNexis UK, 2007) 508–27.

[19] Ss 28, 122.

[20] Ss 111, 112.

[21] Home Affairs Select Committee, *First Report*, HC 351 (2001–02).

[22] A Simpson, *In the Highest Degree Odious: Detention Without Trial in Wartime Britain* (Oxford, Clarendon Press, 1992).

security grounds. However, the suspect could be represented by a security-cleared 'special advocate', who had access to the classified information upon which the detention was based, although this could not be discussed with the detainee.[23] In the event 16 persons were detained, although as some of these were prosecuted or released on stringent bail conditions, the number had by January 2005 reduced to 7[24]

These detentions were – famously – found to be unlawful in the *Belmarsh* detainees case handed down by the House of Lords in December 2004. To long-term students of national security jurisprudence[25] the *Belmarsh* decision came as a welcome surprise. There was little reason beforehand to be confident that the HRA would produce change in judicial attitude towards national security claims.

Indeed, in a decision given weeks after 9/11 the House of Lords in *Rehman* had in effect undone some of the recent work to subject national security deportation decisions to additional scrutiny.[26] *Rehman* was the first challenge to reach the Appellate Committee from SIAC – the body established to bring the procedure into conformity with Article 6 following the European Court of Human Rights adverse ruling in the *Chahal* case.[27] The clear intention had been that SIAC would be a judicial forum in which deportation decisions based on intelligence material could be challenged effectively. This was why special innovative procedures for closed hearings (with the possibility of excluding the deportee in part) and special advocates were introduced:[28] to overcome the conundrum usually facing a court in such cases. The House of Lords, however, invoked the separation

---

[23]   Report, Privy Counsellor Review Committee, *Anti-Terrorism, Crime and Security Act 2001 Review*, 18 December 2003.

[24]   See the annual reviews by Lord Carlile of Berriew QC, under Anti-Terrorism Crime and Security Act 2001, Pt IV, s 28.

[25]   See L Lustgarten and I Leigh, *In From the Cold: National Security and Parliamentary Democracy* (Oxford, Clarendon Press, 1994) ch 12 for a survey of earlier decisions from several jurisdictions.

[26]   *Secretary of State for the Home Department v Rehman* [2001] UKHL 47; [2002] 1 All ER 122.

[27]   *Chahal v UK* (1996) 23 EHRR 413.

[28]   Special Advocates were introduced by the Special Immigration Appeals Commission Act 1997 s 6. They have access to closed material and represent the deportees interests but may not take instructions from the deportee: see the   Special Immigration Appeals Commission (Procedure) Rules 2003 SI 2003/1034 (as amended), rr 36–38. Comparable procedures have been introduced in several other areas of law where national security interests are at stake. For a detailed and critical study see C Forcese and L Waldman, *Seeking Justice in an Unfair Process: Lessons from Canada, the United Kingdom, and New Zealand on the Use of 'Special Advocates' in National Security Proceedings* (Ottawa, 2007) <http://aix1.uottawa.ca/~cforcese/other/sastudy.pdf> accessed 18 May 2008. See also: *Treasury Solicitor, Special Advocates: a Guide to the Role of Special Advocates* (London, 2005); Constitutional Affairs Select Committee, *Seventh Report for 2004–5, The operation of the Special Immigration Appeals Commission (SIAC) and the use of Special Advocates*, HC 323-I; Bonner, *Executive Measures* 276–286; 215–16 below.

of powers doctrine[29] to hold that a judicial body like SIAC had to defer to the executive's assessment of national security (in this instance, concerning the damage to UK interests from alleged terrorist-related activities in the Indian sub-continent) if Rehman were not deported. Lord Hoffmann, in a passage bearing little resemblance to his celebrated dissent three years later, reasoned:

> in matters of national security, the cost of failure can be high. This seems to me to underline the need for the judicial arm of government to respect the decisions of ministers of the Crown on the question of whether support for terrorist activities in a foreign country constitutes a threat to national security. It is not only that the executive has access to special information and expertise in these matters. It is also that such decisions, with serious potential results for the community, require a legitimacy which can be conferred only by entrusting them to persons responsible to the community through the democratic process. If the people are to accept the consequences of such decisions, they must be made by persons whom the people have elected and whom they can remove.[30]

Only Lord Steyn referred to the HRA and, while he acknowledged that the Convention was relevant in determining the scope of SIAC's appellate jurisdiction, and that under Convention jurisprudence the courts could review national security decisions, he argued that nevertheless a doctrine of deference towards the executive applied.[31] There was little sign here that the HRA would make any difference to the attitude of deference towards the executive in national security matters that stretched in an unbroken line of cases going back to the First World War.[32]

Against this background the celebrated decision of December 2004 of the House of Lord in the *Belmarsh* detainees case is all the more striking. As is well known, a majority of the House of Lords found that the measures providing for detention without trial of foreign nationals under the Anti-Terrorism Crime and Security Act 2001 violated the Convention.[33] Hence the derogation entered under Art 15 of the Convention and by an order under the HRA were not operative. With that hurdle removed there was a clear violation of Article 5, since the detention was neither

---

[29] See especially Lord Hoffmann in *Rehman* at paras 50 ff.

[30] *Ibid*, para 62.

[31] Para 31. Lord Slynn stated: 'There must be material on which proportionately and reasonably he [the Secretary of State] can conclude that there is a real possibility of activities harmful to national security ...' (para 22).

[32] For examples relating to detention and deportation on national security grounds see: *R v Halliday ex p Zadig* [1917] AC 260; *Liversidge v Anderson* [1942] AC 206; *R v Secretary of State for the Home Department ex p Hosenball* [1977] 1 WLR 766; *R v Secretary of State for the Home Department ex p Cheblak* [1991] 2 All ER 319. See further L Lustgarten and I Leigh, *In From the Cold: National Security and Parliamentary Democracy* (Oxford, Clarendon Press, 1994) chs 7, 12.

[33] *A (FC) and Others (FC) v Secretary of State for the Home Department* [2004] UKHL 56, Lord Walker of Gestinthorpe dissenting. See further (2005) 68 *MLR* 672.

prior to deportation or to trial: rather, it was as an alternative to both. The House issued a quashing order in respect of the Human Rights Act 1998 (Designated Derogation) Order 2001 and a declaration of incompatibility finding section 23 of the 2001 Act[34] to be incompatible with Articles 5 and 14 insofar as it was disproportionate and discriminated on grounds of nationality.[35] Was the unexpectedly sceptical attitude on the part of the judiciary attributable to the HRA? It would appear so.

Lord Bingham rejected the Attorney-General's argument that on constitutional grounds the courts should not review whether measures were *strictly required* by the exigencies of the situation:

> It is of course true that the judges in this country are not elected and are not answerable to Parliament. It is also of course true ... that Parliament, the executive and the courts have different functions. But the function of independent judges charged to interpret and apply the law is universally recognised as a cardinal feature of the modern democratic state, a cornerstone of the rule of law itself. The Attorney General is fully entitled to insist on the proper limits of judicial authority, but he is wrong to stigmatise judicial decision-making as in some way undemocratic. .... The 1998 Act gives the courts a very specific, wholly democratic, mandate.[36]

Lord Nicholls and Lord Hope emphasised that the courts had a responsibility to subject the authorisation of indefinite detention by the executive to the closest scrutiny because of interference with the fundamental right of liberty.[37]

In contrast, Lord Walker, dissenting, found that the derogating measures were neither disproportionate having regard to the exigencies of the emergency nor unjustifiably discriminatory. He pointed to the safeguards inserted by Parliament into the scheme, especially the availability of judicial review of the Secretary of State's powers before SIAC (which not was also required under to review every certificate at regular intervals), the temporary nature of the legislation and periodic parliamentary review of extensions of the power, and the reports on its operation by the independent assessor (Lord Carlile QC) appointed under section 28.

---

[34] The provision enabling indefinite detention of a person who could not be deported, following the Home Secretary's certifying that he reasonably believed that the person's presence in the United Kingdom constituted a threat to national security and that he suspected the person to be a terrorist.

[35] Para 73. See generally D Moeckli, 'The Selective "War on Terror": Executive Detention of Foreign Nationals and the Principle of Non-Discrimination' (2006) 31 *Brook J of Int Law* 495.

[36] Para 42. For further discussion of the impact of the HRA on the separation of powers see ch 5 above.

[37] Lord Nicholls, para 81; Lord Hope, para 100.

All these safeguards seem to me to show a genuine determination that the 2001 Act, and especially Pt 4, should not be used to encroach on human rights any more than is strictly necessary.[38]

For the majority of their Lordships, however, two features of the government's stance were fatal to justifying these powers. First, that they did not apply to those UK citizens (on the Government's estimate, in excess of a thousand) who had engaged in comparable behaviour to the target group of foreign nationals, for example, by attending training in jihadist camps. As Lord Rodger put it:

> The acute question was whether the exigencies of the situation strictly required a small number of foreign suspects to endure indefinite detention of this kind while, in the judgment of the Government and Parliament, an undisclosed number of British suspects could safely be allowed to remain at liberty.[39]

The Government's failure to take comparable measures against this group of British citizens doubly undermined its case: it cast doubt on the necessity of acting against non-UK citizens and was, moreover, discriminatory (contrary to Art 14 of the European Convention). Whereas a difference in the treatment of the two groups could be justified for the purposes of immigration,[40] when seen from the perspective of security measures (as the House of Lords argued to be the correct viewpoint[41]), it could not. Secondly, the foreigners were in a prison with three walls only: if they could find another state prepared to accept them, they could leave the United Kingdom at any time. The fact that the UK Government was prepared to allow them to regain their liberty and freedom of action in this way again cast doubt on the seriousness of threat assessment in the judges' minds.

Lord Hoffmann was prepared to go further than the majority and to find that Article 15 was not engaged since there no emergency threatening the life of the nation.[42] While willing to accept that credible evidence of terrorist plots existed, he found that SIAC had been incorrect to accept the Attorney-General's submission that a threat of serious physical damage

---

[38] Para 217.

[39] Para 178. Cf Lord Hope at para 129: 'the indefinite detention without trial of foreign nationals cannot be said to be strictly required to meet the exigencies of the situation, if the indefinite detention without trial of those who present a threat to the life of the nation because they are suspected of involvement in international terrorism is not thought to be required in the case of British nationals.'

[40] On this basis the Court of Appeal had rejected the argument that there was a breach of Art 14: *A, X and Y and Others v Secretary of State for the Home Department* [2002] EWCA Civ 1502, [2003] 1 All ER 816, [56] (Lord Woolf), [102], [132] (Brooke LJ).

[41] Lord Bingham explained, 'Suspected international terrorists who are UK nationals are in a situation analogous with the appellants' because, in the present context, they share the most relevant characteristics of the appellants.' [53].

[42] Paras 95–97.

and loss of life was sufficient. Quoting Milton[43] and referring by way of comparison to the threat from Hitler during the Second World War, he reached a crescendo:

> Terrorist violence, serious as it is, does not threaten our institutions of government or our existence as a civil community. ... The real threat to the life of the nation, in the sense of a people living in accordance with its traditional laws and political values, comes not from terrorism but from laws such as these. That is the true measure of what terrorism may achieve. It is for Parliament to decide whether to give the terrorists such a victory.[44]

Lord Hoffmann's speech rivals Lord Atkin's famous dissent in *Liversidge v Anderson*[45] for its rhetorical force, but it is worth pointing out carefully the place of the HRA in his argument. As commentators have noted, his Lordship all but ignored the Convention authority on Article 15, describing it as not particularly helpful.[46] This could be seen as an example of a domestic judge choosing to go further than the strict boundaries of the Convention jurisprudence in defence of rights.[47] Moreover, because he reached the conclusion that he did, Lord Hoffmann did not go on to consider whether the measures were either proportionate or discriminatory. The Human Rights Act was relevant, however, in allowing judges for the first time to question the need for emergency powers through a declaration of incompatibility:

> Parliament may then choose whether to maintain the law or not. The declaration of the court enables Parliament to choose with full knowledge that the law does not accord with our constitutional traditions.[48]

It is misplaced to criticise the shortcomings of this approach[49] for what is really a design feature of the HRA. As his comments make clear, what Lord Hoffmann envisaged was constitutional dialogue rather than judicial supremacism – a point lost in the critical reaction by ministers towards his speech. Indeed, Professor Conor Gearty has argued that the limited power available to the courts under the Act (they could not in the end result free the detainees) gave scope for a more libertarian and restricted interpretation of Home Secretary's powers.[50]

---

[43] 'Lords and Commons of England, consider what nation it is whereof ye are, and whereof ye are the governours'.

[44] Paras 96–97.

[45] [1942] AC 206.

[46] Para 92. D Dyzenhaus, 'An Unfortunate Burst of Anglo-Saxon Parochialism' (2005) 68 *MLR* 673; Bonner, op. cit., 295.

[47] Ch 2 above.

[48] Para 90.

[49] See, eg, Dyzenhaus above.

[50] C Gearty, 'Human Rights in an Age of Terrorism: Injurious, Irrelevant or Indispensable?' (2005) *CLP* 25, 35.

It is clear also that reluctance to accept the government's case among the other Law Lords cannot be attributed to the HRA alone. Lord Scott, while deferring to the Secretary of State on whether there was a public emergency within Article 15, expressed 'very great doubt' whether it threatened the life of the nation and referred to the 'faulty intelligence assessments' prior to the Iraq war.[51] It can be safely assumed that, not just the widespread public discussion of intelligence material over the previous three years – to a large extent initiated by the government itself in order to enlist public support[52] – but also the close familiarity of first Lord Scott himself and then a brother Law Lord, Lord Hutton, with intelligence material as a result of each conducting inquiries with a substantial intelligence component,[53] may have contributed to this scepticism at the highest judicial levels. The mystery surrounding a government invocation of national security that would at one time have awed the courts and led them to defer to government had been considerably lifted through increased public and professional familiarity with the secret world.

Lord Bingham's speech in *A* points out that, in large part

> the correctness of the Secretary of State's choice of immigration control as a means to address the Al-Qaeda security problem ... is the issue to be resolved.[54]

It is not fanciful to argue that the government's choice of this approach was a *political* one, based on a calculation of what Parliament would accept and tempered by previous experience of public hostility towards internment measures (both in Northern Ireland and during the First and Second World Wars).[55] The first Gulf War may have also been a model for the use of immigration powers: on that occasion several hundred foreign nationals were detained pending deportation although, because of the short-lived nature of the conflict, they were mostly released before their cases could be determined.[56] Following 9/11 the same powers were applied – this time much more selectively – but with more serious consequences for

---

[51] Para 154. Cf Lord Hoffmann's reference to 'the widespread scepticism which has attached to intelligence assessments since the fiasco over Iraqi weapons of mass destruction' (para 94) and Baroness Hale (at para 226) pointing out that the Government and its advisers 'may, as recent events have shown, not always get it right'.

[52] The Government had chosen to publish two controversial dossiers of intelligence material in September 2002 and January 2003: P Gill, 'The Politicization of Intelligence: Lessons from the Invasion of Iraq', in H Born, L Johnson and I Leigh (eds), *Who's Watching the Spies: Establishing Intelligence Service Accountability* (Dulles, Virginia, Potomac Books, 2005).

[53] *Report of the Inquiry into the Export of Defence Equipment and Dual-Use Goods to Iraq and Related Prosecutions*, HC 115 (1995–96); *Report of the Inquiry into the Circumstances Surrounding the Death of Dr David Kelly*, available at: <http://www.the-hutton-inquiry.org.uk> accessed 19 May 2008.

[54] Para 53.

[55] Cf. Lord Nicholls in *A(FC) v SSHD* at para 203.

[56] I Leigh, 'The Gulf War Deportations and the Courts' [1991] *PL* 331.

those affected, since they faced indefinite detention. What is clear, however, is that having chosen to use immigration powers in this way, rather than to bring in internment by name, or to bring Al-Qaeda sympathisers to criminal trial, that the government was then severely constrained by the existing Convention jurisprudence.

The domestic judges are certainly not to blame for the disastrous but predictable legal results of this policy choice: the Government brought the *Belmarsh* defeat upon itself through its unwise choice of legal weapons. It had chosen to ignore a succession of warnings from the Joint Committee on Human Rights, Amnesty International, JUSTICE, Liberty and the UN Human Rights Committee concerning whether the derogation was defensible, before the 2001 Act reached the statute book.[57] This is why shrill criticism from politicians of the judiciary for in effect sabotaging the counter-terrorist strategy[58] was at best ill-informed and misguided or, at worst, a disingenuous populist attempt at diverting public attention. Moreover, if the House of Lords had not found as it did then, it was likely that the European Court of Human Rights would have done so. At least one of the objectives of incorporation of the Convention – avoiding criticism before an international tribunal – can have been said to have been achieved. Criticism of the European Court of Human Rights is equally misplaced, however. The jurisprudence establishing that a state deporting or extraditing a person to a country where his or her human rights are abused bears responsibility[59] and that national security considerations cannot be balanced against or override the real risk of mistreatment contrary to Article 3[60] was clear and well-established at the time that the Blair Government introduced the HRA. The Government is perfectly entitled to invite the Strasbourg court to reconsider its stance (as indeed it did[61]) but it could not credibly claim to have been ambushed by the courts, either in the UK or in Strasbourg.

The Government and parliamentary response to the House of Lords' ruling was confused. So far as the detainees were concerned, a substantial delay ensued while the Government contemplated its options. Although, strictly, the release of the Belmarsh detainees was not required by the ruling, when for some weeks the Government took no steps to respond and the detainees continued to languish in prison, the senior special advocate

---

[57] Joint Committee on Human Rights, *Second Report for 2001–02*, HL37/HC 372; Joint Committee on Human Rights, *Fifth Report for 2001–2*, HL51/HC 420.

[58] Eg 'Reid Warning to Judges Over Control Orders', *Guardian* 25 May 2007.

[59] *Soering v UK* (1989) 11 EHRR 439.

[60] *Chahal v UK* (1996) 23 EHRR 413.

[61] It intervened in pending cases brought against the Netherlands and Italy to argue that the possibility of torture must be balanced against other considerations: *Ramzy v Netherlands*, Appl no 25424/05; in *Saadi v Italy* Appl no 37201/06, Grand Chamber, 28 February 2008, the ECtHR rejected this argument (see paras 139ff).

resigned in protest.[62] After nearly four months' delay and nearing the point at which the powers under the 2001 Act were to lapse under the 'sunset clause' imposed when the 2001 Bill was before Parliament, the courts lost patience with the process and began to release the detainees themselves. This flurry of activity in March 2005 coincided with a full-blown constitutional crisis over the Prevention of Terrorism Bill 2005, in which the Upper House rejected the Bill no fewer than four times and amended the proposals intended to fill the legal gap following the *A* judgment.

Before considering the 2005 Act once again it is worth pointing out the road *not* taken. Prior to the *Belmarsh* judgment a review of the 2001 Act had been conducted by a Committee of Privy Counsellors, the Newton Committee. It concluded that:

> Terrorists are criminals, and therefore ordinary criminal justice and security provisions should, so far as possible, continue to be the preferred way of countering terrorism.[63]

The Committee strongly recommended the repeal of the powers allowing for indefinite detention of foreign nationals. As an alternative it argued that the government should examine removing the blanket ban on the use of intercepted communications being given as evidence and the scope for more intensive use of surveillance to prevent and disrupt terrorism.[64] In emphasizing criminalisation rather than militarisation in this way the

---

[62] Ian Macdonald, 'Why I feel I have no option but to resign', *Mail on Sunday*, 19 December 2004. See generally Constitutional Affairs Select Committee, *Seventh Report for 2004–05, The Operation of the Special Immigration Appeals Commission (SIAC) and the use of Special Advocates*, HC 323-I.

[63] Privy Counsellors Review Committee, *Anti-Terrorism Crime and Security Act 2001 Review*, 18 December 2003.

[64] The UK is unusual among legal systems in barring evidence obtained by telephone tapping and other forms of interception of communications from being given in court. The reason is less concern about the invasion of privacy than the wish to maintain some element of secrecy concerning the procedures. However, there are some unjustifiable anomalies: eg, evidence obtained by bugging can be given and the ban does not apply to all tribunals (a notable exception being SIAC). A debate has been raging inconclusively within government departments for several years about removing the ban on evidential use of intercepted material: ISC, *Annual Report for 2004–05*, Cm 6510 (May 2005), paras 92–94. The apparent reason for failure to agree has been continuing concern over the scope of disclosure likely to be ordered by the courts and, in particular, the fact that this cannot be predicted in advance, with the risk that confidential sources might therefore be compromised. A Bill to remove the bar on interception evidence for terrorist offences was introduced by Lord Lloyd of Berwick (a former Interceptions Commissioner) in 2006/07: Interception of Communications (Admissibility of Evidence) Bill 2006/07. In a careful comparative review, JUSTICE has described the ban as 'archaic, unnecessary and counter-productive': JUSTICE, *Intercept Evidence: Lifting the ban* (London, 2006), at para 168. A review by a committee of Privy Counsellors cautiously recommended allowing intercept evidence provided a regime could be devised that sufficiently safeguarded national security: *Privy Council Review of Intercept as Evidence*, Cm 7324 (2008).

Committee were effectively reprising arguments from the early days of the Northern Ireland troubles.

CONTROL ORDERS

As eventually passed, the 2005 Act replaced the controversial detention without trial provision with an equally controversial new weapon: the control order. Although non-custodial these orders allow for the imposition of draconian restrictions on a person's liberty, amounting to house arrest. Control orders may be made against any suspected terrorist, whether the terrorist-related activity is international or domestic.[65] The Home Secretary must normally apply to the courts, and where the order is made the case will be automatically referred for a judicial review of the decision. At least 10 of those formerly detained became the immediate subject of these new orders. In compliance with the letter of the *A* judgment the 2005 Act added a new ingredient by allowing for control orders to be made against UK citizens, thus addressing the discrimination point.

Control orders may involve a variety of detailed restrictions on a person's movement, communication (including use of the phone and internet), and on whom they meet.[66] In the case of the severest restrictions – under 'derogating control orders'[67] – parliamentary approval of the use of the powers is required,[68] as would a further derogation from Article 5 of the European Convention be. The power to make derogating control orders has not so far been used and is unlikely to be invoked unless in response to further major threat or attack.

It was inevitable that that this scheme too would be challenged under the HRA. In the first decision a challenge was made to the judicial procedure for supervising non-derogating control orders. These allow for parts of the proceedings to be closed to the person against whom the order is proposed and for the appointment of a Special Advocate.[69] The Prevention of Terrorism Act 2005 Act gives the court a limited role in supervising

---

[65]   In at least one case, that of Rauf Abdullah Mohammed, a control order has been made immediately following an *acquittal* by court on terrorist charges: *The Times*, 30 August 2006.

[66]   Section 1(4) of the 2005 Act lists no fewer than 17 different *types* of restriction that may be imposed by control order. For an example see 216–17 below.

[67]   The balance of power between the Secretary of State and the courts is different in these cases: derogating control orders may only be made by the court on the application of the Secretary of State (ss 1(2)(b), 4) whereas non-derogating orders may be made by the Secretary of State, with the court's permission (which can be dispensed with in cases of urgency, s 3(1)) and are subject to review in the courts (ss 3(7)–(14)).

[68]   S 6(3).

[69]   Prevention of Terrorism Act 2005 Sch 1.

whether the Secretary of State's decisions were flawed, according to judicial review principles.[70]

In *Secretary of State for the Home Department v MB*[71] the majority of the Law Lords (Lord Hoffmann dissenting) used section 3 to refer back to the trial judge a non-derogating control order case in which special advocates were used. This followed a different course to either of the courts below.

In the High Court, Sullivan J found that these procedures were too limited to satisfy Article 6 of the Convention and issued a declaration of incompatibility. In his view there was a denial of Article 6 since the controlee's rights were being determined not by an independent court but rather under a 'conspicuously unfair' procedure by 'executive decision-making untrammelled by any prospect of effective judicial supervision'[72] The Court of Appeal, however, used section 3 of the HRA to find that the court should consider the evidence available at the date of the hearing, rather than being limited (as the statute appeared to state) to review of the factual basis for the Secretary of State's determination of reasonable grounds that the person was involved in terrorist-related activity.[73] The argument in the lower court had overlooked section 11(2) of the 2005 Act, which made it the appropriate tribunal for any Convention rights arguments concerning the making of control orders. The effect of that provision, the Court of Appeal held, was that the court had a duty to ensure that Article 6 was complied with. Consequently it 'read down' the relevant provision (section 3(10)) to achieve this effect.[74] Moreover, it stressed the Strasbourg[75] and domestic[76] authority establishing that closed procedures employing Special Advocates could comply with Article 6.[77] A similar approach by Lord Hoffmann in the House of Lords led him to dismiss the appeal.

While the Court of Appeal upheld the compatibility of the 2005 Act procedure for using intelligence material to lead to detention as an alternative to a criminal trial, nevertheless it also used the Convention to

---

[70] Ss 3(2), (6), (8), (10) and (11).

[71] [2007] UKHL 46.

[72] *SSHD v MB* [2006] EWCA Civ 1140, [2006] 3 WLR 839, [96].

[73] *SSHD v MB* [2006] EWCA Civ 1140, [2006] 3 WLR 839.

[74] *Ibid*, [44]–[46].

[75] *Chahal v UK* (1996) 23 EHRR 413 [113]; *Tinnelly & Mc Elduff v UK* (1997) 27 EHRR 249; *Rowe v UK* (2000) 30 EHRR 1 [61].

[76] *R v H* [2004] UKHL 3; [2004] 2 AC 134; *A v SSHD* [2002] EWCA Civ 1202; [2004] QB 335, para 57 (Lord Woolf); *R (Roberts) v Parole Board* [2005] UKHL 45; [2005] 2 AC 738.

[77] See n 28 above.

strengthen judicial supervision in a way that departed from traditional judicial deference over national security.[78]

This was also the practical outcome of the House of Lords' decision, although the majority used section 3 of the HRA in a different way. They ruled that the issue must be referred back to the trial judge with the provisions reinterpreted to give greater emphasis to the Article 6 rights of the person appealing the order.[79] This involved reading a proviso[80] into the duty that the judge otherwise had not to order intelligence material to be disclosed where it would be contrary to the public interest. This interpretation admittedly ran counter to the statutory scheme, which impliedly anticipated that the judge would rely on the undisclosed material. However, to follow the scheme could bring conflict with Article 6 and, if possible, their Lordships ruled the scheme should be made to work in a way that was Convention compatible. This is another instance of strong use of the section 3 power and one that consciously parallels the rape shield judgment discussed in chapter 3.[81]

In a second decision (*JJ*) the House of Lords by a majority of three to two found that a 'non-derogating' control order breached ECHR Article 5 because of the onerous-ness of the conditions imposed on the controlee.[82] The Court of Appeal's judgment summarises their effect and is worth repeating:

> Each respondent is required to remain within his 'residence' at all times, save for a period of six hours between 10 am and 4 pm ... During the curfew period the respondents are confined in their small flats and are not even allowed into the common parts of the buildings in which these flats are situated. Visitors must be authorised by the Home Office, to which name, address, date of birth and photographic identity must be supplied. The residences are subject to spot searches by the police. During the six hours when they are permitted to leave their residences, the respondents are confined to restricted urban areas, the largest of which is 72 square kilometres. These deliberately do not extend, save in the case of GG, to any area in which they lived before. Each area contains a mosque, a hospital, primary health care facilities, shops and entertainment and sporting facilities. The respondents are prohibited from meeting anyone by

---

[78] In holding that Art 6 requires the courts to inquire into whether the factual basis justifying the control order exists the Court of Appeal in *MB* struck a blow for substantive review of these decisions, despite wording in the Act that limited the court's role to judicial review; cf 154ff. above.

[79] See especially Baroness Hale at [72]–[74].

[80] '[E]xcept where to do so would be incompatible with the right of the controlled person to a fair trial'.

[81] *R v A* [2002] 1 AC 45.

[82] *Secretary of State for the Home Department v JJ* [2007] UKHL 45. Another appeal heard at the same time involving less onerous conditions was dismissed: *Secretary of State for the Home Department v E* [2007] UKHL 47.

pre-arrangement who has not been given the same Home Office clearance as a visitor to the residence.[83]

To refer to this as house arrest is misleading, since that downplays the element of compulsory relocation also involved, in view of fact that five of the six applicants were prevented from returning to their previous homes and were required to live in accommodation provided by the authorities in a different area. The majority of the House of Lords confirmed Sullivan J's finding that, applying the relevant Convention authority,[84] the collective impact of the conditions went beyond a mere restriction and amounted to a deprivation of liberty. Moreover, under the 2005 Act, only the court, rather than the Secretary of State, could make an order having this effect, within the regime for 'derogating' control orders. The orders were therefore quashed. By preventing the Home Secretary from making control orders that breached Article 5, the House of Lords in effect reinforced the element of democratic accountability within the scheme: if the government wishes to restrict the liberty of controlees to this extent it will need to invoke 'derogating' control order powers. (This requires parliamentary approval of the scheme and then transfers the making of the order to the court.)[85] Important as this principle is, in practice the judgment is no more than an inconvenience and will only necessitate future fine-tuning of the conditions of the orders.

Quite apart from the seriousness of the legal restrictions imposed on some of those subject to these orders, their effectiveness is questionable in other less restrictive instances: by June 2007 four (maybe six) of the 17 people subject to control orders had absconded.[86]

BROADER ASPECTS OF THE 'WAR ON TERROR'

Impressive as the detention rulings are, where the courts have been faced with other aspects of the 'war on terror' they have not spoken so consistently in vindication of human rights.

---

[83] *Secretary of State for the Home Department v JJ, KK, GG, HH, NN, LL* [2006] EWCA Civ 1141 [2006], 3 WLR 866 [4].

[84] *Guzzardi v Italy* (1980) 3 EHRR 333.

[85] The Joint Committee on Human Rights had also criticised the 'non-derogating' provisions of the 2005 Act for allowing orders to be made that breached Art 5: Joint Committee on Human Rights, *12th Report for 2005–06*, para 38.

[86] Quarterly statement by Tony McNulty, 10 June 2007.

Stop and Search Powers

In *R (Gillan) v Commissioner of Police for the Metropolis*[87] the House of Lords found that the use of police stop and search powers (of a protester and a journalist at an arms fair in London) under the Terrorism Act 2000 did not violate Convention rights. It was noteworthy that the power expressly did *not* require the police officer to have reasonable suspicion of the presence of articles connected with terrorism[88], that the power extended to the whole metropolitan police area (all of London in effect) and that, despite procedural safeguards, it had been renewed monthly for more than two years. Nevertheless, their lordships found that that there was no breach of Articles 5 or 8 in detaining and searching in this way: the power was authorised by law and necessary in a democratic society. Reliance was placed on the fact that the applicants had made no attempt to contradict evidence based on intelligence material of the value of such searches, despite an invitation to do so through a closed hearing process.[89] Although, not directly in issue, in comments supported by the remaining law lords, Lord Brown used the occasion to pronounce on public concerns over racial and religious profiling in the face of evidence that the powers were used substantially more frequently to stop and search people of Asian appearance.[90] He found that:

> Ethnic origin accordingly can and properly should be taken into account in deciding whether and whom to stop and search provided always that the power is used sensitively and the selection is made for reasons connected with the perceived terrorist threat and not on grounds of racial discrimination.[91]

Moreover, he concluded:

> [N]ot merely is such selective use of the power legitimate; it is its *only* legitimate use. To stop and search those regarded as presenting no conceivable threat

---

[87]   [2006] UKHL 12, [2005] Crim LR 414.

[88]   Terrorism Act 2000 s 45(1).

[89]   See, for instance, Lord Scott's speech at paras 63–4.

[90]   A junior Home Office minister conceded that 'the fact that at the moment the threat is most likely to come from those people associated with an extreme form of Islam, or falsely hiding behind Islam, if you like, in terms of justifying their activities, inevitably means that some of our counter-terrorist powers will be disproportionately experienced by people in the Muslim community': Hazel Blears MP, Home Affairs Select Committee, *Uncorrected Minutes of Evidence,* 1 March, 2005, HC 156-v. On the impact of counter-terrorist powers on the Muslim community, see A Blick, T Choudhury, S Weir, *The Rules of the Game: Terrorism, Community and Human Rights* (York, Joseph Rowntree Reform Trust, 2006).

[91]   Para 81. Contrast *R v Khawaja* [2006] OJ No 4245, in which the Ontario Superior Court of Justice ruled that the inclusion of 'religious purpose, objective or cause' in counter-terrorism powers violated the Charter of Rights because of the chilling effect on Muslims groups generally.

whatever (particularly when that leaves officers unable to stop those about whom they feel an instinctive unease) would itself constitute an abuse of the power.[92]

Gillan suggests that in the face of an open-ended war on terror the senior judiciary has accepted that minor restrictions on liberty (compared in any event to indefinite detention) do not infringe human rights.

International aspects of the wider 'war on terror' have also raised human rights challenges. A senior judge, Lord Steyn, in an unusual break with judicial protocol described Guanatanamo Bay in a public lecture as a legal 'black hole'.[93] This same concern was reflected, but without tangible results, in litigation brought upon behalf on British citizens detained in Guanatanamo Bay. In the *Abassi* case[94] a legal challenge was brought to compel the Foreign Secretary to make representations on behalf of several of them. The Court of Appeal rejected the claim, although stating its

> deep concern that, in apparent contravention of fundamental principles of law, Mr Abbasi may be subject to indefinite detention in territory over which the United States has exclusive control with no opportunity to challenge the legitimacy of his detention before any court or tribunal.[95]

Following diplomatic negotiations, however, five UK citizens held in Guantanamo were returned to the UK in March 2004 and a further four were released in January 2005 (Feroz Abassi was among the latter group), with additional releases of non-citizen British residents negotiated by the new Brown Government in 2007.

Mistreatment and Evidence Obtained by Torture

A key feature of the response to 9/11 has been international co-operation between the security and intelligence agencies of different countries, pairing the traditional allies of the anglo-saxon countries with new European and Middle Eastern partners. This has been given rise to suspicions of sub-contracting or exporting dubious information-gathering practices, including torture, and so-called 'extraordinary renditions': the forcible removal and transportation of terrorist suspects without due legal process.[96] Rendition came before the UK courts somewhat indirectly in the

---

[92] Para 92.

[93] Lord Steyn, 'Guantanamo Bay: The Legal Black Hole' (2004) 53 *ICLQ* 53.

[94] *R (Abbasi) v Secretary of State for Foreign and Commonwealth Affairs & Secretary of State for the Home Department* [2002] EWCA Civ 1598.

[95] Para 107 (Lord Phillips); see also para 64, referring to Guantanamo Bay as a 'legal black-hole'.

[96] Amnesty International, *United States of America Below the Radar: Secret Flights to Torture and Disappearances (2006)*, Committee on Legal Affairs and Human Rights, Council

Al-Rawi case[97] in which the Court of Appeal rejected claims from two UK residents (Al-Rawi and el-Banna) who had been taken to Guantanamo Bay from Gambia, via Afghanistan, following apparent collusion between the UK, Gambian and US authorities, that the Foreign Secretary should be required to intervene on their behalf. The court found that there was no such duty in the case of non-citizens (the case was even weaker than *Abassi*) and that the Foreign Secretary's refusal was not contrary to Articles 3, 8 or 14 of the Convention. The Intelligence and Security Committee later concluded that conditions imposed on information given by the Security Service (MI5) and the Secret Intelligence Service (MI6) to the CIA had been ignored by the latter agency.[98] This episode demonstrates the relative impenetrability of intelligence diplomacy to legal scrutiny, although in this respect UK courts are not exceptional: the US courts have also disallowed attempts to sue for rendition on procedural grounds.[99] Indirectly, however, the proceedings did contribute to the Foreign Secretary's later decision to make representations to the US authorities (leading to Al-Rawi's release from Guantanamo in April 2007 and el-Banna's in December 2007).

Revelations of the abuse of prisoners at Abu Ghraib, together with concerns over the condition of those held at the US base at Guantanamo Bay, and reports of secret CIA detention centres and 'extraordinary renditions' have led to worldwide concern over the use of torture to obtain evidence from suspected terrorists.[100] The UK courts have been faced with these issues only indirectly, however. Where the person concerned is in the

---

of Europe (rapporteur Mr Dick Marty), *Secret Detentions and Illegal Transfers of Detainees Involving Council of Europe Member States: Second Report*, Council of Europe Parliamentary Assembly Doc 11302 rev (11 June 2007); Council of Europe, *Follow-Up to the Secretary-General's Reports under Article 52 ECHR on the Question of Secret Detention and Transport of Detainees suspected of Terrorist Act, Notably by or at the Instigation of Foreign Agencies* (SG/ Inf(2006)5 and SG/Inf(2006)13 (30 June 2006) (SG (2006)01). *European Parliament's Temporary Committee on the alleged use of European countries by the CIA for the transport and illegal detention of prisoners*, 24 November 2006: <http://www.europarl. europa.eu/comparl/tempcom/tdip/default_en.htm> accessed 19 May 2008. Experts' report: <http://www.europarl.europa.eu/comparl/tempcom/tdip/studies/cfr_cdf_opinion3_2006_en.· pdf> accessed 19 May 2008. European Commission for Democracy through Law (Venice Commission), *Opinion on the International Legal Obligations of Council of Europe Member States in Respect of Secret Detention Facilities and Inter-State Transport of Prisoners* (CDL-AD (2006) 016).

[97] *R (Al Rawi and others) v Secretary of State for Foreign and Commonwealth Affairs and Secretary of State for the Home Department (United Nations High Commissioner for Refugees intervening)* [2006] EWCA Civ 1279.

[98] Intelligence and Security Committee, *Rendition*, Cm 7171 (July 2007), paras 111–147.

[99] *El-Masri v Tenet*, 479 F 3d 296 (4th Cir 2007); *Arar v Ashcroft*, 414 F Supp 2d 250 (EDNY 2006).

[100] See generally, K Greenberg and J Dratel (eds), *The Torture Papers: The Road to Abu Ghraib* (Cambridge, CUP, 2005).

United Kingdom or in the hands of UK military or security officials, or their actions are directly involved[101], there is a strong case for application of the HRA.

Nevertheless, the House of Lords has thwarted attempts by relatives of civilians allegedly killed by British troops in Iraq to have an independent inquiry established to look at the circumstances of their deaths. In June 2007 their Lordships ruled that the HRA did not apply extra-territorially in these cases: consequently Article 2 did not apply to require such an inquiry.[102]

The House of Lords' judgment of December 2005 in *A (No 2)*[103] that evidence obtained by torture could not be used in legal proceedings in the United Kingdom was seen by many as a historic pronouncement of principle, especially when viewed against the backcloth of allegations concerning the actions of foreign intelligence services in the 'war on terror'. Although there is much in their Lordships' speeches to justify pride in the outcome, when examined more closely, however, the ruling's practical effect is substantially more limited.[104] Nor have the high sentiments of *A (No 2)* translated fully into practical redress against torture. In *Jones*[105] the House of Lord held that British nationals could not sue Saudi officials in the UK for torture they underwent in Saudi Arabia. This decision mirrors the unfortunate conclusion at Strasbourg that the operation of state immunity in such cases does not constitute a violation of Article 6.[106]

To begin with the credit side in *A (No 2)*, however: the proceedings elicited statements from the Home Secretary that evidence obtained by torture should be excluded not only if UK authorities were responsible but also if they were complicit in the torture (this goes some way to meet

---

[101] A report by the Intelligence and Security Committee into the interviewing of detainees in Afghanistan, Guatanamo Bay and Iraq found that ministers should have been consulted before staff from UK agencies had interviewed captives in the hands of the US military in Afghanistan and that ministers should be informed 'immediately' where an official had concerns about the treatment of such detainees: ISC, *The Handling of Detainees by UK Intelligence Personnel in Afghanistan, Guantanamo Bay and Iraq*, Cm 6469 (March 2005).

[102] *R(Al-Skeini) v SS for Defence* [2007] UKHL 26, discussed further at 00–00. In one instance of a civilian who died in an army base following mistreatment it was agreed between the parties that the case be remitted. A lengthy and expensive court martial ended in 2007 with the commanding officer of the Queen's Lancashire Regiment, Col Jorge Mendonca, being cleared of negligence. Charges of manslaughter against a number of other soldiers were withdrawn. Corporal Donald Payne subsequently pleaded guilty to treating Iraqi civilians inhumanely, making him the first member of the British armed forces to admit a war crime. 'Iraqi Civilians Bring Abuse Claim to the High Court', *Independent* 9 June 2007.

[103] *A (No 2) v Secretary of State for the Home Department* [2005] UKHL 71.

[104] N. Grief, 'The Exclusion of Foreign Torture Evidence: a Qualified Victory for the Rule of Law', [2006] *EHRLR* 201; Bonner, op. cit., 332–341.

[105] *Jones v Ministry of the Interior of the Kingdom of Saudi Arabia* [2006] UKHL 26; [2007] 1 AC 270.

[106] *Al-Adsani v UK* (2002) 34 EHRR 11, in which the doctrine operated to prevent a similar civil claim (for abduction and torture) against the Emir of Kuwait.

concerns over 'outsourcing' torture to less scrupulous states). The contested area concerned the actions of foreign states, not at the request of authorities in the United Kingdom, leading to information given in evidence in proceedings here (so-called 'third party torture evidence').

Lord Brown captured the dilemma of third party torture evidence best:

> Torture is an unqualified evil. It can never be justified. Rather it must always be punished. So much is not in doubt. It is proclaimed by the Convention against Torture and many other international instruments and now too by s 134 of the Criminal Justice Act 1988. But torture may on occasion yield up information capable of saving lives, perhaps many lives, and the question then inescapably arises: what use can be made of this information? Unswerving logic might suggest that no use whatever should be made of it: a revulsion against torture and an anxiety to discourage rather than condone it perhaps dictate that it be ignored: the ticking bomb must be allowed to tick on. But there are powerful countervailing arguments too: torture cannot be undone and the greater public good thus lies in making some use at least of the information obtained, whether to avert public danger or to bring the guilty to justice.[107]

As we shall see, his comments are particularly relevant to the *indirect* use of information obtained by torture, for example where it leads to other compelling and admissible evidence: the ticking bomb with the terrorist's fingerprints, to adapt his metaphor.

So far as the direct use was concerned, however, all seven of the Law Lords hearing the appeal agreed that if the evidence was *known* to have been obtained by torture abroad it was inadmissible. Lord Hoffmann was strong in condemnation:

> The use of torture is dishonourable. It corrupts and degrades the state which uses it and the legal system which accepts it. When judicial torture was routine all over Europe, its rejection by the common law was a source of national pride.[108]

Lord Hope likened the effect to an infectious disease that once allowed a toe-hold in the legal system would spread to harden and brutalise those acclimatised to it.[109]

Lord Bingham stated:

> The principles of the common law, standing alone. ... compel the exclusion of third party torture evidence as unreliable, unfair, offensive to ordinary standards of humanity and decency and incompatible with the principles which should animate a tribunal seeking to administer justice..[110]

---

[107] Para 160.

[108] Para 72 (reference omitted). He added, 'In our own century, many people in the United States, heirs to that common law tradition, have felt their country dishonoured by its use of torture outside the jurisdiction and its practice of extra-legal "rendition" of suspects to countries where they would be tortured.'

[109] Lord Hope at [113].

[110] Para [52].

It might be thought curious that a common law system that rejected torture in the 17th century should have taken a further three-and-a-half centuries to rule third party torture evidence to be inadmissible. The explanation is that the rule against hearsay prevented evidence from third parties not present in court from being admitted in most cases, and so the issue simply did not arise.[111] It arose at this point because, although SIAC is a judicial body, the strict rules of evidence do not apply to it (enabling a variety of intelligence material to be considered by it under restricted conditions).[112]

As Lord Bingham noted, matters did not end with the common law, however: they had to be considered also with reference to the ECHR and the UN Convention Against Torture.[113] Lord Bingham treated the right to a fair trial under the ECHR as requiring the exclusion of evidence obtained by torture as in effect an exception to the general principle that evidence is a matter for national courts, rather than a common Convention approach.[114]

Their Lordships' ruling against third party torture evidence is general in effect, rather than one limited merely to the type of proceedings (before SIAC) in which the issue was raised. This then is a notable if limited exception to the general trend examined in chapter 7 that the courts have disappointingly failed to use the HRA to develop principles for the exclusion of evidence obtained through violation of Convention rights.

We should note some limitations, nevertheless, that the Law Lords were careful to point out. As explained above, the judgments are more concerned with the direct use of statements obtained by torture in legal proceedings. First, they do not prohibit the use of such statements for action by the executive or the police (for example, as the basis for making an arrest, instigating surveillance or a search).[115] Secondly, further evidence that arises as result will not be tainted: English law has no equivalent to the

---

[111] See, however, *R (Saifi) v Governor of Brixton Prison* [2001] 1 WLR 1134.

[112] Lord Bingham (at [51]) referred to the 'legality principle' to rebut on the argument that its statutory discretion could allow SIAC to admit torture evidence: '[I]t would of course be within the power of a sovereign Parliament (in breach of international law) to confer power on SIAC to receive third party torture evidence. But the English common law has regarded torture and its fruits with abhorrence for over 500 years, and that abhorrence is now shared by over 140 countries which have acceded to the Torture Convention. I am startled, even a little dismayed, at the suggestion (and the acceptance by the Court of Appeal majority) that this deeply-rooted tradition and an international obligation solemnly and explicitly undertaken can be overridden by a statute and a procedural rule which make no mention of torture at all.'

[113] Art 15 of the Torture Convention provides: 'Each State Party shall ensure that any statement which is established to have been made as a result of torture shall not be invoked as evidence in any proceedings, except against a person accused of torture as evidence that the statement was made.'

[114] Paras 23–26.

[115] Lord Nicholls (para 71); and see Lord Bingham (paras 47–8) and Lord Hoffmann (paras 92–7).

US 'fruit of the poisoned tree' doctrine.[116] Although to allow material knowingly derived from torture to this extent may represent a 'pragmatic compromise',[117] it gives less than a clear priority to human rights. After all the Convention against Torture requires states not to 'permit or tolerate' torture or other cruel, inhuman or degrading treatment or punishment (Article 3) and to take 'effective measures' to prevent it (Article 4).

It is when the question of evidence that *may* have been obtained (ie when it is not certain) by third party torture is examined, however, that the full limitations of the decision in *A (No 2)* become apparent. Realistically this was the issue that confronted SIAC and – as the Director-General of MI5 had explained in an affidavit to the court – is most likely to occur in practice. Lord Hoffmann, dissenting, was dismissive concerning the Nelsonian policy of the Secretary of State:

> [I]t leaves open the question of how much inquiry the Secretary of State is willing to make. It appears to be the practice of the Security Services, in their dealings with those countries in which torture is most likely to have been used, to refrain, as a matter of diplomatic tact or a preference for not learning the truth, from inquiring into whether this was the case. It may be that in such a case the Secretary of State can say that he has no knowledge or belief that torture has taken place. But a court of law would not regard this as sufficient to rebut real suspicion and in my opinion SIAC should not do so.[118]

The majority (Lords Hope, Rodger, Caswell and Brown) ruled that the evidence would only be inadmissible if SIAC were satisfied on the balance of probabilities that the evidence had been obtained by torture. Lord Hope argued that this was the only realistic test:

> SIAC may be required to look at information coming to the attention of the security services at third or fourth hand and from various sources, the significance of which cannot be determined except by looking at the whole picture which it presents. The circumstances in which the information was first obtained may be incapable of being detected at all or at least of being determined without a long and difficult inquiry which would not be practicable ... Our revulsion against torture ... must not be allowed to create an insuperable barrier for those who are doing their honest best to protect us. A balance must be struck between what we would like to achieve and what can actually be achieved in the real world in which we all live.[119]

The minority (Lords Bingham, Hoffmann, and Nicholls) argued that the evidence must be excluded if SIAC was satisfied there was a real risk that

---

[116] See further Lord Hoffmann at para 88 and Lord Brown at para 161.
[117] Lord Bingham's expression (at para 16).
[118] Para 98.
[119] Para 119.

the evidence had been obtained by torture.[120] They dismissed the majority's approach, because of its impracticality in requiring the detainee to discharge an unrealistic burden of proof in a situation where he had no access to the relevant information. Lord Bingham likened this to blindfolding a man and then imposing a standard that the sighted could not hope to meet. He argued that the inevitable consequence would that 'despite the universal abhorrence expressed for torture and its fruits, evidence procured by torture will be laid before SIAC because its source will not have been "established"'.[121] Lord Nicholls described the majority test as largely nullifying and merely paying 'lip-service' to the principle that torture evidence should not be admitted.[122]

The Rules are Changing[123]

On 7 July 2005, 52 people were killed and around 700 hundred injured by four bombs in central London, three of them on London underground trains and a fourth upon a bus. Investigations quickly established that the attacks were not the work of overseas terrorists targeted by Pt IV of the 2001 Act but that of British suicide bombers: in each case British Muslims without a clear previous history of involvement in terrorism.[124] On 21 July 2005 a further series of 4 small explosions on the transport system took place; this time, however, only the detonators exploded. Nevertheless, the attempts resulted in the largest investigation ever conducted by the Metropolitan Police, resulting in the conviction in 2007 of six defendants.[125]

After '7/7', as it became known, the Government has been prepared overtly to target radical Islamic groups in a way that it was not before in

---

[120] 'It must be for SIAC, if there are reasonable grounds for suspecting that to have been the case (eg, because of evidence of the general practices of the authorities in the country concerned) to make its own inquiries and not to admit the evidence unless it is satisfied that such suspicions have been rebutted.' (Lord Hoffmann, para 98).

[121] Para 59.

[122] Para 80. Lawyers acting for the Home Secretary in subsequent SIAC proceedings have, however, adopted a 'pragmatic' practice, although not compelled to do so, the spirit of which is nearer to the minority position. This involves withdrawing reliance on material which the Special Advocates argue, or may argue, may have been obtained by torture, generally from detainees in countries where there is arguably a real possibility that statements may have been the result of torture: *Abu Qatada v Secretary of State for the Home Department* [2007] UK/SIAC 15/2005, para 73.

[123] And see A Blick, T Choudhury and S Weir, *The Rules of the Game: Terrorism, Community and Human Rights* (York, Joseph Rowntree Reform Trust, 2006).

[124] Intelligence and Security Committee *Report into the London Terrorist Attacks of 7 July 2005*, Cm 6785 (2006).

[125] 'Four Guilty over 21/7 Bomb Plot', *BBC News*, 10 July 2007 <http://news.bbc.co.uk/1/hi/uk/6284350.stm> accessed 19 May 2008. 'Fifth 21/7 London bomber jailed', *BBC News*, 20 November 2007 <http://news.bbc.co.uk/1/hi/uk/7101514.stm> accessed 19 May 2008.

the face unmistakeable evidence of a small core of home-grown violent radical Muslims. However, the inevitable difficulty is in setting the boundaries for state activity so as not to interfere with legitimate dissent, for example concerning UK foreign policy, or religious freedom. The issue of young Muslims who attend madrassas in Pakistan (as had the 7/7 bombers), people who visit jihadist websites, or Islamic bookshops stocking militant literature, or who raise money for the conflicts in Palestine or Chechnya are all examples of the problem.

In his now famous 'the rules of the game are changing' speech of 5 August 2005 Prime Minister Tony Blair announced a series of proposals impacting on Muslim individuals and communities. These included increased use of citizenship and immigration powers,[126] proscription of additional Islamist groups,[127] renewing the effort to deport violent radical Islamists, proposed new police powers to hold terrorist suspects for up to 90 days before charge and to close a place of worship 'which is used as a centre for fomenting extremism', and a new offence justifying or glorifying terrorism anywhere in the world. Some but by no means all of these proposals were included in a draft Terrorism Bill published in September 2005 and enacted as the Terrorism Act 2006.

Among the new offences created by the 2006 Act were offences of encouragement (glorification) of terrorism[128], relating to bookshops and other disseminators of terrorist publications[129], preparation of terrorist acts[130], and further terrorist training offences.[131] The Act also extended the powers of the Secretary of State relating to proscription, to allow for the proscription of groups which glorify terrorism or the activities of which associate it with acts that glorify terrorism, and to deal with proscribed

---

[126] Extending the powers to remove citizenship to naturalised citizens 'engaged in extremism'; reviewing the threshold requirements for citizenship and establishing in consultation with the Muslim community a Commission on better integration; in consultation with Muslim leaders in respect of those clerics who are not British citizens, drawing up a list of those not suitable to preach who will be excluded from Britain.

[127] In his August 5 statement the Prime Minister announced the government's intention to ban a further two Islamic groups the Hizb ut Tahrir organisation and Al-Muhajiroun. The Prime Minister's statement provoked wide condemnation in the Muslim community and by May 2007 neither group had in fact been proscribed. Al-Muhajiroun has disbanded since 2005, although in July 2006 the Home Secretary announced the proscription of two of its alleged offshoots, Al-Ghurabaa and the Saved Sect: 'Groups Banned by New Terror Law', *BBC News*, 17 July 2006. <http://news.bbc.co.uk/1/hi/uk_politics/5188136.stm> accessed 19 May 2008. See further: Terrorism Act 2000 (Proscribed Organisations) (Amendment) Order 2005 SI 2005/2892. An unsuccessful Human Rights Act challenge to proscription was brought in *Kurdistan Workers Party v Secretary of State for the Home Department* [2002] EWHC 644 (Admin).

[128] S 1.

[129] S 2.

[130] S 5.

[131] S 6.

organisations that change their names.[132] Controversially it also allowed the extension of detention of terrorist suspects (with judicial approval for up to 28 days).[133]

Overall, the measures amount to an attempted – arguably overdue – to tackle the causes and spread of radical Islamist terrorism directly. The measures aimed at 'preachers of hate' are clearly in this category. These included the 'Code of Unacceptable Behaviours', intended as public statement of the Home Secretary's policies on use of his 'public good' powers to refuse entry or to deportation non-nationals.[134] In a linked move the Foreign Office expanded the 'warnings index' of people who might come to the UK to foment terrorism and who could be prevented from entry under the Home Secretary's powers. The first target of this new approach was the radical preacher Omar Bakri Mohammed. After he left Britain for Lebanon in August 2005, the Home Secretary announced he would not be allowed back. In the light of earlier cases involving denial of entry to controversial religious speakers it is likely that the courts will be deferential over the use of these powers.[135] Even at this late stage, however, ministers were curiously ambivalent about taking steps that could be seen as singling out the Muslim community. For example, the controversial proposal (dropped before the Bill was introduced) of a power for the police to apply to close places of worship applied to all religions,[136] despite the fact that it was framed with the clear evidence of events of the North Finsbury Mosque in mind.[137] Working groups convened by the Home Secretary came forward in September 2005 with proposals for National Advisory Council on Imams and Mosques, a forum against extremism and Islamaphobia, and a 'roadshow' of populist speakers to expound 'the concept of Islam in the West' and to condemn extremism.[138] The initiatives are underwritten with a £5m 'capacity building fund' from the Home Office 'to support all faith communities to play an active role in building a cohesive society'.

---

[132] Ss 21–22.

[133] Ss 23–24.

[134] Evidence to the Home Affairs Select Committee on 13 September 2005. 'It covers any non-UK citizen whether in the UK or abroad who uses any means or medium, including: writing, producing, publishing or distributing material; public speaking including preaching; running a website; or using a position of responsibility such as teacher, community or youth leader to express views which foment, justify or glorify terrorist violence in furtherance of particular beliefs; seek to provoke others to terrorist acts; foment other serious criminal activity or seek to provoke others to serious criminal acts; or foster hatred which might lead to inter-community violence in the UK.'

[135] *R (Farrakhan) v SSHD* [2002] QB 1391.

[136] Home Office, *Preventing Extremism Together: Places of Worship*, 6 October 2005.

[137] *BBC News*, 'Abu Hamza and the Mosque', 28 May 2004. <http://news.bbc.co.uk/1/hi/uk/3756675.stm> accessed 19 May 2008.

[138] Home Office Press Release, 'Tackling Extremism Together: Working Groups report back to Home Secretary' 22 September 2005.

The attempts announced by the Prime Minister to ease the path to deportation of terrorist suspects who themselves face potential human rights abuses in the country to which their return is sought have followed a twin-track. On the one hand the Government has sought to remove the obstacle posed by the European Court of Human Rights *Chahal* doctrine by intervening in cases pending in Strasbourg to invite the Court to soften its approach in favour of state interests, for example, by allowing balancing by the Home Secretary and the domestic courts of the risk to the deportee's human rights and that state security.[139]

The second track is to attempt to sidestep *Chahal* by entering memorandums of understanding with other states, designed to overcome the Convention obstacles by giving diplomatic assurances against torture.[140] Concern has been expressed about the effectiveness of these agreements by international bodies and human rights NGOs.[141] The Strasbourg court has, however, accepted such assurances on occasion in the past[142] while the UN Committee Against Torture has been sceptical.[143] Each case turns on its own circumstances and the post 7/7 strategy has had a mixed record before domestic courts and tribunals. It succeeded when SIAC accepted a memorandum of understanding with Jordan as satisfying Article 3 concerns in proceedings concerned with the deportation of Abu Qatada.[144] Assurances have also been accepted in the case of Algeria.[145] In the case of Libya, however, SIAC has ruled that memorandums of understanding do not allay human rights concerns, holding that there remained a real risk of breach of Articles 3 and 6 if the deportees were returned to Libya, notwithstanding diplomatic assurances.[146] Bearing in mind the attitude of the European Court of Human Rights, these judgments are impressive for their close and

---

[139]   Unsuccessfully: see *Saadi v Italy* (n 142 below).

[140]   See also C Walker, 'The Treatment of Foreign Terror Suspects' (2007) 70 *MLR* 427, 441 ff.

[141]   Human Rights Watch, *Still At Risk: Diplomatic Assurances No Safeguard Against Torture* (New York, 2005).

[142]   *Abu Salem v Spain*, Appl No 26844/04, 9 May 2006; *Mamatkulov v Turkey*, [2005] 41 EHRR 25 [75]; *Saoudi v Spain*, Appl No 22871/06, 18 September 2006. See *Saadi v Italy*, Appl 37201/06, Grand Chamber of the ECtHR, 28 February 2008, parass 147–48

[143]   *Agiza v Sweden*, CAT/C/34/D233/2003, 24 May 2005, concerning diplomatic assurances received by Sweden from Egypt.

[144]   *Abu Qatada v Secretary of State for the Home Department* [2007] UK/SIAC 15/2005 The Court of Appeal allowed appeal and returned the case to SIAC on other grounds: *Othman v Jordan* [2008] EWCA Civ 290.

[145]   *BB v SSHD*, SC/39/2005, SIAC 5 December 2006; *G v SSHD*, SC/02/2005 SIAC 8 February 2007. Two other SIAC decisions involving the return to Algeria of persons who allege that there is real risk of ill treatment have been remitted to SIAC by the Court of Appeal on procedural grounds: *MT (Algeria) v Secretary of State for the Home Department* [2007] EWCA Civ 808. SIAC subsequently dismissed their appeals: *Y, BB and U v Secretary of State for the Home Department* [2007] UKSIAC 32/2005.

[146]   *DD v SSHD* Appeal No SC/42 and 50/2005 (SIAC, 27 April 2007); see also *AS and DD (Libya) v SSHD* [2008] EWCA Civ 289.

conscientious scrutiny of the legal and political climate of the countries concerned and detailed consideration of the agreements.

The provisions of the 2006 Act that attracted most concern on human rights grounds were the new offence of glorification of terrorism[147] and the extension of detention pending charge.

The glorification offence was the Government's response to the public offence caused by some radical Muslims clerics condoning the 7/7 bombings. Abu Uzair (of the Saviour Sect) had reportedly claimed that the bombings 'raised the banner of jihad in the United Kingdom' and Abu Izzadeen (of the al-Ghurabaa group) described the bombers' actions as 'completely praiseworthy'. These remarks prompted a bizarre excursion into legal history when in, August 2005, the Attorney-General's office confirmed that the Crown Prosecution Service was considering whether prosecutions could be brought for treason. When that proved to be a blind alley attention turned to the creation of a tailor-made offence.[148] The new offence is committed if a person publishes a statement likely to be understood to give direct or indirect encouragement or other inducement to other people in the commission, preparation or instigation of acts of terrorism.[149] It is enough that the maker of the statement intends or is reckless[150] whether this will be the result. The breadth of the provision is demonstrated by section 1(3):

> the statements that are likely to be understood by members of the public as indirectly encouraging the commission or preparation of acts of terrorism or Convention offences include every statement which –
>
> (a) glorifies the commission or preparation (whether in the past, in the future or generally) of such acts or offences; and
>
> (b) is a statement from which those members of the public could reasonably be expected to infer that what is being glorified is being glorified as conduct that should be emulated by them in existing circumstances.

Furthermore it is irrelevant whether the statement relates to any specific act of terrorism or indeed whether anyone else is in fact encouraged or induced.[151] 'Glorification' of terrorism includes any form of praise or

---

[147] D Barnum, 'Indirect Incitement and Freedom of Expression in Anglo-American Law' [2006] *EHRLR* 258; C Brants, 'Glorifying Terrorism', in M Loenen and JE Goldschmidt (eds), *Religious Pluralism and Human Rights in Europe: Where to Draw the Line?* (Antwerp, Intersentia, 2007) 279 ff; H Fenwick and G Phillipson, *Media Freedom under the Human Rights Act* (Oxford, OUP, 2006) 527–33.

[148] The Lord Chancellor dampened speculation, however, in a radio interview, making clear that he thought treason prosecutions unlikely: BBC Radio 4, 'The World at One' 9 August 2005.

[149] Terrorism Act 2006 s 1(1), (2).

[150] The Bill was amended, however, to remove the original proposal that objective recklessness (gross negligence) was sufficient mens rea.

[151] S 1(5).

celebration:[152] prompting speculation that celebration of bonfire night could fall within the definition, as a commemoration of the failed Gunpowder plot of 5 November 1605.[153]

Strong reservations were expressed in Parliament over the need for the new offence and concerning its vagueness and possible chilling effect on free speech.[154] It could be argued that *direct* encouragement of terrorism was already constituted the criminal offence of incitement and that some general comments encouraging violence could constitute the offence of soliciting murder.[155] Critics (including Cherie Booth QC) argued that the effect of combining the vague notion of glorification with the already vague statutory definition of 'terrorism' would be that many forms of support for freedom fighters against repressive regimes would become an offence. The wording referring to indirect encouragement produced a sharp conflict between the two Houses of Parliament in which the Commons finally prevailed, although the Lords for its part insisted on amending the Government's original proposal that gross negligence alone would suffice by way of intention.

There was similar parliamentary conflict (although this time involving a backbench revolt in the House of Commons) over the government's plan to extend the permissible period that a suspect could be detained before charge to 90 days. Despite assertions (including the intervention of the Metropolitan Police Commissioner) that such an extended period was necessary in order to allow for the gathering of evidence, including the decryption of computer disks, the Government was unable to produce convincing evidence that the existing period (it had been extended to seven days by the 2000 Act and then to 14 days by the 2001 Act) had resulted in the collapse of any investigations. The House of Common defeated the proposals by a majority of 31[156] although it did agree to an extension to 28 days, depending on judicial authorisation.[157]

---

[152] S 20.

[153] Cf Lord Goodhart, referring to 'glorification' of Robin Hood and the War of American Independence: *HL Debs*, vol 443, col 143 (28 February 2006).

[154] Joint Committee on Human Rights, Third Report (2005–06), *Counter-Terrorism Policy and Human Rights: Terrorism Bill and Related Matters*, Hl 75-i/ HC 561.

[155] Eg, Abu Hamza was convicted in February 2006 and sentenced to seven years' imprisonment for soliciting murder and inciting racial hatred, as well as possessing a 'terrorist encyclopaedia': 'Abu Hamza Jailed for Seven Years' *BBC News*, 7 February 2006. <http://news.bbc.co.uk/1/hi/uk/4690224.stm> accessed 19 May 2008.

[156] HC Debs, vol 439, col 386 (9 November 2005).

[157] S 23(7). , On 11 June 2008 the House of Commons voted in favour of 42 days detention in proceedings on the Counter-Terrorism Bill 2008; HC Debs vol 477, col 405 (11 June 2008).

CONCLUSION: WAR ON TERROR/WAR ON THE JUDGES

To return to the question posed in the Introduction to this chapter: what difference has the HRA made to the United Kingdom's response to 9/11?

So far as the Government is concerned the conclusion must be that it has not made a difference. From the review in this chapter there is little evidence that ministers have regarded the Act as anything more than an inconvenience. On the one hand, politically opportunist legislative proposals only tangentially related to the 'war on terror' have continued to flow unabated out of the Home Office: incitement to religious hated, duties to retain communications data, ever-widening and ever-vaguer terrorist offences, all duly certified that they comply with the Convention. On the other hand, when challenged, ministers assert that the world changed on 11 September 2001 and that a new balance must be struck between civil liberties and national security.

Two aspects of the European Convention system have proved a significant constraint on the Government's counter-terrorist measures.[158] It is a longstanding interpretation by the European Court of Human Rights that the expulsion of an asylum seeker by a Contracting State may give rise to an issue under Article 3 where substantial grounds are shown for believing that the person concerned faces a real risk of being subjected to torture or degrading treatment or punishment in the country to which he is returned.[159] In addition, the Court held in a decision from the 1990s[160] that a person facing deportation on grounds of national security had to be given an effective means of challenging this before a judicial body. This lead to the creation of the special forum in which intelligence material can be presented: the SIAC. Together these aspects have severely limited the UK government's ability to remove from the country radical Islamic teachers, especially those in the country as political refugees. To circumvent these constraints the government was driven, firstly, to enter a controversial derogation to Article 5 of the Convention and, when that strategy failed, to intervene in pending litigation to ask the European Court of Human Rights to reconsider, and to seek diplomatic means of ensuring the safety of those it wishes to deport on national security grounds.

If anything the derogation entered in respect of the Anti-Terrorism Crime and Security Act 2001 was a consequence of the government's reluctance to use the criminal courts, rather than a necessary response to

---

[158] Department of Constitutional Affairs, *Review of the Implementation of the Human Rights Act* (London, 2006) found that, although there had been an impact on counter-terrorism legislation, 'The main difficulties in this area arise not from the Human Rights Act, but from decisions of the European Court of Human Rights.'

[159] *Soering v UK* (1989) 11 EHRR 439, 467–468, para 88; *Cruz Varas v Sweden* (1992) 14 EHRR 1, 33–34, paras 69–70.

[160] *Chahal v UK* (1997) 23 EHRR 413.

an emergency. In opting to use executive measures rather than criminal trials the government reversed the clear previous trend, for example under the Terrorism Act 2000, which had been away from such measures and towards prosecuting wherever possible.

One effect of the HRA has, however, been to produce a heightened sensitivity to human rights issues in Parliament. All legislation is now vetted by the influential Joint Parliamentary Committee on Human Rights. Several important changes were insisted upon to the 2001 Anti-Terrorism Crime and Security Bill because of human rights concerns and the Prevention of Terrorism Bill produced a full-blown confrontation between the two houses in April 2005. Despite that it remains the case that Parliament has substantially and repeatedly added to already voluminous anti-terrorism legislation by enacting some powers previously unimaginable in peacetime: indefinite detention without trial on ministerial certificate and detention before charge for up to 28 days, to name but two.

If it is a war, then it has been a relatively good one for the judges. Armed with the new weapon of proportionality they have been able to ask probing questions about the justification for the more extreme of counterterrorist measures: executive detention and control orders. The *Belmarsh* decision drew worldwide admiration and has emboldened courts in other countries, notably Canada, in a newly assertive questioning of national security.[161] Equally acclaimed, though with less justification in view of the majority's reasoning, was the torture evidence judgment.

Ministers' outrage at the *Belmarsh* decision was artificially manufactured: they were accurately warned of precisely these consequences when the 2001 Bill was introduced. The courts' response to the derogation was widely predicted and legally conventional according to the European Convention jurisprudence; it was not an impermissible usurpation of political power or anti-democratic. Ministerial attacks on the judiciary over counter-terrorism have bordered on the irrational, since the judges have merely applied orthodox doctrine that the Government itself was well aware of before introducing its counter-terrorist measures. Moreover, a number of the difficulties ministers faced stemmed from the Government's legislative choices (in particular, not pursuing criminal justice alternatives) or were of Parliament's making (for example, in insisting on a sunset clause for Pt IV of the 2001 Act), rather than the responsibility of the courts. If the judiciary *has* become politicised as a result it is because of the

---

[161] In *Charkaiou v Canada (Minister of Citizenship and Immigration)* 2007, SCC 9 the Supreme Court of Canada held that the procedure under the Immigration and Refugee Protection Act for issuing security certificates leading to the detention of national security of foreign nationals who were inadmissible to Canada on security grounds breached s 7 of the Charter of Rights: <http://scc.lexum.umontreal.ca/en/2007/2007scc9/2007scc9.html> accessed 19 May 2008.

intemperate reaction of a succession of government ministers, from the Prime Minister downwards. This is democratic dialogue of a kind, but conducted with threats and megaphones.

Chapter 9

'Horizontal Rights'

INTRODUCTION

IN THIS CHAPTER we discuss whether human rights also apply where the alleged infringer of the liberty is a *private* person or a company (for instance, an employer), rather than a public body. This issue, which is hotly debated in a number of legal systems, is often referred to as one of 'horizontal rights' (the vertical axis referring to the enforcement of constitutional rights against the state).[1]

In the UK's case, questions of the applicability of the Human Rights Act 1998 (HRA) to private persons are necessarily connected with debates about the nature of Convention rights themselves. Are they merely international human rights 'incorporated' into domestic law? Or do they have some distinct status under domestic law?

Taking the first perspective: traditionally, international law has been enforced only against states and international organizations, even where private individuals may have had a right of petition, as under the European Convention machinery. Individuals lack standing to take proceedings against other individuals under the Strasbourg machinery: only complaints by individuals, NGOs or groups of individuals claiming to be a victim of a violation 'by one of the High contracting Parties' may be bought under Article 34.[2] The same discipline requires applicants to characterise their claims in Strasbourg as a failure by the state (including its courts) to secure their Convention rights (as required under Article 1), even where more naturally, the legal dispute would be with another private individual, were that route open.[3]

The issue of whether the Convention has 'horizontal' effect to create rights between private individuals has been considered repeatedly at the

---

[1] See generally, A Clapham, *Human Rights in the Private Sphere* (Oxford, OUP, 1993); D Friedmann and D Barak-Erez, *Human Rights in Private Law* (Oxford, Hart Publishing, 2001).

[2] Under Art 35 the court shall consider a application inadmissible if it is incompatible with the Convention, manifestly ill-founded, or an abuse of the right of petition.

[3] Eg, a family breakdown was characterised as a state's failure to respect or interference with family life under Art 8 because of the unavailability of an order of judicial separation: *Airey v Ireland*, Series A, vol 32, paras 31–2.

Strasbourg level.[4] The Court has argued that in some instances, and especially with regard to Article 8, a member State must protect the positive rights of individuals, rather than merely refraining from interfering itself with their rights.[5] On occasion it has been held that the State may be responsible for failing to prevent lawful action by a private individual which impedes the exercise of another's Convention rights.[6] In one case a failure to provide for the possibility of prosecution for sexual assault on a mentally handicapped woman was held to violate Article 8. The Court stated that respect for Article 8 'may invoke the adoption of measures designed to secure respect for private life even in the sphere of the relations between the individuals themselves'.[7] In the recent *Von Hannover* case this was found to require a domestic remedy to prevent publication of photographs of a public figure engaged in everyday activities such as shopping.[8]

The main method for protection of horizontal rights has been the recognition by the Strasbourg court of 'positive obligations' where the state has a duty to protect an individual's rights from incursion, including incursions from other private individuals.[9] The duty clearly lies with the state but at the municipal level it is likely to discharge it by imposing corresponding duties on private individuals either by legislation or under the common law. Positive obligations are not synonymous with horizontality, however. From the Strasbourg court's perspective what matters is that the state protects the right in question, not the means of doing so; it is not necessary therefore that domestic courts explicitly invoke the Convention to do so. Moreover in some of the more important instances the positive obligation may be discharged by the state imposing domestic criminal rather than civil liability on individuals.[10]

---

[4] For a full account analysing the potential for horizontal effect of each Article of the Convention, see A Clapham, op. cit., ch 7; also, A Clapham, 'The Privatisation of Human Rights' [1995] *EHRLR* 20.

[5] See especially *Airey v Ireland* Series A 32 (1979); *Marckx v Belgium* (1979–80) 2 EHRR 330 on the scope of 'respect for family life' in Art 8; and *Lopez Ostra v Spain* (1995) 20 EHRR 277, paras 51–58 (state responsible under Art 8 for environmental pollution to neighbour from waste reprocessing plant, since municipality allowed it to be built and failed to take legal action against it, but on the facts some direct state responsibility due to public subsidy).

[6] Eg, Art 11 violated by power of trade union: *Young, James and Webster v UK* (1982) 4 EHRR 38; duty to take reasonable and appropriate measures to protect demonstrators from counter-demonstrators: *Platform Ärzte für das Leben v Austria*, Series A 139 (1988).

[7] *X and Y v The Netherlands*, Series A 91 (1985), para 23.

[8] 249 below.

[9] A Mowbray, *The Development of Positive Obligations under the European Convention on Human Rights by the European Court of Human Rights* (Oxford, Hart Publishing, 2004).

[10] In one instance the Court found that the UK had violated Art 3 in failing to protect a victim of physical abuse from his step-father because a jury, applying the 'reasonable

Although no question of private liability for human rights violations arises at the international level, it may nevertheless do so in domestic courts. UK courts may be free, for example, in some sense to apply the Convention rights between private individuals even where Strasbourg jurisprudence does not require this.

Whether Convention rights under the HRA are regarded as a species of constitutional rights is a question again closely connected to the issue to their status in private law. Legal systems typically accord constitutional rights *some* form of higher status over other legal rights, although the precise extent and method of doing so varies enormously between countries according to the constitutional text and judicial interpretation.[11] It rarely involves straightforwardly treating a private party as bound in identical fashion to a state entity. Nevertheless, evidence that some such development was occurring under the HRA would point to the treatment of Convention rights as a species of constitutional rights, despite some obvious distinctions between the HRA and a constitutional Bill of Rights.[12]

However, at the domestic level a conceptually watertight distinction between constitutional or human rights enjoyed against the state and private law rights is problematic. It is worth briefly explaining the problem in general before turning to the various ways in which constitutional or human rights may be given some effect in private law.

It may seem that the law is only directly involved in private law situations where one person has a clear legal remedy against another, such as breach of contract or negligence. This is misleading, however, as becomes clear once one considers a more sophisticated account of legal rights other than one treating all rights as corresponding to another person's legal duty (so called 'claim-rights'). The work of the jurist Wesley Hohfeld[13] reminds us that the law (and state institutions, notably the courts) is no less concerned with protecting an individual's rights when the rights in question are *liberties* and *immunities* claimed against another person, than when they are *claim-rights*. Take, for example, the freedom at

---

chastisement' exception for assault, acquitted at trial: *A v UK* (1998) 27 EHRR 611. Subsequently English law was clarified: Children Act 2004 s 58.

[11] See S Gardbaum, 'The "Horizontal Effect" of Constitutional Rights' (2003) 103 *Mich LR* 387; S Gardbaum, 'Where the (State) Action Is' (2006) *IJCL* 760.

[12] Ch 1 above.

[13] WN Hohfeld, *Fundamental Legal Conceptions as Applied in Judicial Reasoning* (New Haven, Yale University Press, 1923). Hohfeld distinguished between situations in which one person owes another a legal *duty* and, therefore, a correlative *claim-right* applies, and where the first person has an absence of such a duty (a '*privilege*', called by later writers a '*liberty*') and the second therefore has a '*no-right*'. Under Hohfeld's scheme a second set of jural relations concerns the presence or absence of a legal *power* (the capacity to change the legal relations between two individuals). Where one party has a *power*, the second is described as being under being subject to a '*liability*'. The absence of such a power Hohfeld described as a '*disability*'; the other party enjoys a corresponding *immunity*.

common law to discriminate against another person on grounds of their race, sex, sexual orientation or religion. The law was no less implicated between the parties under the common law in allowing such discrimination (in the form of a *liberty* for the discriminator), than if a statutory remedy is provided – as is now commonly the case in many countries – in the form of a *right* not to be discriminated against for the victim. Recognising with Hohfeld that rights are more than claim-rights entails that a court may, therefore, give effect to a constitutional document either granting a right or an immunity from state action by using it to form the basis for rights or immunities against another private individual.[14]

Hohfeldian analysis also draws attention to a second key issue: when dealing with private law, the human rights rarely (if ever) fall all on the one side of the dispute. In the example above of discriminatory behaviour, for example, providing a statutory remedy for discrimination will necessarily limit the discriminator's liberty, autonomy, privacy and control of property. Many countries have found the case for doing so compelling (for instance to combat the societal effects of acts of private discrimination), but this does not mean that discriminators have no such rights in the first place: rather, that there are good reasons to override them.

Frequently, however, debates about the application of human rights to powerful economic and other private interests are conducted in naïve terms that suggest that it follows automatically that once the mantra of human rights is invoked the interests of the weak, marginalised or oppressed must prevail. As a political strategy it may of course be rhetorically effective to argue in this way. In the legal sphere, however, multi-national companies (to take one favourite target) have human rights to property just as workers and communities have human rights of their own. Newspapers have rights of freedom of expression, just as celebrities have rights to privacy, and so on. Applying human rights horizontally therefore is unlikely to settle such disputes determinatively and is more likely instead to change the terminology in which they are conducted so that the interests of each party are described in human rights terms.

THE CONSTITUTIONAL FOUNDATIONS OF HUMAN RIGHTS

Many legal systems have faced the question of the impact, if any, to be given to constitutional rights in private law. In comparing them, several

---

[14] A close comparison with this form of reasoning exists under the 'state action' doctrine under the 14th Amendment in US Constitutional law but the argument is of more general application.

common modes of argument recur,[15] although, inevitably, there are important differences between the status and applications of the various Bills of Rights.

One argument is that since the common law, in the private law field, is applied by the courts and these are state institutions, the courts are therefore bound to apply constitutional rights to the private law disputes that come before them. Sometimes the constitutional document in question makes clear whether it binds the courts: for example, section 6 of the UK's Human Rights Act 1998 includes courts and tribunals among the category of public authorities which must not violate a person's Convention rights. Similarly, section 3 of the New Zealand Bill of Rights Act 1990 refers to 'acts done' by the 'judicial branch'.[16] Conversely, section 32 of the Canadian Charter refers expressly to Federal and Provincial legislatures and governments, thereby implicitly *excusing* the courts from direct compliance.[17]

Even where courts are expressly included there is scope for considerable debate about the implications. Does it mean that the courts are required to re-configure the common law to create new rights of action based on constitutional rights? (In practice, as we explain below, this has emerged as the major controversy in the UK in relation to the protection of privacy). Alternatively, it may be argued that the adaptation of existing legal principles by using such rights to extend the circumstances in which a tort may be established or where a defence may apply is sufficient.[18] More modest still is 'remedial horizontality',[19] which requires only that judges respect constitutional rights in the discretionary orders that they make on evidential, procedural and remedial matters.

In the absence of the explicit inclusion of the courts, it may nevertheless be argued that constitutional documents have an indirect impact, for

---

[15] See also I Leigh, 'Horizontal Rights, the Human Rights Act and Privacy: Lessons from the Commonwealth?' (1999) 48 *ICLQ* 57.

[16] This has been treated as importing the Bill of Rights into decisions about judicial orders even in civil cases: see *Auckland Area Health Board v Television New Zealand* [1992] 3 NZLR 406, 407 (Cooke P). See also *Hosking v Runting* [2005] 1 NZLR 1, in which the majority of the NZ Court of Appeal held that the recognition of a tort of privacy would not be a reasonable limit (s 5) on freedom of speech (s 14). See further P Rishworth, G Huscroft, S Optican and R Mahoney, *The New Zealand Bill of Rights* (Auckland, OUP, 2003), 102–109. A Butler and P Butler, *The New Zealand Bill of Rights: A Commentary* (New Zealand, LexisNexis, 2006) 94–109.

[17] See *Retail Wholesale and Department Store Union Local 580 et al v Dolphin Delivery Ltd* (1985) 33 DLR (4th) 174: [1986] 2 SCR 573, 600–601, discussed in A Hutchinson and A Petter, 'Private Rights Public Wrongs: the Libel Lie of the Charter' (1982) 38 *Toronto LJ* 278; B Slattery, 'The Charter's Relevance to Private Litigation' (1987) 32 *McGill LJ* 905. A similar conclusion was reached by the South African Constitutional Court in interpreting the Interim Constitution: *Du Plessis v De Klerk*, 1996 (3) SA 850.

[18] See the discussion of the new tort of misuse of personal information: 00–00 below.

[19] See Leigh, above n 15.

example, by guiding the courts as to underlying principles or public policy considerations.[20] In this way the Supreme Court of Canada has referred to Charter 'values' (rather than Charter 'rights') in the context of defamation.[21] Drawing on German constitutional terminology,[22] judges of the Constitutional Court of South Africa have variously referred to 'diagonal' effect, 'seepage' or 'radiating' effect of constitutional rights.[23] In the light of the HRA, academic literature and judges in the UK have spawned yet more terms to describe this phenomenon.[24]

A *second* common mode of argument concerns legislation applicable between private parties, such as statutes in the field of family or employment law. This arises because constitutional guarantees bind the legislature and commonly do not differentiate between legislation concerning the government and the individual and legislation that operates solely in the private sphere. This is the case, for example, with the New Zealand and UK provisions.[25] Consequently, where the relationship between the private parties is founded on legislation, UK courts would be bound, as far as possible, to interpret it consistent with the parties' Convention rights.[26]

A *third* type of argument focuses on the definition of a governmental body. Even where the common law generally is not subject to constitutional interpretation and adjudication, this may nevertheless be appropriate in common law cases in which a governmental body is a party, since governments are bound in this way.[27] Inevitably, this will give an incentive for a plaintiff to argue that the other party is 'governmental' so as to bring into play constitutional rights that would not otherwise apply. Consequently, boundary disputes are endemic. Under the HRA the definition of a 'public authority' under section 6 has been the pressure point for these conflicts.[28]

---

[20] For a pre-HRA example see in relation to Art 9, see *Blathwayt v Baron Cawley* [1976] AC 397 (considering public policy as a reason for not giving effect to the forfeiture of a gift in a will should the beneficiary be or become a Roman Catholic).

[21] See *Retail Wholesale and Department Store Union Local 580 et al v Dolphin Delivery Ltd* [1986] 2 SCR 573, 603 (MacInyre J), and *Hill v Church of Scientology of Toronto* [1995] 2 SCR 1130.

[22] The terminology of 'drittwirkung' is not, however, so easily transferable into a UK context because of the absence of a separate Constitutional Court and a unitary constitution (rather than a Federal one).

[23] *Du Plessis v De Klerk*, 1996 (3) SA 850.

[24] For a clear overview see A Young, 'Horizontality and the Human Rights Act 1998' in K Ziegler (ed), *Human Rights and Private Law: Privacy as Autonomy* (Oxford, Hart Publishing, 2007).

[25] See, respectively, NZ Bill of Rights Act 1990 s 6 and HRA s 3, creating interpretive obligations applicable to all legislation.

[26] HRA s 3.

[27] McIntyre J in *Dolphin Delivery* [1986] 2 SCR 573, 598–99.

[28] 138–149 above.

Debates about the private law impact of human rights, even if answered affirmatively, lead only to further questions such as: is the right in question capable of applying horizontally?;[29] and are there any reasons to limit it having regard to the position of the other party? The South African Constitution is unusual in explicitly addressing such key issues. It adopts a sophisticated contextual approach.[30] Section 8(2) states:

> A provision of the Bill of Rights binds a natural or juristic person if, and to the extent that, it is applicable, taking account of the nature of the right and the nature of any duty imposed by the right.[31]

The HRA has no equivalent provision. Even where these questions remain implicit rather than explicit, it is nonetheless vital to discuss them.

An initial question is whether the right claimed has any relevance to private legal relations. The issue of whether a private party is capable of enjoying the right in question (for instance, whether a company can benefit from freedom of religion) is, in principle, the same whether the claim is made against the state or against another private party. However, plainly some constitutional rights (the right to a fair trial, for example) apply paradigmatically against the state.

A second question is the impact of a claim of this kind on the other party who allegedly bears the burden of the right. Plainly, it would be invidious to allow the claim of a horizontal right to restrict the other party's constitutional rights and, arguably, other rights that he or she may enjoy in private law. It is not at all obvious that a constitutional right should for example override a freely exercised private law right under a contract or a will. Rights of this kind are important in the common law even if not usually denoted as 'constitutional'. Conversely, if other explicitly constitutional rights are permitted to trump them in private litigation this will merely have the effect of creating incentives to rephrase these private interests in constitutional terms (for example, as property rights).[32] To

---

[29] For an argument that Convention rights 'conceptually' have 'unmediated direct applicability' and therefore should be given direct horizontal effect under the HRA, see D Beyeleveld and S Pattinson, 'Horizontality applicability and horizontal effect' (2002) 118 *LQR* 623. While we do not subscribe to this view, to engage with it here would be a substantial diversion, and an unnecessary one in view of the development of the jurisprudence.

[30] Following the approach advocated by Madala J *in Du Plessis*, 1996 (3) SA 850, 925ff that direct horizontal effect should be considered in the context of each specific constitutional right rather than according to a general principle.

[31] The courts' duty in such cases is dealt with in detail in s 8(3), which requires the development of the common law if legislation does not give effect to the right in question, but also permits the common law to be developed to limit rights, if the test of reasonable and justifiable limitation in s 36(1) is satisfied. See H Cheadle and D Davis, 'The Application of the 1996 Constitution in the Private Sphere' (1997) 13 *SAJHR* 50, 60–65.

[32] Eg, *Syndicat Northcrest v Amselem* 2004 SCC 47, in which a co-ownership dispute over the erection of temporary religious structures on the balconies of condominiums was

translate private law disputes into the language of constitutional rights in this way may achieve little beyond making the law less stable and predictable as the courts apply new terminology to old issues. Especially when deciding whether to superimpose a newly operative Bill of Rights on earlier legal agreements concluded between private parties there are important considerations of legal certainty at stake. These interests of legal certainty and contractual expectations can also re-phrased also in human rights terms of protection from retroactivity and deprivation of property.

TYPES OF HORIZONTAL APPLICABILITY UNDER THE HRA

One of the shortcomings of the policy debate that preceded the introduction of the HRA in the UK was the failure to address the well-known issues concerning private law that had arisen in other countries such as Germany, Ireland, Canada and South Africa. In the quarter-century long debate about incorporation of the Convention into UK law the questions had been recognised at an early point but were then seemingly lost to sight. A Home Office consultation paper from 1976 had argued that the position could either be left open, or that a Bill of incorporation could embody a 'state action' doctrine, whereby the courts assumed responsibility for ensuring adequate protection of citizens' rights, whatever the source of the threat.[33] From the same period the House of Lords' Select Committee on a Bill of Rights had argued in favour of leaving the issue open under any legislation.[34] In contrast the Northern Ireland Standing Advisory Commission on Human Rights preferred a clear statement that the Bill was not intended to apply between private individuals.[35]

This discussion appears to have been forgotten, however, two decades later. The Labour Party's 1996 consultative document, *Bringing Rights Home*, came out generally against horizontal rights. It argued that the Convention's purpose was to protect individuals against the misuse of state power, rather than against each other. Nevertheless, one paragraph slightly qualified this general approach:

> Individuals would in certain circumstances be able to use the new Act to seek to
> secure effective action by public authorities to protect them against abuse of

dealt with by the Supreme Court of Canada as a clash between rights of freedom of religion and property (the former prevailing); see further T Allen, *Property and the Human Rights Act 1998* (Oxford, Hart Publishing, 2005) 243–45.

[33] *Legislation on Human Rights With Particular Reference to the European Convention: A Discussion Document* (1976) paras 2.18–2.19 and 4.14–4.15

[34] *Report of the Select Committee on a Bill of Rights*, HL 176 (1977–78) para 41.

[35] *The Protection of Human Rights by Law in Northern Ireland*, Cmnd. 7009 (1977) para 7.11.

human rights by private bodies or individuals. Nevertheless, this new legislation is not intended to alter existing legal relationships between individuals.[36]

The White Paper *Rights Brought Home*,[37] on the other hand, made no mention of the possible use of Convention rights against other private individuals, even via the indirect route of alleging failure on the part of a public authority to give protection to the victim. When the text of the Human Rights Bill was published it made no explicit mention of the issue. The drafting did, however, leave open variations on the three basic types of horizontal arguments described earlier: arising from the duties of the courts as public authorities under section 6; under the interpretative obligation (s 3) in legislation applicable between private parties; and by imposing duties on 'hybrid' public authorities (ie those with mixed private/public functions), again under section 6. These possibilities were of immediate concern to two groups of potential non-governmental defendants – the press and religious organisations and charities – both of which mounted partially successful campaigns to amend the Bill.[38]

Much of the press comment at the time of publication of the Human Rights Bill speculated on the possibility of creating a new right of privacy in UK law, enforceable, for example, against intrusive reporters and newspapers. Fear of the possibility was sufficient to rouse the Chairman of the Press Complaints Commission, Lord Wakeham, to air misgivings over the potential restraint of the press. In response, during the Second Reading debate on the Bill, the Lord Chancellor gave a somewhat confused and contradictory account of the government's intention: while it was not intended to create new rights against private individuals, incorporation of Article 8 might make the creation by the judges of a new right of privacy against newspapers easier, but in doing so the courts would be merely following the emerging direction of the common law.[39] In the ensuing controversy, amendments were made to the Bill to protect the press from ex parte injunctions protecting privacy. The Government introduced a new clause (now s 12), which applies wherever a court is considering granting relief which might affect the exercise of the Convention right of freedom of expression.[40] It applies mainly to applications for pre-publication injunctions for breach of confidence. Section 12 requires that if the newspaper is not present or represented the court must be satisfied that all practicable steps have been taken to notify them, or that there are compelling reasons why they should not be notified. The court is not permitted to grant an order unless at trial the applicant is 'likely to establish' that the publication

---

[36] *Bringing Rights Home* (London, Labour Party, 1996) 7.
[37] Cm 3782 (1997).
[38] The result was the inclusion of ss 12 and 13.
[39] Lord Irvine of Lairg, HLDebs, vol 582, cols 1231–32 (3 Nov 1997).
[40] HC Debs, vol 315, cols 534 ff (2 July 1998).

should not be allowed (this in contrast to the 'arguable case' test for interlocutory injunctions). The court is required to have 'particular regard' to Article 10 and must also consider the extent to which the information has been or is about to become available to the public, the public interest in publication, and any relevant privacy code (eg from the Press Complaints Commission, Ofcom or the broadcaster itself). In practice, the provision has had little impact except – due to a mischievous judicial interpretation – as an acknowledgement of potential horizontal impact, so opening consideration of Article 8 as well as Article 10 in these cases.[41] Lord Irvine's predictions concerning privacy turned out to be nearly accurate as, notwithstanding section 12, the courts took inspiration from Article 8 to fashion a tort of misuse of private information out of breach of confidence.[42] Professor Gavin Phillipson is correct to conclude that the press were 'fobbed off' with section 12.[43]

A rather similar process occurred in relation to the concerns of religious organisations over the potential application of the Act to them. The Strasbourg jurisprudence draws a clear line between state institutions, which can be liable for human rights violations, and non-state actors, which cannot. Even established churches are treated as being in the latter category[44] as potential human rights claimants, both of collective religious liberty and freedom of association. Similarly religious dissenters are not entitled to invoke individual religious liberty against the group they belong to: their liberty comprises the freedom to join or leave a religious organization, rather than to make it conform to their individual beliefs and practices.[45] Nevertheless, religious organisations had serious misgivings that the HRA could be used to bring claims against them. Would a church, for example, be required by secular courts to ordain or admit to membership persons who did not subscribe to its doctrinal positions or whose lifestyle it regarded as inconsistent with its beliefs? Would a religious charity such as a hospice be required to employ pro-euthanasia staff?

In response to such concerns (both real and exaggerated) there was a vigorous campaign to amend the Human Rights Bill to include specific recognition of religious group autonomy.[46] An attempt to exclude churches

---

[41] *Douglas v Hello!* [2001] QB 967, 1003 (Sedley LJ).

[42] 248ff. below.

[43] G Phillipson, 'Clarity Postponed: Horizontal Effect After Campbell', in H Fenwick, G Phillipson and R Masterman (eds), *Judicial Reasoning under the UK Human Rights Act* (Cambridge, CUP, 2007) 148.

[44] *Hauanemi v Sweden* (1996) 22 EHRR CD 155.

[45] Eg, the European Commission rejected a complaint from the UK in which a vicar alleged that the Church of England's decision to ordain women priests violated his rights under Art 9: see *Williamson v UK*, Appl No 0027008/95, 17 May 1995.

[46] For a detailed analysis, see I Leigh, 'Towards a Christian Approach to Religious Liberty' in P Beaumont (ed), *Christian Perspectives on Human Rights and Legal Philosophy* (Carlisle, Paternoster Press, 1998) 64–71; P Cumper, 'The Protection of Religious Rights

from the definition of public authority failed in the House of Lords.[47] Three more limited exemptions (designed to give conscience exemptions for those acting on religious teachings and for church courts) met with short-lived success: they were passed by the House of Lords only to be removed, at the Government's request, by the House of Commons at the Committee Stage. The Government argued that the amendments were unnecessary since the concerns were either adequately addressed through the incorporation of Article 9, or under the existing Convention jurisprudence, or subject to specific UK legislative safeguards which would take precedence in the event of conflict. In the end the Government put forward a broad compromise solution to assuage the religious groups' persistent concerns. Section 13 was the result:

> (1) If a court's determination of any question arising under this Act might affect the exercise by a religious organisation (itself or its members collectively) of the Convention right to freedom of thought, conscience and religion, it must have particular regard to the importance of that right.

The Home Secretary, Jack Straw, conceded that this fell short of according primacy to Article 9 over other rights, such as privacy or free speech, but argued that to do so would itself contravene the Convention. Nonetheless, he believed that the section would 'send a clear signal to the courts that they must pay due regard to the rights guaranteed by article 9',[48] reminding them that rights attach not only to individuals but to the churches (or other associations with religious objectives).[49] The sparse reference to section 13 in subsequent religious liberty cases,[50] however, confirms the view of several commentators that the provision was primarily symbolic and would not have a significant impact.[51]

Leaving aside the history of these amendments, more generally the variety of potential avenues under the HRA for pursuing horizontal claims

---

under Section 13 of the Human Rights Act 1998' [2000] *PL* 254; J Rivers, 'From Toleration to Pluralism: Religious Liberty and Religious Establishment under the United Kingdom's Human Rights Act' in R Ahdar (ed), *Law and Religion* (Aldershot, Dartmouth Publishing, 2000) ch 7.

[47] HL Deb., vol 584, col 1263 (19 January 1998).

[48] HC Deb., vol 312, col, 1024 (20 May 1998).

[49] HC Deb., vol 312, col, 1023 (20 May 1998).

[50] Eg, s 13 was given little attention by either the Court of Appeal ([2003] 1 All ER 385, 402, 440 and 464) or the House of Lords in *R v Secretary of State for Education and Employment ex p Williamson* [2005] UKHL 15 [55]. In *R (Amicus – MSF Section) v Secretary for State for Trade and Industry* [2004] EWHC 860 (Admin), [41], Richards J stated that s 13 does not give greater weight to religious rights protected by Art 9 than would otherwise be enjoyed under the Convention.

[51] Cumper, 'Protection of Religious Rights' 265; I Leigh, 'Freedom of Religion: Public/Private, Rights/Wrongs' in M Hill (ed), *Religious Liberty and Human Rights* (Cardiff, University of Wales Press, 2002) 148.

quickly gave rise to a vigorous debate.[52] At the poles are the views of the late Sir William Wade[53] and of Sir Richard Buxton,[54] who argued respectively for comprehensive horizontal application of the Convention rights under the Act and that it has no application to private litigation.

For Wade the decisive provision was section 6(3) which treats all courts and tribunals as public authorities and so requires them to uphold Convention rights wherever they are claimed. This argument has difficulty in explaining why therefore the Act carefully refers to public authorities, which on Wade's thesis is otiose (as he acknowledged), and to the interpretation of statutory provisions but not to the common law. In short Wade's argument radically subverts the architecture of the Act. Buxton, on the other hand, stressed that the ECHR is a treaty regarding the rights of individuals against the state and argues that it retains that character when incorporated into domestic law. As we have seen, however, the first premise is an over-simplification since in limited spheres the Convention organs themselves have recognised a positive obligation on the state (including its courts) to protect individuals from incursion of their rights by other private individuals.[55] Moreover, the reference in section 2 to taking Strasbourg jurisprudence into account gives domestic courts latitude to develop rights in ways not limited by the ECHR jurisprudence, provided they do not contradict it.[56] As we shall see, each of these extreme positions has been in effect ruled out by the UK courts in their HRA judgments.

In contrast to this controversy the case for *statutory* horizontality has proved un-contentious, so much so that some major instances of courts acting in this way to import human rights into private law risk being overlooked. Where the relationship between the private parties is founded on legislation, UK courts would be bound under HRA section 3 to interpret the legislation, as far as possible, consistently with the parties'

---

[52] See, eg, M Hunt, 'The "Horizontal Effect" of the Human Rights Act' [1998] *PL* 423; Leigh, 'Horizontal Rights'; B Markensinis, 'Privacy, Freedom of Expression and the Human Rights Bill: Lessons from Germany' (1999) 115 *LQR*. 47; G Phillipson, 'The Human Rights Act, "horizontal effect" and the Common Law: a Bang or a Whimper?' (1999) 62(6) *MLR* 824; A Lester and D Pannick, 'The Impact of the Human Rights Act on Private Law: the Knight's Move' (2000) 116 *LQR* 380; N Bamforth, 'The True Horizontal Effect of the Human Rights Act' (1998) *PL* 423; I Hare, 'Vertically Challenged: Private Parties, Privacy and the Human Rights Act' [2001] *EHRLR* 526.

[53] H Wade, 'The United Kingdom's Bill of Rights' in I Hare and C Forsyth (eds), *Constitutional Reform in the United Kingdom: Practice and Principles* (Oxford, Hart Publishing, 1998) 63–4 and 'Horizons of Horizontality' (2000) 116 *LQR* 217; and C Forsyth and H Wade , *Administrative Law* (8th ed) (Oxford, OUP, 2000), App 2. See also J Morgan, 'Privacy, Confidence and Horizontal Effect: 'Hello' Trouble' (2003) 62 *CLJ* 444, 467–8 and 'Questioning the True Effect of the Human Rights Act' (2002) *LS* 259.

[54] R Buxton; 'The Human Rights Act and Private Law' (2000) 116 *LQR* 48.

[55] Ch3 above.

[56] The practice of the courts in using s 2 has, however, been disappointing: see ch 3 above.

Convention rights: the Act makes no distinction in applying the interpretative obligation between litigants that are public or private in nature. There have been numerous instances of the courts applying the HRA to legislation in the private sphere in this way, for example: in an action for breach of copyright under the Copyright, Designs and Patents Act 1988;[57] in the case of a hire purchase agreement under the Consumer Credit Act 1974;[58] when considering if a dismissal is unfair under the Employment Rights Act;[59] and to the question of who is entitled to succeed to a statutory tenancy under the Rent Act 1977.[60] The first three of these arguments failed on the facts but without judicial dissent from the principle that the HRA could assist the plaintiff in an appropriate case.

Similarly it seems generally accepted that whatever else the inclusion of courts and tribunals within the definition of public authorities under section 6(3)(a) may mean it certainly requires judges exercising discretionary powers in private litigation to do so in conformity with the parties' Convention rights ('*remedial horizontality*').[61] A controversial but clear illustration of this duty concerned the injunctions to protect the notorious child murderers of Jamie Bulger: Thompson and Venables.[62] In an unprecedented ruling Butler-Sloss J granted an injunction *contra mundum* to prevent their whereabouts after release or new identities being revealed. In two respects the decision broke entirely new ground. Previously, and quite exceptionally, injunctions had been issued to protect convicted notorious child and juvenile criminals from further intrusive publicity until they reached adulthood under the wardship jurisdiction.[63] Once Thompson and Venables reached majority wardship could no longer apply. The court found the basis for further restriction of publicity in the law of confidence. Secondly, the court order was directed at people who are not parties to the action – contrary to the well-established principle[64] that an injunction cannot be granted except against a party to the suit. In the words of Butler-Sloss J:

> we are entering a new era, and the requirement that the courts act in a way that is compatible with the Convention, and have regard to European jurisprudence, adds a new dimension to those principles.[65]

---

[57] *Ashdown v Telegraph Group plc*[2001] EWCA Civ 1142.
[58] *Wilson v First County Trust (No 2)* [2003] 3 WLR 568 (see 254–6 below).
[59] *X v Y* [2004] EWCA Civ 662 [2004] ICR 1634 (258 below).
[60] *Ghaidan v Godin-Mendoza* (see 253ff. below).
[61] Alison Young points out that HRA s 12 also enacts a form of remedial horizontality in cases involving freedom of expression: 'Horizontality and the Human Rights Act 1998' in K Ziegler (ed), *Human Rights and Private Law: Privacy as Autonomy* (Oxford, Hart Publishing, 2007) 38.
[62] [2001] 1 All ER 908 (F).
[63] *Re X (a minor) (wardship: injunction)* [1985] 1 All ER 53.
[64] Lord Eldon in *Iveson v Harris* (1802) 7 Ves 251; 32 ER 102.
[65] [2001] 1 All ER 908, 939 (para 100).

SPECIFIC AREAS OF PRIVATE LAW

In this section we move from general arguments to the particular. The discussion that follows considers the impact of arguments concerning the horizontal application of Convention rights under the HRA in several specific fields of substantive private law: under the common law in protecting privacy, in contractual disputes, in employment and, finally, property law[66]

Privacy and Protection From Misuse of Personal Information

As we have seen, one of the major controversies at the time of enacting the HRA concerned whether it would lead the courts to create a common law right of privacy. Press fears concerning this had led to the inclusion of section 12. The story after the Act came into force has been one of less dramatic but nonetheless significant incremental development of the law. The courts have declined to create a privacy tort; through a series of decisions they have, however, transformed the existing breach of confidence action into a new tort of misuse of personal information which provides substantial protection for personal privacy. This process demonstrates several points about the horizontal effect of the Act.

The place of European Convention jurisprudence in this unfolding story has been ambiguous. Since 2000 the jurisprudence itself has significantly developed in the direction of requiring states to provide protection to individuals whose privacy is infringed by other individuals.[67] The text of Article 8 is silent on this issue, referring in Art 8(2) to limitations by *public authorities* on the right to respect for private life. The European Commission on Human Rights appeared to regard protection from private individuals as outside Article 8.[68] At the time of commencement of the Act the only hint of the developments to come were some under-developed comments in decisions in which such applications were declared *inadmissible*:[69] there were no concrete examples of the European Court of Human Rights upholding an Article 8 complaint for failing to prevent an intrusion by another private individual. This breakthrough came in 2004 in *Von*

---

[66] One area not discussed here for lack of space is the applicability of the Convention in family law disputes. For a detailed treatment concluding that there has been 'entrenched hostility' towards rights-based discourse in private law cases arising under the HRA see: S Harris-Short, ' Family Law and the Human Rights Act 1998: judicial restraint or revolution?' in H Fenwick, G Phillipson and R Masterman (eds), *Judicial Reasoning under the UK Human Rights Act* (Cambridge, CUP, 2007) 334 ff.

[67] H Fenwick and G Phillipson, *Media Freedom under the Human Rights Act* (Oxford, OUP, 2006) ch 13.

[68] *Winer v UK*, 1986, Appl No 10871/84, 48 *D&R* 154.

[69] *Earl Spencer v UK* (1998) 25 EHRR CD 105, 112; *Barclay v UK* (1999) Appl No 35712/97.

Hannover when it was found that the failure of the German courts to grant a remedy to Princess Caroline of Monaco to prevent publication of paparazzi shots of her in everyday public situations breached Article 8.[70] Although thinly reasoned the *Von Hannover* decision amounts to a clear extension of the Article 8 jurisprudence and lays a positive obligation on member states subject to a fair balance with other rights within the margin of appreciation.

Turning to the attitude of the domestic courts, prophecies of the development of a tort of privacy using Article 8 have turned out to be unfounded. The House of Lords conclusively rejected this possibility in *Wainwright*[71] in finding that there was no remedy for a strip search of visitors by prison officers. In doing so their Lordships affirmed that earlier long-standing authority that no such general tort exists in English law[72] remained unchanged. Indeed Lord Hoffmann argued that the introduction of the HRA had *weakened* the case for any such common law development because of the possible extended liability of public authorities.[73] When *Wainwright* reached Strasbourg, however, the European Court of Human Rights found that Article 8 had been breached and that the failure of the domestic courts to offer redress breached Article 13.[74] In response to this ruling the parliamentary Joint Committee on Human Rights has questioned whether the government is considering introducing a statutory tort of privacy invasion.[75] The need for a general tort does not necessarily follow: *Wainwright* involved actions by prison officers in breach of the Prison Rules and it may be that either public law remedies or the tort of misfeasance in a public office could be extended to give a remedy to satisfy the Convention.[76] What seems clear, however, is that, unlike in New

---

[70] *Von Hannover v Germany* (2005) 40 EHRR 1. See also *Sciacca v Italy* (2006) 43 EHRR 20 (release to press of photo obtained for tax evasion investigation). An earlier decision, *Peck v UK* (2003) 36 EHRR 41, involving the broadcast of CCTV footage of the applicant, turned on the involvement of a state body (the local council) in disclosing the film.

[71] *Wainwright v Home Office* [2004] 2 AC 406 [2003] UKHL 53.

[72] *Kaye v Robertson* [1991] FSR 62; *Malone v Metropolitan Police Commissioner* [1979] Ch 344.

[73] *Wainwright* at [34]. Strictly the argument concerning Art 8 circumvented the HRA (which did not apply since the search took place in 1997) and proceeded on the basis that development of the common law was necessary to comply with the UK's international obligations: see Lord Hoffmann's speech in *Wainwright* at para 7.

[74] *Wainwright v UK* (App No 12350/04) ECtHR, 26 September 2006, para 55.

[75] Joint Committee on Human Rights, *Sixteenth Report (2006–7)*, App 10. For earlier discussion of a general statutory tort of privacy see the Lord Chancellor's discussion paper, *Infringement of Privacy* (London, 1993).

[76] Cf Lord Hoffmann at para 51 in *Wainwright v Home Office*: 'Article 8 may justify a monetary remedy for an intentional invasion of privacy by a public authority, even if no damage is suffered other than distress for which damages are not ordinarily recoverable. It does not follow that a merely negligent act should, contrary to general principle, give rise to a claim for damages for distress because it affects privacy rather than some other interest like bodily safety.'

Zealand where their brethren have recently developed a tort of invasion of privacy,[77] *Wainwright* signals the great reluctance of UK judges to do so. Such a step is more likely to occur as a result of parliamentary intervention than by judicial invocation of the HRA.[78]

This outcome has been explained by several senior judges on the basis that the HRA does not authorise the creation of new causes of action between private parties. This was the clear conclusion of Lady Hale in *Campbell v MGN*:

> The 1998 Act does not create any new cause of action between private persons. But if there is a relevant cause of action applicable, the court as a public authority must act compatibly with both parties' Convention rights.[79]

The courts have thus in the case of Article 8 rejected Wade's argument for full or direct horizontal effect.[80] The only apparent indirect endorsement of Wade's position comes from decisions that speak of the court's jurisdiction (to restrain publicity in some cases) being founded on Convention rights. On closer analysis, however, the judges appear to be describing either a form of remedial horizontality or where the court has been placed an intermediate position to protect the rights of both parties founded on section 6. The former explains Butler-Sloss LJ's comments in *Thompson and Venables* that seized of threats to the plaintiffs (the killers of Jamie Bulger) she was obliged to issue injunctions that broke new ground in that they gave protection to them as *adults* from publicity and were made against all the world, rather than only parties to the litigation.[81]

The courts have, however, proved markedly more receptive to arguments in favour of extending existing causes of action, notably breach of confidence. In recent years that action has been transformed so that there is no longer any requirement of any obligation of confidentiality between the parties.[82] The result has been the creation of a tort of misuse of personal

---

[77] *Hosking v Runting* [2005] NZLR 1; *Television New Zealand v Rogers* (NZCA) 7 August 2006 (CA 12/06); *Andrews v Television New Zealand*, (NZHC) 15 December 2006, CIV 2004–404–3536. A successful claim requires the existence of facts in respect of which there is a reasonable expectation of privacy and that publicity is given to those private facts that would be considered highly offensive to an objective reasonable person.

[78] Cf Buxton LJ in the Court of Appeal *Wainwright v Home Office* [2002] QB 1334, 1365, referring to democratic and practical considerations favouring development by Parliament rather than the courts.

[79] *Campbell v MGN* [2004] 2 AC 457 [2004] UKHL 22, para 132. See also Lord Phillips MR

[80] 246 above,

[81] [2001] 1 All ER 908 (F) 932 (para 78). Butler-Sloss LJ doubted that the Act created a free-standing cause of action based directly on the Convention: *Ibid*, 918 (para 27).

[82] Compare *Coco v AN Clark Engineers* [1969] RPC 41 and *AG v Guardian Newspapers (No 2)* [1990] 1 AC 109 with *Campbell v MGN* [2004] 2 AC 457.

information.[83] The case brought by the model Naomi Campbell against the *Daily Mirror* newspaper was decisive in this development. It concerned details that the newspaper had published of her treatment for drug addiction, including clandestinely taken photographs of her leaving a Narcotics Anonymous meeting. A majority of the House of Lords held that publication of the photographs amounted to a breach of confidence.[84] Even the minority agreed that breach of confidence no longer required an initial confidential relationship.[85] Although there were signs that the law had been developing in this direction before the HRA, it is clear that reference to Article 8 was decisive in determining the private information to be protected.[86]

This is clearly an example of the *indirect* horizontality of Convention rights, although differences in the way that individual judges have explained the process have led to academic debate about whether what is involved is strong or weak indirect effect.[87] On the one hand are some judges who speak of Convention 'values' (rather than rights) informing the development of the common law – a form of weak indirect horizontality. Thus in his minority speech in *Campbell* Lord Nicholls stated:

> The values embodied in articles 8 and 10 are as much applicable in disputes between individuals or between an individual and a non-governmental body such as a newspaper as they are in disputes between individuals and a public authority.[88]

In the same decision Lord Hoffmann argued similarly:

> What human rights law has done is to identify private information as something worth protecting as an aspect of human autonomy and dignity. And this recognition has raised inescapably the question of why it should be worth protecting against the state but not against a private person. I can see no logical ground for saying that a person should have less protection against a private individual than he would have against the state for the publication of personal information for which there is no justification.[89]

---

[83] *Campbell* at para 14 (Lord Nicholls); *McKennit v Ash* [2006] EWCA Civ 1714, para 8 (Buxton LJ).

[84] *Campbell v MGN* [2004] 2 AC 457.

[85] Lord Nicholls at paras 13–14.

[86] For a detailed account, see H Fenwick, *Civil Liberties and Human Rights* (4th ed) (Abingdon, Routledge Cavendish, 2007) 895–915.

[87] For detailed analysis see G Phillipson 'Clarity Postponed: horizontal effect after Campbell', in H Fenwick, G Phillipson and R Masterman, *Judicial Reasoning under the UK Human Rights Act* (Cambridge, CUP, 2007).

[88] *Campbell* at para 17.

[89] *Campbell* at para 50.

On the other hand other judges (such as Lady Hale in *Campbell*[90]) describe this in terms of a more concrete *obligation* on the court to give effect to Convention rights. And in *Re S (A Child)* Lord Phillips stated:

> The court should, insofar as it can, develop the action for breach of confidence in such a manner as will give effect to both Article 8 and Article 10 rights.[91]

A variety of metaphors abounds to describe the process: 'absorbing the rights' into breach of confidence,[92] re-phrasing or translating the common law, pouring the Convention articles into the empty shell of breach of confidence, and so on.

Although much attention has been devoted to finding differences between these positions, they are not of great practical significance, for two reasons: first, the judges regard themselves as performing the same exercise although they express it in different ways; secondly, more important than the subtle difference in indirect influence is the question of what the Convention rights or values *are*. While there was no clear pronouncement from Strasbourg on horizontality and the need for a domestic remedy for breach of privacy the distinctions were largely esoteric. Now that the European Court of Human Rights has held in *Von Hannover* that a domestic remedy for infringements of privacy by private individuals is *required* by Article 8 further talk of Convention values would appear to have been superseded by that positive duty to give effect to Article 8. The key question for the future is whether further adjustments will be required to give full effect to *Von Hannover* since it is clearly to this jurisprudence that English courts must now look in determining what counts as private information.[93]

We turn now to consider the applicability of the HRA to a second field of the common law – contract.

Contract, Certainty and Horizontality

The common law has developed a delicate balance for dealing with issues of fairness, whereas the Convention does not on its face govern private contractual, tortious or property relations at all.[94] One of the dangers of

---

[90] n 79 above. And see Lord Hope in *Campbell* at para 114 and Lindsay LJ in *Douglas v Hello! (No 2)* [2003] 3 All ER 996, para 186 (1).

[91] *Re S* at para 53.

[92] Woolf, LCJ in *A v B Plc* [2002] 3 WLR 542, 546.

[93] See *Mckennit v Ash* [2006] EWCA Civ 1714; *Murray v Express Newspapers*, [2007] EWHC 1908 (Ch), discussed in ch 3 above.

[94] A rare exception in the jurisprudence is *Pla v Andorra* [2004] FCR 630, a challenge under Arts 8 and 14, in which the European Court of Human Rights found that the Andorran courts should have interpreted a will to prevent discrimination against the testator's adopted son. Richard Kay notes that '*Pla* displaces the national rules on interpretation ... [and] raises

importing human rights standards into contractual relations therefore is of undermining certainty and the intentions of the parties. Whereas HRA section 3(1) requires Convention-friendly interpretation of statutes, including those preceding the Act, there is no corresponding provision for contracts and leases. The question of whether of whether a private contract[95] entered into prior to the HRA should be interpreted in a way that the parties could not have envisaged is therefore problematic.[96] There is also the further complication that the parties may have relied upon earlier precedents from the courts interpreting the statute applying to their arrangements that now might be revisited under the HRA.

Both factors were arguably present in *Ghaidan v Godin-Mendoza*.[97] Mr Ghaidan, the defendant, was the landlord of flat leased to Mr Wallwyn-James, whose surviving partner was the plaintiff, Mr Godin-Mendoza. The House of Lords read the definition of 'spouse' in the Rent Act 1977 so as to include same-sex partners in order to comply with Articles 8 and 14 ECHR. The effect was to recognise the rights of Mr Godin-Mendoza as a statutorily protected tenant against Mr Ghaidan. This is a striking interpretation for several reasons. The definition of spouse under the Rent Act 1977 was 'a person living with the original tenant as his or her wife or husband'. It was clear, however, that the provision had been intended when enacted to give to heterosexual cohabitees the same rights as married couples.

In view of the fact that the tenancy pre-dated the HRA it would have been open to the House of Lords to hold that the obligations on landlords should not be extended without clear statutory approval. At the time of judgment neither the Equality Act 2006 (providing for anti-discrimination legislation on grounds of sexual orientation in the field of goods and services) nor the Civil Partnerships Act 2004 (conferring recognition on registered same-sex partnerships) had been passed: the latter was, however, before Parliament. From the point of view of legal certainty the decision in *Ghaidan* is open to criticism. Four years earlier the House of Lords had, before the coming into force of the HRA, held that a surviving same-sex partner of a tenant did *not* qualify to succeed to the tenancy under the provision benefiting co-habitees.[98] In the intervening period (and shortly

the possibility that the Convention may apply, by its own force, to the relations of private parties inter se': R Kay, 'The European Convention on Human Rights and the Control of Private Law' (2005) *EHRLR* 466, 468.

[95] Where one contracting party is a public authority HRA s 6 may be invoked: see, eg, *R (Haggerty) v St Helens BC* [2003] EWHC 803, [26]ff; *Lee v Leeds CC* [2002] EWCA Civ 6, [24]ff. In a case of this kind the Act deals explicitly with retrospectivity in s 22.

[96] On normal principles contracts are to be construed according to the factual context at the time that they are entered into.

[97] [2004] 3 WLR 113 [2004] UKHL 30. See further ch 3 above.

[98] *Fitzpatrick v Sterling Housing Association Ltd* [2001] 1 AC 27. However, by a majority the House held that the plaintiff could qualify for as a 'family member' for an

before *Ghaidan* itself) the Strasbourg court had ruled that denial of equivalent tenancy rights to same-sex couples as those available to unmarried different sex couples amounted to discrimination contrary to Article 14.[99] From the landlord's point of view *Ghaidan* was an abrupt reversal in the application of the law since, unlike the decision to extend Rent Act protection to cohabitees which was taken by Parliament prospectively,[100] the effect of the Lords decision was retrospectively to change the consequences of the agreement entered to between the parties.[101] These considerations pointed in the direction of making of a declaration of incompatibility under section 4, rather than the radical *re-interpretation* of the Rent Act,[102] undertaken by the majority in the House of Lords. Lord Nicholls, however, rejected this argument in brief terms by pointing that the interpretive duty had to be undertaken at the time when the statute fell to be applied.[103]

In contrast to the ruling in *Ghaidan* the difficulties arising from post HRA re-interpretation of statutes applicable to private transactions were squarely faced by the House itself in *Wilson v First County Trust*.[104] The issue was applicability of the HRA to a hire purchase agreement for a car. The agreement failed to comply with the statutory conditions, with the result that, under Consumer Credit Act 1974 section 127(3), it was unenforceable. The Court of Appeal found that a statutory bar on the enforcement of security was incompatible with Article 6 or Article 1 of the First Protocol to the Convention (the right to peaceful enjoyment of one's possessions).[105] The Court of Appeal was unable either to read the provision to comply with the Convention or to find an adequate explanation (either from the parliamentary material or otherwise) for why such a draconian provision had been enacted. Accordingly, it found that the section did not fall within what it otherwise recognised would have been a wide discretionary area of legislative judgment to be respected in matters

---

assured tenancy. *Fitzpatrick* did not address the discrimination argument that prevailed in *Ghaida*, For comparison of the two decisions, see A Kavanagh, 'Judicial Reasoning after *Ghaidan v Mendoza*' in Fenwick, Phillipson and Masterman op. cit.

[99]   *Karner v Austria*, Appl no. 40016/98 (2003) 2 FLR 203.

[100]   These provisions were enacted in 1988 and came into force in 1989.

[101]   As Lord Millett point out in his dissenting speech para 99, referring to the uncertainty over the date the change in the law took effect.

[102]   There were clear dicta in *Fitzpatrick* that 'living with the original tenant as his or her wife or husband' could not refer to a same-sex couple: Lord Nicholls, 43; Lord Clyde, 47; Lord Slynn, 34.

[103]   Para 23, citing *Wilson v First County Trust (No 2)* [2003] 3 WLR 568, 587.

[104]   [2003] UKHL 40.

[105]   *Wilson v First County Trust (No 2)* [2001] EWCA Civ 633; argument had earlier been adjourned to allow argument on the incompatibility point: *Wilson v First County Trust* [2001] 2 WLR 302, CA.

of social policy,[106] and made a declaration of incompatibility. The consequence was that the HRA was applied in the purely private context of a consumer loan because it was governed by a statutory provision which fell to be interpreted under section 3.

A complicating factor was that both the hire purchase agreement and the county court judgment under appeal had been made before the commencement of the HRA. The Court of Appeal had found that the relevant date was not that of either event but rather when the issue came before the Court itself, since as a public authority it was obliged not to act in a way that violate a person's Convention rights.[107] On appeal, however, Lord Rodger pointed out that even disregarding the inconsistency with the House of Lords' approach to retrospectivity, this approach ignored the effect of section 6(2)(a), which exonerated the public authority (here the Court of Appeal and House of Lords) when the authority was obliged by statute to violate Convention rights. The way his Lordship approached the retrospectivity question was to apply the presumptions against retrospective operation and against interference with vested interests.[108] While HRA section 3 could have the effect of changing the interpretation of legislation already in force (even to the extent of reconsidering and revising pre-HRA interpretations),[109] this could cause 'considerable difficulties':

> It would mean that parties' rights under existing legislation in respect of a transaction completed before the Act came into force could be changed overnight, to the benefit of one party and the prejudice of the other. This change, moreover, would operate capriciously, with the outcome depending on whether the parties' rights were determined by a court before or after 2 October 2000.[110]

Lord Rodger concluded therefore that

> in general the principle of interpretation set out in section3(1) does not apply to causes of action accruing before the section came into force. The principle does not apply because to apply it in such cases, and thereby change the interpretation and effect of existing legislation, might well produce an unfair result for one party or the other.[111]

---

[106] *Ibid*, paras 33–40.

[107] [2001] EWCA Civ 633, para 18.

[108] Citing Staughton LJ in *Secretary of State for Social Security v Tunnicliffe* [1991] 2 All ER 712, 724: 'Parliament is presumed not to have intended to alter the law applicable to past events and transactions in a manner which is unfair to those concerned in them, unless a contrary intention appears. It is not simply a question of classifying an enactment as retrospective or not retrospective. Rather it may well be a matter of degree – the greater the unfairness, the more it is to be expected that Parliament will make it clear if that is intended.'

[109] Para 17.

[110] Para 18.

[111] Para 20. See also Mummery LJ in *Wainwright v Home Office* [2001] EWCA Civ 2081, [2002] QB 1334, 1352, para 61.

The consequence was that the HRA had no effect upon the prior agreement between Mrs Wilson and First County Trust.

We can now reconsider *Ghaidan* in the light of this approach. Mead has pointed out it is a significant omission that in *Ghaidan* there is no discussion of why a similar presumption did not apply for the benefit of the landlord.[112] One argument might be that this was because the plaintiff's cause of action did not 'accrue' until the death of the statutory tenant in 2001. This, however, is not fully convincing since Godin-Mendoza's legal status was clearly derived from an agreement between his partner and the landlord that pre-dated the HRA. David Mead argues persuasively that both *Wilson* and *Ghaidan* are examples of pre-HRA contracts 'infused with statutory underpinning'. As such they raise a difficulty left unanswered by the Act and unaddressed by the House of Lords in *Ghaidan*: whereas the text of section 3 makes clear that is to apply to earlier legislation by using the expression 'whenever enacted', it is silent as to the effect on earlier private agreements.[113]

A convincing treatment of this issue would have to take notice first of all of the public policy considerations favouring certainty in agreements of this kind between private parties and then to address these points within the Convention framework (in this instance of Article 14). If it had done so in *Ghaidan* the House of Lords would inevitably have confronted a second issue that the speeches overlook: the impact of extending entitlement to succession to the tenancy on the landlord's right to enjoyment of his possessions (Protocol 1, Article 1 of the Convention).[114] To deal with these issues the House would have needed to consider whether deprivation of possessions by retrospective interpretation was in the words of that Article 'in the public interest' and 'provided by for law', on the one hand, and whether, on the other, any resulting discriminatory treatment was capable of 'reasonable and objective justification' under Article 14.[115] These points receive no mention (still less resolution) in the Law Lords' speeches. Viewed then from the perspective of horizontality *Ghaidan* is an unsophisticated decision that fails to engage with the landlord's Convention rights or to make any attempt to reconcile the restriction of those rights with the protection of the successor to the tenancy.[116]

---

[112] D Mead, 'Rights, Relationships and Retrospectivity: the impact of the Convention rights on pre-existing private relationships following *Ghaidan* and *Wilson*' [2005] PL 459.

[113] By contrast the question of retrospectivity as regards s 6 was specifically addressed in s 22(4)

[114] It appears that the landlord did not raise an argument of this kind.

[115] *Belgian Linguistics Case* (1986) 1 EHRR 252, 284.

[116] As Professor Tom Allen points out the carefully balancing of rights on both sides of the argument that the Supreme Court of Canada has engaged in applying human rights to property disputes simply does not feature in either *Ghaidan* or *Wilson*: T Allen, *Property and the Human Rights Act 1998* (Oxford, Hart Publishing, 2005) 243.

Section 3 will have no impact, of course, if the relationship between the parties is not at least partly dependent on statutory obligations. In such cases it may nevertheless be argued that the court as a public authority has a duty under section 6 not to act in violation of a person's Convention rights. Conceivably this duty could even extend to allowing non-parties to the agreement to raise Convention arguments. An ingenious, though unsuccessful, attempt to do so was made by residents living near to Biggin Hill airport in litigation involving the construction of a lease in an action between the landlord (Bromley LBC) and the airport operator (the tenant).[117] The residents argued that the court had a duty to construe the lease compatibly with *their* Convention rights and so to respect their private lives and homes by prohibiting scheduled air services from the airport. Alternatively, they claimed an implied term prohibiting Bromley from interfering with their Convention rights should be read in to the lease or the user clause should be read down after the coming into force of HRA in so far as it interfered with Convention rights.[118] The judge rejected these arguments since the HRA did not require a Convention-friendly interpretation of leases and therefore declined to allow the residents to be joined in the proceedings. As the facts of the case demonstrate permitting claims by third parties in this way it would bring a host of new problems about privity of contract and reconciling the claims of the tenant and alleged victims, not least because in these situations it would be the council's *failure* to include certain terms or to enforce alleged rights or duties against the tenant which would threaten the victim's Convention rights.

Employment Law

Like the area of landlord-tenant law, employment law is a specialised form of contract, heavily overlaid with statutory rights and obligations. One of most important of these concerns unfair dismissal. A tribunal or court is required to assess the reasonableness of the employer's action in determining whether a dismissal is unfair.[119] A controversial aspect of the pre-HRA doctrine was that the dismissal of an employee for activities outside of work could, depending on the circumstances, nevertheless be fair.

In the HRA era employees have sought, unsuccessfully, to argue that a dismissal of this type interferes with their right to respect for their private life. The two leading cases concern dismissal involving sexual activities outside the workplace. In both instances it was accepted that the unfair

---

[117] *Biggin Hill Airport v Bromley London BC, The Times,* January 9, 2001.
[118] These arguments were presumably premised on the fact that the landlord was itself a public authority.
[119] Employment Rights Act 1996 s 98(4).

dismissal legislation should be interpreted with effect to the employee's Convention rights, but when Article 8 came to be applied this did not assist either claimant. In *X v Y*[120] the claimant was dismissed from his job as a youth worker with a not-for-profit organisation when it was discovered that he had been cautioned by the police for indecency in a public toilet with another man: something he had not disclosed when applying for the post. The Court of Appeal accepted his Convention rights were engaged, but went on to find that Article 8 did not protect sexual acts in a public lavatory which were contrary to the criminal law. Although the reasoning has been criticised it is unsurprising; there is no inconsistency here, for example, with the European Court of Human Rights rulings giving the protection of Article 8 to *private* homosexual acts.[121] In the second example a probation officer was dismissed for well-publicised out-of-work activities of performing bondage shows in sex clubs and running a business selling sex aids.[122] The Employment Appeal Tribunal found the dismissal to be fair, concluding that the publicity that the claimant had given to his own activities took them out of the realm of private life under Article 8.

A further example of the relevance in the Convention to unfair dismissal legislation following the HRA came in *Copsey v WWB Devon Clays Ltd*.[123] Here the Court of Appeal found that an employee's freedom to manifest his religion under Article 9 ECHR was not infringed when he was dismissed for refusing to work on Sundays. Mummery LJ applied the so-called 'non-interference' line of jurisprudence from the European Commission of Human Rights, and held that Article 9(1) was not engaged because Mr Copsey was entitled to resign if his employer's work requirements were incompatible with manifesting his religion.[124] He found that, although much-criticised, this line of authority was clear and, in the absence of a change of heart at Strasbourg or a different view from the House of Lords, should apply.[125] Rix LJ stressed that this approach had the virtue of giving primacy to the autonomy of the parties and concluded that he had

> no difficulty with the general thesis that contracts freely entered into may limit an applicant's room for complaint about interference with his rights.[126]

---

[120] [2004] EWCA Civ 662.

[121] Eg *Dudgeon v UK* (1981) 4 EHRR 149.

[122] *Pay v Lancashire Probation Service* [2004] ICR 187.

[123] [2005] EWCA Civ 932.

[124] See especially *Stedman v UK* (1997) 23 EHHR CD168; R Ahdar and I Leigh, *Religious Freedom in the Liberal State* (Oxford, OUP, 2005) 176–179, 298 ff; and G Morris, 'Exclusion of Fundamental Rights by Agreement' (2001) 30 *Ind LJ* 49.

[125] Mummery LJ [2005] EWCA Civ 932, paras 26–39.

[126] See especially para 52, referring to *Ahmad v ILEA* [1978] QB 36 and *Ahmad v UK* (1981) 4 EHRR 126 (refusal of time off for Muslim teacher to attend Friday prayers did not violate Art 9).

He went on to find that unfair dismissal legislation could, even disregarding Article 9, contain a concept of reasonable accommodation of religion.[127] For those who hoped that the UK courts would give a broader interpretation of religious freedom to overcome the limitations of the Article 9 jurisprudence *Copsey* came as a disappointment.[128]

The employment cases demonstrate that establishing horizontal applicability is merely the first hurdle that a claimant must leap. She then faces the unsympathetic Strasbourg jurisprudence on horizontal claims in the employment sphere. The European Court of Human Rights has sometimes allowed claims by public sector employees under Article 8 because their employers' actions can be attributed to the state.[129] Similar claims under Article 9 or Article 10 have, however, been met with the response that any restriction on the employees' rights is self-imposed and can be avoided by changing jobs. In this climate it is unsurprising that the domestic courts have tended to dismiss horizontal claims in the employment field.

Property Law

As with other matters of horizontality, the key to understanding the potential effect of the Convention in private property disputes is the question of state involvement. The main provision to be discussed here is the right to peaceful enjoyment of one's possessions under Article 1 of the First Protocol.[130]

In some circumstances it is not hard to identify an interference by the state. The Strasbourg court has, for example, found that the statutory scheme enabling long leaseholders to purchase the freehold under the Leasehold Reform Act 1967 should be considered as a state deprivation of the freeholders' property.[131] Similarly, a requirement that landowners in France transfer hunting rights over their land (despite their opposition to hunting) has been found to violate Article 1.[132]

---

[127] Paras 67–73. Cf. the judgment of Neuberger LJ.

[128] A case on similar facts would now be treated as an example of indirect religious discrimination under the Employment Equality (Religion or Belief) Regulations 2003, SI 2003/1660. For post regulations caselaw: See R Sandberg, 'Flags, Beards and Pilgrimages: A Review of Early Cases on Religious Discrimination' (2007) 9 *Ecc LJ* 87.

[129] *Halford v UK* (1997) 24 EHRR 523; *Lustig-Preen and Beckett v UK* (1999) 29 EHRR 548; *Young, James and Webster v UK* (1982) 4 EHRR 38.

[130] P van Dijk, F van Hoof, A van Rijn, and L Zwaak, *Theory and Practice of the European Convention on Human Rights* (4th edn, Antwerp, Intersentia, 2006) ch 17.

[131] *James v UK* (1986) 8 EHRR 123. It went on, however, to find that the 1967 Act fell within the margin of appreciation since compulsory transfer of property between private individuals could be a legitimate means of promoting public interest and (on the detail of the legislation) was not disproportionate.

[132] *Chassegnou v France* (2000) 29 EHRR 615. Note that in *R (Countryside Alliance and others and others)v Her Majesty's Attorney General and another* [2007] UKHL 52 the House

On other occasions, however, the enforcement of private property rights has been regarded by the Convention organs as the mere consequence of the actions of individuals under private law to which the Convention has no application. The former Commission found, for example, that there is nothing that concerns the Convention when a court merely applies the terms of lease agreed between the parties so as to order forfeiture against a tenant.[133]

The line between these two approaches has not been clearly articulated. Conceptually it could turn on whether the obligation enforced by the court derives from legislation (clearly the product of state action) or from a private agreement.[134] This, however, would not deal satisfactorily with agreements enforceable under common law rules.[135] Moreover, it can also be argued that the state has a positive obligation to prevent breaches of Convention rights arising from some private transactions.[136]

In decisions under the HRA the domestic courts have on the whole found that either that the Convention right of peaceful enjoyment of possessions is not engaged in private property disputes, or if engaged, that any limitations are in the public interest.

In *Wallbank*[137] the question concerned the nature and compatibility with the Convention of an obligation running with the plaintiffs' land for chancel repairs to a parish church. The duty was governed by the Chancel Repairs Act 1932 under which the defendants (the parish church council of the church concerned) had levied a demand for payment.[138] In part the HRA challenge was based on an ultimately unsuccessful attempt to argue that the PCC was a public authority.[139] Despite finding that section 6 did not apply the speeches in the House of Lords deal with the question of the applicability of Article 1 of the First Protocol. The Court of Appeal had treated the liability as a form of tax, which contravened the right to peaceful enjoyment of possessions.[140] The House of Lords, however,

---

of Lords rejected arguments that the prohibition of fox hunting in England and Wales under the Hunting Act 2004 violated Arts 8, 11 and 14 ECHR and Art 1 of the First Protocol.

[133]   *Application 1194/86 v UK* (1988) 10 EHRR 149 (admissibility decision). See also *Bramelid v Sweden* (1983) 5 EHRR 249.

[134]   In *JA Pye (Oxford) v UK* Appl No 44302/02 (below) the majority judgment of the Grand Chamber (at para 57) found that the state was not *directly* responsible for the loss but rather was responsible for legislation which was then in effect activated by private parties.

[135]   237 above (Hohfeld) .

[136]   Cf *Pla v Andorra* [2004] FCR 630 (n 94 above).

[137]   [2001] 3 WLR 1323.

[138]   The liability to pay for the repairs arose prior to the HRA but the Church of England did not advance an argument concerning retrospectivity so that the court would be free to determine the issue of Convention compatibility; and see Lord Hope in *Wallbank* at para 29 ff.

[139]   See further 140–42 above.

[140]   [2002] Ch 51.

affirmed the view of Ferris J at first instance that liability was simply an incident of owning the land.[141] Lord Hobhouse pointed out that:

> The liability is a private law liability which has arisen from the voluntary acts of the persons liable. [the plaintiffs] have no Convention right to be relieved of that liability. Nor do they have a Convention right to be relieved from the consequences of a bargain made, albeit some 200 years earlier, by their predecessors in title.[142]

The same question of how to categorise the impact of rules governing private property has arisen in extensive litigation concerning adverse possession of land. A series of challenges under the HRA have attacked the rule which allows a squatter or trespasser to acquire title to land by continuing in open possession of the land for a period, currently 10 years, on grounds of Convention incompatibility with the rights of the registered title holder. In *JA Pye (Oxford) Ltd v Graham* the House of Lords[143] found that that there was no need to consider the HRA since the events in question took place before commencement and, applying the principles of adverse possession to the facts, awarded possession to the respondent. This was in contrast to the Court of Appeal's finding that the Act did apply[144] but that there was no violation of Article 1 of the First Protocol. The Court of Appeal found limitation periods such as the one applicable here to bar the original registered owner's claim could be compatible with the Convention and the extinction of title was in the public interest and not disproportionate.[145]

A quite different approach was taken by Strauss J in *Beaulane Properties v Palmer*[146] in which he gave a Convention-friendly reading to section 17 Limitation Act 1980 and section 75 Land Registration Act 1925. Inventively, he used section 3 in effect to reinstate a line of earlier decisions on the meaning of adverse possession[147] in order to protect the registered owner. The consequence was that a claim of adverse possession which would otherwise have succeeded was defeated.

The uncertainty over the correct approach to applying the Convention to adverse possession claims can, however, now be regarded as settled following the recent decision of the Grand Chamber of the European Court of Human Rights in the *JA Pye* case. The court made clear that even

---

[141] *Wallbank*, Lord Hope at para 71. Cf Lord Scott at para 134, describing it as a liability at common law.

[142] Para 91.

[143] *JA Pye (Oxford) Ltd. v Graham* [2002] UKHL 30.

[144] [2001] Ch 804.

[145] See also *Family Housing Association v Donnellan* [2002] 1 P&CR 34, holding that adverse possession was a private matter rather than a state expropriation of property.

[146] [2006] Ch 79.

[147] *Leigh v Jack* (1879) 5 Ex D 264, requiring the adverse possession to with any expressed or implied intention concerning future use of the land by the landowner.

if the Convention were considered, there was no breach of right to property.[148] The Grand Chamber upheld the UK Government's argument that the risk of adverse possession was a normal and well-established limitation on ownership of land: the rule amounted to state control of property rather than deprivation and did not upset the fair balance between communal interests and the applicants' rights

Jean Howell argues that the HRA cases on Article 1 have failed to 'explain how and why it allows actions to be taken, or how to reconcile conflicting claims'.[149] She concludes that the attempts to apply the Act have merely sown uncertainty: '[T]he introduction of human rights values is a wild card which is wholly unpredictable in effect'.[150] In the light of the litigation concerning adverse possession, which produced what Oliver Jones described as 'a cacophony of decisions and reasons in the English courts'[151] only to bring the law full-circle, it is hard to disagree.

CONCLUSION

The relatively conservative approach of the domestic courts to the applicability of the HRA in a private context can be attributed partly to the Convention jurisprudence and partly their own disinclination.

As we have seen, the Convention text is silent on many matters affecting private parties and the European Court of Human Rights has only recognised horizontal effect in limited fields through the development of positive obligations upon member states. It has done so, for example to now require a domestic remedy for private interferences with another person's reasonable expectation of privacy (*Von Hannover*). As regards property obligations, however, these have been left for the most part as a zone free of Convention obligations (as in the recent *JA Pye* case).

The UK courts have on the whole shown little appetite to go beyond this limited Strasbourg recognition of horizontal rights.

Even in the much-discussed area of privacy, developments have proceeded cautiously. Despite numerous predictions to the contrary the courts have not used the HRA to develop a new tort of privacy. Instead they have maintained the pre-HRA position that no such general tort exists.[152] They have, however, drawn inspiration from the Convention in refashioning the

---

[148] *JA Pye (Oxford) v UK* Appl No 44302/02, Grand Chamber 30 August 2007. A Chamber had found initially that there was a violation of the applicant's right to property (*JA Pye (Oxford) v UK* (2005) 43 EHRR 3).

[149] J Howell, 'The Human Rights Act 1998: Land, private citizens, and the common law' (2007) 123 *LQR* 618 , 626.

[150] *Ibid*, 634.

[151] O Jones, 'Down With the squatters! The European Court of Human Rights and *JA Pye (Oxford) Ltd v United Kingdom*' (2006) 25 *Civil Justice Quarterly* 404, 405.

[152] *Wainright v Home Office* [2004] 2 AC 406.

common law remedy of breach of confidence into a tort of misuse of personal information. This development was not strictly a requirement of the Convention: indeed it pre-dated and anticipated the Strasbourg court's own finding that Article 8 requires states to give some protection to individuals against incursions into their private lives from other private individuals in *Von Hannover v Germany*.[153] The point is underlined by the fact that the New Zealand courts (without the inspiration of the Convention) have in the same period developed from the common law a tort of privacy as such.[154] The Convention has been the pretext rather than the reason for the common law developments in the UK.[155] As a result the Strasbourg court in *Von Hannover* outstripped the House of Lords in *Campbell*, dealing with the identical issue of media intrusion into the lives of public figures.

Apart from dismissing the more extreme positions the courts have largely disregarded the voluminous theoretical literature on the horizontal application of rights, much of it due to the debate over privacy.[156] It is clear that the HRA will not be given direct horizontal application: it does not found new causes of action. While undoubtedly giving some indirect effect to the HRA in modifying the common law applicable between private persons, judges have repeatedly stated that is unnecessary to resolve many of the theoretical points in the academic literature.

Other routes to horizontal applicability have proved more straightforward: for example, the use of Convention rights to interpret statutes applying between private individuals (such as landlord and tenant and family members and in employment law). Arguably an over-attention to cases involving breach of confidence has led to neglect of these more prosaic forms of horizontality. In these fields the judges have been speaking in prose without always realising it – and without commentators usually noticing it either. Perhaps as a consequence important questions concerning the impact Convention rights on earlier agreements remain under-theorised.[157]

Overall, we can say that, in their measured approach to horizontal questions, as in other areas, the domestic courts are giving limited effect to Convention rights within the constraints both of the Strasbourg jurisprudence and the HRA itself. There is no evidence here of treating Convention

---

[153] *Von Hannover v Germany* (2005) 40 EHRR 1.

[154] N 77 above.

[155] As predicted in I Leigh, 'Horizontal Rights, The Human Rights Act and Privacy: Lessons from the Commonwealth?' (1999) 48 *ICLQ* 57.

[156] G Phillipson, 'Clarity Postponed: horizontal effect after Campbell', in H Fenwick, G Phillipson and R Masterman, *Judicial Reasoning under the UK Human Rights Act* (Cambridge, CUP, 2007).

[157] See the discussion of *Ghaidan* above.

right as a set of overriding, higher law norms that displace other obligations – not as constitutional rights, in other words.

Chapter 10

Civil Law Remedies

INTRODUCTION

ACTIONS IN PRIVATE law have long provided an avenue for the individual seeking a remedy for wrongs committed by public authorities. Key to the Diceyan conception of the rule of law was the assertion that:

> every man, whatever his rank or condition, is subject to the ordinary law of the realm and amenable to the jurisdiction of the ordinary tribunals.[1]

As such, for example, actions for trespass,[2] unlawful imprisonment[3] and so on have historically offered the individual an opportunity to seek redress against an officer of the state under a cause of action which could equally be brought against a private individual.[4] Developments in administrative law in the latter stages of the 20th century saw the private law action against public officials become less common in the face of the expansion of the judicial review jurisdiction.[5] But the Human Rights Act 1998 (HRA) has brought about subtle changes in the nature of remedies available against the state, giving 'civil law' remedies an increased prominence in the scheme of rights protection adopted.

Article 13 of the European Convention on Human Rights provides the victim of a breach of a Convention right with the right to an effective remedy for that breach.[6] Article 13 does not however fall within those of

---

[1] AV Dicey, *Introduction to the Study of the Law of the Constitution* (Indianapolis, Liberty Fund, 1982) 114.

[2] *Entick v Carrington* (1765) 19 St Tr 1030; *Raleigh v Goschen* [1898] 1 Ch 73.

[3] *Liversidge v Anderson* [1942] AC 206.

[4] As Ewing and Gearty describe however, the civil liberties record of the courts under such causes of action is patchy at best (see KD Ewing and CA Gearty, *The Struggle for Civil Liberties: Political Freedom and the Rule of Law in Britain, 1914–1945* (Oxford, OUP, 2000), ch 1 for an overview).

[5] Lord Woolf, J Jowell and A Le Sueur, *De Smith, Woolf and Jowell's Principles of Judicial Review* (London, Sweet and Maxwell, 1999) 609–610. While actions in tort and contract became available against the Crown directly following the Crown Proceedings Act 1947.

[6] Art 13 provides, 'Everyone whose rights and freedoms as set forth in this Convention are violated shall have an effective remedy before a national authority notwithstanding that the violation has been committed by persons acting in an official capacity.'

the Convention Rights given further effect in domestic law under section 1(1) HRA.[7] Instead the HRA furnishes domestic courts with what appears to be a broad discretion over the availability of remedies for unlawful action under the Act. Section 8 HRA provides courts and tribunals with a power to grant a range of remedies against public authorities for action which is, or would be, unlawful under the Act.[8]

The question of remedies may arise following an action brought directly via section 7(1)(a) HRA, or indirectly via an existing cause of action. Section 7 of the HRA creates a free-standing action against public authorities for unlawful action in contravention of a Convention Right as defined by section 6(1). Under section 7(1) the 'victim' of claimed unlawful action may bring proceedings either directly against the public authority in question, or rely on the Convention point in proceedings under another cause of action.[9] In either scenario, any remedy awarded would, by virtue of the courts' duty under section 6(3) HRA, have itself to be Convention-compliant.

In the event of a finding of unlawful action, section 8(1) provides that a court 'may grant such relief or remedy, or make such order, within its powers as it considers just and appropriate.' The clause seems to be a wide one, allowing a court to 'grant any order within its jurisdiction.'[10] As Lord Irvine indicated during the debates on clause 8 of the Human Rights Bill – as it then was – was of the 'widest amplitude.' By way of explaining the absence of Article 13 ECHR, he indicated that he could not countenance a situation in which the range of remedies available in English law 'would be unable to provide an effective remedy' for the victim of a public body's unlawful action or inaction.[11]

Alongside sections 3(1) and 4 of the HRA, section 8 provides the courts with supplementary remedial powers for breach of the Convention Rights. In this chapter we will examine the use of two civil law remedies: damages

---

[7]   Although it has been suggested that in the event of uncertainty, domestic courts 'should be able to refer to the rule in *Pepper v Hart*, and interpret the remedial provisions of the [Human Rights Act] in a way that meets the requirements of Art 13, taking account of the jurisprudence of the Court and Commission': D Feldman, 'Remedies for violations of Convention Rights under the Human Rights Act' [1998] *EHRLR* 691, 692.

[8]   Section 6(1) HRA provides: 'It is unlawful for a public authority to act in a way which is incompatible with a Convention right.' Section 6(6) provides further that, '"An act" includes a failure to act'. For discussion of the definition of 'public authority' under the HRA see pp 138–149 above.

[9]   S 7(1) HRA reads: 'A person who claims that a public authority has acted (or proposes to act) in a way which is made unlawful by section 6(1) may – (a) bring proceedings against the authority under this Act in the appropriate court or tribunal, or (b) rely on the Convention right or rights concerned in any legal proceedings, but only if he is (or would be) a victim of the unlawful act.'

[10]   HL Debs, vol 583, col 479 (18 November 1997) (Lord Kingsland).

[11]   HL Debs, vol 583, col 1266 (19 January 1998); HL Debs, vol 583, col 479 (18 November 1997).

and injunctive relief. First, however, issues surrounding the scope of section 8 HRA and the Convention concept of 'just satisfaction' will be examined.

THE BREADTH OF SECTION 8

In contrast to the HRA, the New Zealand Bill of Rights Act 1990 contains no specific clause dealing with remedies.[12] However, the New Zealand Court of Appeal has implied a number of novel remedies into the Bill of Rights Act, most notably, in *Simpson v Attorney-General*, commonly known as *Baigent's Case*.[13] In that case, the New Zealand Court of Appeal found that the absence of an express remedies clause should not be 'an impediment to the court's ability to "develop the possibilities of judicial remedy."'[14] Without the power to 'grant appropriate and effective remedies,' commented Hardie Boys J, the commitment to rights protection embodied in the New Zealand Bill of Rights Act would be nothing more than an 'empty statement'.[15] As Lord Cooke later wrote, in providing a clear remedies clause, 'the United Kingdom Act may be seen as making explicit what the New Zealand Court found to be implicit.'[16] As such, section 8 HRA avoids exposing domestic courts to the controversies of 'discovering' remedial provisions inherent in the HRA.[17]

Section 8(1) envisages the use of a wide range of judicial remedies, subject to the qualification that the court have jurisdiction to grant the remedy in question and that to do so it be 'just and appropriate' in the circumstances. Among the range of available remedies is the potential award of monetary compensation. Although section 8(1) makes no specific mention of the award of damages, it is clear from what follows that damages were to be available as compensation for the breach of a Convention right by a public authority in certain circumstances. Section 8(2) makes clear that damages were not however to available in all proceedings: 'damages may be awarded only by a court which has power to award damages, or to order the payment of compensation, in civil

---

[12] See generally: P Rishworth, G Huscroft, S Optican and R Maloney, *The New Zealand Bill of Rights* (Oxford, OUP, 2003) ch 29.

[13] *Simpson v Attorney-General (Baigent's Case)* [1994] 3 NZLR 667. See also: *Moonen v Film and Literature Board of Review* [2000] 2 NZLR 9.

[14] *Ibid*, 691 (Casey J).

[15] *Ibid*, 702 (Hardie Boys J).

[16] Lord Cooke of Thorndon, 'The British Embracement of Human Rights' [1999] *EHRLR* 243, 257.

[17] For criticisms of the approach of the New Zealand Court of Appeal in *Baigent's Case*, see: J Allan, 'The Effect of a Statutory Bill of Rights where Parliament is sovereign: the lesson from New Zealand' in T Campbell, KD Ewing and A Tomkins, *Sceptical Essays on Human Rights* (Oxford, OUP, 2001) 381–382; JA Smillie, '"Fundamental" rights, parliamentary supremacy and the New Zealand Court of Appeal' (1995) 111 *LQR* 209.

proceedings.' As such, a court hearing a criminal case would have no such power in the event of a finding of a breach of the Convention rights of the accused, any such claim would have to proceed by way of a separate action in the county or High Court.[18] This appears to mark something of a departure for English public law; until the enactment of the HRA, English courts had

> been instinctively hostile to the idea that public funds are better spent on compensating those who have temporarily been wronged, rather than in properly executing the legislative purpose in future.[19]

As such, damages were only generally available against public authorities for private law wrongs, such as trespass and breach of contract, rather than as a remedy under the established heads of judicial review.[20] This issue was raised by Lord Lester of Herne Hill during the parliamentary debates on the Human Rights Bill. During the debates, Lord Lester asked the Lord Chancellor whether damages would in future be available as of right against public authorities by way of judicial review proceedings. As Lord Lester observed, in the absence of misfeasance in public office, English law has not typically awarded damages as a remedy for public authority illegality.[21] Declining to give a statement which could have been

---

[18] Law Commission and Scottish Law Commission, *Damages under the Human Rights Act 1998* (Law Com No 266; Scot Law Com No 180) (Cm 4853), October 2000, para 2.16. The Law Commission report also points to the uncertainty created by the use of language in s 8(2): 'An unresolved issue concerns the position of the Court of Appeal (in England and Wales) when exercising its criminal jurisdiction. The apparent intention of the section is to confine claims for damages to civil proceedings. However, the language focuses on the powers of the court, rather than the nature of the particular proceedings. Criminal appeals are heard by a separate division of the Court of Appeal, rather than a separate court. Accordingly, on a literal reading of the section, it is a court which, in civil proceedings, would have power to award damages. On this view, it would have power to award damages under the HRA, eg where it quashes a conviction in breach of the Convention.' Government statements on this issue during the passage of the Human Rights Bill were inconclusive: 'More difficult is a case where the Criminal Division of the Court of Appeal allows an appeal against conviction because of a breach of human rights. That court probably does have power to award damages under s 8(2) because the Court of Appeal, generally, does have "power to award damages ... in civil proceedings"' (HL Debs, vol 583, col 855 (24 November 1997) (Lord Irvine of Lairg)). See also I Dennis, 'Fair Trials and Safe Convictions' (2003) 57 *Current Legal Problems* 211. However, contrast *R v Plinio Galfretti* [2002] EWCA Crim 1916, para 42: 'it is accepted that this court does not have power to award damages under s 8(2) of the 1998 Act, because damages may be awarded only by a court which has power to award damages in civil proceedings.'

[19] I Leigh and L Lustgarten, 'Making Rights Real: The Courts, remedies and the Human Rights Act' (1999) 58 *CLJ* 509, 527.

[20] See *R v Secretary of State for Transport ex p Factortame (No 2)* [1991] 1 AC 603, 672 (Lord Goff), and generally, P Cane, *Administrative Law* (4th ed) (Oxford, Clarendon Press, 2004) 94–100.

[21] HL Debs, vol 583, col 854 (24 November 1997).

used under *Pepper v Hart*,[22] and quoting from clause 8(3), Lord Irvine enigmatically responded that

> an award of damages will be made if ... 'the court is satisfied that the award is necessary to afford just satisfaction to the person in whose favour it is made.'[23]

Lord Irvine's failure to commit to resolving the issue over damages led to a degree of uncertainty over the parameters of this new form of public law illegality. At closer inspection however, despite making the award of damages a possibility under the Act, the HRA continues the general trend against awarding damages in public law proceedings, by imposing further limitations on the circumstances in which a court might award damages for unlawful action.

Under section 8(3), a court's power to award damages is curtailed by the direction that 'no award of damages is to be made' unless the court is 'satisfied that the award is necessary to afford just satisfaction to the person in whose favour it is made.' In addition, in determining whether the grant of damages is 'necessary' the court must consider 'any other relief or remedy granted, or order made, in relation to the act in question', and 'the consequences of any decision ... in respect of that act.'[24] It is clear therefore from section 8(3) – taken with section 8(1)'s enjoinder that the award of any remedy be 'just and appropriate' – that the court would need to find a compelling reason to support an award of damages in preference to another remedial order.[25] In determining whether such a remedy will be granted, it was clearly within the Government's intentions that the interests of the victim were not to be the courts' sole concern; as much was outlined in the White Paper, *Making Rights Real*:

> what remedy is appropriate will ... depend on both the facts of the case and on a proper balance between the rights of the individual and the public interest.[26]

This much has been noted, extra-judicially, by Lord Woolf, who commented that

> the ECHR is all about securing our civil liberties and not promoting a public law damages culture. The primary result that the [Human Rights] Act should seek to achieve is the reinforcement of standards of public administration

---

[22] *Pepper v Hart* [1993] AC 593.
[23] HL Debs, vol 583, col 856 (24 November 1997).
[24] HRA s 8(3).
[25] Cf the position in private law torts: Lord Lester of Herne Hill and D Pannick, *Human Rights Law and Practice* (London, Butterworths, 1999), para 2.3.8.
[26] *Rights Brought Home* (October 1997), Cm 3782, para 2.6.

with the aim of reducing those occasions on which Convention rights are infringed by the actions of public bodies.[27]

As noted above, an action against a public authority might proceed either by way of an existing cause of action or directly under section 7(1)(a) HRA. Commentators' predictions that the vast majority of cases against public authorities would proceed on an application for judicial review have been confirmed.[28] But the question of whether the judiciary would formulate a new 'government' or 'constitutional' tort on the basis of the HRA raised the question of whether applicants might be more likely to pursue actions directly under section 7(1)(a). Commentators noted that the Government's silence on the issue of damages in judicial review actions had given the judiciary a 'free hand' to expand and develop a 'constitutional tort' for breach of a Convention right which would support an award of damages as of right.[29] The status of the new cause of action under section 7 was therefore also the source of some confusion. The Law Commission characterised the new cause of action as 'in effect a form of action for breach of statutory duty,' which would provide a discretionary remedy in damages.[30] Lester and Pannick described section 7 HRA as giving rise to:

a new cause of action against public authorities (widely defined) for a new public law tort of acting in breach of the victim's Convention rights.[31]

While Lord Woolf felt 'uncomfortable' applying the epithet 'tort' to a cause of action which would only support a discretionary award of monetary compensation.[32] Wade and Forsyth cut through the confusion with typical ease:

Infringements of human rights under the HRA may be regarded as a new species of tort or else as an additional form of breach of statutory duty or else as *sui generis*. This is merely a matter of words. Whatever classification is adopted, the Convention requirement of 'just satisfaction' ... makes it clear that compensation equivalent to money damages may be awarded.[33]

---

[27] Lord Woolf, 'The Human Rights Act and Remedies' in M Andenas and D Fairgrieve (eds), *Judicial Review in International Perspective* (The Hague, Kluwer Law International, 2000) 433.

[28] *Ibid*, 431. See also: *Anufrijeva v Southwark LBC* [2004] QB 1124, para 53. *Van Colle*, discussed below at pp 279–280, was brought under s 7(1)(a).

[29] See, eg, I Leigh and L Lustgarten, 'Making Rights Real: The courts, remedies and the Human Rights Act' (1999) 58(3) *CLJ* 509, 529.

[30] Law Commission and Scottish Law Commission, *Damages under the Human Rights Act 1998* (Law Com No 266; Scot Law Com No 180) (Cm 4853), October 2000, para 4.20.

[31] D Pannick and A Lester, 'The impact of the Human Rights Act on private law: the knight's move' (2000) *LQR* 380, 382.

[32] Woolf, above n 27, 432.

[33] HWR Wade and CF Forsyth, *Administrative Law* (9th ed) (Oxford, OUP, 2004) 749. See also: P Craig, *Administrative Law* (5th ed) (London, Sweet and Maxwell, 2003) 886.

On the face of the Act therefore, it appeared that the remedy of damages would be available in actions under section 7(1) HRA *and* by way of judicial review. The cases explored below however, demonstrate that the award of damages in *either* scenario will be an exceptional result.

'JUST SATISFACTION'[34]

Section 8(3) of the HRA adopts the specific terminology of the Convention in stating that an award of damages should be 'necessary to afford *just satisfaction*' to the victim of the breach.[35] Section 8(4) provides further that, in determining whether to award damages, or the sum of damages to be awarded, the court must:

> take into account the principles applied by the European Court of Human Rights in relation to the award of compensation under Article 41 of the Convention.

As Article 41 is not one of the 'Convention Rights' for the purposes of section 1(1) of the HRA, section 8(4) serves as a direction to domestic courts to 'take into account' case law which would not ordinarily fall within their section 2(1) obligation.

Grosz, Beatson and Duffy have pointed to the interpretative difficulty posed by the specific use of the term 'just satisfaction' in section 8(3). Just satisfaction, they argue, is 'a concept unfamiliar to domestic law' and making explicit reference to the principle in the Act has the effect of 'incorporating' that notion, and its attendant case law, into domestic law.[36] This, they suggest, has the effect of strengthening the direction to 'take into account' relevant case law and principles by supplanting it with the direction to give effect to the principle of 'just satisfaction' in domestic law. As they observe, in this regard section 8(3):

> does not sit entirely comfortably with the weaker direction to 'take account' of the principles applied by the Strasbourg court, which is the ultimate arbiter of the meaning of just satisfaction.[37]

---

[34] On which see generally: DJ Harris, M O'Boyle and C Warbrick, *Law of the European Convention on Human Rights* (London, Butterworths, 1995) 682–688; P Van Dijk and GJH Van Hoof, *Theory and Practice of the European Convention on Human Rights* (3rd ed) (The Hague, Kluwer Law International, 1998) 239–259.

[35] Art 41 – formerly Art 50 – reads: 'If the Court finds that there has been a violation of the Convention or the protocols thereto, and if the internal law of the High Contracting Party concerned allows only partial reparation to be made, the court shall, if necessary, award just satisfaction to the injured party.'

[36] S Grosz, J Beatson and P Duffy, *Human Rights: The 1998 Act and the European Convention* (London, Sweet and Maxwell, 1999) 143.

[37] *Ibid*. Although the stronger direction suggested by the Grosz, Beatson and Duffy bears much in common with the approach to s 2(1) as interpreted by the courts under the HRA: as outlined in ch 3, the prevailing approach under s 2(1) HRA dictates that when determining a

Questions over whether the principles of just satisfaction are to be applied in domestic courts, or simply taken account of, are arguably secondary concerns for the domestic court. The more pressing issue for domestic courts is identifying just what those 'principles' might be. There is almost universal consensus among commentators that is it virtually impossible to discern *any* consistent principles emerging from the European Court's case law on Article 41.[38] On an area of the Strasbourg case law in which the Law Commission's report on *Damages under the Human Rights Act* pointed to a number of 'irreconcilable inconsistencies,'[39] Grosz, Beatson and Duffy have commented that

> [t]he Court's decisions contain regrettably little hard reasoning and in consequence it is difficult to distil any consistent statement of principle from its judgments.[40]

More scathingly, they continue,

> the student of the Court's practice is left wondering whether the process by which the Court arrives at its judgments is anything more sophisticated than sticking a finger in the air or tossing a coin.[41]

For those seeking to rely on the decisions of the Strasbourg organs to inform their arguments in domestic courts, the task is seemingly no easier; as Sullivan J commented in *R (Bernard) v Enfield LBC*:

> If the parties are agreed upon one thing in this case it is the difficulty of identifying any principles upon which the European Court of Human Rights decides whether it is necessary to afford just satisfaction under Article 41.[42]

The European Court of Human Rights affords just satisfaction under Article 41 on an 'equitable basis.'[43] There is no entitlement to compensation – Article 41 only requires damages to be paid 'if necessary' to afford just satisfaction – and the court's discretion 'is guided by the particular

---

question arising in connection with a Convention right, the domestic court should *follow* jurisprudence of the Convention organs.

[38] See, eg, AR Mowbray, 'The European Court of Human Rights' approach to just satisfaction' [1997] *PL* 647; P Leach, *Taking a Case to the European Court of Human Rights* (Oxford, OUP, 2005), ch 9; Lord Woolf, 'The Human Rights Act and Remedies', above n 27, 432–433.

[39] Law Commission and Scottish Law Commission, *Damages under the Human Rights Act 1998* (Law Com No 266; Scot Law Com No 180) (Cm 4853), October 2000, para 3.5. See generally paras 3.4–3.15.

[40] Grosz, Beatson and Duffy, above n 36, 144.

[41] *Ibid*, 145.

[42] *R (Bernard) v Enfield LBC* [2003] HRLR 4, para 35. See also *R (KB) v South London and South and West Region Mental Health Tribunal* [2004] QB 936, para 24.

[43] See, eg, *Modinos v Cyprus* (1993) 16 EHRR 485; *Pine Valley Developments v Ireland* (1993) EHRR 379; *Öneryildiz v Turkey* (2005) 41 EHRR 20.

circumstances of each case having regard to equitable considerations.'[44] The European Court has awarded damages for both pecuniary and non-pecuniary loss, although has to date not awarded punitive, exemplary or aggravated damages.[45] In general terms, any award of compensation made by the Strasbourg court is likely to be low in comparison to comparable damages awarded by domestic courts.[46] In determining the quantum of damages, the European Court has looked to domestic awards as comparators, although is not bound to follow them.[47]

In its extensive survey of the case law under Article 41 of the Convention, the Law Commission was able to identify five guiding principles which the European Court of Human Rights considers when contemplating an award of damages:

1) A finding of a violation may constitute just satisfaction.
2) The degree of loss suffered must be sufficient to justify an award of damages.
3) The seriousness of the violation will be taken into account.
4) The conduct of the respondent will be taken into account. This may include both the conduct giving rise to the application, and a record of previous violations by the State.
5) The conduct of the applicant will be taken into account.[48]

THE AWARD OF DAMAGES UNDER THE HUMAN RIGHTS ACT

The number of cases in which damages have actually been awarded in cases under the HRA is remarkably few. At the time of writing only three cases have seen compensation awarded to the applicant(s) in question: *R (Bernard) v Enfield LBC*,[49] *R (KB) v South London and South and West Region Mental Health Review Tribunal*[50] and *Van Colle v Chief Constable*

---

[44] Harris, O'Boyle and Warbrick, above n 34, 684. Damages may be denied in spite of a breach of the Convention where, eg, the conduct of the applicant was reprehensible (see, eg, *McCann v UK* (1996) 21 EHRR 97, para 219).

[45] As Leach observes however, it has not ruled out awarding such damages (Leach, above n 38, 400).

[46] As a result Lord Lester of Herne Hill and Lydia Clapinska have argued that the direction under s 8(4) to have regard to the European Court's jurisprudence on Art 41 can be attributed to 'Treasury concerns over public expenditure': 'Human Rights and the British Constitution' in J Jowell and D Oliver (eds), *The Changing Constitution* (5th ed) (Oxford, OUP, 2004) 84.

[47] See Leach, above n 38, 400 (where the example given is of *Z and others v UK* (2002) 34 EHRR 3, para 120).

[48] Law Commission and Scottish Law Commission, *Damages under the Human Rights Act 1998* (Law Com No 266; Scot Law Com No 180) (Cm 4853), October 2000, para 4.44. See further, paras 3.31–3.78, 4.43–4.91.

[49] *R (Bernard) v Enfield LBC* [2002] EWHC 2282 (Admin); [2003] HRLR 4.

[50] *R (KB) v South London and South and West Region Mental Health Tribunal* [2004] QB 936.

of Hertfordshire.[51] That two of those awards were made pursuant to an application for judicial review should put beyond doubt at least one of the uncertainties described above.

In *R (Bernard) v Enfield LBC*[52] a couple were awarded £10,000 following a breach of Article 8 by the London Borough Council. The first and second claimants – one of whom was profoundly disabled, the other her effective carer[53] – had been living in local authority accommodation that had been deemed to be unsuitable for their needs by the Social Services department of Enfield LBC in September 2000. Enfield's Housing Department failed to act upon the recommendation to adapt the accommodation, and did not respond to letters from the claimants' solicitors. It was not until a hearing in March 2002 that the LBC admitted that it was under a duty pursuant to section 21(1)(a) of the National Assistance Act 1948 to house the couple in suitable accommodation, and it was not until October 2002 that the claimants were able to move into accommodation which was appropriate to their needs. The failure of the local authority to act showed, in the words of Sullivan J:

> a singular lack of respect for the claimants' private and family life ... The claimants and their family had to live in deplorable conditions, wholly inimical to any normal family life, and to the physical and psychological integrity of the second claimant for a considerable period of time.[54]

Indicating that the conduct of the public authority would be relevant to the assessment of whether damages should be awarded, Sullivan J added that the lack of any indication that the 'defendant's procedures have been improved so that the same kind of mistake ... is less likely to happen in the future' compounded by the fact that the LBC had offered neither explanation nor apology for its actions, made such an award necessary.[55] Such a finding raises the suspicion of there being a punitive element to the damages awarded in *Bernard*. As described above, such an award would have no grounding in the Strasbourg approach to just satisfaction.

R (KB) v South London and South and West Region Mental Health Review Tribunal comprised eight conjoined cases brought on behalf of persons detained under the Mental Health Act 1983.[56] Each of the eight applicants had suffered breaches of Article 5(4) of the Convention due to

---

[51]   *Van Colle v Chief Constable of Hertfordshire* [2006] HRLR 25.

[52]   *R (Bernard) v Enfield LBC* [2002] EWHC 2282 (Admin); [2003] HRLR 4.

[53]   The second claimant had virtually no use of her right arm or leg, and was reliant on an electrically operated wheelchair following a stroke. She was doubly incontinent and also a diabetic. Her husband, the first claimant, was her carer and also responsible for looking after their six children.

[54]   *Ibid*, paras 34 and 36.

[55]   *Ibid*, paras 36 and 41.

[56]   *R (KB) v South London and South and West Region Mental Health Tribunal* [2004] QB 936.

unlawful delay to the hearing of their cases before the Mental Health Review Tribunal, remaining detained throughout the periods of delay.[57] The court awarded damages in the region of £400–£750 for 'frustration and distress', and in two cases found that the finding of the breach in question was sufficient to afford just satisfaction.

In both *Bernard* and *KB* it was stated that the finding of a breach will, in many cases, of itself provide just satisfaction.[58] In awarding compensation, both courts were guided by the principle of *restitutio in integrum*, but failed to gain useful guidance from the Strasbourg case law on just satisfaction beyond the level of general principle.[59] In *KB* Stanley Burnton J observed a difference between the wording adopted by Parliament in sections 2(1) and 8(4) HRA, the former requiring a court to take into account 'decisions' of the Strasbourg organs, the latter requiring a court to take into account 'principles' applied by the European Court in awarding just satisfaction.[60] In the view of the judge, the only explanation for this difference was to allow domestic courts a greater degree of freedom in their reliance on the Strasbourg case law on just satisfaction.[61] Considering the lack of consistency in the Strasbourg case law this would allow the domestic courts to pursue a 'more analytical approach' in line with the demands of legal certainty imposed by our 'legal culture.'[62] The court conducted a lengthy survey of the Strasbourg case law, from which it was able to discern no 'clear and constant' authority.[63] Instead, Stanley Burnton J saw no reason why damages under the HRA should be lower than 'for a comparable tort,'[64] and accordingly sought guidance from a number of domestic cases concerning unlawful detention.

In *Bernard* Sullivan J was not convinced that damages be 'minimal', preferring a

---

[57] *R (KB) v Mental Health Review Tribunal* (2002) 5 CCLR 458.

[58] In *KB* Stanley Burnton J held that damages were not an entitlement, and that a threshold must be crossed before the claimants would have been eligible for damages: '[E]ven in the case of mentally ill claimants, not every feeling of frustration and distress will justify an award of damages. The frustration and distress must be significant: "of such intensity that it would in itself justify an award of compensation for non-pecuniary damage." In my judgment, an important touchstone of that intensity in cases such as the present will be that hospital staff considered it to be sufficiently relevant to the mental state of the patient to warrant its mention in the clinical notes' (para 73). See also *Bernard* above n 49, para 39.

[59] In *Bernard* Sullivan J drew on the principles outlined in the Law Commission report referred to at n 49 above (para 35). *R (KB) v South London and South and West Region Mental Health Tribunal* [2004] QB 936, paras 21–25.

[60] *R (KB) v South London and South and West Region Mental Health Tribunal*, para 22.

[61] *Ibid.* See also the findings of the Law Commission Report, above n 48.

[62] *Ibid*, para 25.

[63] *Ibid*, paras 26–47

[64] *R (KB) v South London and South and West Region Mental Health Tribunal* [2004] QB 936, para 53.

'restrained' or 'moderate' approach to quantum [which would] provide the necessary degree of encouragement while not depleting the funds available to the defendant for the benefit of others in need of care.'[65]

The judge also looked to domestic comparators in determining the quantum of damages, and found that useful guidance was to be gleaned from the decisions of the Local Government Ombudsman, as – notwithstanding the differences in the nature of the award – the case in question was, 'in essence, an extreme example of maladministration.'[66]

Anufrijeva v Southwark London Borough Council

Anufrijeva v Southwark LBC[67] – concerning conjoined cases brought by asylum-seekers claiming damages for breach of their rights under Article 8 – provided the Court of Appeal with its first opportunity to consider the award of damages under the HRA. The Court of Appeal, comprising Lord Woolf CJ, Lord Philips of Worth Matravers MR, and Auld LJ, attempted to clarify the principles under which the European Court awards just satisfaction, and those under which a domestic court should do the same under the HRA. Lord Woolf, giving the judgment of the court, found that it was possible to discern a number of broad propositions arising out of Article 41. First, the 'fundamental principle underlying the award of compensation' by the Strasbourg court was that of *resitutio in integrum*.[68] Secondly, where the infringement of a Convention right has given rise to a 'significant' pecuniary loss, this will usually be assessed and awarded. However, Lord Woolf found that where the loss caused is incapable of being calculated in financial terms, the European Court's jurisprudence is unclear:

> The primary object of the proceedings will be to bring the adverse treatment to an end. If this is achieved is this enough to constitute 'just satisfaction' or is it necessary to award damages to compensate for the adverse treatment that has occurred? More particularly, should damages be awarded for anxiety and distress that has been occasioned by the breach? It is in relation to these questions that Strasbourg fails to give a consistent or coherent answer.[69]

---

[65] *Bernard*, above n 49, paras 58–59. The point relating to quantum however, appears to have been overruled by *R (Greenfield) v Secretary of State for the Home Department* [2005] UKHL 14; [2005] 1 WLR 673, see pp 278–279.

[66] *Ibid*, para 60. See generally the analysis at paras 42–62.

[67] *Anufrijeva and Another v Southwark London Borough Council* [2003] EWCA Civ 1406; [2004] QB 1124.

[68] *Ibid*, para 59.

[69] *Ibid*, para 60.

Further, Lord Woolf noted the Strasbourg court's reluctance to award damages for procedural errors, unless resulting in 'serious consequences.'[70] And finally, the court noted that the 'scale and manner of the violation' could be relevant to the question of whether to award monetary compensation.[71]

In seeking to calculate the quantum of damages to be awarded, Lord Woolf noted with approval the attempts by the courts in *Bernard* and *KB* to seek out domestic comparators.[72] In addition he appeared to distance himself from comments made extra-judicially to the effect that 'damages should be on the low side in comparison to those awarded for torts in our courts,' noting that this stance had been criticised by the Law Commission and had not been followed in either *Bernard* or in *KB*.[73] This advice, he noted, 'should in future be ignored'.[74]

Returning to the issue of balancing the need for individual and constitutional justice raised by Sullivan J in *Bernard*, Lord Woolf noted that:

> in considering whether to award compensation and, if so, how much, there is a balance to be drawn between the interests of the victim and those of society as a whole.[75]

He continued:

> There are good reasons why, where the breach arises from maladministration, in those cases where an award of damages is appropriate, the scale of such damages should be modest. The cost of supporting those in need falls on society as a whole. Resources are limited and payments of substantial damages will deplete the resources available for other needs of the public including primary care.[76]

Lord Woolf in other words suggested that the need for effective enforcement of the Convention rights via the provision of damages needed to be balanced with the broader concern not to damage the enjoyment of Convention rights for others. Richard Clayton has asserted that this 'limitation' on the courts' powers to award damages has no basis in the law of the Convention, in spite of his concession that the 'principle of fair

---

[70] *Ibid*, para 62.

[71] *Ibid*, paras 67–69.

[72] Identifying guidelines issued by the Judicial Studies Board, awards made by the Criminal Injuries Compensation Board, and awards of damages made by the Parliamentary Ombudsman and Local Government Ombudsman as providing 'rough guidance' (para 74).

[73] *Ibid*, para 73. See also Lord Woolf, above n 27, 434.

[74] *Ibid*.

[75] *Ibid*, para 56. Lord Woolf went on to quote the following passage from the White Paper: 'What remedy is appropriate will of course depend both on the facts of the case and on a proper balance between the rights of the individual and the public interest. In some cases, the right course may be for the decision of the public authority in the particular case to be quashed. In other cases, the only appropriate remedy may be an award of damages': *Rights Brought Home: The Human Rights Bill* (1997) (Cm 3782), para 2.6.

[76] *Ibid*, para 75.

balance is, of course, inherent to the Convention as a whole.'[77] Not only, however, is the notion of balance inherent in the Convention, it is also apparent in the design of the HRA itself.[78] For Lord Woolf, concern over the repercussions of an award of damages on the ability of a public authority to prevent against further future breaches led him to the conclusion that damages under the HRA should be a measure of 'last resort'.[79]

R (Greenfield) v Secretary of State for the Home Department

The leading case on the award of damages under the HRA is now the House of Lords decision in *Greenfield*.[80] Greenfield was serving a two-year sentence in HM Prison Doncaster. He was charged under the Prison Rules of a drug offence, and was sentenced, after an internal hearing before the deputy controller of the prison, to serve an additional 21 days imprisonment.[81] At this hearing, Greenfield was denied legal representation. Judicial review proceedings before the Divisional Court and Court of Appeal – in which Greenfield had contended that internal hearing was in breach of his rights under Article 6 ECHR – had been unsuccessful. However, the decision of the European Court of Human Rights in *Ezeh and Connors v United Kingdom*[82] had caused the Secretary of State to concede that

> the proceedings against the appellant did involve the determination of a criminal charge within the meaning of Art 6 of the Convention, that the deputy controller was not an independent and impartial tribunal and that the appellant was wrongly denied legal representation.[83]

As such, the only remaining issue for the House of Lords was whether Greenfield was entitled to damages.

The House of Lords found that in the vast majority of Article 6 cases, the finding of a violation alone would provide the applicant with just

---

[77] R Clayton, 'Damage Limitation: The Courts and Human Rights Act Damages' [2005] *PL* 429, 435.

[78] On which see ch 4.

[79] *Anufrijeva*, above n 67, para 56.

[80] *R (Greenfield) v Secretary of State for the Home Department* [2005] UKHL 14; [2005] 1 WLR 673.

[81] HM Prison Doncaster was a private prison, with the 'Deputy Controller' being the equivalent to a 'Deputy Governor'.

[82] *Ezeh and Connors v UK* (2003) 39 EHRR 1, in which the Grand Chamber of the European Court of Human Rights held that the denial of legal representation during prison disciplinary proceedings amounted to a violation of Art 6(3)(c).

[83] *Greenfield*, above n 65, para 1.

satisfaction.[84] Beyond the scope of Article 6 cases, Lord Bingham – with whom the remaining Law Lords agreed – added that:

> The routine treatment of a finding of violation as, in itself, just satisfaction for the violation found reflects the point ... that the focus of the Convention is on the protection of human rights and not the award of compensation.[85]

Lord Bingham echoed the findings of Lord Woolf in *Anufrijeva* by suggesting that the primary concern of the domestic court should be to put a stop to the treatment causing the violation.[86]

In response to the suggestions that awards of damages under the HRA should reflect domestic scales of damages, and the parallel concern, that domestic courts should be free to depart from the so-called 'principles' of just satisfaction in Strasbourg cases, Lord Bingham advocated a restrained approach. First, he said, the HRA 'is not a tort statute.'[87] 'Secondly, the purpose of incorporating the Convention in domestic law through the 1998 Act was not to give victims better remedies at home than they could recover in Strasbourg but to give them the same remedies without the delay and expense of resort to Strasbourg.'[88] Finally, section 8(4) obliged a domestic court to consider the Strasbourg approach to just satisfaction not only in determining the amount of any award, but also in determining whether there should be award at all. As Lord Bingham added, 'there could be no clearer indication that courts in this country should look to Strasbourg and not to domestic precedents.'[89] In language reminiscent of the 'no less/no more' approach of *Ullah*,[90] Lord Bingham went on to add that, '[domestic courts] are not inflexibly bound by Strasbourg awards in what may be different cases. But they should not aim to be significantly more or less generous than the Court might be expected to be, in a case where it was willing to make an award at all.'[91] In Greenfield's application, the House found 'no special feature' to merit an award of compensation.[92]

Van Colle v Chief Constable of Hertfordshire Police[93] is the only case since *Greenfield* in which HRA damages have been awarded. In Novemmber 2000, Giles Van Colle was murdered by Daniel Brougham, days before Van Colle was due to give evidence in a criminal trial in which

---

[84] *Ibid*, para 8. Adding further, at para 30, that 'the pursuit of damages should rarely, if ever, be an end in itself in an Article 6 case.'
[85] *Ibid*, para 9.
[86] *Ibid*.
[87] *Ibid*, para 19.
[88] *Ibid*.
[89] *Ibid*.
[90] On which see ch 3 at pp 66–71.
[91] *Greenfield*, above n 65, para 19.
[92] *Ibid*, para 29.
[93] *Van Colle v Chief Constable of Hertfordshire* [2006] ECHC 360; [2006] HRLR 25 (QB).

Brougham was the defendant. Prior to his murder, Van Colle had been subject to an 'escalating situation' of 'threats and incidents of witness intimidation by Brougham' about which the police force were – or should have been – aware. However, no action was taken by Hertfordshire police to secure the safety of Van Colle in the face of this serious threat to his well-being. Van Colle's parents brought an action under section 7(1) HRA against the Chief Constable of Hertfordshire for the failure of officers acting under him to act compatibly with Articles 2 and 8 ECHR. In the High Court, Cox J found that both Articles 2 and 8 had been violated. In determining the quantum of damages, Cox J attempted to distinguish the findings of the House of Lords in *Greenfield*, noting that the context of the breach was notably different from that of the present case.[94] Preferring a 'fact-sensitive approach, having regard to the justice of a particular case' Cox J awarded the applicants a total of £50,000 in damages.[95]

On appeal, the Court of Appeal – following *Greenfield* in making an award more clearly grounded in Strasbourg decisions[96] – reduced the sum to a total of £25,000.[97]

Conclusion

Contrary to the claims of critics of the HRA, the movement towards the Government's predicted 'culture of rights' has manifestly not contributed to the symbiotic development of a 'culture of compensation' in our legal system. In a reality far removed from that described by a number of critics of the HRA, damages under section 8 have been awarded in a mere three instances since October 2000 – hardly the weight of authority alluded to by Michael Howard MP when he claimed in 2005 that a culture of compensation, fuelled by the HRA, was 'running riot' in the United Kingdom.[98] Equally, when those three cases in which damages have been

---

[94]   *Ibid*, para 103.

[95]   *Ibid*, paras 105, 107–119. £15,000 in relation to the distress suffered by the applicant's son in the weeks prior to his death, £35,000 for that caused to the applicants themselves.

[96]   The Court of Appeal considered *Edwards v UK* (2002) 35 EHRR 487; *Akkoç v Turkey* (2000) 34 EHRR 1173; *Tas v Turkey* (2000) 33 EHRR 325; and *Şemsi Önen v Turkey* (App No 22876/93) (unreported), 14 May 2002. Of particular influence over the Court of Appeal's decision was the award of approximately £40,000 in *Akkoç*, in which the deceased had been unlawfully detained for 10 days prior to his death, during which time he was tortured. The Court of Appeal found the facts in *Akkoç* to be on a 'wholly different scale from the breaches established in the present case, in terms of both seriousness and culpability' (para 108).

[97]   *Van Colle v Chief Constable of Hertfordshire* [2007] EWCA Civ 325; [2007] 1 WLR 1821. The quantum of damages breaks down as follows: £10,000 for the distress suffered by Giles Van Colle, and £7,500 to each of the applicants (paras 119–129).

[98]   'Time to liberate the country from Human Rights Laws', 18 March 2005, available at <http://www.conservatives.com/tile.do?def=news.story.page&obj_id=120747> accessed 20 May 2008.

awarded under the HRA are examined, it is hard to sustain fellow Conservative MP David Davies' assertion that the HRA 'rewards compensation chasers and criminal troublemakers.'[99]

In fact the few cases in which damages have been awarded – and the narrow interpretation of section 8 put forward by *Greenfield* – seem to have surprised both the Government and commentators. As the 2006 review of the HRA conducted by the Department for Constitutional Affairs observed:

> [section 8] has been interpreted so strictly by the courts that the general view of legal commentators is that it is now very difficult to obtain damages under the HRA. The House of Lords has held that a finding of breach is generally sufficient redress under the HRA.[100]

Similarly, as Richard Clayton has argued, the interpretation of section 8 as advanced in *Anufrijeva* and in *Greenfield* is 'more restrictive than the terms of the Act itself would mandate'[101] in terms of both availability and quantum. In addition, such an approach may well give rise to the interpretative difficulty of attempting to shape a consistent domestic approach to human rights damages on the basis of the notoriously unprincipled Strasbourg jurisprudence on just satisfaction.

For the House of Lords however, the restrained approach to the award of damages against public authorities under the HRA is entirely in keeping with the intent behind the Act itself.[102] As Lord Bingham observed in *R (SB) v Denbigh High School*, the purpose of the HRA was

> not to enlarge the rights or remedies of those in the United Kingdom whose Convention rights have been violated but to enable those rights and remedies to be asserted and enforced by the domestic courts of this country and not only by recourse to Strasbourg.[103]

Put simply, the victim of a breach should not be entitled to a more generous remedy in domestic courts than would be provided at Strasbourg. Equally, however, the damages cases under the HRA reflect a long-standing hesitance on the part of the courts to award damages against public

---

[99] 'Conservatives condemn growing compensation culture', 20 August 2004, available at <http://www.conservatives.com/tile.do?def=news.story.page&obj_id=114677> accessed 20 May 2008.

[100] Department for Constitutional Affairs, *Review of the Implementation of the Human Rights Act* (July 2006) 18.

[101] Clayton, above n 77, 430.

[102] Lord Irvine commented during the Parliamentary debates that successful applicants 'should receive damages equivalent to what they would have obtained had they taken their case to Strasbourg.' (HL Debs, vol 582, col 1232 (3 November 1997)).

[103] *R (SB) v Denbigh High School* [2006] UKHL 15; [2007] 1 AC 100, para 29.

authorities for fear that while the remedy might benefit the individual, the community at large would suffer.[104] As Lord Browne-Wilkinson stated in *X v Bedfordshire*:

> if a liability in damages were to be imposed, it might well be that local authorities would adopt a more cautious and defensive approach to their duties.[105]

While the wording of section 8(3) is vague enough to support consideration of the public authority's financial position – requiring the court to consider 'all the circumstances of the case' – there is an arguable tension here with the general position that scarcity of resources should not justify the failure to discharge a statutory obligation, in this case under section 6(1) HRA.[106] It would be unusual to say the least if the victim of unlawful activity which would otherwise warrant an award of compensation were denied a remedy on the basis of the impoverishment of the public body at fault. Nevertheless, in the emergent case law under the HRA, the courts have begun to show that, in the few cases in which damages will be available, generosity to the individual victim has to be reconciled with bringing rights home for the wider community.

INJUNCTIVE RELIEF

The weakness of the remedy of damages is of course that any award will post-date the infringement and not prevent it. Injunctive relief provides would-be victims of breaches with the opportunity to assert their rights prior to any interference, and as such is a potent judicial mechanism of rights protection. Further, injunctions can be employed in a broad range of circumstances; under section 37(1) of the Supreme Court Act 1981, the High Court is entitled to award injunctions where it is 'just and convenient do to so.' One of us has written elsewhere that:

> Of all the weapons in the judicial arsenal, the injunction is the most coercive of civil remedies. It can be used either to negate or protect human rights more directly and effectively than any other. Particularly where time and immediacy are vital, the ability to obtain or fend off an injunction will often determine whether a paper right becomes a real one.[107]

---

[104] For a sketch see: M Fordham, 'Reparation for Maladministration: Public Law's Final Frontier' [2003] *Judicial Review* 104.

[105] *X (Minors) v Bedfordshire County Council* [1995] 2 AC 633, 750.

[106] See: *R v Sussex county court ex p Tandy* [1998] AC 714. Cf *R v Gloucester County Council ex p Barry* [1997] AC 584.

[107] Leigh and Lustgarten, above n 19, 531.

While injunctions are available against public authorities,[108] the most significant developments in their use under the HRA have been visible in disputes between private parties. As observed above, the horizontal effect of the HRA has not been such as to develop new common law causes of action based on the actual or future infringement of the Convention rights, but the duty of the court under section 6 ensures that a degree of horizontal influence is becoming apparent, including in the grant of remedies.[109] That the Convention would be indirectly horizontally applicable was made evident in the case of *Venables and Thompson v News Group Newspapers*, heard just one month after the coming into effect of the HRA.[110] The horizontal effects of that case have been described in more detail above, but at this stage, it is the scope of the injunctions awarded and the grounds on which the court felt able to make the award that are pertinent.

Venables and Thompson required the court to assess the balance between the rights of the applicants under Articles 2, 3 and 8 against those of the newspapers under Article 10.[111] Dame Elizabeth Butler-Sloss P felt able – as a result of section 6(1) and 6(3)(a) HRA – to assert that while the applicants could not rely on a 'free-standing application under the Convention,'[112] the court itself was under an obligation to act compatibly with the Convention rights. This duty, she outlined, 'includes both a positive as well as a negative obligation.'[113] In other words, not only was the court to seek to avoid the infringement of rights, it could also impose measures actively designed to protect them. Such was the threat to the Articles 2 and 3 rights of the applicants that Butler-Sloss P granted injunctions *contra mundum* in respect of the disclosure of a wide range of information pertaining to their identity, appearance and whereabouts.[114]

In the view of the court, the restriction on the freedom of the press the injunctions would entail was entirely proportionate to the need to protect the claimants from 'serious and possibly irreparable harm.'[115] Butler-Sloss P recognised that the decision was ground-breaking, but justified the scope of the orders made on the basis of the 'real and substantial' risk to the 'uniquely notorious' applicants.[116] That the court was able to grant the

---

[108] Including Ministers and officers of the Crown: *M v Home Office* [1994] 1 AC 377.
[109] See ch 9.
[110] *Venables v News Group Newspapers; Thompson v News Group Newspapers* [2001] Fam 430. See further: *Venables v News Group International (Breach of Injunction)* The Times, 7 December 2001.
[111] See further pp 247–248, 250.
[112] *Venables v News Group Newspapers; Thompson v News Group Newspapers*, above n 110, 447.
[113] *Ibid*, 446.
[114] *Ibid*, 470–471 (on the information protected).
[115] *Ibid*, 463.
[116] *Ibid*, 467.

unprecedented remedies sought has been referred to as 'a notable extension of judicial power'[117] demonstrating the potential for the court to shape novel remedies in defence of human rights based on its duty under HRA section 6(3).

Subsequent cases have seen the scope of this novel jurisdiction cemented and broadened. Confirmation that such a wide-ranging injunction could be granted in cases other than those in which there existed a direct risk to the life of the applicant was found in *X (A woman formerly known as Mary Bell) v O'Brien*.[118] In the latter case, injunctions *contra mundum* were granted to protect the Article 8 rights of the applicant (who had, as a minor, been convicted of the killing of two boys) and her daughter, who had on five occasions been forced to move home following the discovery of their whereabouts and harassment by the press. In *Carr v News Group Newspapers* similarly broad injunctions were granted. Maxine Carr had become notorious after providing a false alibi for her then partner, Ian Huntley, who was subsequently convicted of the murder of two children in Soham in 2002. She was convicted of perverting the course of justice and on her release was granted injunctions on grounds of Articles 2 and 8 ECHR to protect against disclosure of information relating to her new identity, movements and the psychiatric treatment she was receiving.[119]

Section 12 HRA and Press Freedom

While the recent history of the common law disclosed a less than robust approach to the rule against prior restraint, the influence of the Strasbourg jurisprudence promised a more rigorous analysis of measures designed to restrict press freedom.[120] In spite of this, and with a press fearful of the chilling effect of a newly developed privacy remedy, the Government was persuaded to amend the Human Rights Bill to include a provision designed to bolster protection for freedom of expression yet further. As outlined above, the provision puts beyond doubt the horizontal application of at least one of the Convention rights, and in so doing – under the 'rights of others' exception – brings the other Convention rights into play.[121] Section

---

[117] L Clark, 'Injunctions and the Human Rights Act 1998: Jurisdiction and Discretion' (2002) 21 *Civil Justice Quarterly* 29, 36.

[118] [2003] EWHC 1101; [2003] EMLR 37.

[119] *Carr v News Group Newspapers* [2005] EWHC 971 (QB). On which see: P Dougan, 'Anonymity orders and media censorship in the "new era" of human rights' (2005) *Ent LR* 150.

[120] Contrast, eg, *AG v Guardian Newspapers* [1987] 1 WLR 1248 with *Observer and Guardian v UK* (1992) 14 EHRR 153.

[121] See pp 247–248. Section 12 HRA applies to 'the press, broadcasters or anyone whose right to freedom of expression might be affected. It is not limited to cases to which a public authority is a party' (HC Debs, vol 314, col 535 (2 July 1998) (Jack Straw MP)).

12 HRA applies to 'any relief which, if granted, might affect the exercise of the Convention right to freedom of expression.'[122] Section 12(2) is designed to reduce the number of *ex parte* injunctions granted in this area by stipulating that 'no such relief is to be granted' unless it is established that 'the applicant has taken all practicable steps to notify the respondent' or 'compelling reasons' exist 'why the respondent should not be notified.' Further, the section provides that:

> no such relief is to be granted so as to restrain publication before trial unless the court is satisfied that the applicant is *likely* to establish that publication should not be allowed.[123]

And where the subject of the application is journalistic, literary or artistic material, the court should have 'particular regard to the importance of the Convention right to freedom of expression.'[124]

The application of section 12 has raised two particular issues of note: the extent to which the established *American Cyanamid* test is modified where the Convention rights are in play, and the question of whether that provision gives Article 10 rights a 'presumptive priority' over the other Convention rights given effect under the HRA. Each will be discussed in turn.

Likelihood of Success at Trial

The process of determining whether interim injunctive relief should be granted has been described as a judicial 'guessing game'.[125] This is for the reason that the judge is required to make an assessment of the prospects of the action at trial, on the basis of incomplete evidence and submissions. For the applicant, the interim stage is of particular importance; despite being designed to maintain the status quo pending trial, in many cases it is 'effectively the disposition of the matter.'[126] Prior to the implementation of the HRA, this area of the law had been governed by the 1975 House of

---

[122] HRA s 12(1).
[123] HRA s 12(3) (emphasis added).
[124] HRA s 12(4), the full text of which reads: '(4) The court must have particular regard to the importance of the Convention right to freedom of expression and, where the proceedings relate to material which the respondent claims, or which appears to the court, to be journalistic, literary or artistic material (or to conduct connected with such material), to –
(a) the extent to which –
 (i) the material has, or is about to, become available to the public; or
 (ii) it is, or would be, in the public interest for the material to be published;
(b) any relevant privacy code.'
[125] Clark, above n 117, 29.
[126] Leigh and Lustgarten, above n 19, 533.

Lords decision in *American Cyanamid v Ethicon Co*[127] In that case, the House of Lords held that an interim injunction should be granted where the applicant could show that the issues disclosed a serious issue to be tried, that damages would not provide an adequate remedy should an injunction be refused, and that the balance of convenience lay in favour of granting the injunction.[128] On the basis of establishing a 'serious issue to be tried' the court could exercise its discretion to grant an interlocutory injunction, without placing an onerous burden on the applicant and without having to assess the substance of the case made in the absence of full evidence, cross-examination of witnesses and so on.

On its face, the HRA appears to raise this threshold where freedom of expression is in play. Section 12(3) HRA provides that in cases where freedom of expression is at issue interim relief should not be provided unless that applicant has shown a *likelihood* of success at full trial. Not only is the question of threshold arguably altered, so – as Devonshire has argued – is the degree to which the court will have to engage with the substance of the case made:

> The *American Cyanamid* test is plainly at odds with s 12(3). The former discourages the assessment of substantive issues, conflicts of evidence or difficult questions of law. The latter requires a determination of the merits of a case to evaluate the prospects of eventual success.[129]

The question therefore arose whether, in applying section 12 HRA in practice, how far the courts should amend the established *American Cyanamid* approach.

As Andrew Keay has observed, the early case law under section 12(2) HRA displays a degree of confusion.[130] Initially, courts had recognised that in giving effect to section 12 HRA they would have to depart from *American Cyanamid*, as Keene LJ noted in *Douglas v Hello!*:

> [T]he court must look beyond conventional *American Cyanamid* principles and seek to discern where the balance of justice lies ... [T]he court has to look ahead to the ultimate stage and to be satisfied that the scales are likely to come down in the applicant's favour.[131]

---

[127] [1975] AC 396.

[128] *Ibid*, 406–408. As Lord Diplock outlined in his speech: 'The court ... must be satisfied that the claim is not frivolous or vexatious; in other words, that there is a serious question to be tried' (407).

[129] P Devonshire, 'Restraint on Freedom of Expression under the Human Rights Act: *Cream Holdings Ltd v Banerjee* in the House of Lords' (2005) *Civil Justice Quarterly*, 194, 197–198.

[130] A Keay, 'Whither *American Cyanamid*?: Interim injunctions in the 21st century' (2003) *Civil Justice Quarterly* 133, 144–146. See also Devonshire, above n 129, 194.

[131] *Douglas v Hello!* [2001] QB 967, 1007–1008. Keay also refers to the decisions of Cresswell J in *Lakeside Homes Ltd v BBC* (14 November 2000), and Ouseley J in *Theakston*

However, in *Imutran v Uncaged Campaigns* however, Sir Andrew Morritt VC remarked that the *American Cyanamid* approach and that in section 12(3) were so similar as to have little (if any) effect in practice.[132]

The leading case is now the decision of the House of Lords in *Cream Holdings v Banerjee*.[133] Banerjee had been an accountant for the Cream Holdings Company. Upon leaving her post she had taken documents which, she claimed, disclosed financial impropriety on the part of the company, and handed them to the second defendants, the publishers of the *Liverpool Daily Post* and *Liverpool Echo*. The second defendants published information relating to the materials obtained by Banerjee, and Cream Holdings applied for an interim injunction to prevent further publication.

At first instance, an injunction was granted, with Lloyd J treating the test of likelihood as being synonymous with the applicants showing a 'real prospect of success'.[134] The Court of Appeal, dismissed the defendants' appeal, and endorsed the use of the test as applied at first instance, while distancing themselves from the application of the *American Cyanamid* test in cases under the HRA.[135] As Arden LJ recognised, section 12(3) requires that the courts engage with the merits of the application.[136] For the reason the test under section 12 HRA is more exacting than that set down by Lord Diplock in *American Cyanamid*, as Arden LJ observed, when applying section 12 HRA, the test in *American Cyanamid* should be 'put … firmly to one side.'[137]

The defendant's appeal to the House of Lords, on the ground that the judge had misdirected himself in applying the 'real prospect of success' test,[138] was unanimously allowed. Lord Nicholls, with whom the remaining Law Lords agreed, held that the purpose of section 12 HRA was to protect freedom of expression by setting a more onerous threshold test for the grant of interlocutory injunctions. The purpose of section 12(3) was to:

> buttress the protection afforded to freedom of speech at the interlocutory stage.
> It sought to do so by setting a higher threshold test for the grant of interlocutory

---

v MGN [2002] EWHC 137 (QB); [2002] EMLR 22 as supporting the view that a departure from *American Cyanamid* was necessary for the purposes of s 12.

[132] [2001] EMLR 21, para 17.

[133] [2004] UKHL 44; [2005] 1 AC 253.

[134] *Ibid*, para 6, where Lloyd J is quoted as saying, in holding that the s 12(3) test was satisfied, 'I do not say it is more likely than not, but there is certainly a real prospect of success.'

[135] [2003] EWCA Civ 103; [2003] Ch 650.

[136] *Ibid*, para 103.

[137] *Ibid*, para 123. See also the comments of Simon Brown LJ at para 56.

[138] The defendants' argued that to apply a test of 'real prospect of success' under s 12(3) would be to 'read down' that provision and give it a narrow construction which would 'lower rather than raise the threshold for interim restraint on freedom of speech in comparison to the pre-Human Rights Act state of the law.' The arguments of the defendants are set out at [2005] 1 AC 253, 254–256.

injunctions against the media than the *American Cyanamid* guideline of a 'serious question to be tried' or a 'real prospect' of success at the trial.[139]

The threshold would be crossed if established to the court's satisfaction that the 'applicant is likely to establish that publication should not be allowed.' Lord Nicholls conceded that the word 'likely' 'has several different shades of meaning,'[140] but denied that a uniform interpretation of 'more likely than not' would be appropriate in all circumstances.[141] As the test set down by Parliament in section 12 was one of 'universal application' Lord Nicholls held that it should be applied with a degree of flexibility so as to avoid causing injustice in exceptional cases:

> where the potential adverse consequences of disclosure are particularly grave, or where a short injunction is needed to enable the court to hear and give proper consideration to an application for interim relief pending the trial or any relevant appeal.[142]

The 'general approach' to the grant of interim injunctions under section 12(3) under *Cream Holdings* appears to gives effect to the higher threshold to be reached before the courts will grant interim relief.[143] Subject to the limited exception outlined by Lord Nicholls above, the *American Cyanamid* test has been replaced by the more exacting standard of likelihood of success at trial in cases where freedom of expression is at issue. While this appeared to herald a movement towards a more robust protection for freedom of expression, Article 10 is not the only consideration to be exposed to judicial scrutiny under section 12. As Lord Nicholls observed, the discretion to grant an interim injunction would be exercised, 'duly taking into account the relevant jurisprudence on Article 10 *and any countervailing Convention rights*.' Judicial consideration of section 12(3) cannot be fully understood without exploring the approach of the courts to section 12(4) and the arguably more complex technical question of how to reconcile conflicts between two competing Convention rights.

---

[139] *Ibid*, para 15.
[140] *Ibid*, para 12.
[141] *Ibid*, para 20.
[142] *Ibid*, para 22.
[143] *Ibid*. Where Lord Nicholls indicated 'that the courts will be exceedingly slow to make interim restraint orders where the applicant has not satisfied the court he will probably (more likely than not) succeed at the trial.'

'Parallel Analysis'[144]

On its face, the direction in section 12(4) HRA that courts have 'particular regard to the importance' of freedom of expression appears to give that right primacy in those cases in which journalistic materials are before the court. Based on statements in Parliament however, it is certainly debatable whether it was in the intentions of the Government at least to tip the scales in this way. Then Home Secretary Jack Straw initially observed that

> we cannot assert as a contracting party, that one part of [the Convention] wholly trumps another part ... [T]he whole part of the Convention is that it balances one article with another.[145]

However, it is hard to see how this can be entirely reconciled with his later statement that section 12 would 'enhance press freedom in a wider way than would arise simply from the incorporation of the Convention into our domestic law.'[146]

As we have described above, the inclusion of section 12 was almost certainly a sop to press freedom, but uncertainty over its practical application soon became evident once the Act came into force. As much was acknowledged by Bracewell J early in the life of the HRA, who found that judicial analysis under section 12(4)

> is not a balancing exercise in which the scales are evenly positioned at the commencement of the exercise. On the contrary, the scales are weighted at the beginning so that Art 10 prevails unless one of the defined derogations applies when given a narrow interpretation.[147]

It must be conceded that this may well be the natural intent to be inferred from the provision in question, but to give effect to the 'presumptive priority' of Article 10 regardless of the circumstances of the case would at least distort the requirements of – and would likely be incompatible with – the Convention. As Sedley LJ observed in *Douglas v Hello!* it 'cannot have been Parliament's design' to effectively allow Article 10 to trump competing Convention rights regardless of context:

---

[144] For more detailed consideration of this topic than space allows here see: H Rogers and H Tomlinson, 'Privacy and Expression: Convention Rights and Interim Injunctions' [2003] *EHRLR* 37; H Fenwick, 'Clashing Rights, the welfare of the child and the Human Rights Act' (2004) 67(6) *MLR* 889; H Fenwick, 'Judicial Reasoning in clashing rights cases' in H Fenwick, G Phillipson and R Masterman (eds), *Judicial Reasoning under the UK Human Rights Act* (Cambridge, CUP, 2007). For analysis of the conflict between Art 8 and Art 1 of Protocol 1 see: L Fox, *Conceptualising Home: Theories, Laws and Policies* (Oxford, Hart Publishing, 2007) ch 10.

[145] HC Debs, vol 314, col 415 (17 June 1998).

[146] HC Debs, vol 314, col 536 (2 July 1998).

[147] *In the Matter of X (A Child)*, judgment of 13 October 2000 (unreported) (cited in H Fenwick, 'Judicial Reasoning in Clashing Rights Cases' in Fenwick, Phillipson and Masterman, above n 144, 274).

The European Court of Human Rights has always recognised the high importance of freed media of communication in a democracy, but its jurisprudence
does not – and could not consistently with the Convention itself – give Art 10(1)
the presumptive priority which is given, for example, to the First Amendment in
the jurisprudence of the United States' Courts.[148]

In spite of this, early cases under the HRA took the position that those
rights which clashed with Article 10 should be treated as narrow exceptions to the right to freedom of expression. Fenwick and Phillipson have
charted this trend back to the decision of Butler-Sloss P in *Venables and
Thompson*.[149] While this may be ironic considering the wide-ranging
restrictions on freedom of expression imposed by that decision, it is
nevertheless the case that Butler-Sloss P stated:

> I am satisfied that I can only restrict the freedom of the media to publish if the
> need for those restrictions can be shown to fall within the exceptions set out in
> Article 10(2). In considering the limits to the law of confidence, and whether a
> remedy is available to the claimants within those limits, I must interpret
> narrowly those exceptions.[150]

An approach such as this would treat other Convention rights as narrowly-
construed exceptions to freedom of expression and would, as a result, have
the practical effect of treating Article 10 as being at the top of a hierarchy
of Convention rights. Such an approach would produce the

> striking asymmetry whereby the protection of the right to privacy would have to
> be justified in as necessary in a democratic society, while the claims of free speech
> would be simply assumed.[151]

Needless to say, such an approach offers an unbalanced view of the
requirements of Article 8, which also requires justification to ensure the
legitimacy of any restriction on its enjoyment.

Subsequent cases began to show signs of an acknowledgement that the
courts were required to undertake a 'balancing exercise' to properly
discharge their obligations under section 6 HRA. In *A v B plc* Lord Woolf
recognised the 'tension between the two articles' and noted that the court
must achieve the correct balance between the rights by attaching the
'proper weight' to each competing claim.[152] In spite of this however, that
case arguably followed the example of earlier cases in failing to fully

---

[148]   *Douglas v Hello!* [2001] QB 967, 1004.
[149]   H Fenwick and G Phillipson, *Media Freedom under the Human Rights Act* (Oxford,
OUP, 2006) 700–706.
[150]   *Venables v News Group Newspapers; Thompson v News Group Newspapers* [2001]
Fam 430, 461.
[151]   Fenwick and Phillipson, above n 149, 701.
[152]   *A v B Plc* [2002] EWCA Civ 337; [2003] QB 195, para 6.

analyse the legitimacy of any purported restriction of the Article 8 right which would result from publication of the information in question.[153]

Analysis of competing rights claims is now founded on the presumptive equality of the rights at issue, and the Convention-compliant process of 'parallel analysis' first expounded by Lady Justice Hale – as she then was – in the Court of Appeal decision in *Re S (A Child)*.[154] The subsequent endorsement of such an approach can be seen in the House of Lords decisions in *Campbell v MGN*,[155] and in *Re S (A Child)* on appeal to the Law Lords.[156] On the basis of those decisions, any reconciliation of Articles 8 and 10 must now proceed on the basis that, '[a]s each is a fundamental right, there is evidently a "pressing social need" to protect it.'[157] As Baroness Hale suggested in *Campbell*, the correct approach to 'balancing' those competing claims

> involves looking first at the comparative importance of the actual rights being claimed in the individual case; then at the justifications for interfering with or restricting each of those rights; and applying the proportionality test to each.[158]

The subsequent endorsement of this approach by the House in *Re S* saw the key principles of parallel analysis described by Lord Steyn:

> First, neither article has as such precedence over the other. Secondly, where the values under the two articles are in conflict, an intense focus on the comparative importance of the specific rights being claimed in the individual case is necessary. Thirdly, the justifications for interfering with or restricting each right must be taken into account. Finally, the proportionality test must be applied to each.[159]

Conclusion

The issue of injunctions under the HRA has not only seen the courts deploy novel remedies based on their own duties under section 6 HRA but has also seen the resolution of a number of issues of technical difficulty arising out of the HRA. While the question of the extent to which the *American Cyanamid* test would be amended following the implementation of the HRA caused a degree of uncertainty, the resolution of the method by which conflicting rights should be 'balanced' against each other is an

---

[153] Fenwick and Phillipson, above n 149, 702–703.

[154] *In Re S (A Child) (Identification: Restrictions on Publication)* [2003] EWCA Civ 963; [2004] Fam 43. Although the term 'parallel analysis' appears to have been coined by Rogers and Tomlison, above n 144.

[155] *Campbell v MGN* [2004] UKHL 22; [2004] 2 AC 457.

[156] *In Re S (A Child)* [2004] UKHL 47; [2005] 1 AC 593.

[157] *Campbell v MGN*, above n 155, para 140.

[158] *Ibid*, para 141.

[159] *In Re S (A Child)*, above n 156, para 17.

important development for domestic law under the HRA which is becoming an accepted feature of cases involving competing rights claims.[160] Not only has the development of the technique of parallel analysis resolved the difficulty posed by section 12(4) HRA,[161] it has also done so without explicit guidance from Strasbourg. As Baroness Hale noted in *Campbell*:

> The European Court of Human Rights has been concerned with whether the State's interference with privacy ... or a restriction on freedom of expression ... could be justified in the particular case. In the national court, the problem of balancing two rights of equal importance arises most acutely in the context of disputes between two private persons.[162]

In contrast to the occasionally gloomy picture painted above of domestic courts hesitating to act without explicit guidance from Strasbourg, this area of domestic law shows the ability of domestic courts to both shape Convention-compliant remedies which are both novel in their scope and achieved through technically novel judicial reasoning.

---

[160] See, eg, *Re LM (Reporting Restrictions: Coroner's Inquest)* [2007] EWHC 1902 (F); [2007] CP Rep 48; *HRH Prince of Wales v Associated Newspapers Ltd* [2006] EWHC 522 (Ch); [2007] 3 WLR 222; *CC v AB* [2006] EWHC 3088 (QB); [2007] EMLR 11.

[161] 'Whatever the intention behind section 12(4), it has not been accepted as binding in extra weight on the side of freedom of expression at the expense of other Convention rights' (Fenwick and Phillipson, above n 149, 131).

[162] *Campbell v MGN*, above n 155, para 140.

Chapter 11

Conclusion

TEN YEARS AFTER the passing of the Human Rights Act 1998 (HRA), what been achieved and what might lie ahead?

It is something of a truism to describe the HRA as unique, a hybrid, or as a 'third wave' rights system. Commentators emphasise (as did the Government in proposing it) the novelty of the compromise between strong judicial review (in which judges have the last word) and political protections of rights.

This same concern over judicial interference with the democratic process has predominated in discussion of the HRA during its first decade. Tension over this matter is in fact a design feature of the Act and manifests itself in the inter-connectedness of the strong pro-rights interpretative duty and the declaration of incompatibility process (sections 3 and 4 respectively). On the one hand, section 3 has produced, as expected, some innovation in statutory interpretation. On the other hand, a degree of institutional modesty by the judiciary over what interpretations are 'possible' even with the backing of section 3 has resulted in a greater than expected number of cases in which the issue is in effect handed back to the political process through section 4. The maturity and sensitivity of the senior judiciary in discussing deference has seldom been matched, however, by that of politicians in responding to individual judgments.

In our view, however, the attention devoted to this issue has lead to a somewhat distorted view of the Act. By focusing almost exclusively on the conflict between law and politics the result has been to neglect the broader context in which the HRA operates.

The HRA functions in the shadow of Strasbourg. Neither Parliament nor domestic judges have the freedom to start with a clean sheet concerning what Convention rights mean: the law-making ability of both branches is constrained. More than 40 years' worth of Strasbourg jurisprudence elucidates, elaborates and confines their meaning. The further that domestic interpretation departs from that canon the more it undermines one of the other objectives of the HRA – to bring rights home – since the last word does not lie with the UK courts. In this conversation at any rate human rights do *not* have a Humpty-Dumpty quality – they cannot mean whatever we like since for the most part the meanings have already been stipulated.

Nor can we say that Parliament has the final word over judicial interpretations of Convention rights. Parliamentary disregard of the Convention will end in an adverse ruling at the European Court of Human Rights. The suggestions sometimes heard that the Westminster Parliament could defy the Court by refusing to implement a ruling disagreeable to it, or that the UK Government could denounce the Convention, leave the Council of Europe, or persuade the 46 other member states to renegotiate the Convention to resolve a national difficulty have a decided air of unreality despite their strict legal pedigree.

To portray the two systems as operating in complete isolation from each other would however also be a mistake – the Convention system relies on the European Court of Human Rights considering 'the changing conditions in contracting states' and responding 'to any emerging consensus as to the standards to be achieved.'[1] In 2005, Lord Steyn wrote of a developing 'creative dialogue' between domestic institutions and the European Court of Human Rights, referring to the decision of *Z v UK*[2] in which the Strasbourg court had departed from its earlier ruling in *Osman v UK*.[3] While it may be debated whether the HRA was directly responsible in this specific instance,[4] following the implementation of the HRA there are indications of domestic decisions having a growing influence at the Strasbourg level. In 2006 the Department for Constitutional Affairs reported that:

> the close analytical attention paid by the English courts to the European Convention on Human Rights case law is respected by the European Court of Human Rights and is influential on the way that it approaches English cases.[5]

More encouragingly, there are also signs of a corresponding – albeit slow – improvement of the United Kingdom's record as a respondent before the European Court of Human Rights.[6] These are undoubted successes of the Act – but so long as the 'no less/no more' doctrine continues to hold sway there will continue to be doubts over the ability of our judges to

---

[1] *Stafford v UK* (2002) 35 EHRR 32, para 68.

[2] (2002) 34 EHRR 3.

[3] *Osman v UK* (1998) 29 EHRR 245: See Lord Steyn, '2000–2005: Laying the foundations of human rights law in the United Kingdom' [2005] *EHRLR* 349.

[4] The decision which prompted the European Court's change of position – *Barrett v Enfield LBC* [2001] 2 AC 550 – had been made prior to the HRA coming into operation.

[5] Department for Constitutional Affairs, *Review of the implementation of the Human Rights Act* (2006) 11. See, eg, *Evans v UK* (2006) 43 EHRR 21; *Roche v UK* (2006) 42 EHRR 30; *Dickson v UK* (2007) 44 EHRR 21.

[6] On which see: M Amos, 'The impact of the Human Rights Act on the United Kingdom's performance before the European Court of Human Rights' [2007] *PL* 655.

constructively 'contribute to [the] dynamic and evolving interpretation of the Convention' at the Strasbourg level.[7]

The excessive focus on debates concerning judicial supremacism and deference has also led to neglect of what should be, we argue, the most important measure of the HRA's success: its effectiveness in granting accessible remedies to individuals claiming that their human rights have been violated. This after all, was the benchmark set by the White Paper *Rights Brought Home* and by the Act's short title: 'An Act to give *further effect* to the rights and freedoms guaranteed under the European Convention on Human Rights ...'[8]

What we *can* say is that the particular constitutional status of the HRA has to some extent undermined its usefulness in providing effective domestic remedies. Thus the HRA's unique constitutional status is reflected in the minimal impact of the Convention in criminal justice. As we saw in chapter 7, by a series of choices over the scope of a 'criminal charge' and, in particular, because of the failure to develop evidential protections against official conduct violating human rights, the courts have minimised the HRA's application in criminal trials. By comparison with countries with a *constitutional* right of fair trial the impact of Article 6 has been barely noticeable.

Similarly, although much debate has surrounded the horizontal application of the HRA to private law disputes (chapters 9 and 10), on a balanced assessment the developments, while worthwhile, are clearly cautiously incremental in character. Notably – and despite many predictions to the contrary – a tort of invasion of privacy has *not* been created. The more limited remedy for misuse of personal information already lags behind Strasbourg protection in some respects.

Here as in judicial review (chapter 6) the HRA has tended to nudge further common law trends already underway rather than producing a bold change of direction. After a hesitant start the courts have intensified the standard of review (especially in the case of unqualified rights) – all the while agonising over whether they are crossing the constitutional rubicon into merits review.

Our conclusions so far may appear a little downbeat in comparison to the euphoria and expectation that greeted the HRA a decade ago. Nevertheless, it is worth noting that they also borne out by the Government's own mid-term report on the Act, published by the Department of Constitutional Affairs in 2006. This concluded that the Act had 'not significantly altered the constitutional balance between Parliament, the Executive and the Judiciary' and 'had no significant impact on criminal

---

[7] The White Paper, *Rights Brought Home: The Human Rights Bill* (October 1997), Cm 3782, para 2.5.
[8] Emphasis added.

law', while in other fields of substantive law it had had a 'generally beneficial' effect.[9] Data on the use of the Act in the appellate courts was revealing: in the period up until the report only two per cent of cases on appeal could be described as 'human rights' cases. Although the House of Lords had made greater use of the Act (it had been considered in around a third of appeals in the period) it was judged to have had a decisive impact in only 10 per cent of the cases in which it was considered by the House (ie in around three per cent of the total appeals).

The gorilla in the room is, of course, counter-terrorism policy and legislation.[10] It is here that the Act has faced its biggest challenges. No one could have predicted that, a year after the Act came into force, Parliament would be debating proposals to detain indefinitely without trial foreign terrorist suspects and the package of other measures that became the Anti-Terrorism Crime and Security Act 2001. Although the specific circumstances of 9/11 *were* unforeseeable it was to be expected that sooner or later a major international crisis would present challenges for human rights comparable to those of First and Second World Wars. The Government's failure was in promoting (as some ministers have continued to) the idea that the challenges post 9/11 were so novel and exceptional that the necessary response could only come outside rather than within the framework of human rights. This was barely credible for anyone with a sense of history: the Convention was after all born in the ruins of a continent literally torn apart by events of an entirely different magnitude and under the threat of imminent resumption of global conflict during the early years of the Cold War. If 9/11 demonstrated that that for some politicians the commitment to human rights culture was only skin-deep, it has also, surprisingly, shown that the judiciary has absorbed and internalised the message more profoundly. Judgments such as the *Belmarsh* detainees case and those on control orders are a radical break with previous judicial practice in cases of national security and have given teeth to the HRA. They show that the current generation of judges at least has learned the lessons of past conflicts – that governments in crises tend to make excessive legal claims and that vulnerable and unpopular groups can suffer severe injustice as result.

In the field of anti-terrorism we can observe also the extent to which human rights have become part of the part of the public discourse since 1998. Even while restricting and derogating from human rights, ministers

---

[9] Department of Constitutional Affairs, *Review of the Implementation of the Human Rights Act* (2006) 10.
[10] The Department of Constitutional Affairs review concluded also that the Act 'has had an impact upon the Government's counter-terrorism legislation. The main difficulties in this area arise not from the Human Rights Act, but from decisions of the European Court of Human Rights' (*Ibid*, 9).

felt it necessary to attempt to justify these measures in terms of the function of the state positively to protect the human rights of its citizens. In that sense we can say that there are limited signs of a new human rights culture. The formal parliamentary machinery for promoting that culture is (as we explained in chapter 2) weak but despite that the contribution of the Joint Committee on Human Rights has been significant.

As we look ahead the Equality and Human Rights Commission (which came into operation on 1 October 2007) may prove itself to be a significant new actor on the domestic human rights stage.[11] Significantly, the powers and duties of the new Commission give it a prime opportunity to revive belatedly the movement towards a culture of respect for, and awareness of, human rights. Alongside its role in monitoring the effectiveness of human rights laws,[12] it has broader duties to 'promote understanding of the importance of human rights' and to 'encourage good practice in relation to human rights', specifically concerning the compliance of public authorities with section 6 HRA.[13] In the exercise of these duties the Commission has a range of powers at its disposal, not least the ability to bring or intervene in legal proceedings relating to any of its functions.[14]

As the HRA became increasingly seen within Government as a direct obstacle to the deployment of policies on anti-terrorism, asylum seekers and criminal justice, a series of damaging misconceptions about the Act were allowed to germinate.[15] In the absence of an independent body with a significant public profile willing to promote human rights values, public support for the HRA – already arguably lacking – was allowed to wither. In this sense, the campaign to 'bring rights home' has been a categorical failure. It is to be hoped that, for the HRA at least, the establishment of the Equality and Human Rights Commission is not too little, too late.

Yet the Conservative party is already committed to the repeal of the HRA and to its replacement with a 'modern British Bill of Rights.'[16] David Cameron's party argue that the HRA is 'hampering the fight against crime and terrorism',[17] and has promised to:

---

[11] Under the Equality Act 2006, Pt 1. See: Lord Lester of Herne Hill and K Beattie, 'The New Commission for Equality and Human Rights' [2006] *PL* 197; C O'Cinneide, 'The Commission for Equality and Human Rights: a new institution for new and uncertain times' [2007] *Ind. LJ* 141.

[12] *Ibid*, s 11.

[13] *Ibid*, s 9.

[14] *Ibid*, ss 13–32.

[15] Department of Constitutional Affairs, above n 9, 32–34. See also: F Klug, 'A bill of rights: do we need one, or do we already have one?' [2007] *PL* 701.

[16] See: D Cameron, 'Balancing freedom and security – a modern British Bill of Rights': speech to the Centre for Policy Studies, London, 26 June 2006 (available at <http://www.conservatives.com/tile.do?def=news.story.page&obj_id=130572> accessed 20 May 2008).

[17] *Ibid*.

scrap the Human Rights Act and replace it with a British Bill of Rights that sets out rights and responsibilities ... and which allows us to take the action we need to defend our citizens against serious crime and our country against terrorism.[18]

The proposal is both openly Euro-sceptical – in promising to jettison 'European' rights and codify 'British' freedoms – and incoherent; it would at the same time involve the UK remaining a party to the European Convention.

The Government too remains concerned about its ability to counter terrorist threats under the Convention – as indicated by its attempted intervention in the *Ramzy v Netherlands* litigation.[19] It too has proposed a Bill of Rights and Responsibility.[20] However, it also appears, following the Department for Constitutional Affairs 2006 review of the Act, to remain committed to the HRA.[21] Under the Government's proposals, the HRA will continue to operate in parallel with the new Bill of Rights, with the latter document – we are told – to operate as a symbolic statement of values reminiscent of the US and South African Bills of Rights.[22]

At the time of writing the contents of these proposed 'Bills of Rights' remain unclear. The Government's proposal appears to seek to catch the opportunity lost under the HRA: the generation of popular support for the aims of the constitutional reform. But in the current political climate both parties' claims contain the potential to water down the protections of liberty that the HRA undoubtedly provides. Under either the Labour or Conservative options, claims to be able to codify 'responsibility' should be treated with scepticism if they are to simply act as a façade for another raft of criminal justice and anti-terrorism measures.

The HRA faces an uncertain future: an uncertain life beyond the next general election, or an uncertain role alongside a new Bill of Rights.

---

[18] N Herbert, 'Time to repair our broken politics', speech to the Conservative Party Conference, 2 October 2007 (available at <http://www.conservatives.com/tile.do?def=news.story.page&obj_id=139318> accessed 20 May 2008).

[19] *Ramzy v Netherlands* App No 25424/05; and see pp 228–229, 231.

[20] Ministry of Justice, *The Governance of Britain*, Cm 7170 (2007), paras 204–210. See also: J Straw, The MacKenzie Stuart Lecture, Faculty of Law, University of Cambridge, 25 October 2007 (available at <http://www.justice.gov.uk/news/sp251007a.htm>) accessed 12 May 2008.).

[21] See: J Straw, 'Towards a Bill of Rights and Responsibility', 21 January 2008 (available at <http://www.justice.gov.uk/news/sp210108a.htm> accessed 20 May 2008). In his lecture Straw referred to the HRA as 'an enormously important and defining piece of legislation.'

[22] *Ibid.*

Select Bibliography

REPORTS AND OFFICIAL PUBLICATIONS

Constitutional Affairs Select Committee, 'Seventh Report for 2004–5, The operation of the Special Immigration Appeals Commission (SIAC) and the use of Special Advocates' HC 323-I.

Department for Constitutional Affairs, 'Review of the Implementation of the Human Rights Act' (July 2006).

Home Affairs Select Committee, 'First Report for 2001–2' HC 351.

Home Office, 'Interception of Communications in the United Kingdom' (Cm 4368, 1999).

—— 'Human Rights Act Guidance for Departments' (2nd edn, 2000).

—— 'Preventing Extremism Together: Places of Worship' (6 October 2005).

'Inquiry into Legislation against Terrorism' (Cm 3420, 1996).

Intelligence and Security Committee, 'Annual Report for 2004–5' (Cm 6510, May 2005).

—— 'The Handling of Detainees by UK Intelligence Personnel in Afghanistan, Guantanamo Bay and Iraq' (Cm 6469, March 2005).

—— 'Report into the London Terrorist Attacks of 7 July 2005' (Cm 6785, 2006).

—— 'Rendition' (Cm 7171, July 2007).

Joint Committee on Conventions, 'Conventions of the UK Parliament, 2005–2006' HL 265-I; HC 1212-I.

Joint Committee on Human Rights, 'Counter-Terrorism Policy and Human Rights: 28 days, intercept and post-charge questioning, Nineteenth Report for 2006–7' HL 157, HC 790.

—— 'Second Report for 2001–2' HL 37/HC 372.

—— 'Fifth Report for 2001–2 of the Joint Committee' HL 51, HC 420.

—— 'Sixth Report for 2001–2' HL 57, HC 472.

—— 'First Report for 2002–3' HL 24, HC 191.

—— 'Third Report for 2005–6, Counter-Terrorism Policy and Human Rights: Terrorism Bill and Related Matter' HL 75, HC 651-I.

—— 'Twelfth Report for 2005–6' HL 122, HC 915.

—— 'Twenty-Third Report for 2005–06, The Committee's Future Working Practices' HL 239, HC 1575.

—— 'Sixteenth Report for 2006–7, Monitoring the Government's Response to Court judgments finding breaches of human rights' HL 128, HC 728.

—— 'Second Report for 2007–8, Counter-Terrorism Policy and Human Rights: 42 days' HL 23, HC 156.

Law Commission and Scottish Law Commission, 'Damages under the Human Rights Act 1998' (Law Com No 266; Scot Law Com No 180; Cm 4853, 2000).

Lord Chancellor's discussion paper, 'Infringement of Privacy' (London, 1993).

Northern Ireland Human Rights Commission, 'Making a Bill of Rights for Northern Ireland' (2001).

Northern Ireland Standing Advisory Commission, 'The Protection of Human Rights by Law in Northern Ireland' (Cm 7009, 1977).

'Privy Council Review of Intercept as Evidence' (Cm 7324, 2008).

Privy Counsellor Review Committee, 'Anti-Terrorism, Crime and Security Act 2001 Review' (18 December 2003).

Public Administration Committee, 'Fifth Report for 2001–2' (Cm 494).

'Report of the Inquiry into the Circumstances Surrounding the Death of Dr David Kelly' HC 247 (2004).

'Report of the Inquiry into the Export of Defence Equipment and Dual-Use Goods to Iraq and Related Prosecutions' HC 115 (1995–6).

'Report of the Select Committee on a Bill of Rights' HL 176 (1977–8).

Richard Commission, 'The Powers and Electoral Arrangements of the National Assembly for Wales' (2004).

'Rights Brought Home: the Human Rights Bill' (Cm 3782, 1997).

Royal Commission on the House of Lords, 'A House for the Future' (Cm 4534, 2000).

'The Governance of Britain' (Cm 7170, July 2007).

Treasury Solicitor, 'Special Advocates: a Guide to the Role of Special Advocates' (London, 2005).

Council of Europe

Committee on Legal Affairs and Human Rights, Council of Europe (rapporteur Mr Dick Marty), 'Secret Detentions and Illegal Transfers of Detainees Involving Council of Europe Member States: Second Report', Council of Europe Parliamentary Assembly Doc 11302 rev (11 June 2007).

Council of Europe, 'Follow-Up to the Secretary-General's Reports under Article 52 ECHR on the Question of Secret Detention and Transport of Detainees suspected of Terrorist Act, Notably by or at the Instigation of Foreign Agencies' (SG/Inf(2006)5 and SG/Inf(2006)13, 30 June 2006).

European Commission for Democracy through Law (Venice Commission), 'Opinion on the International Legal Obligations of Council of Europe Member States in Respect of Secret Detention Facilities and Inter-State Transport of Prisoners' (CDL-AD (2006) 016).

'European Parliament's Temporary Committee on the alleged use of European countries by the CIA for the transport and illegal detention of prisoners' (24 November 2006).

New Zealand

New Zealand Law Commission, 'Evidence: Evidence Code and Commentary' (Report 55, Vol 2, Wellington, 1999).

BOOKS

AHDAR, R (ed), *Law and Religion* (Aldershot, Ashgate, 2000).

AHDAR, R and LEIGH, I, *Religious Freedom in the Liberal State* (Oxford, Oxford University Press, 2005).

ALLEN, T, *Property and the Human Rights Act 1998* (Oxford, Hart, 2005).

ALSTON, P (ed), *Promoting Human Rights through Bills of Rights* (Oxford, Oxford University Press, 1999).

AMNESTY INTERNATIONAL, *United States of America Below the Radar: Secret Flights to Torture and Disappearances* (London, Amnesty International, 2006).

ANDENAS, M and FAIRGRIEVE, D (eds), *Judicial Review in International Perspective* (The Hague, Kluwer Law International, 2000).

BAMFORTH, N and LEYLAND, P (eds), *Public Law in a Multi-Layered Constitution* (Oxford, Hart Publishing, 2003).

BEAUMONT, P (ed), *Christian Perspectives on Human Rights and Legal Philosophy* (Carlisle, Paternoster Press, 1998).

BLICK, A, CHOUDHURY, T and WEIR, S, *The Rules of the Game: Terrorism, Community and Human Rights* (York, Joseph Rowntree Trust, 2006).

BONNER, D, *Executive Measures, Terrorism and National Security* (Aldershot, Ashgate, 2007).

BORN, H, JOHNSON, L and LEIGH, I (eds), *Who's Watching the Spies: Establishing Intelligence Service Accountability* (Dulles, Virginia, Potomac Books, 2005).

BRADLEY, AW and EWING, KD, *Constitutional and Administrative Law* (London, Longman, 2003).

BRITISH INSTITUTE OF HUMAN RIGHTS, *The Human Rights Act—Changing Lives* (London, British Institute of Human Rights, 2007).

BUTLER, A and BUTLER, P, *The New Zealand Bill of Rights: A Commentary* (Wellington, LexisNexis, 2006).

CAMBRIDGE CENTRE FOR PUBLIC LAW, *Constitutional Reform in the United Kingdom: Practice and Principles* (Oxford, Hart Publishing, 1998).

CANE, P, *Administrative Law* (4th edn, Oxford, Clarendon, 2004).

CAMPBELL, T, EWING, K and TOMKINS, A, *Sceptical Essays on Human Rights* (Oxford, Oxford University Press, 2001).

CLAPHAM, A, *Human Rights in the Private Sphere* (Oxford, Oxford University Press, 1993).

LORD COOKE, *Turning Points of the Common Law* (London, Sweet & Maxwell, 1997).

CRAIG, P, *Administrative Law* (5th edn, London, Sweet & Maxwell, 2003).

CRAIG, P and RAWLINGS, R (eds), *Law and Administration in Europe* (Oxford, Oxford University Press, 2003).

CROFT, J, *Whitehall and the Human Rights Act 1998* (London, Constitution Unit, 2000).

—— (2002) *Whitehall and the Human Rights Act 1998: the First Year* (London, The Constitution Unit).

DICEY, AV, *Introduction to the Study of the Law of the Constitution* (Indianapolis, Liberty Fund, 1982).

VAN DIJK, P *et al*, *Theory and Practice of the European Convention on Human Rights* (4th edn, Antwerp, Intersentia, 2006).

DWORKIN, R, *A Bill of Rights for Britain* (London, Chatto and Windus, 1990).

EMERSON, B and ASHWORTH, A, *Human Rights and Criminal Justice* (London, Sweet & Maxwell, 2001).

EWING, K and GEARTY, C, *Freedom Under Thatcher* (Oxford, Oxford University Press, 1990).

—— (2000) *The Struggle for Civil Liberties: Political Freedom and the Rule of Law in Britain, 1914–1945* (Oxford, Oxford University Press).

EWING, K, GEARTY, C AND HEPPLE, B, *Human Rights and Labour Law: Essays for Paul O'Higgins* (London, Mansell, 1994).

FELDMAN, D (ed), *English Public Law* (Oxford, Oxford University Press, 2004).

FENWICK, H, *Civil Liberties, New Labour, Freedom and the Human Rights Act* (London, Longman, 2000).

—— *Civil Liberties and Human Rights* (4th edn, London, Routledge-Cavendish, 2007).

FENWICK, H and PHILLIPSON, G, *Media Freedom under the Human Rights Act* (Oxford, Oxford University Press, 2006).

FENWICK, H, PHILLIPSON, G and MASTERMAN, R (eds), *Judicial Reasoning under the UK Human Rights Act* (Cambridge, Cambridge University Press, 2007).

FINNIE, W, HIMSWORTH, CMG and WALKER, N (eds), *Edinburgh Essays in Public Law* (Edinburgh, Edinburgh University Press, 1991).

FORCESE, C and WALDMAN, L, *Seeking Justice in an Unfair Process: Lessons from Canada, the United Kingdom, and New Zealand on the Use of 'Special Advocates' in National Security Proceedings* (Ottawa, Canadian Centre for Intelligence and Security Studies, 2007).

FORSYTH, C and WADE, H, *Administrative Law* (8th edn, Oxford, Oxford University Press, 2000).

FOX, L, *Conceptualising Home: Theories, Laws and Policies* (Oxford, Hart Publishing, 2007).

FREEDMAN, L (ed) *Superterrorism: Policy Responses* (Oxford, Blackwell, 2002).

FRIEDMANN, D and BARAK-EREZ, D, *Human Rights in Private Law* (Oxford, Hart, 2001).

GEARTY, C, *Principles of Human Rights Adjudication* (Oxford, Oxford University Press, 2004).

—— *Can Human Rights Survive?* (Cambridge, Cambridge University Press, 2006).

GOLDSWORTHY, J, *The Sovereignty of Parliament: History and Philosophy* (Oxford, Clarendon Press, 1999).

GREENBERG, K and DRATEL, J (eds), *The Torture Papers: The Road to Abu Ghraib* (Cambridge, Cambridge University Press, 2005).

GRIFFITH, J, *The Politics of the Judiciary* (London, Fontana Press, 1991).

GROSZ, S, BEATSON, J and DUFFY, P, *Human Rights: The 1998 Act and the European Convention* (London, Sweet & Maxwell, 2000).

LORD HAILSHAM, *The Dilemma of Democracy* (London, Collins, 1978).

HARRIS, D, O'BOYLE, M and WARBRICK, C, *Law of the European Convention on Human Rights* (London, Butterworths, 1995).

HILL, M (ed), *Religious Liberty and Human Rights* (Cardiff, University of Wales Press, 2002).

HOGG, P, *Constitutional Law of Canada* (5th edn, Scarborough, Carswell, 2006).

HOHFELD, W, *Fundamental Legal Conceptions as Applied in Judicial Reasoning* (New Haven, Yale University Press, 1923).

HUMAN RIGHTS WATCH, *Still At Risk: Diplomatic Assurances No Safeguard Against Torture* (New York, Human Rights Watch, 2005).

HUNT, M, *Using Human Rights Law in English Courts* (Oxford, Hart Publishing, 1997).

HUSCROFT, G and RISHWORTH, P (eds), *Litigating Rights: Perspectives from Domestic and International Law* (Oxford, Hart Publishing, 2002).

LABOUR PARTY, *A New Agenda for Democracy: Labour's Proposals for Constitutional Reform* (London, Labour Party, 1993).

—— (1996) *Bringing Rights Home: Labour's Plans to Incorporate the European Convention on Human Rights into United Kingdom Law* (London, Labour Party).

—— (1997) *New Labour: Because Britain Deserves Better* (London, Labour Party).

LORD IRVINE, *Human Rights, Constitutional Law and the Development of the English Legal System* (Oxford, Hart Publishing, 2003).

JOWELL, J and OLIVER, D (eds), *The Changing Constitution* (5th edn, Oxford, Oxford University Press, 2004).

—— (eds) (2007) *The Changing Constitution* (6th edn, Oxford, Oxford University Press, 2007).

KLUG, F, *Values for a Godless Age: the Story of the United Kingdom's New Bill of Rights* (London, Penguin, 2000).

LEACH, P, *Taking a Case to the European Court of Human Rights* (Oxford, Oxford University Press, 2005).

LOENEN, M and GOLDSCHMIDT, J (eds), *Religious Pluralism and Human Rights in Europe: Where to Draw the Line?* (Antwerp, Insentia, 2007).

LESTER, A, *Democracy and Individual Rights* (London, Fabian Society, 1969).

LESTER, A and PANNICK, D, *Human Rights Law and Practice* (London, Butterworths, 1999).

LUSTGARTEN, L and LEIGH, I, *In From the Cold: National Security and Parliamentary Democracy* (Oxford, Clarendon Press, 1994).

MARKESINIS, B (ed), *The Gradual Convergence: Foreign Ideas, Foreign Influences and English Law on the eve of the 21st Century* (Oxford, Clarendon Press, 1994).

MAY, R, *Criminal Evidence* (4th edn, London, Sweet & Maxwell, 1999).

LORD MCCLUSKY, *Law Justice and Democracy* (London, Sweet & Maxwell, 1987).

MOWBRAY, A, *The Development of Positive Obligations under the European Convention on Human Rights by the European Court of Human Rights* (Oxford, Hart Publishing, 2004).

OLIVER, D, *Common Law Values and the Public-Private Divide* (London, Butterworths, 1999).

PADFIELD, N, *Beyond the Tariff: Human Rights and the Release of Life Sentence Prisoners* (Devon, Willan Publishing, 2002).

RISHWORTH, P et al, *The New Zealand Bill of Rights* (Oxford, Oxford University Press, 2003).

ROBERTS, P and ZUCKERMAN, A, *Criminal Evidence* (2nd edn, Oxford, Oxford University Press, 2004).

RUSSELL, M, *Reforming the House of Lords: Lessons From Overseas* (Oxford, Oxford University Press, 2000).

LORD SCARMAN, *English Law—The New Dimension* (London, Stevens and Sons, 1974).

SIMPSON, A, *In the Highest Degree Odious: Detention Without Trial in Wartime Britain* (Oxford, Oxford University Press, 1992).

STARMER, K, *European Human Rights Law: The Human Rights Act 1998 and the European Convention* (London, LAG, 1999).

STEVENS, R, *The English Judges* (Oxford, Hart Publishing, 2002).

WADE, HWR and FORSYTH, CF, *Administrative Law* (9th edn, Oxford, Oxford University Press, 2004).

WALKER, C, *The Prevention of Terrorism in British Law* (2nd edn, Manchester, Manchester University Press, 1992).

WALKER, C and STARMER, K (eds), *Miscarriages of Justice: A Review of Justice in Error* (London, Blackstone Press, 1999).

WOODHOUSE, D, *The Office of Lord Chancellor* (Oxford, Hart Publishing, 2001).

LORD WOOLF, JOWELL, J and LE SUEUR, A, *De Smith, Woolf and Jowell's Principles of Judicial Review* (London, Sweet & Maxwell, 1999).

ZANDER, M, *A Bill of Rights?* (London, Sweet & Maxwell, 1997).

—— (2005) *The Police and Criminal Evidence Act 1984* (5th edn, London, Sweet & Maxwell).

ZIEGLER, K (ed), *Human Rights and Private Law: Privacy as Autonomy* (Oxford, Hart Publishing, 2007).

JOURNAL ARTICLES

ALLAN, J, 'Bills of Rights and Judicial Power—A Liberal's Quandary' (1996) 16(2) *OJLS* 337.

—— 'Portia, Bassanio or Dick the Butcher? Constraining Judges in the Twenty-First Century' (2006) 17 *KCLJ* 1.

ALLAN, TRS, 'Human Rights and Judicial Review: A Critique of "Due Deference"' (2006) *CLJ* 671.

AMOS, M, '*R v Secretary of State for the Home Department, ex p Anderson*—Ending the Home Secretary's Sentencing Role' (2004) 67(1) *MLR* 108.

—— 'The Impact of the Human Rights Act on the United Kingdom's performance before the European Court of Human Rights' [2007] *PL* 655.

ASHWORTH, A, 'Excluding Evidence as Protecting Rights' [1977] *Crim LR* 723.

BAMFORTH, N, 'Parliamentary Sovereignty and the Human Rights Act 1998' [1998] *PL* 572

—— 'The True Horizontal Effect of the Human Rights Act' (1998) *PL* 423.

BARENDT, E, 'Separation of Powers and Constitutional Government' [1995] *PL* 592, 601.

BARNUM, D, 'Indirect Incitement and Freedom of Expression in Anglo-American Law' [2006] *EHRLR* 258.

BEYLEVELD, D, KIRKHAM, R and TOWNEND, D, 'Which Presumption? A Critique of the House of Lords Reasoning on Retrospectivity and the Human Rights Act' (2002) *LS* 185.

BEYELEVELD, D and PATTINSON, S, 'Horizontality applicability and horizontal effect' (2002) 118 *LQR* 623.

BINGHAM, T, 'The European Convention on Human Rights: Time to Incorporate' (1993) 109 *LQR* 390.

BONNER, D, 'Managing Terrorism While Respecting Human Rights? European Aspects of the Anti-Terrorism Crime and Security Act 2001' (2002) 8 *European Public Law* 497.

BONNER, D, FENWICK, H and HARRIS-SHORT, S, 'Judicial Approaches to the Human Rights Act' (2003) 52 *International and Comparative Law Quarterly* 549.

BRADLEY, A, 'Judicial Independence under Attack' [2003] *PL* 397.

BUXTON, R, 'The Human Rights Act and Private Law' (2000) 116 *LQR* 48.

CHEADLE, H and DAVIS, D, 'The Application of the 1996 Constitution in the Private Sphere' (1997) 13 *South African Journal of Human Rights* 50.

CLAPHAM, A, 'The Privatisation of Human Rights' [1995] *EHRLR* 20.

CLARK, L, 'Injunctions and the Human Rights Act 1998: Jurisdiction and Discretion' (2002) 21 *Civil Justice Quarterly* 29.

CLAYTON, R, 'Developing Principles for Human Rights' [2002] *EHRLR* 175.

—— 'The Limits of what's Possible: Statutory Construction under the Human Rights Act' [2002] *EHRLR* 559.

—— 'Judicial Deference and "Democratic Dialogue": The Legitimacy of Judicial Intervention under the Human Rights Act 1998' [2004] *PL* 33.

—— 'Damage Limitation: The Courts and Human Rights Act Damages' [2005] *PL* 429.

LORD COOKE, 'The British Embracement of Human Rights' [1999] *EHRLR* 243.

—— 'The Road Ahead for the Common Law' (2004) 53 *International and Comparative Law Quarterly* 273.

CRAIG, P, 'Contracting Out, the Human Rights Act and the Scope of Judicial Review' (2002) 118 *LQR* 551.

CRAIG, P and WALTERS, M, 'The Courts, Devolution and Judicial Review' [1999] *PL* 274.

CUMPER, P, 'The Protection of Religious Rights under Section 13 of the Human Rights Act 1998' [2000] *PL* 254.

DAVIES, H, 'Public Authorities as "Victims" under the Human Rights Act' (2005) 64 *CLJ* 315.

DENNIS, I, 'Fair Trials and Safe Convictions' (2003) 57 *Current Legal Problems* 211.

LORD DEVLIN, 'Judges and Lawmakers' (1976) 39 *MLR* 1.

DEVONSHIRE, P, 'Restraint on Freedom of Expression under the Human Rights Act: Cream Holdings Ltd v Banerjee in the House of Lords' (2005) *Civil Justice Quarterly* 194.

DOUGAN, P, 'Anonymity orders and Media Censorship in the "New era" of Human Rights' (2005) *Entertainment Law Review* 150.

DYZENHAUS, D, 'An Unfortunate Burst of Anglo-Saxon Parochialism' (2005) 68 *MLR* 673.

EDWARDS, R, 'Generosity and the Human Rights Act: the right interpretation?' [1999] *PL* 400.

—— 'Judicial Deference under the Human Rights Act' [2002] 65(6) *MLR* 859.

EWING, K, 'The Human Rights Act and Parliamentary Democracy' (1999) 62 *MLR* 79.

—— 'The Futility of the Human Rights Act' [2004] *PL* 829.

EWING, K and GEARTY, C, 'Rocky Foundations for Labour's New Rights' (1997) EHRLR 146.

FELDMAN, D, 'Remedies for violations of Convention Rights under the Human Rights Act' [1998] *EHRLR* 691.

—— 'The Human Rights Act and Constitutional Principles' (1999) 19 *LS* 165.

—— 'Parliamentary Scrutiny of Legislation and Human Rights' [2002] *PL* 323.

—— 'The Impact of the Human Rights Act on the UK Legislative Process' (2004) 24 *Statute Law Review* 91.

FENWICK, H, 'The Anti-Terrorism, Crime and Security Act 2001: A Proportionate Response to September 11?' [2002] 65 *MLR* 724.

—— 'Clashing Rights, the Welfare of the Child and the Human Rights Act' (2004) 67(6) *MLR* 889.

FENWICK, H and PHILLIPSON, G, 'Public Protest, the Human Rights Act and Judicial Responses to Political Expression' [2000] *PL* 627.

—— 'Direct Action, Convention Values and the Human Rights Act' (2001) 21 *LS* 535.

FORDHAM, M, 'Reparation for Maladministration: Public Law's Final Frontier' [2003] *Judicial Review* 104.

GARDBAUM, S, 'The "Horizontal Effect" of Constitutional Rights' (2003) 103 *Mich LR* 387.

—— 'Where the (State) Action Is' (2006) *International Journal of Constitutional Law* 760.

GEARTY, C, 'Reconciling Parliamentary Democracy and Human Rights' (2002) 118 *LQR* 248.

—— 'Human Rights in an Age of Terrorism: Injurious, Irrelevant or Indispensable?' (2005) *Current Legal Problems* 25.

GRIEF, N, 'The Exclusion of Foreign Torture Evidence: a Qualified Victory for the Rule of Law' [2006] *EHRLR* 201.

GRIFFITH, J, 'The Political Constitution' (1979) 42 *MLR* 1.

HAMMOND, A, 'The Human Rights Act and the Government Legal Service' 20(3) *Statute Law Review* 230.

HARE, I, 'Vertically Challenged: Private Parties, Privacy and the Human Rights Act' (2001) *EHRLR* 526.

—— 'Crosses, Crescents and Sacred Cows: Criminalising Incitement to Religious Hatred' [2006] *PL* 520–37.

T HICKMAN, 'Constitutional Dialogue, Constitutional Theories and the Human Rights Act 1998' [2005] *PL* 306.

—— 'The Courts and Politics after the Human Rights Act: A Comment' [2008] *PL* 84.

HIEBERT, J, 'Parliament and the Human Rights Act: Can the Joint Committee on Human Rights help facilitate a culture of rights?' (2006) *Int J of Constitutional Law* 1.

LORD HOFFMANN, 'Human Rights and the House of Lords' (1999) 62(2) *MLR* 159.

HOGG, P and BUSHELL, A, 'The Charter Dialogue between Courts and Legislatures (Or Perhaps The Charter of Rights isn't Such a Bad Thing After All' (1997) 35 *Osgoode Hall Law Journal* 75.

HOOD PHILLIPS, O, 'A Constitutional Myth: Separation of Powers' (1977) 93 *LQR* 11.

LORD HOPE, 'The Human Rights Act 1998: The Task of the Judges' (1999) 20(3) *Statute Law Review* 185.

HOWELL, J, 'The Human Rights Act 1998: Land, Private Citizens, and the Common Law' (2007) 123 *LQR* 618.

HUNT, M, 'The "Horizontal Effect" of the Human Rights Act' [1998] *PL* 423.

HUTCHINSON, A and PETTER, A, 'Private Rights Public Wrongs: the Libel Lie of the Charter' (1982) 38 *Toronto LJ* 278.

LORD IRVING OF LAIRG, 'The Development of Human Rights in Britain under an Incorporated Convention on Human Rights' [1998] *PL* 221.

—— 'Activism and restraint: human rights and the interpretative process' [1999] *EHRLR* 350.

—— 'The Impact of the Human Rights Act; Parliament, the Courts and the Executive' [2003] *PL* 308.

JONES, O, 'Down With the squatters! The European Court of Human Rights and *JA Pye (Oxford) Ltd v United Kingdom*' (2006) 25 *Civil Justice Quarterly* 404.

JOWELL, J, 'Beyond the Rule of Law: Towards Constitutional Judicial Review' [2000] *PL* 671.

—— 'Judicial Deference: servility, civility or institutional capacity?' [2004] *PL* 592.

KAVANAGH, A 'Statutory Interpretation and Human Rights after Anderson: A More Contextual Approach' [2004] *PL* 537.

—— 'The Elusive Divide between Interpretation and Legislation under the Human Rights Act 1998' (2004) 24 *OJLS* 259.

—— 'Unlocking the Human Rights Act: The "Radical" Approach to Section 3(1) Revisited' [2005] *EHRLR* 259.

KAY, R, 'The European Convention on Human Rights and the Control of Private Law' (2005) *EHRLR* 466.

KEAY, A, 'Whither American Cyanamid?: Interim Injunctions in the 21st Century' (2003) *Civil Justice Quarterly* 133.

KLUG, F, 'The Human Rights Act 1998, *Pepper v Hart* and All That' [1999] *PL* 246.

—— 'The Human Rights Act—A "Third Way" or "Third Wave" Bill of Rights' [2001] *EHRLR* 361.

—— 'Judicial Deference under the Human Rights Act' [2003] *EHRLR* 125.

—— 'The Long Road to Human Rights Compliance' (2006) 57(1) *Northern Ireland Legal Quarterly* 186.

—— 'A Bill of Rights: Do We Need One, or Do We already Have One?' [2007] *PL* 701.

KLUG, F and WILDBORE, H, 'Breaking new ground: the Joint Committee on Human Rights and the role of Parliament in human rights compliance' [2007] *EHRLR* 231.

LAWS, J, 'Is the High Court the Guardian of Fundamental Constitutional Rights?' [1993] *PL* 59.

—— 'The Limitations of Human Rights' [1998] *PL* 254.

LEIGH, I, 'The Gulf War Deportations and the Courts' [1991] *PL* 331.

—— 'Horizontal Rights, The Human Rights Act and Privacy: Lessons from the Commonwealth?' (1999) 48 *International and Comparative Law Quarterly* 57.

—— 'Taking Rights Proportionately: Judicial Review, the Human Rights Act and Strasbourg' [2002] *PL* 265.

—— 'Bias, Necessity and the Convention' [2002] *PL* 407.

LESTER, A, 'English Judges as Law Makers' [1993] *PL* 269.

—— 'The European Convention in the New Architecture of Europe' [1996] *PL* 5.

—— 'Developing constitutional principles of public law' [2001] *PL* 684.

—— 'Parliamentary Scrutiny of Legislation under the Human Rights Act 1998' [2002] *EHRLR* 432.

—— 'The Utility of the Human Rights Act: a reply to Keith Ewing' [2005] *PL* 249.

LESTER, A and BEATTIE, K, 'The New Commission for Equality and Human Rights' [2006] *PL* 197.

LESTER, A and PANNICK, D, 'The Impact of the Human Rights Act on Private Law: the Knight's Move' (2000) 116 *LQR* 380.

LE SUEUR, A, 'The Rise and Ruin of Unreasonableness' [2005] *Judicial Review* 32.

LEWIS, J, 'The European Ceiling on Human Rights' [2007] *PL* 720.

LEWIS, T, 'Political Advertising and the Communications Act 2003' [2005] 3 *EHRLR* 290.

—— 'Rights Lost in Translation? Fact-insensitive Laws, the Human Rights Act and the United Kingdom's Ban on Political Advertising' [2007] *EHRLR* 663.

LOVELAND, I, 'War Against the Judges' (1997) 68 *Pol Q* 162.

—— 'Making it up as they go along? The Court of Appeal on Same Sex Spouses and Succession Rights to Tenancies' [2003] *PL* 222.

LUSTGARTEN, L and LEIGH, I, 'Making Rights Real: The Courts, Remedies and the Human Rights Act' (1999) 58(3) *CLJ* 509.

LYELL, N, 'Wither Strasbourg? Why Britain should Think Long and Hard before Incorporating the European Convention on Human Rights' [1997] *EHRLR* 132.

MAHONEY, R, 'Abolition of New Zealand's Prima Facie Exclusionary Rule' [2003] *Crim LR* 607.

MANFREDI, CP and KELLY, JB, 'Six Degrees of Dialogue: A Response to Hogg and Bushell' (1999) 37 *Osgoode Hall Law Journal* 513.

MARKENSINIS, B, 'Privacy, Freedom of Expression and the Human Rights Bill: Lessons from Germany' (1999) 115 *LQR* 47.

MARSHALL, G, 'The Lynchpin of Parliamentary Intention: Lost, Stolen or Strained?' [2003] *PL* 236.

JUDGE SIBRAND KAREL MARTENS, 'Incorporating the European Convention: The Role of the Judiciary' [1998] *EHRLR* 5.

MASTERMAN, R, 'A Supreme Court for the United Kingdom: two steps forward, but one step back on judicial independence' [2004] *PL* 48.

—— 'Section 2(1) of the Human Rights Act 1998: Binding Domestic Courts to Strasbourg?' [2004] *PL* 725.

—— 'Taking the Strasbourg Jurisprudence into Account: Developing a "Municipal Law of Human Rights" under the Human Rights Act' (2005) 54 *International and Comparative Law Quarterly* 907.

—— 'Determinative in the Abstract? Article 6(1) and the Separation of Powers' [2005] *EHRLR* 628.

MCCRUDDEN, C, 'A Common Law of Human Rights?: Transnational Judicial Conversations on Constitutional Rights' (2000) 20(4) *OJLS* 499.

MEAD, D, 'Rights, Relationships and Retrospectivity: The Impact of the Convention Rights on Pre-existing Private Relationships following Ghaidan and Wilson' [2005] *PL* 459.

MOECKLI, D, 'The Selective "War on Terror": Executive Detention of Foreign Nationals and the Principle of Non-Discrimination' (2006) 31 *Brook J of Int Law* 495.

MORGAN, J, 'Questioning the True Effect of the HRA' (2002) *LS* 259.

—— 'Privacy, Confidence and Horizontal Effect: "Hello" Trouble' (2003) 62 *CLJ* 444.

MORRIS, G, 'Exclusion of Fundamental Rights by Agreement' (2001) 30 *Ind LJ* 49.

MOWBRAY, A, 'The European Court of Human Rights' Approach to Just Satisfaction' [1997] *PL* 647.

NICOL, D, 'Are Convention rights a no-go zone for Parliament?' [2002] *PL* 438.

—— 'Statutory Interpretation and Human Rights after Anderson' [2004] *PL* 274.

—— 'The Human Rights Act and the politicians' (2004) 24(3) *LS* 451.

—— 'Gender Reassignment and the Transformation of the Human Rights Act' (2004) 120 *LQR* 194.

—— 'Law and Politics after the Human Rights Act' [2006] *PL* 722.

O'CINNEIDE, C, 'Democracy, Rights and the Constitution—New Directions in the Human Rights Era' (2004) 57 *Current Legal Problems* 175.

—— 'The Commission for Equality and Human Rights: a new institution for new and uncertain times' [2007] *Ind LJ* 141.

OLIVER, D, 'Chancel Repairs and the Human Rights Act' (2001) *PL* 651.

—— 'Functions of a Public Nature under the Human Rights Act' [2004] *PL* 329.

O'NEILL, A, '"Stands Scotland where it did?": Devolution, Human Rights and the Scottish Constitution Seven Years On' (2006) 57 (1) *Northern Ireland Legal Quarterly* 102.

OPTICAN, S and SANKOFF, P, 'The New Exclusionary Rule: A Preliminary Assessment of *R v Shaheed*' (2003) *New Zealand Law Review* 1.

ORMEROD, D and BIRCH, D, 'The Evolution of the Discretionary Exclusion of Evidence' [2004] *Crim LR* 767.

PANNICK, D, 'Principles of Interpretation of Convention Rights under the Human Rights Act and the Discretionary Area of Judgment' [1998] *PL* 545.

PHILLIPSON, G, 'The Human Rights Act, "horizontal effect" and the Common Law: a Bang or a Whimper?' (1999) 62(6) *MLR* 824.

—— 'Transforming Breach of Confidence: Towards a Common Law Right to Privacy under the Human Rights Act' (2003) 66 *MLR* 726.

—— '(Mis-)Reading Section 3 of the Human Rights Act' (2003) 119 *LQR* 551.

—— 'Judicial Reasoning in Breach of Confidence Cases under the Human Rights Act: Not Taking Privacy Seriously?' [2003] *EHRLR* (Special Issue: Privacy 2003) 54.

—— 'Deference, Discretion and Democracy in the Human Rights Era' (2007) *Current Legal Problems* 40.

QUANE, H, 'The Strasbourg Jurisprudence and the Meaning of a "Public Authority" under the Human Rights Act' [2006] *PL* 106.

RAWLINGS, R, 'Hastening Slowly: The Next Phase of Welsh Devolution' [2005] *PL* 824.

LORD REID, 'The Judge as Law Maker' (1972) 12 *Journal of the Society of Public Teachers of Law* 22.

ROACH, K, 'Constitutional and common law dialogues between the Supreme Court and Canadian Legislatures' (2001) 80 *Canadian Bar Review* 481.

ROGERS, H and TOMLINSON, H, 'Privacy and Expression: Convention Rights and Interim Injunctions' [2003] *EHRLR (Special Issue Privacy 2003)* 37.

SANDBERG, R, 'Flags, Beards and Pilgrimages: A Review of Early Cases on Religious Discrimination' (2007) 9 *Ecclesiastical Law Journal* 87.

SCOTT, A, '"A Monstrous and Unjustifiable Infringement"? Political Expression and the Broadcasting Ban on Advocacy Advertising' (2003) 66 *MLR* 240.

SEDLEY, S, 'Human Rights: A Twenty-First Century Agenda' [1995] *PL* 386.

—— 'Wringing Out the Fault: Self-Incrimination in the 21st Century' (2001) 52 *Northern Ireland Legal Quarterly* 107.

SINGH, R, 'The Declaration of Incompatibility' [2002] JR 237.

SLATTERY, B, 'The Charter's Relevance to Private Litigation' (1987) 32 *McGill LJ* 905.

SMILLIE, J, '"Fundamental" Rights, Parliamentary Supremacy and the New Zealand Court of Appeal' (1995) 111 *LQR* 209.

SMIT, JVZ, 'The New Purposive Interpretation of Statutes: HRA Section 3 after *Ghaidan v Godin-Mendoza*' (2007) 70(2) *MLR* 294.

DE SMITH, S, 'The Separation of Powers in New Dress' (1966) 12 *McGill LJ* 491.

SPENCER, J, 'Quashing Convictions for Procedural Irregularities' (2007) *Crim LR* 835.

SPJUT, R, 'Internment and Detention without Trial in Northern Ireland 1971–1975: Ministerial Policy and Practice' (1986) 49 *MLR* 712.

STARMER, K, 'Two years of the Human Rights Act' [2003] *EHRLR* 14.

STARMER, K and KLUG, F, 'Incorporation through the Back Door' [1997] *PL* 223.

LORD STEYN, 'The New Legal Landscape' [2000] *EHRLR* 549.

—— 'Dynamic Interpretation amidst an orgy of statutes' [2004] *EHRLR* 245.

—— 'Guantanamo Bay: The Legal Black Hole' (2004) 53 *International and Comparative Law Quarterly* 53.

—— 'Deference: A Tangled Story' [2005] *PL* 346.

—— '2000–2005: Laying the foundations of human rights law in the United Kingdom' [2005] *EHRLR* 349.

—— 'Democracy, the Rule of Law and the Role of Judges' [2006] *EHRLR* 243.

SUNKIN, M, 'Pushing Forward the Frontiers of Human Rights Protection: The Meaning of Public Authority under the Human Rights Act' [2004] *PL* 643.

TAYLOR, N and ORMEROD, D, 'Mind the Gaps: Safeness, Fairness and Moral Legitimacy' [2004] *Crim LR* 266.

TIERNEY, S, 'Devolution Issues and s 2(1) of the Human Rights Act 1998' [2000] *EHRLR* 380.

TOMKINS, A, 'Legislating Against Terror: the Anti-Terrorism, Crime and Security Act 2001' [2002] *PL* 106.

TREMBLAY, LB, 'The Legitimacy of Judicial Review: The Limits of Dialogue between Courts and Legislatures' (2005) 3 *International Journal of Constitutional Law* 617.

TRENCH, A, 'The Government of Wales Act 2006: The Next Steps on Devolution for Wales' [2006] *PL* 687.

TURENNE, S, 'The Compatibility of Criminal Liability with Freedom of Expression' (2007) *Crim LR* 866.

WADE, H, 'Horizons of Horizontality' (2000) 116 *LQR* 217.

WALDRON, J, 'A Rights-Based Critique of Constitutional Rights' (1993) 13(1) *OJLS* 18.

WALKER, C, 'The Treatment of Foreign Terror Suspects' (2007) 70 *MLR* 427.

LORD WINDLESHAM, 'The Constitutional Reform Act 2005: Ministers, Judges and Constitutional Change: part I' [2005] *PL* 806.

—— 'The Constitutional Reform Act 2005: the politics of constitutional reform: part II' [2006] *PL* 35.

WINETROBE, B, 'Scottish Devolved Legislation in the Courts' [2002] *PL* 31.

WINTEMUTE, R, 'The Human Rights Act's First Five Years: Too Strong, Too Weak, or Just Right?' (2006) 17 *KCLJ* 209.

LORD WOOLF, 'Droit Public—English Style' [1995] *PL* 57.

—— 'The Rule of Law and a Change in the Constitution' (2004) 63(2) *CLJ* 317.

YOUNG, A, 'A Peculiarly British Protection of Human Rights?' (2005) 68 *MLR* 858.

—— '*Ghaidan v Godin-Mendoza*: Avoiding the Deference Trap' [2005] *PL* 23.

Index